THE SPEAK ANGEL SERIES

ALSO BY ALICE NOTLEY

THE SPEAK ANGEL SERIES

ALICE NOTLEY

FONOGRAF EDITIONS

Portland, OR

Fonograf Editions
Portland, OR

Cover and text design by Kit Schluter

First Edition, First Printing
FONO23

Published by Fonograf Editions
www.fonografeditions.com

For information about permission to reuse any material from this book,
please contact Fonograf Ed. at info@fonografeditions.com.

ISBN: 978-1-7378036-2-1
LCCN: 2021951794

CONTENTS

ILLUSTRATION BY ALICE NOTLEY

"Angels? I say   Wings he says   I flew over the   time when I died"

PREFACE | *Alice Notley*

Welcome to *The Speak Angel Series*. It is long and perhaps idiosyncratic, but friendly. It is a good book for now—a time of covid and environmental crisis, wars and panicky immigration—since it offers a future. There always is one, a future; speaking cosmically, everything is immortal because there's no nowhere for something to become nothing in . . . I think. Anyway, I offer a future made of recombination like a collage, a pasting on of things by a massive regrouping of the dead and alive in order to begin again, at this point, whatever you think this point is. I'm quickly going to tell you there are six books in *The Speak Angel Series*, *The House Gone*, *Opera*, *Healing Matter*, *To Paste On*, *Out of Order*, and *The Poem*.

I begin with a dream about my mother's recent death—this is 2013— and a desire to use long lines for awhile. So the first book, *The House Gone*, becomes a journey in which I begin to lead everyone and -thing (people and mountains, quasars and whoever) to newness. One will keep forgetting what's happening, because whatever's happening at any time is Not the illustration of what's happening, it's what's happening. You don't always know who's speaking, because a conversation is like that. So I become the leader and I lead to a point zero, where the current description, on earth, of the cosmos, ceases to exist. We are finally on the "other side of the story." There are inset poems and also a tale with variants—as usual I didn't know what I was doing until I'd done it. I saw this first book as somewhat literal happenstance, even though it obviously isn't. That I believed everything that was happening became the mode, for me, of the whole series. I don't remember when I knew I was writing a "series." Somewhere, though, in this first book the phrase "the speak angel series" was given to me in a dream.

The second book, *Opera*, is a kind of extension of Book I, a celebration of leading and arriving and a series of pasting-on's—what could be included in the new collage. Everyone led comes to stand at the edge of a void, conversing. Gradually I began using caps for poetic stress, but emphasizing unexpected strings of words or phrases—not according to orthodox English verse patterns, but presenting what I was hearing in my mind. When I undertook to read extracts aloud to myself, I realized my voice was automatically being pitched into a sort of chanting or even singing. So the second book became an "opera."

In the third book, *Healing Matter*, the protagonist, who is myself, takes off on her own, leaving all the "led" on the precipice of "ice" above the "abyss," remaking. The protagonist enters the abyss. Writing this book I fell into a measure somewhat like that of my book *The Descent of Alette*, without the quotation marks of that book, as if there were no distance between my mind and the book itself. For the quotation marks in *The Descent of Alette* had created space between the author and the story, but in *Healing Matter* I felt no distance, though the events of the book are equally visionary. Two-thirds of the way through someone tells the protagonist (me) that he has been killed. That someone is Michael Brown, the young man who was shot, notoriously, in Ferguson, Missouri in the summer of 2014 while I was writing this particular book. He becomes a recurring presence in the series.

To Paste On, the fourth book, is more referential to the "real world" and contains a number of individual poems and forms. It isn't straight narration, though what has become the general narrative of the series constitutes the background. But there are dreams of (my) friends, references to the war in Syria, and to Ebola; and Michael Brown is here. A number of longish poems about the remaking of the universe are offered as events of remaking and healing; the pressure to do that continues. To heal the universe.

The fifth book, *Out of Order*, is itself a deliberate collage. I wrote in a notebook, out of order, not filling the pages chronologically and sometimes cutting and pasting. I don't remember exactly how I determined the final order, not by a method. The book is just out of order—everything is, isn't it? Unapologetically, here and in *To Paste On* I present myself as intermittently crucified. Anyone is, aren't they? I know I am.

Book VI, *The Poem*, is deliberately modeled on *The Descent of Alette*, that is formally, again without the quotation marks. It's divided into four sections—which in this case are titled—and each section contains roughly the same number of pages as the corresponding section of *The Descent of Alette*. I don't remember exactly why I did that. The book contains encounters with the dead and descriptions of how the dead make art; references to contemporary events—various people whose deaths occurred during the compositional process join the poem. There is a battle—between the conscious and the unconscious, there is resolution and restatement of the need to remake, the ability to remake, the idea that we are and will be surrounded by the broken, but pieces are there to remake with, the dead are there, perhaps time isn't any more.

Though I do use "I" throughout these books it might be useful to the reader to know that I'm influenced by older public forms of art: Greek epic and drama, Latin rhetoric and epic, the plays of Racine. I'm always conscious of foundation myths and stories that keep getting told, within cultures and also from culture to culture. One way to look at this work might be as a posited myth—in the myth I posit myself as the leader of a reconstruction. It is fictive, but I'm not doing fiction. Take it as you want, as you certainly will.

At this point my forms are simply whatever I'm using *at this moment*. Probably there are two Alette-form books to balance each other, there's an opera because I started singing. There's a big collage because I keep saying collage is the form of everything, the way *you* are a monkey, a horse mane, a bird-throated breasted-mammal flower-organed species-eater. In the midst of writing the sixth book, in Paris in the year of various terrorist attacks, 2015, I was jogging at dawn in the Parc des Buttes-Chaumont and heard a man praying out loud in anguish and tears, hidden by trees and darkness, to the Seigneur, praying, as I remember it, for himself and his family. That is part of this book too. I don't know what happened to this man, and I'm not sure what "happen" is. This book, though he would never read it, is for him.

Alice Notley
January 1, 2022

FOREWORD: "A BROKEN HEART STAYS OPEN" | *Robert Dewhurst*

Nature is a Haunted House—but Art—a House that tries to be haunted.
EMILY DICKINSON

It's not a normal experience, to write a poem.
ALICE NOTLEY

"Listen to people and make a poem," Alice Notley once guided a group of young writers, in a summer 1978 presentation at the Naropa Institute, recorded to audiocassette and now archived in the garrulous ether of the internet.[1] Eavesdropping is poetry's oldest trick—practically, its origin—and, she knew, as endless a source of information as Borges's Library of Babel. All-knowing already, Notley counseled the class to stick with this exercise, a workshop perennial, of making a poem from the overheard. "If you've done this assignment before, or thought about these things before, don't simply think you've done it and thought about it," she insisted. "You'll be doing it and thinking about it forever."[2] True to this teaching, the enjoinder to write by ear has been perhaps *the* guiding imperative of Notley's work in the nearly half century since, her vast and polyhedral oeuvre charting her own lifelong process of doing and thinking listening. *The Speak Angel Series*, an epic in six books written over two years and then revised for another five, is her most supreme act of listening yet.

Oracular and sometimes opaque, *Speak Angel* is an imposing work, spanning some six hundred and fifty pages and an array of poetic forms, its decidedly *un*apostrophic "I" inhabited by an ossuary of disembodied voices who speak to, and through, the poet. But here Notley's readers will find themselves at home, in a "grand house of creation" disobedient to the apparent laws of the universe (never mind those of governments and genres), limited only by human imagination and courage.[3] *Speak Angel*, by its own testimony, is an "epic of the dead," and thus the magnum opus which yokes what have been Notley's two primary avenues of investigation—epic poetry and death—since her dramatic turn to longer and more visionary forms in the late 1980s. Its strategies, though, run even deeper than that, to her origins as a poet of acute attunement to speech and the ambient.

---

1. Ted Berrigan and Alice Notley, "Visiting Poetics Academy: Ted Berrigan and Alice Notley," reading and workshop, Naropa Institute, May 31, 1978, Boulder, CO, audiocassette 2 of 6, MPEG copy, Jack Kerouac School of Disembodied Poetics Audio Archive, Naropa University, http://archives.naropa.edu/digital/collection/p16621coll1/id/1567/rec/3.

2. Ibid.

3. Here and below, unattributed quotations are from *Speak Angel* itself.

"We're simultaneous," she tells us in *Speak Angel*, as she draws on seemingly all of her own past and present resources, and the entire history of poetry, to lead us—that is, write us—into a future exorcised of all dogma.

Then, at Naropa, Notley was talking about talking: about her practice of pulling others' words, like found art (or at least art supplies), from out of the air and into her poems. Elevating the ephemeral oral into poetry with a single, alchemic gesture, Notley's talk technique came right out of American modernism, an offspring of Stein's aesthetic of "using everything" and the strong preference of certain post–World War II poets, via Williams, for the vernacular.[4] Lew Welch, perhaps, best put across the latter view: "Language is what goes on when you open the door of a banquet-room and there are 300 ladies having lunch. . . . Language is speech. Any other form, the printed one or the taped one, is a translation of language. All poems are translations."[5] (This attitude, more or less emblematic of the entire countertradition of the New American Poetry, also had its corollaries in the emergent world of conceptual art; Notley has told the scholar Nick Sturm that she read "all of Andy Warhol's *A* when it came out in 1969.")[6] Living throughout the 1970s and early '80s with the poet Ted Berrigan and their two sons (Anselm and Edmund, now poets) in a small New York apartment that she would later describe as a "doorless railroad flat" whose occupants experienced daily life "simultaneously in each's consciousness," Notley's poems opened themselves to include the chatter of her family members—translating, in Welch's sense, from her home's "polyphonic voicefulness" to the page.[7] While Notley often integrated others' voices into her poems silently, using a logic

---

4. Gertrude Stein, "Composition as Explanation," in *Selected Writings of Gertrude Stein*, ed. Carl Van Vechten (New York: Vintage Books, 1990), 511–23 (518–22 passim). For some discussion of Notley's affinity with the all-inclusivity of both Stein and Williams, see Heather H. Thomas, "Spectacular Margins: Women Poets Refigure the Epic; Transfigured Self in Innovative Long Poems of Alice Notley and Anne Waldman" (PhD diss., Temple University, 1999), 45–46. The progenitive metaphor is Notley's own. Her 1980 lecture "Doctor Williams' Heiresses" includes a letter which imagines that she and Bernadette Mayer were two granddaughters of a marriage between Stein and Williams: see Alice Notley, *Doctor Williams' Heiresses* (Berkeley: Tuumba Press, 1980), n.p.

5. Lew Welch, "Language Is Speech," in *Ring of Bone: Collected Poems of Lew Welch*, ed. Donald Allen (San Francisco: City Lights, 2012), 235–49 (236).

6. Nick Sturm, "Seeing the Future: A Conversation with Alice Notley," Poetry Society of America, n.d. [2017], https://poetrysociety.org/features/interviews/seeing-the-future-a-conversation-with-alice-notley. (Sturm's personal website indicates that this interview was conducted on September 16, 2017, and contains some additional raw material from the transcript: see Nick Sturm, "'It's Not the Way You're Taught': From an Interview with Alice Notley," *Crystal Set* (blog), October 28, 2017, https://www.nicksturm.com/crystalset/2017/10/26/from-an-interview-with-alice-notley.)

7. Alice Notley, entry in *Contemporary Authors Autobiography Series*, vol. 27, ed. Shelly Andrews (Detroit: Gale Research, 1997), 221–40 (227–28). The apartment was located at 101 St. Mark's Place, on the Lower East Side, and its polyphony included more than the family's own voices: as Notley writes, "I lived there altogether for sixteen years [March 1976–September 1992] and it was always full, of voices

of collage rather than narrative to make poetry from the materials at hand, the voices of her sons are particularly distinct in her works from this time. The daybook-style entries of Notley's 1981 collection *Waltzing Matilda*, for example, record a running commentary from the boys which makes for quick shifts and surprise endings, such as this hypnagogic exchange used to put one energetic poem to rest: "Mom / why don't / people read in the dark? They can't see the words in the / dark. I can. Please go to sleep now. Please, honey."[8] Like a medieval amanuensis, Notley also trained herself during these years to memorize, for use in poems, conversations she encountered outside the apartment, her ears always open to the possibilities for spinning the straw of "spoken American" into gold.[9]

Notley's listening, though, has never been only naturalistic. As early as 1978, at least in ways rhetorical and whimsical, she began testing the idea of mediumship—writing, that is, as if poetry could communicate with the dead. "Jack Would Speak through the Imperfect Medium of Alice," a posthumous message from Kerouac to his own biographers delivered (if "imperfectly") by Notley, is still a fan favorite. ("So I'm an alcoholic Catholic mother-lover," it memorably begins, eager to arrest the pedantry and small-mindedness of the living.)[10] Another poem from this time, "A True Account of Talking to Judy Holliday, October 13," entertains a dialogue with that deceased actress (and, of course, Frank O'Hara) in which the two women's voices become indistinguishable through the medium (as in art form) of "playing" (as in acting).[11] Teasingly, the adjectives in these poems' titles—*imperfect, true*—make a big difference, calling into question the veracity of all that follows. In 2014, interviewed by Corey Zeller, Notley preferred to leave that question open: "I wrote ['Jack Would Speak'] in defense of [Kerouac's] writing as if spoken by him—who

and bodies and objects, sometimes seemingly haunted by the dead" (ibid., 227). For a reading of Notley's "doorlessness" in terms of an "intersubjectivity" with philosophical resonances, see Thomas, "Spectacular Margins," 56–57.

8. Alice Notley, "Waltzing Matilda," in *Grave of Light: New and Selected Poems 1970–2005* (Middletown, CT: Wesleyan University Press, 2006), 116–34 (118). For a brief reading of these lines in the context of a critical essay on Notley's whole career (up to about *Disobedience*), see Maggie Nelson, "Dear Dark Continent: Alice Notley's Disobediences," in *Women, the New York School, and Other True Abstractions* (Iowa City: University of Iowa Press, 2007), 131–67 (144). My thinking in this foreword is indebted to Nelson's insight that "many, if not most, of the concerns and tropes of Notley's recent epics have been alive and at play throughout her career" (ibid., 135).

9. Alice Notley, interview by Michael Silverblatt, *Bookworm*, KCRW, July 10, 2014, https://kcrw.co/3tAlkOq; and Berrigan and Notley, "Visiting Poetics Academy."

10. Alice Notley, "Jack Would Speak through the Imperfect Medium of Alice," in *Grave of Light*, 71–72 (71).

11. Alice Notley, "A True Account of Talking to Judy Holliday, October 13," in *Grave of Light*, 91–93 (93). Notably, "Jack Would Speak" and "Talking to Judy Holliday" share a publication history: both were written in 1978, first published in *Mag City 6* (1979), and collected in Notley's *How Spring Comes* (West Branch, IA: Toothpaste Press, 1981).

knows? maybe he told me what to say."[12] Even if neither "Jack Would Speak" nor "Talking to Judy Holliday" takes its mediumship completely seriously, both show Notley leaning into the idea, turning her ear from the domestic toward the departed, early on.

Since her entrance into epic poetry beginning in the late 1980s, Notley's concern for speaking with and for the dead has deepened considerably, evolving from these early forays to take on a gravitas and global scope befitting the genre. As Notley herself has narrated, her turn to epic was inextricable from grief, compelled by the deaths of her stepdaughter, Kate Berrigan, in 1987, and her brother, Albert Notley Jr., in 1988.[13] Notley developed the distinctive "chorale-like" line of her celebrated first epic, *The Descent of Alette*, while writing a pair of elegies for Kate and Albert: respectively, *Beginning with a Stain* (a thirty-one page sequence) and "White Phosphorus."[14] (This line, subdivided into smaller foot-like units which spotlight "infraline phrasing," is reprised throughout *Speak Angel*.)[15] Later, while writing *Alette* itself, Notley gradually came to understand it, too, as a sustained response to her brother's death; Albert, not Alice, is the eponym for her protagonist.[16] "Though I was writing it because of him, all along, I'd forgotten, because the poem isn't personal, it's public," she has said of composing *Alette*.[17] *Beginning with a Stain* and *The Descent of Alette* were first published together in Notley's 1992 "compendium of books" with Douglas Oliver, *The Scarlet Cabinet*.[18] In her remarkable introduction to this collection, Notley envisaged what has been her artistic agenda for the last thirty years: "The poet must prophesy the future, speak to it, educate it. . . . *Someone*, at this point, must take in hand the task of being everyone, & no one, as the first poets did. Someone must

---

12. Corey Zeller, "A Quick Interview with Alice Notley," *Ampersand Review*, May 11, 2014. This online interview is no longer available at its original URL, but significant portions of it may be found quoted on other sites: see, for example, "Rachel Zucker on Alice Notley, Alice Notley on Alice Notley," *Harriet* (blog), May 13, 2014, https://www.poetryfoundation.org/harriet-books/2014/05/rachel-zucker-on-alice-notley-alice-notley-on-alice-notley.

13. For Notley's narration of this, see Alice Notley, "The 'Feminine' Epic," in *Coming After: Essays on Poetry* (Ann Arbor: University of Michigan Press, 2005), 171–80 (171–72).

14. Ibid., 173.

15. Alice Notley, "American Poetic Music at the Moment," in *Coming After*, 131–46 (138); for Notley's primary discussion of this poetic line, see 135–37. By "infraline phrasing," Notley means a marked emphasis on individual phrases within each line: as she puts it in *Speak Angel*, "Each line should be as full of events as every forgotten day."

16. Notley, "The 'Feminine' Epic," 178. As Notley adds here, the name also sounds like "owl-ette," establishing Alette's descent, as it were, from the guardian owl she meets underground, a figure modeled on her father (whom her brother was himself named for).

17. Ibid.

18. An earlier version of *Beginning with a Stain* was first published in booklet form as *From a Work in Progress* (New York: DIA Art Foundation, 1988). In 1996, *The Descent of Alette* would be republished by Penguin Books in a standalone volume with a wider distribution.

pay attention to the real spiritual needs of both her neighbors (not her poetic peers) & the future. We must find our voice, we must find a story—something that reproduces itself in the aether, not necessarily in bookstores. There must be a holy story."[19]

Virtually all of Notley's poetry since then has answered this call, in a myriad of forms and "fictions" loosely united in their listening for this "holy story," quite literally, in the voices of the dead.[20] In the wake of *Alette*, Notley first undertook to write the sixty-page verse dialogue *Close to me & Closer . . . (The Language of Heaven)*, seeking to better understand the mysterious "black lake" which figures in *Alette* as "the gate to the rest of the universe, death, infinity, the one place beyond the Tyrant's reach."[21] *Close to me*, by Notley's own description, "is an attempt to contact death."[22] Her interlocutor in the dialogue is her father, Albert Notley Sr., who died in 1975, and her preface to the work testifies that his portions of the text were dictated. "I remember feeling very happy writing it, waking up mornings with my dead father's voice in my head," she details there. "In order to write his speeches properly I had to have faith that that was his literal voice I heard. I let the voice dictate to me exactly what to write with very little interference from 'my' rationalizing self. . . . I'm loath to say he didn't <u>really</u> dictate his part of the poem; and I feel the daughter's parts of the dialogue are nowhere as good as the father's."[23] *Close to me* was published, in 1995, bound with the seventy-page "epic-like" *Désamère*, which similarly channels the voice of the French surrealist poet Robert Desnos.[24] Both books, she writes in their shared preface, "search for a mystical ground common to all life": *Close to me*, by soliciting an account of the afterlife from her father; and *Désamère*, through the narrative arc (and archetype) of a desert vision quest.[25] Since the appearance of this these first post-*Alette* poems, Notley's search for a mystical common ground and its accompanying conversation with the dead

19. Alice Notley, introduction to *The Scarlet Cabinet: A Compendium of Books*, by Alice Notley and Douglas Oliver (New York: Scarlet Editions, 1992), v–vi (vi).

20. For Notley's first use of the term "fiction" to describe her narrative poetry, see her preface to *Close to me & Closer . . . (The Language of Heaven) and Désamère* (Oakland: O Books, 1995), n.p. The term has never been a good fit for what Notley does in these works, as her preface *here* suggests. In a recent interview, she elaborated: "Fiction is a veneer of life—it's fictional and I don't believe it or have any use for it but as escape from my mind. Poetry seems much more beautiful, truthful, and monumental to me" (Erkut Tokman, "Erkut Tokman Talks to Alice Notley," the Poetry Society, Spring 2021, https://poetrysociety.org.uk/interview-erkut-tokman-talks-to-alice-notley). For further reflections by Notley on this topic, see also Laynie Brown, "A Conversation with Alice Notley on the Poet's Novel," *Jacket2*, March 15, 2013, https://jacket2.org/commentary/conversation-alice-notley-poets-novel.

21. Notley, "The 'Feminine' Epic," 179.

22. Ibid.

23. Notley, preface to *Close to me & Closer*, n.p.

24. Notley, "The 'Feminine' Epic," 179.

25. Notley, preface to *Close to me & Closer*, n.p.

have proven themselves immense indeed, motivating many subsequent epics and other, less easily categorizable long works. With a publication history that has lagged, as long as fifteen years, behind her prolific production, in chronological order of composition these include *Mysteries of Small Houses* (written in 1995 and published in 1998); *Disobedience* (written in 1995–96 and published in 2001); *Reason and Other Women* (written ca. 1997–98 and published in 2010); *Benediction* (written in 1998–2000 and published in 2015); *Alma, or the Dead Women* (written in 2001–3 and published in 2006); *In the Pines* (written in 2003–4 and published in 2007); *Songs and Stories of the Ghouls* (written in 2004–5 and published in 2011); *Negativity's Kiss* (written in 2006 and published in 2014); *Eurynome's Sandals* (written in 2006–7 and published in 2019); and *For the Ride* (written ca. 2009–10 and published in 2020).[26] In bardic fashion, each of these works, besides probing the nature of reality, has also addressed political (that is, public) crises: *Désamère*, the desertification of global warming; *Songs and Stories of the Ghouls*, genocides ancient and ongoing; *Eurynome's Sandals*, issues of immigration; *For the Ride*, impending apocalypse; and so on, scaling her epic vision well beyond the bounds of this foreword. As Notley said in a 2014 interview by Karin Schalm: "I am, at this point, an epic poet—I am like Virgil, and everyone had better watch out because I am the one reshaping the myth and defining the world. I am international, interplanetary if you will."[27]

Speak Angel, first drafted in 2013–15 and now Notley's most "current" (not to mention, longest) published epic, certainly expands her spiritual search into cosmogonic dimensions.[28] Like many of her earlier epics, it listens to the dead; and like much of her poetry since *Beginning with a Stain*, it seeks, in essence, to reveal and rewrite the origin of

---

26. The "written" dates in this sentence are reported by Notley, but, she writes, "it's hard to be completely accurate: I would write a book a certain year, then tinker with it for years" (email to author, January 6, 2022). It is similarly tricky to inventory all of Notley's "epics" or even "long works," given the genre-defying nature of her writing and the fact that even her collections of shorter, individual poems are highly conceived, also, as books. In a 2013 interview by Lindsay Turner, Notley said, "Since I wrote ['The "Feminine" Epic' in 1995] I've written a lot of books, and I suppose each one has been a kind of an epic, although *Culture of One* [written ca. 2008 and published in 2011] was more like a novel" (Lindsay Turner, "'At the Mercy of My Poetic Voice': An Interview with Alice Notley," *Boston Review*, November 8, 2013, https://bostonreview.net/articles/lindsay-turner-alice-notley-interview-feminism-mojave-collage). Another book that has appeared since 1995, *Certain Magical Acts* (written in 2005–13 and published in 2016), collects poems made between longer projects. Complicating the big picture further, Notley writes, "I've recently decided that I am now writing the same poem from now on forever and will include everything in it as project, with the stipulation that I can take whole chunks of it out and call them a unit too" (email to author, January 7, 2022).

27. Karin Schalm, "Alice Notley on Ghouls," *CutBank: The Literary Journal of the University of Montana*, January 26, 2014, http://www.cutbankonline.org/interviews/2014/01/interviews-alice-notley.

28. On her asynchronous publishing history, in her interview by Sturm, Notley joked, "I'm usually about ten years ahead of everybody else so if I'm publishing what I wrote ten years ago then I'm current" (Sturm, "Seeing the Future").

things. In a 2009 interview by David Baker, Notley reflected on this persistent interest:

> After a couple of people dear to me died in the '80s, I read a lot of books by Mircea Eliade that asserted that the response of indigenous peoples to any crisis was to recite their creation stories, to sing the world into being once more, but each time being always the first time. I seem to have incorporated this idea into my own procedures. But I'm always, also, trying to find out what really happened at the beginning. I don't accept any of the stories I know, though I find some of them quite interesting: I'm looking for my own, true version. And I'm looking for the perfect singing of it, the exact and perfect rendering.[29]

If anything, *Speak Angel* is Notley's vigorously renewed attempt to render this truer or more perfect creation story. "I'm looking," she writes lucidly in book II, "for an initial relation between all us." Since this "relation," as she will discover in book III, is poetry itself—in its "primal use," as the "organizing principle of spirit"—then the failing terms of our world are necessarily subject to revision. Poetry's highest purpose (and therefore, Notley's own), in other words, is nothing short of world-making.[30] Or, as she puts this more gracefully in book V, "only eloquence will recreate the universe." *Speak Angel* itself *is* this act of "eloquence": Notley's sustained attempt to "sing" so "perfectly" a new world emerges. Really, the book's first three lines say everything, asserting not the so-called materiality of language but something more like an occulted "language of materiality": "Our words are what is they say what we make / They don't stand for the universe what you see as much / Stands for them reality in the thicknesses shimmery."

To refigure reality in suitably thick and shimmery language is the challenge to which *Speak Angel* rises, and the reader should need little more to embark than, maybe, a few signposts. Notley's guides here are many, but they begin with the familiar voices of her father (who tells in book I a "meandering" "uncreation story," starring a possible variant

---

29. David Baker, "Evident Being: A Conversation with Alice Notley," *Kenyon Review*, n.d. [2009], https://kenyonreview.org/conversation/alice-notley. Notley included Eliade on a wide-ranging reading list that she prepared for another class at Naropa, this one in 1989, telling students: "I read the entire repetitive oeuvre of Mircea Eliade. You don't have to do that, but that's something I spent a lot of time doing." Notably, this reading list also included several indigenous creation myths: Harold Courlander, *The Fourth World of the Hopis: The Epic Story of the Hopi Indians as Preserved in Their Legends and Traditions* (Albuquerque: University of New Mexico Press, 1987); *Popol Vuh: The Definitive Edition of the Mayan Book of the Dawn of Life and the Glories of Gods and Kings*, trans. Dennis Tedlock (New York: Simon and Schuster, 1985); and Paul G. Zolbrod, *Diné Bahane': The Navajo Creation Story* (Albuquerque: University of New Mexico Press, 1984). See Alice Notley, "Alice Notley's Writing Workshop," reading and workshop, Naropa Institute, July 9, 1989, Boulder, CO, audiocassette 1 of 2, MPEG copy, Jack Kerouac School of Disembodied Poetics Audio Archive, Naropa University, http://archives.naropa.edu/digital/collection/p16621coll1/id/2101.

30. Speaking of dreams, which she has used to write poetry since 1971's *165 Meeting House Lane*, Notley told Maggie Nelson in 2002 that she believes that "life is a dream; that we construct reality in a dreamlike way; that we agree to be in the same dream; and that the only way to change reality is to recognize its dreamlike qualities and act as if it is malleable" (Nelson, "Dear Dark Continent," 156).

of Alette named the Alphabet) and her brother (who needs, and will receive, healing from the trauma of war). Notley's recently deceased mother, in a dream vision which opens *Speak Angel*, elects her daughter to "lead" the dead, announcing the motif of leadership (and "fate") that Notley will contend with throughout the whole series. More plot summary would spoil the story, and the author's own preface provides the broad strokes you will need. Look, though, for our protagonist, an American poet living in Paris named Alice Notley, to step into the black lake of old (now, a "cracked ice abyss" or "VOID of GRACE"); to reacquire the "universal tongue of creation" at the "zero point zero zero infinite" of all being; to collage together a new universe (or *past eon*?) with a call "to paste on"; to, Samson-like, tear down a false factory, on her way to slaying sadness; to correct the idea of the Big Bang, so that the universe begins not in an act of violence but rather like the stretching open of a wing; to restore chaos from "out of order" (rather than the reverse); to rehabilitate the "olde signes," such as the labyrinth and cross; to be crucified and cursed by rivals, then battle them; to transmute others' guilt ("opaque stuff unwanted stuff") into a particulate prima materia; and to minister healing to all manner of dead souls who arrive in and speak through these poems, from Michael Brown to victims of Ebola, the Syrian civil war, the explosions at the Port of Tianjin, the Kunduz hospital airstrike, and the November 13, 2015, terrorist attacks in Paris.[31] Notley's narrative is not always linear, and it may help to bear in mind that dictum of Stein's about beginnings: "Beginning again and again is a natural thing even when there is a series."[32]

Poetry has always been mediumistic, from Hesiod to Hannah Weiner.[33] The philosopher Avital Ronell has argued that writing itself is intrinsically haunted, a form of conversation that "always comes from elsewhere, at the behest of another."[34] *Angel* means "messenger," and for many years now Notley has been candid about her own messengers, the voices that she listens for in her writing chair each morning. Asked to elaborate on her communication with the dead in a 2016 interview by Shoshana Olidort, Notley said this:

> People in my life kept dying, and each time they died I stood at this chasm, and the wall between the living and the dead collapsed. Gradually I just had the ability to see into this other world because these traumatic things happened to me. . . . Sometimes I think that there is no poetry written without the intervention of the dead. It's their voices speaking to you that allow you to find words

31. Considering *Speak Angel*'s apparently autobiographical qualities, the reader might recall Notley's remark about the protagonist of *Désamère*: "She is myself, a fact that's not interesting except insofar as anyone realizes that one is a product of one's times" (Notley, preface to *Close to me & Closer*, n.p.).

32. Stein, "Composition as Explanation," 516.

33. For a comment on Hesiod's prototypical poetic mediumism, see Jed Rasula, *The American Poetry Wax Museum: Reality Effects, 1940–1990* (Urbana, IL: National Council of Teachers of English, 1996), 45–46. The *Theogony* is an explicit reference for *Speak Angel*.

34. Avital Ronell, *Dictations: On Haunted Writing* (Urbana and Chicago: University of Illinois Press, 2006), xiv.

from nowhere; they are the muse. . . . But also, you do rip yourself open if you go through the experiences I have, and you do stand on the chasm between life and death. There is communication, I am certain of this. I've also been ill and in my illness I've reached out further. The more defective you become the more you learn, the more you know, the more shamanic you'll be.[35]

The Speak Angel Series stands at this same chasm, and dares to describe the view from its icy rim. It may be the most futuristic thing that Notley has ever written—aspiring to "remake the real," to unspeak the living and the dead alike from the "bad art" of our "broken cosmos"—but it also carries forward the ethic of listening that she has led with since her earliest works. "Leave this perverse memorization of the details of / Other people's imaginations and come with me," she urges in this grand epic's final pages. "I promise nothing but // To be in touch forever . . . A broken heart stays open." Notley's promise to stay "in touch" means more than ever in our paradoxically disconnected digital era, "this age of glass- / Fingered outreach that would make the tinman bleed," reminding us of the virtues of more sentient communion and communication. Its six books like the sides of a cube or cosmic dice which might tumble us into a better existence, *Speak Angel* offers to lead us to "the other side." Now, reader, follow.

---

35. Shoshana Olidort, "Between the Living and the Dead: An Interview with Alice Notley," *Los Angeles Review of Books*, December 25, 2016, https://www.lareviewofbooks.org/article/between-the-living-and-the-dead-an-interview-with-alice-notley.

I.

THE · HOUSE GONE

Our words are what is they say what we make
They don't stand for the universe what you see as much
Stands for them reality in the thicknesses shimmery

We are in here and each presents a face eyes closed but is
The only conscious there really is I'm listening
I'll interpret for everyone dead or alive and make the words radiate
The story so thick with breaking up layers
That you have to be in it neweyed feeling your way
The winds I forgot your story you're going to overpower me
A mind is a wind the ancestor of any mind who thinks it's contemporary

The body presses on you until you leave it you're another body
All along why was I there it's the only way
The soul me just me tornout gold and outside it activity
We are all tornout gold

She lay on the bed old her hair in spangled braids
First I couldn't find her and I couldn't find who I was
You need a red one to get into the house of our identity
Said someone and who approved the secret I asked
Later no one knew it now no one knows it at all
You need green or red rectangles to get into the house of knowledge
I am the house of knowledge I say then put on more
Layers someone else says or they'll see how transparent you are
I am the one you think I am and also another
The dying body lay in braids with her soul showing
I'm speaking in my own language
Spangled with the breaking up of gold they come to get me
It's beautiful in death it's substantial
People with jars of being animals with eyes rocks with identity
No one alive permitted to see until now would you like to know something

The first word to know
In the secret language is
Soul I'm your bond
The universe bound to-
Gether its parts speaking
To each other

Denser than matter any mind thrills to know the further mind I am
She says lying on the bed a darker woman sits beside her
My attendant as I would attend you dark and dense as a secret

The dead created the world when they were still dead
I'm frightened don't be you'll just be dead or alive
I'm impoverished momma but you're okay and I'm dead I'm okay
But it's part of my story still that I resisted money and the things
My knowledge is that now you have to speak for us
I'm still poor you have to speak for us you're our leader

You want to know how love's dangerous if it makes us or we make it
I'm sitting in a lovefilled apartment I can't let go of
It's like the most luminous dots or molecules torn as a memory
Or when I loved you was that a memory of something else I say
Your lovetorn leader that is matter as it came to be this shattered story
The broken specificity whose pieces a man could sell I know
How the universe began he says but I myself know it didn't
Walking through layer after layer of distraction in the picture
We the dead were and are the dead walking this life
The warrior knows he can't forget he killed but I know
The exact beauty of my voice and then faltering

The tricks in my hands
Al says were just guns
But I know this story he
says death is full of what
I know

I came home and there was no one there anymore another story
The curse on our family shallow I remember
We have been taught curses I can teach it to you if you want
Death is now full of what I know each one says
Each molecule says and the molecules of death
Each layer of the picture hides another Daddy says I like that
I I say can't remember a thing how can I lead you write
What you're writing it's tall in here though I'm materially bodiless

I've already told all these stories in death we represent them
We can tell them for the first or last time again if we want
In our thoughts to each other and they can change
In the story where we emerge we are emerging from ourselves
As the dead are in a chordal stave of music no one composed
I am composing it hitting random notes on the piano
There is no random there is no chance event here is a piece of change rather

When there was nothing there was something this future on earth
The knowledge we're interested in is our own composition
Which we can't stop working on without clear understanding or method
It floats secretively near that no one's in control of but
We all are and must make beautiful I came home destroyed
We know your story already you don't know how I feel and never will

You needed a red rectangle to enter here's an oval of evil you'll want
I your leader swallowing evil which lights one up but then you have to resist
You needed it then have to resist it you're trying to make me need you
The man says to me but I am not that young this will pass
Before my mind sometimes when I'm dead then I'm running I
Can't come and drink with you yes you're running from something specific
Passing before my mind sometimes when I'm dead in the past or future
When you're dead Dad says a red rectangle is a visible idea
What is the secret he asks again what do you think it is
If we didn't need each other we wouldn't be the universe
The secret is that I've always wanted to be alone because someone
Hurt me bad someone hurt me and isn't very smart either
All this talk is what it's like to be dead he said you still don't have our
Speech though you are our leader our language is quickly thought
I'm trying to get it fast I know you are he says a story's faster here too

One layer he says one smoke-
Screen
One or two in my later
Life but far back the earliest one
Sometimes comes forward
My mother left the children by
My father and took the other two

Away for a few months left us
I'm sometimes forlorn like that I say
I think a piece of so-called unconscious
Matter can be bereft
It breaks something else gets formed
It is by definition the planet is be-
Reft of what once belonged to it they
Came back he says
I don't really have to
Live it again I'm just sad that's
Part of everything luminous

I was out in the mist alone looking for a fiscal stamp
Do you go over it rue du Paradis has changed again
The windows store is still there one year I
Walked that street just trying to find oh anyone
I didn't know perfectly alone and never did
In this line I'm shy a thought leaves things out he says
Will I be allowed dead to hold back your experience
Will fill our land as an atmosphere of shapes and unexpected
Words what we're composed of thinking

No one's more special
I am your leader I
Need that little thought an-
Other says at the be-
Ginning of untime
When you know the
Future but have to play
The stars crumbled up they're
Mixed with water and mud

I came home there was no one there but myself and the dead
This small planet containing many wars fancying its economics
To be of importance do the dead ever think about money
It was a form like a rectangle money and written down or-
Dinary poems not like this immense interchange of
Mental energy where you are leading us that I am already in

I took the métro entered several stores bought objects and returned
In diurnal sense of time as if I waste it I floated outward
All of us kids would huddle under the covers together Daddy says
One of us would fart and we'd see who had to come up for air first
The dead don't fart in case you wanted to know
And I went away to war says anyone and haven't gotten over it
And the universe we are shudders from its explosions and deaths of stars
Its formal thoughts the maintenance of its
Painful designs its patterns as human minds see them
Each line should be as full of events as every forgotten day
I walk through the forest of colors Al says fearfully and I burn
For I'm dead and still traumatized no one can kill me now
But I hope to change though there's no time to change in
And then he changes because this is chaos a mellow state

I took the white rectangle from the
Cube and plugged it into the black one
These are the most transitory of objects
I hold up my fingered hands and com-
Pare mine to the fingers in the painting
More like fingers than mine
My hands are inhuman and old like my experience

What forms there of any thought categories linger
One remembers all animals had eyes but I'd see with my
Hands as well painting someone says in my thought I send
You a new red shape like a console radio or armchair
Rounded like a decade mulberry colored not frontal
To the side for more centrally there's space and it's green
I like the new picture I say there's paint in death he says
The idea of it tactility was in the vaunted mentality oh yes
The secret the own language and the played out story

The secret's probably the language we are what else would I be
No words special though I'm your leader is that a secret
If you can't remember all of yesterday the words for each micro-
Second but then more the memory yours bored and fatigued
How do you remember time in death how do you re-

Member brainlessly opulently present to me your leader
For I am dux never give up on this drawing us out of our dross
All the possible divisions of time oh don't bore me I am the universe
I mean this flatly serious I am your leader

They can film every second the
They death persists in no
Line so how do you organ-
Ize this musical chaos as in
Words I know not always the
Meaning of

I am leading us to freedom the only one with that power
Foreseen I would possess from the beginning for
It is not obvious though now it is that you need someone to tell you
Who you are the ever alive the ever dead you have tried to
Lose your souls ever present I say soul to soul in these words so like you as to be you

You never look at the right thing these days or read the signs
I am your leader I can read them inside the dead mind trans-
Lated into these thoughts coincident with letters my body or both
Bodies yours reading or hearing in this sunlessness temporary this Paris

There are no bigshots or leverage over you in death I was born to be your
Only real and strangest leader I was going to remember everything Al says
It was tall and dark in the mental forest the firefight vague pyro-
Graphic lines what I remember is how I felt a sick depression
Details aren't worth it remembered a hurtful act by me or
You I remember every word I might have hurt a person with
I say I hurt you it no longer matters he says your love has grown
Larger more generous has yours I may still be too wounded he says I'm
Waiting to love more it will be a huge release if I can let myself think
I'm allowed to love then my life will begin though I'm dead
I think you love me I say don't bother to remember the days you
Passed through he says remember permanence our own desert

We saw a road-
Runner through the window

Of the hospital
There'd been a scorpion in one
Patient's room and outside
The mountains
They're here he says for I
Imagine Boundary Cone
I do too in Paris I say
I couldn't live with-
Out it

Our attention has always existed before we were it was like a lake of space
This is the day when the black wind rushes towards me
What you see stands for these words change the line I am changing you
I'm the unrecognized possible standing in your way
We do have our epic Daddy says we the dead taking place towards and from
These lines but not linearly I call to the sea of space and mind
He says I call to the burden of our connectedness the violence of making our-
Selves to oversee this poem in a true medias res to remake
Us are we in chaos as traditionally we fool with it
Each line but of it I came from a background or did it come from me

There has never been any force controlling us except for our imaginations
I'm leading you to the crystality of your complex story I say
And we were always in the grand house of creation
The hotel we could never leave that becomes a shambles but stays
A history of instant transmission though between minds lan-
Guages and structural implacements the origin can only point backwards
He says they walk from the mountains to the river in order to name it all again
Calling it honey or grandad a green not vegetative just green
Is there subjection in death people pattern themselves in known ways til it's
Evident they don't have to be obedient to the mores of life the dreamed past

They walked to the river he says knowing they needn't and couldn't drink
And dead they wore nothing legless a cluster of minds the river was a form un-
Involved itself in lubrication or being water formally it flowed
A torrent of thought a channel of silence or of song it might sing or growl
There is a bat in my ear I say listening for sounds I can't hear
I think fast I can't sing as fast is there a fast song in death

They walk along the river he says as far as the camp where an army brought its
Wounded but who could remember which war and the women leave
We aren't women in death and we won't do anything we once did
Though you may want to listen to this meandering epic without money
Sex or the power of a boss but there are leftover nightmares and lornnesses

I'm listening to
Lead you to more
Intricate sounds still faint
They got in their boats having sacri-
Ficed a woman
To the winds re-
Member that was what life was
Always like public life
I'm so glad
To be dead
He says

And the women he tells me withdrew their minds al-
Most as one in the beginning of death according
To one version I hear I'm listening to the sounds further
Back and forth I say you who have been a victim he says
Professionally I see this by the overpowering of men are now our leader
You can be mine he says because I so much want to go there
As if it were a structure a massive warp in our fabric as we'd ac-
Cepted it until now a collection of power from nothing I
Say though there has never been negation the sounds come closer

When the souls of women leave the souls of men they also leave each other
A universal revulsion everywhere everyone would leave it the fabric you
Do it in your head you don't have a head the mind
You must begin to understand that matter's within the soul
Each of us can have our own legends whatever you'd devise
The rest of dreams are dark polar like my leftover heart

But I could not think even
Dead without admitting of you
I grieve for this inadequacy

Of imagination I would be mono-
Lithic
And I I tried to be that who am con-
Signed to your leadership

A woman walked alone he says to a source-filled basin
And if I would sleep she cried can there be any rest in death
We have to find each other in order to get any rest shouts the ghost
Wind filling the plain the woman approaches the basin backed
By the wind as companion can wind have an afterlife more
Than as thought as much as there can be any claim to origin or
Duty when that is manifestly in death only all us I speak
Through you and there is a form of anything known here in desertion
Mirroring the treason of the formation of stars and nebulae

Because of the way these lines relate within and between each other space
Manifold has not extent but relation and complicity I say and
Dialogue that's true he says you can't speak of something as if you and it
Weren't speaking that's what I see I say we need a new iconography

The woman wants to be
Alone but she is lone-
Ly wants not to sub-
Mit to alteration of thought by
Exposure to another
That you change in a banal
Or group-thought-out manner
That's the last thing I
Want do you want us to
Love you not if I have to be like
You all this was said in an in-
Stant of reflection

Chaos that loved herself for she was what was says the basin
To the woman maybe just a little bit more composition
The woman reluctantly of the dead considers herself to be gold too
I am tornout gold I want my thwarted-in-life unrecognized ac-
Complishments because I was a powerless woman to be worth something now

Oh we are transcendant now I want my honors for I
Was more skilled than any man in articulating our existence
Then you can't be alone she asked the basin of origin who are we it said I don't know
Origin is just another idea and if scientific equations work still they wouldn't if ev-
Eryone were dead oh yes they worked for us as the alive but there are none
For us now let's leave these stories awhile I see that all of you await me what if I
Said I wouldn't lead you further I say unless I were as adequately honored
As the many hacks oh that's part of a story the dead stand around my bed
Imparting their energies to my mind and limbs so I can lead them

Are you our leader a spy
In the night sado-
Masochistic human world
Where we con-
Trive to hurt or be hurt with-
Out sunrise you can eat this
Food I don't want to

Asked to denounce and shatter any basin of stillness
So that no one would rest there isn't enough light in death
There aren't any eyes they're in the back of my head and in my future

This or anywhere mental is space manipulable
In one story she croons to the green void as her poems
Could be for it must she find the minds of the other dead
I will not change for you he says she said only for myself
Little girl you are kind and brave and beautiful echoes in the green death
That was the story you liked he says to me where are we going
And if I'm not sure does it matter from line to line we wander
I met you once whoever viewed like an iconography
Is what the woman said in another version the universe doesn't
Look like anything our words find ourselves in it
Sickeningly enmeshed in the field where all others
Send forth their only minds of former has one tired of them personalities
The impulse toward individuation is older than the basin
The woman or little girl may have been kind and brave and beautiful but
Where our minds prowled that was nothing not for me she
Said struggling along the brooding plain the edge or there are no

Edges no there are none my dad says
These are our cities our connected minds do you mean chaos is our death
The boats dissolved as conveyors to war for we could not kill or
Even attack another's mind why not it would just drift away
Unlocateable there's no certain space to find it in

Let me in I'm
Looking for your
Mind why wasn't my re-
Ligion correct why
Should it have been fol-
Low me across this void
I can't follow a woman
The mind says you are
No longer a man I say
A soul is calm re-
Cede finding it and you'll
Find me why should I
I'm leading you somewhere
Not in space it comes and
Goes you'll be the only
Steady thing you know now
Except for me

I died for my god he says who didn't says another
I died trying to escape from myself says my brother why couldn't I
No one believes they're real I say until they're anguished
And our minds find each other across the cosmos without
Effort for it is impossible to be lost in that which one is
I thought I was commanded to kill each of several minds
Says but others too say other things I shouldn't have died
In an accident but I'm not dead are you content here
Yes because it's reality and it says I was a woman now
Refusing that usage what I like's mobility no sense of danger
Flashes nervesless and I see not an organism into the mind
Or words of the one that permits that and one who had killed says
Everyone I killed is here but I won't know them I
Never knew who it infidel was in the time before my body at-

Tained to its extreme of pain what was that for
Can you lead everyone I seem to be doing that do you still
Hate ones unlike you I can't find the unlikeness
What's the point then what did the woman do next
In the uncreation story I ask my dad and the souls of animals
In a peculiarly pleasureable tone or mood began to follow her
The boats dissolved the boats of the Greeks had dissolved
You are kind and brave and beautiful said the animals to the
Woman for anyone might talk and animals have always
Spoken mentally to each other as any fool might observe
I was walking in snowy Paris in a past tense mind one
Night this week in time nothing happened for why should it
Why should there be anything special or different
When it's snowing one mind enclosing all the minds
One space that doesn't exist nor is your mind visible snow is
Then you have idiot to say that it melts my mind doesn't
I think I want everything that ever happened to me to matter

Alas I am the love but must
Represent solitude
I want you to sleep so I can think
You're just dead the wind
Rails I will finally realize all
That I have been and am
And if you don't allow me my
Mind I'll
Find another entity to be that
You can't relate to

I am myself your leader I can't follow what you say someone says but
I'll follow you I think we're huddling at the shore against an es-
Carpment there's nothing here but a curious perceptual quality
A sort of gritty blankness or when I loved was that then a collective
Memory of love if one says what we are collected in is love that
Word's not it the malleable vast silence with its tones and overtones
For neither do we hear we the dead but we know how to
And so we do and what is audible exists in our death and everywhere
Let's go inside my house says the woman it's up there above the beach
I am the soul who wonders if she has need of her life says I your leader

It's a poem
So I need it
But it's a poem whose de-
Tails are so myriad I can't
Discover them all though may-
Be in an eternity they'll bespangle me
The problem being to know
What a moment or unit of living or
Memory is
There's nothing going on anywhere but an
Ever changing because new
Moments keep being noticed poem
Out of the past connected to the equally trans-
Forming now
Instantly remembered but in death

In death are we still creating memories my father says yes
The dead drift in and out of my mind while I am living
We together are trying to change the universe we want its eternity
And infinity to be more bearable it is so stitched up be-
Tween lines or events that are no longer happening but too are
Can anything happen when there are no boundaries

The denunciation comes and goes like all past happenstance
Or ephemera but is injustice diminished in death
I remember your promises to the weak whose condition you exulted
In in secret will I keep my secret when I'm dead if I find out what
It is you exulted in weakness because it created you
In death I'll continue to denounce you who had held the power I
Desired that I might be of an equal status
My inaugural speech torn and blown by the mortal
Wind following the dead when they repeat in memory their mis-
Takes can there be error in this kind of cosmos would there be
A kind of unity or only us who had split into the kings and overpowered
That I hate you doesn't damage me and soon dead you have
Nothing I would remind you as you shrink or remind me of your
Election we have all been elected to this condition I will be
Able to expose you who were fawned over by both men and women
As a device for we elected to offices machines of appetite (there

Is no food in death) machines of hypocrisy and corruption
What can I have I say what are we women ever to
Have for justice without perpetually naming ourselves
Even in death that meaningless word woman creating us but I
Am uncreated and as such and as the leader denounce forever
The notion that you who never did so might render me equal
To the self-loving possessor of office you are I am far above you so far

I came home and there was
No one there

I am leading you and there is no one there to the thrilling perfection or loss
Of power where death persists and so no one can kill me
And you can't protect or defend me there is no defense against
Me though aspirations of a clear and cutting mentality
I came home there was no one there I didn't have to be
Anyone you are our leader he always reminds me and I change
My secret is my leadership but I must shout it to you
In your minds don't you want to go to this creation without a struggle

Ask your mind if it's its own ancestor if it's its own wind
All there is is yes that's the way it is to move a thought
The spaceless movement between thoughts lets you hear it
I was born for everything to happen to me knowing these details
Rain blown or sprinkled dust they say I was born
My story plays by itself and isn't even old it's supposed to
Be looking for you but is it the first dead person or star

Dad comes bleak here it's too still in the night to whisper
I'm remembering what it's like to feel like this
When I was drunk in the live part of my existence
There are so many people for things to happen to
That the uniqueness of the facts of your suffering just
Gets me one of us says I'm prodigal forgetting my own
I think you know how I feel Dad says rather than that you don't
For as the dead let each other know their minds you though alive
Have seen mine but mine is different my brother Al says
You've killed I say I've tried to imagine myself assassin or feared

It it's immense not banal but if I can be in yours
Your mind and lose mine a little that will be better not peace he says
Relief where a moment lets me forget myself being the
Ground or starlight that someone me has to perceive
I have to perceive it I say

It is perceiving it-
Self I bring you to
Impasse don't for-
Get me it says being
Yourself

Tell me some more of the woman her house is the universe or no
She has her structure so they can't offend her it's all
About memory now existing as itself memories as them-
Selves without a body and bothering me but without them
Could I even know the ground or morning star perceiving
She kept it in a jar or box and in the house memorial photo-

Graphs
Along the walls
Silver-
Framed I remember

Don't at the beginning you get to forget something you always
Know what they are going to do to you don't you get
To forget I just have too much to say being everything and
Your leader across the heavens they can't let you forget what they know

You don't know how I feel running from something and leading
You if I could remember everything I'm running from I'd
Understand the masterwork my life though to remember every in-
Stant and the overlap it's there somewhere unstructured and I
Remember I will rejoice when she dies since she's lived so long
That the brush strokes crossing my vision with their gold flecks
Are counterparts to or not the wind nothing is the thing it is
Maybe an object but not an event I am wearing a white shirt
So your mind can remember to paint on it whatever you imagine

I painted you someone says well you
Painted something
I knew exactly you
With my eyes closed
I can't see myself I say and
What I am isn't an
Image ex-
Cept as made into one by
Others
I don't even have a mirror

When I drank I didn't have to see clearly Dad says but I saw something
Dead I see something do you see me I see your words always so young
You had round eyes and you liked me I like you now
I made such mistakes where are their outlines the only out-
Lines belong to our minds I signed the lobotomy papers
She's freezing she doesn't have a hat she's standing right beside you
And death isn't cold I've been through it again he says

I'm going to carry all of you my mind singing black colors
You need to go north or south or somewhere another inside
I have to be my soul dead he says but I can't get my thought
Free almost but I'm not wholly better more paint on or off
There's something in time always that won't let go of me
I get tired of people I say but you serve them always he says
You have the talent an emphasis within you allowing reception
Of other voices to construct a universal knowledge of ourselves

What do you
Think the secret
Is
It's that it's not as
It seems anything
Isn't
You haven't known a
Thing

That's about it what language are you all speaking thought
I'm wearing a diadem for the pun but seeing it be-
Cause there is sight everywhere the senses are everywhere
Are they and the words are quick to push oh I see your thought
Are we or are we not united the woman in the primal
Story isn't and covers herself in her house or shelter I'm
Dead and can do as I wish you must release me let me go
For you did nothing but diminish me when I lived
There is only us forever we're losing our unpleasantness
It's hard to hold onto things here they come back but then leave
They return to another line or verse our memories our imprint
If I had not been like that but you were she said and I can hold on

They have left bad art in my house against the white walls she said
Made out of coathangers give it back or throw it out I
Refuse to have bad art in my death the woman says it
Has to be as good as a live lily was or a rock or anyone's body
Refuse bad art she shouted that's the end of a primal tale he says of
Course I wouldn't know what bad art is he says
I do I say it isn't the result of suffering to be a form oneself or
Like this poem I'm writing for you we were born when

The universe ex-
Ploded
But I was never
Never born any I
Was never born

You were a fussy baby he says these words from my mouth or hand
Cannot be coathangers or dull plastic they could be old or dis-
Carded like a lost jack or paper rose the poetry's in a beauty con-
Tinuously recognized back and forth between origin and demise
Death and oh these almost used up words like hated
I can hate the woman said I can hate bad art the dead
Shouldn't make it wrongly picturing rain in our nonsensuous
Minds it should be wet and complex strings of like thoughts
Sticking together thunder makes it grow the flash of cognition
A pluvial loving manifestation that's you the rain of death pun oh yes

The woman mentally walked across the yellow sands or remains
Asking you to explain there's really no way to extinguish us
But we aren't what we thought we were thinking everything you
Your ears that don't hear you thinking what hears you thinking
We keep trying to find new forms for ourselves the dead say
Can't open a certain door the woman in the story pines in a deathly
Manner that is ever less but still sometimes with a pang I
Wasn't supposed to long anymore for what for past recog-
Nition now the moment's gone they all are as I move
From line to line looking for the one word to rest in across
The navy blue heavens constellations that shift
The lack of the four directions you don't have to be fertile here
Someone said to her forming forms the old way
I want to formulate she says my historical loss and at last focus your
Attention there the wind scatters it but doesn't destroy it for it
Is ever thought and seeds are here as ideas glowing
I don't know how to live here and I don't know if I want to

My body doesn't
Hurt any-
More nor is weak
I can like that
I don't stop
Being conscious
I think this uni-
Verse is only a
Moment old no I
Mean the whole thing's
Right now a
Voice says

I'm still living out what you did to me though I'm dead the
Woman said in the story he says so the final part
Can be in the one moment of the universe you're knowing
It wasn't you it was me what do you mean think
About it she said think about what that means
My mind says things as I hear them with what soundlessly
There is a form here of any thing any size desert breeze

I would allow an ungendered voice to build a massive shape of
Compacted black energy to lead you to speaking
Here the woman might have had a new bag large and beige
I am details you are learning to perceive lead you to
Consciousness wherein is the astral wind or the moon one word or an-
Other lit and breathy from my running away

I'm less haunt-
Ed there's desert
In me and the minds
Often Dad says
Tell their own stories
Do you acquire more
Stories there are
Dreams everywhere
To be in or not
Why are we any-
Thing you're sup-
Posed to I
Think tell us
Without refer-
Ing to anything else
Any other uni-
Verse

The woman in the story said my dad says there is nothing to
Refer to but my experience this is the beginning of the cos-
Mos a voice said and also its end she said I like that part he says
It means there's neither one like when I did the snake dance
And its head and tail drooped down from the middle in my mouth
I acquired this language but since I am it it's tell-
Ing me what it's thinking that old wind or winding one in the mouth

There's nothing to
Refer to except us

Blue and circle say the word blue it's a black circle is
This a poem or a performance of origin maybe the word isn't blue it's

A single though one sound like star not iris the poem I'm
Reading or am I went there I was there come along
Blam black the late turquoise flash your or his message to me
My old friend dead it's blueness flashing a black circle
I wonder if it should hold still who knows more than I
The weather in this room is over if the woman has to wake up if
She wakes up dead I'm sorry but you're not my teacher
Did anyone ever teach you anything says my dad if you knew it
In an instant as if you already knew it as you did

The Greeks have
Come to show me
How different and
Sad they are
The Greeks mad-
Deningly destroy
The tantric flash
Blue black red af-
Ter glow

As fast as I know it the universe begins without precedent
When it comes from nowhere and no one could do anything but be in it
Who wanted me to be theirs but mostly are scared of not
Having currency blam flash blue or if you were only dead someone
Says I could have all of it all the words and shapes
But they're there because there's more than one of us

I'm always between the woman said the origin of the dead and our ultimate
Form do you understand that so she returned to the basin he says
And regarded it she had no reflection and its outlines wavered was it small
Or pond-sized you're supposed to be the ideal basin no it said I'm
The basin of origin I may be an idea but I'm not sure you can see me
Can I reflect everything all at once but which things are there at
Zero rule out chance mostly the inked-in tires or cycles of the
Weary old vehicles the taking of blood what's left it was when I and
She said when I was free but what of the fact they have contempt for me
A woman down the line and if you're free says the basin you can have
Everything in your own power without linguistic hoax I'm the language
I and I thought it before I said it we return in death to original telepathy

And so the
Words
Come to me
I'm leav-
Ing this house
For another
Which
House for which

I'm haunted in Paris by leavingness but I don't leave
I'm wearing rust my manuscripts are packed up in a
Mental coffin like oh it's too big to be a
Person the universe is casting off words to me cells or
Firebombs the first knowing between parts of the unity would
Have needed no pieces like words until gradually I and you
Were and now you won't even speak to me though I
Still want you but I'm your leader why you you think
Because I'm the only one thinking you're
As distant as spring or death as distant as the con-
Stellation Aries marry someone to recreate the beginning
A man shoots with a pistol a ring onto my finger then weeps
Whose little baby will you be I'm your leader not he
But I'm dead the socalled Native American said to me
Last night I know I said I don't know if I can live with you he
Said well I think you have to we're all dead together
He wore goldrimmed glasses sure you can write like this but
On the other hand you can't no clue how to because I'm really
Hearing the dead and if you were you wouldn't know it

Be good to us they
Said
Don't use us we're
You but oh didn't
We use you
Vomit and lotuses I
Mean a man
In an under-
Shirt on the métro and
In this weather

A grave ac-
Cident to a passenger
At Sully-Morland
Was it me
Says a dead voice a bit
Of vocal
Disarray
With
Melodious a
Temporal or de-
Ceptive lin-
Gering it's only
There
In your head

I wasn't allowed to be alone with you always like that nor
Can I be alone for I am your leader he ties a string he's
Tying me to the tree of life a dream or vision a thought I'm
Cultivating can the dead become smarter than they were alive yes
Anyone can in any moment of this vast one moment aching
To improve she lay there dying not in braids
I was holding her hand both ours old hers older small the
Both I couldn't remember her skin from before she was wrinkled
She was always light-filled I didn't know how to die she says now
I keep an eye on you and listen to your heart what do you mean
I don't exactly know it's that I hear when your feelings cry out
But you did that when you were alive I didn't know I did then

The basin rippled across itself no wind or a phantomic one
I'm thinking it said I've become self-conscious that would
Be one version I prefer the one where I always was self-conscious
I like the basin better than people the storied woman said though
I'm afraid it is people and everything else a helicopter crashes
In a street near the beginning of time for time is a mush
And I'm dead the woman said everything you people said was
History in your wrinkled hand a flesh of possible story the
Outlines wherever you decided you saw them you suckers
One of the most important concepts is vengeance she said if

Vengeance be in the future on earth it's now if you're dead
I'm listening vengeance said as impressionable as the basin
The basin's the size of an oasis do you mean a large or small oasis

Do you re-
Member says my
Mother
The one just across the railroad tracks at
That junction
Small the water's full
Of tadpoles
On the
Way to Vegas

Nothing will ever be more important than that one stretch of road
As far as Searchlight traveling on it an event transpiring
Many times whose boundaries I care about I might
Lead you to it I'm leading you to other shapes lines in
Chaos to create what we think to each other
I'm going to create says my brother Al a large desert thought
Like a bounty of transpiring without incessant payback
I can't pay back anymore somewhere on the map I'm done

To heal being
All the patients
Galactic
Planetary live
Or dead in
Unrecorded until
Now dimension
Cry out
To
Be
Healed

Where are you the dimension's in the mind is it not anywhere if
Speaking the woman must have done something else she's still
In the story and its variants for I he says was in debt I owe someone

Something the woman said I don't owe anyone anything I
Am owed that's where we were on her map I am the owed one

This is the line she walks to leave you whom she can't stop addressing
Along a railroad track in death everyone knows that train
It might come for you in forest or city but if you live in the desert
You might wait at a named little house with its switch as if it were a
Town in alphabetical order Aborigine Boreal Cadiz Damascus Elizabethan I could
Have waited at Fort Emptier but I walked on the tracks to meet the train counting
Crossties at the beginning and forever counting the way to nowhere
Progress of a life my compadres and in death I'm still a cynic she said
There is such variation in emptiness this story scares
Me I say me too my brother says even though I'm dead and know
It isn't empty or like counting all the rocks in the gully
What is it like then it's like these lines in opposition to the winding
Story and as you or we are making it chaos straightens out a little
Always simmering behind things what makes your dreams

What you use
Our us we use
To make the us
We choose

The woman said I did not choose to be made a woman now in
Death I have a choice for you can't kill me again why did
I live my brother says so the one that was you could exist
Didn't I exist before I was you weren't in the play and you were
Playing I always played and war was playing a meteor
Shower an entirely destructive beginning of an age

Where are we going in our mind the basin said you
Can't walk the woman said neither can you you're dead
I've been walking for forever the woman said my dad says
A gigantesque epic made for men become mine and I tell you
According to the exactions of my dreams I say we must live
This new epic not paperdoll cutout poems omitting all of thunder and
Flash communication among billions of light years across

The body of the quasar are we going there he says well we
Are it I'm still not sure where we have to go within us song of our shadows

The dead woman still walked as if trying to die along the railroad tracks
What about her house I say he says that's in a variant where
She keeps trying to clear it of the terrible presents others bring
But as the others get used to being dead their gifts change
Yet she still declaims we need a new iconography so
You can't see me this way I don't look like anything anyway
Chaos depicted as swamp water or image of pulsations
The overtone series or space something non-existent

To tell you what it's
Like he says
I'm exactly where you are
Right now but it's
Where we
Are the dead and also
I and you
You are a location
Of conviction and sounds
Rays warping out
A bundle of light but I
See your
Mind
We are the place of mind
And I can find you
Because you're al-
Ready where we are
And you know this

There's no proof of anything in death the woman said
There's no proof even that I'm dead and I loved you she said
There was never any proof of an event there were no
Events and are there now I'm locked into vastness forever
As if walking and walking though in the house variant
She keeps finding foolishness icons she dislikes left for

Her in the house with fuzzier and fuzzier outlines disappearing frames
I grow up already knowing most of it as if I'd lived my life
Now your leader since I was four because you aren't clear
What would a leader be what kind of word I've ascertained
No adults live by their principles the little girl and the older
Woman both know this because you must concentrate all your
Intelligence giving up much that others value
Thus the universe a sloppy mess violent and weepy
Meteoric tears fall nothing coheres sensibly you see outlines
Name them to feel secure patterns a million years for that to orbit this
The universe destroyer self-mutilator age four I walk about my block visiting
Grownups I know in the sunlight eccentric and abandoned women
With their sons sex mad there's nothing else known to be
Broken cosmos sex and power the only mind I can trust is mine
It is our house there's no god we must be able to change

And I am
Changing he
Says by
Being in this
Poem

In simultaneous time enacting the beginning and ending but in
Individual time having one's own version and difference un-
Interested in community determinism or your blue or brown or
Pale white ghost eye I am leading you and no one else is
In individual time I accept nothing previously thought the
Woman said at the beginning he says how did we make it
For it is nothing but one big grotesque it without bounds
Our limits a perceptual idea originating in eyes
Only the wind at my back denies I forget what she was doing

End of the day cold in a little girl's swimsuit near Wetmore's it's
End of the end of the day blue and pink my mother's dead in the
River my father has returned to the sky and I'm alone
It's sad but necessary because at the beginning I was be-
Fore us I remember the gradual encroachment of darker color
Something tries to make your eyes react causing sentiment

We sit on the
Grass he shows her a
Check
Has she had the
Lobotomy or
Not

I don't want to be all the same thing of you nor the woman
The woman said you can't give me a lobotomy in death
Dad says this version's sad can you bear it I say I
Said it didn't I I say doctors and scientists will tell you
Something's true a good idea I only want to take you to
To to I will always have done that he says though she's here my
Sister beside me she says I too am trying to find my beginning
Before the world took me in or took me over

I sat in the water holding pink desert flowers there's a photo
At the beginning of time I told you to stay away from me
But I knew I had to save you later violently in love
How horrible that seems a seizure and the water colder
The sky could be yellow-white the edgy more-real-than-oneself
Mountain averring one didn't exactly exist one might want that faceoff
As a consciousness I think it is a consciousness she says
The mountain faces me down but I face it down too

Once I was nothing but I know it while nothing I knew it conscious
That I was nothing this is possible without judgment or desire
As you'll find yourself being that nothing in certain in-between
Moments of your in-life life how quickly you've said or conveyed
That he says I'm sorting it out why does my brioche taste like
Fish this morning in individual time I don't care if I'm be-
Having like others or not I'm searching for a certain tongue
That first time you spoke directly in my head I say to him
Your words were careful we speak in a kind of static here he
Says about every fourth or fifth word is heard everything
Else is erased sentence structure the shape of music we
Need we don't need the meaning it's in the coincidence of our
Minds as if from a million billion years ago it's what

I or we always was or were that staticky overtoney mind-
Sound speaking a language that no one knows just language
When you're nothing that kind of conscious it hums is this
True I don't know I hear you my mother says

I just hear
You
I'd say one
Word and you'd
Know
The rest of the
Sentence
Or rather what
I meant
The sentence could
Have been re-
Arranged but
That one
Word

Nothing linear the ache after you in a smeary shape
My eyes sort out the room I bought the objects to
Use them in ways their forms suit them to my contact
Lenses rearrange astigmatism but sometimes I'm not here
Who are you then the cabinet full of my and Ted's
Poems has no meaning then long white hairs on the polka-
Dot chair who are you now you've stopped thinking
The tiny Greek woman holds up iconographically a cup
In black space and speaks in Linear B I hear
Assurances it's a big outfit my mother would say

These hyacinths this bowl these designated gods
The designated curse or christ for one's already ageless ad-
Herence press against the hips of the crucified one
Why so you can bring him the gift of your self and not have one
Shallow as a krater may you be the woman brings the
Suffering man primroses his pain and understanding
Always of the most depth as if there were depth they

Board their primitive black ships for the only war ever
Fought do you call yourself primitive I call the whole
Cosmos primitive and only my own thought of suf-
Ficient sophistication to remake it listen says the voice
I have watched within a span of thousands of years
Nothing progressing but techné fine detail momentary
People alive in the smallest corner of time im-
Properly perceived the only knowing always suppressed

Whatsoever
Heard not
Prevailing but
Writ
In mute air

Knowing but this counter melody we or I ar-
Rive it is I in the broken water placid then rippled
But was I the placidity to find between their
Hysterical fits what else is combat what they feared
In us this quiet the language or background pat-'
Tern of exactly my mind listen with a different
Changing ear to my project the memory
And this crackling graph the verity of material
The material of death that they would too have
Killed but couldn't find ever though riding its sound

No line none of these lines the way out of the maze
My project the memory can't help me leave what house
The cursed house says the Greek what about this syntax
Pull it up or together try to keep its crackle the sense is
All in the mind I'm leaving you earrings I always say
Blind in the dark as the new line starts your project's the mem-
Ory the whole one expressed by the supposition what we see ma-
Terially but are these shapes thee shapes that I've cursed
Who hasn't try to remember without the given structure of
Remembering walking near poplars toward the road that leaves
What can I ever leave when the line goes backwards too
I don't know what to leave progressing backwards the same seg-

Ment of the maze changes into a possible exit
Give me the words of it who ask the shorter sorrow
Spate of words extension to ancient dark green trees I
Will never cease to be myself no matter how far back though
I change utterly I will always be thee consciousness
Out of my first mouth words I don't know but say freely
Can you remember them that I have pressed it the seal so
The outlines in wax can dissolve the air itself is
Dark the molecules of air are dark here as if we were
Light figures inside it that I was the illuminative
Faculty of this dubious cloying and watery extent
I moved upon it before the ships came to cry for battle
I was the consciousness and had no wish
This progress backwards made of words stamp on
The clayey element that may be death Dad it's more like
The dark-colored air and do I have a form of language
Or image or house you can live properly here
Moving over the waters like god and some words

A spine of
Diamond-
Like
Lights
The words are al-
Ways already
There

Language that anything speaks in order to ad-
Here for we are involved in sticking together it all hums
He told you with his mind he was someone else but we were
Pieces of the quasar the sun itself told her they were pieces
Of a mind this is a dead sun hundreds of thousands of light
Years away it is the icon but in death not precisely hot do you re-
Member heat I ask everything's here he says in different combination

And the dark sounds I hear in the February morning are you
Locating me thinking everything is as I move or sleep
I'm leading you all of you who ever lived are you listening

Go to a mind is a wind that we're elected is no food there's
No food here the woman dispatched walking those tracks
I don't have to eat in death but in life we eat lobotomies
I died for my god eat it he isn't even of course he isn't here
There's no god every god you ever appeased was yourself
Every heaven you found shiftingness she said the original tele-
Pathy when I have the first thought ever thought why
Are we going to form into them the images the linear let-
Ters curse by the wind treason of formation of giant
Stars the grief of killing off your mirror masochistic
Now I have to lead you that's why you have sprinkled my blood

I mean we did it together without knowing what it was
The woman walking the tracks said I don't believe I did
It Dad says counting the tracks one billion and Andromeda one
Is it this track that changes everything or is it the
Next I am waiting she said for the pleasure in death to
Overtake me when I am finally justified you our
Leader he says are supposed to justify her I say all
The old dead shamans stood around me last night awaiting my
Call but I want them to strengthen me it is you
He says he really says leading the flickery bacterial let-
Ters existing from our origin inside the oasis

I've passed the
Oasis she
Said and I've passed
The poison white
Flowers in
Death they're
Abstract a
Fris-
Son

And then the voices all of them we have been poisoned
It's seductive yet there is no cause or effect we're poi-
Soned we're just ruined as if we wanted to be but did we
The language the skittery spidered bacteria I was one I

Swam to the shore the smallest thing there was in the black
Purple red black there was only this iota I was but I per-
Ceived the pulsating immensity of waves I was tossed by
Heard as a dream of the separated out was I the large or
Small and which am I now is now separated out

They broke into
My apart-
Ment and stole my
Computer
With this po-
Em on it their
Own e-
Pic

Look for me the voice said are you there write with
The fire of the first in the space between lines soldier
I wrote with my mortar volcanic no space in this
Fight at the first hat dwellt at a word scratch it in black
Kilroy kill the king but he's already dead in this death
So I say that to the woman said which is now her name
It is the future how much beauty can there be now with-
Out suffering I'm traveling to get to your heart the woman
Said to the basin of origin I'm right here the basin said
But I can't get there without walking dead when I was about
Twenty-three years old I wrote a story about Marie
Many years later the protagonist of my book Culture of One
She was walking to Africa counting crossties one-
Thousand-and-Africa-one I had just been in Morocco

Look for me I'm fighting in fire Nam I can't breathe
You must be dead it was exactly at that time
It wasn't a sport I couldn't take any of it with me
Any of the pieces of my body and yet I arrived in death
I think we reconstituted you soul but how oh you loved me
I've spent a lot of time thinking how all of us were
Good together the mountains part of it our group
When we were about twelve but you're

Saying our love holds it together yes he says
This love deposited everywhere keeping too planets in
Space you know I still hear your voice I say
That was my old friend Tony Garcia

In the night
I helped
Them heal some-
One when his gauz-
Y or mobile -- it re-
Sembled water in
Motion but in
Formal place -- soul
Left his body
To sit by me while they
Healed it I held
His hand you don't
Believe this and they
Healed the outer form he
Slipped back inside then
In return
They healed me of cer-
Tain afflictions

Come to a country to absolve fractious counter-
Part but we all sing the same opera and could heal it
Step into the uninvidious nonvoid inter alia especially be-
Tween the live and dead for I have been there often and know it
Here hold his hand sometimes for months one who could not
Be healed but could be accompanied most of the way

The woman Dad says the woman said she still only wanted
To count crossties walking I'm changing what about the one
With the house it has an expansive interior first orange then blue
Orange is a danger color is it dangerous to enter my house
You're about to go as far inside as anyone can anywhere
You have a new necklace of tiny skulls whose I don't know
Flowers and you huge will only ever be a certain one dead the

Universe he says that you are healing as yourself the people
Want to worship something the woman said tell them to
Go to hell the basin said he says that is in the variant
The basin is personal because one not dead is tired tired
This morning in a turquoise sweater you can't know a-
Bout the afterlife because you might want to go there too
Quickly that presupposes rules he says I'm not sure that
There are any rules anywhere in this universe on
Either side of the wall though there is a unitive language

I can't al-
Ways find the
Poetry in
This poem
It comes as
If ac-
Cidentally
I'm trying to
Find you
Poetry replies
I'm through-
Out though
You're mistaken
I
Don't always
Come as you've
Known me
Look
Underneath
What you've
Written
Every-
Thing every-
One is speak-
Ing to you I
Am the primal
Principal the
Tone of
Voice

I'm bringing you to the crazy quasar that may be singing
Failure fabulous place me in your heart and listen
Someone sits crying and trembling the quaver in all us
I went to the past emptiness of deep or dumped space
Around surrounding me icons in focus then failing
We're shorthanded my attic staff's uncalm I feel very very
Bad the murderess a word whispered this is my
Secret you're talking to way down in my I D she
Says you can remember but it's me not you I remember
No one told me I and then I'm past and in word flame
The word is joy from my vantage as god if you carve the
Letters after you speak that's at the same time as the first
Where the maze the cooler sounds a no cash advantage
Are you faking it I don't know I never do someone said
My name a woman last night intrusively people I don't
Like are now trying to get in you may have to let them
The woman said collapsed in the flame colored part of her
Quasi house the ground was multiple intense
With righteousness for we the ground too speak the
Original language I need a moment of rest to rock you

The ob-
Ject is an
Ob-
Long shad-
Ow
Perpendic-
Ular to
Our
Idea
Of a
Ground
That is my
Guilt
One
Says

If you couldn't see where we're going if you can't it's what as an
Astronomer one sees with human eyes since it's inhuman really

But the dead they do see ideas they see dreams anything
The way oneself is save in the memory project for we invented
Memory it used to be spread throughout our mass as one thing
Large and it yours was anywhere because the past (that at
The beginning is the future) was anywhere everywhere you don't
Have to have the concentrated one in you I work at so hard lead-
Ing you to places within where the lacy chaotic upright layers
Are always shifting go on one-billion-and-Antares-one til the tracks
Stop I could just as easily see this cosmic flesh as words
What are they then that I am speaking in your mind always trans-
Lated says this is sshhh I see that the qualities are like in
A body where my words begin preternatural foretaking this smal-
Ler life chronos to distribute it among my dead dimensions
Eyes flashing searchlights charring the words like foliage grow

It presupposes you have eyes the universe does but what kind
Inside the words my eyes and ears don't focus I jingle and tremble
Every word piece of what we are salutes you we could be walk-
Ing black deathcold space but we're yes I am in this
Trajectory because I have a damaged what consciousness or
Will to live that's prattle the interpretations of those who need to
Be led can there be those I can't wait for them to be more intelligent

All
Approa-
Cheth
Anal-
Pha-
Betically
As if
They
Hummed

There are white cars from the late 40s wrecked in moonlight
We are letters they say and the flesh of my heart that
Exterior to me beats because I'm outside it dead
You can smear the space night air on it's silent and shakes
I hear palpitations earless is it because I already know or

Why do I see the journey it's been taken before words see and
Hear themselves from another time and climate also from the first

There it is calmer than a troubled mountain I mean within us
It would use me then what for it is troubled some-
Thing I approach a mash of language or saying
You can hear something windlike telling you you're
Here I'm always here I'm always doing this this seeking
If I find it what point if I continue on counting crossties
People following me single file ticking off their minutes
This and then so what whistles I'm just these words it
Says anything alike straightforward mine my
Can't you talk to me qualities it's a problem that simply I
There's us it says and anticlimatically I just start talk-
Ing are you a structure I think so are you in the
Earliest days of itself I say and in the latter days of strife
Everything would seem to be a given we are the divine it
Says what good's that at first when you circle around to the be-
Ginning door I was there with my musical tremor
The words are formed from I hear your own vastness count-
Ering you don't have to translate anything I know

I went
To the for-
Tune teller
And she told
Me I would
Have two
Loves
I went to the
And told me
She didn't
Say who
You are a
Border-
Line gen-
Ius she
Said why set-

39

Tle for border-
Line I
Didn't
But she
Didn't
Tell
Me
I would have
To suffer
Suffer in
Order
To
Cross
That
Border

All the borders are confused it says except
For between us you can cross it but it's
Not confused it says between words or tones I say be-
Tween the betweens get smaller then we coin-
Cide what and I've done that before what do I do a-
Bout that I can't remember why I came here the green void
Or voice it is the first one of me I say my first voice

I'm not really here where I say I am the trouble is you are
Where else would you be somewhere unconstrained also indi-
Vidual to me no one else wanted where I began I
Say if we're in death where are we and is it the structure dead
I haven't kept life and death separate of course not it says I
In the iconography of senses and science am a quasar group
And I don't want to decide what you might be that is
An individual choice too death isn't but you can name your
Own death whatever you want to it says I guess I am a we
I'm not sure I say what you are for me I might be look-
Ing for something like caritas or to be that I'm not really
A scientifically defined entity it says I don't want that either

It
Doesn't
Matter that
I'm large and
Old I'm
Not I'm
Right now

You might I say to it half chanting be a suicide
Room you might be a death of the universe room you might
You might be so old that because you're so big you're at the
End except you're maybe so big you're endless as I am
Extending myself I say from before the beginning to af-
Ter the end in your it says iconography it says I'm finite but
Don't feel that way like you several of my gigantic times
Loaded on but sing too past all boundaries
Of time trembling everyone can always remember the
Sound of my voice for as you or someone just said
Memory is everywhere everywhere no one can kill it-
Self or selves I have embraced as much as I
Could it says of the structure we are but there's so much
They tried to make me enter I say the suicide room but
I wouldn't go in turn on the lights my selves like yours
My decades my children cry out with me turn on the lights

The parent
Of the
Universe any
Of us
Ex-
Tends its
Icono-
Graphic arms
To em-
Brace
All of
It though the

Stone's worn a-
Way
You
Know
It
Holds you
It
Who is
You

Noise sounds of a language one of you I old am been
The tacky gods and before them as I hit time you have to
Hm hm to untime speech to get what I hum or say
Or speak all at once I say without a where this it says
Maybe in the basement I when it pees the bed or the thing
What a quasar shouldn't no shouldn't have become this
Large and bizarre I get it I we're it not out of control but it hap-
Pens when it happens not as in your eyes or a little
Inside a Latin word I say like exultantque we're that
It was inflection but also a piling up I'm inside
But if you're light it says I might eat you I'm in your thought

And I
Go there it's
Not in my
Head but
I
Don't know
Where

Any it thing you say and they'll quote it I found you
I found another you billions of light years across
There's an ending in the middle and then I go on outside
Cracked contact lenses in my eyes still when you see me you
Say tragic but privately I say genius for I got what I wanted
To experience fully my talent as large as anyone's who's ever lived

Language I wrote it on your back the woman said to the ghost
Wind companion along the tracks and veering off to a small spring
It was another form of the basin of origin I speak origin
It said you must be what my dad is like I say no the
Woman said he is like himself it said and so am I it said
I'm not yours I'm myself and there is no great selflessness to
Exult in are you sure the woman said and it said as you
Are the woman said I am the basin or basis a separation
From what I'm the basis of but we understand each other
The woman said but others less and less at this time or one
Time it said I caught something and forgot it the wind that
Someone would love me a long long time ago the woman said

People on the
Yellow or green
Plain
Frantic
To migrate or bat-
Tle but they
Can't they're dead
And must com-
Municate for-
Ever instead like a
Turbulence
Gradually
Calmer so you
Can enter into com-
Plexity with its
Thought
Patterns of thought

The language came across the expanse creating as it
Led us was us making time and no time presupposing al-
Ternatives that weren't and nonexistence for it could do that at
Least later in its degraded form the dark full of letters
Images dreams and invocations of truths how did I get here
It's a big language my mother says every letter's big be-

Cause my mind is a different size now I shrink them
To speak to you but it's easy is this true kind of
They heard them in their own language at Pentecost
Because the minds first came when upheavals forced
Them to cry out to each other not to lose their each otherness

All of the future beings and forms their souls cross the plain to be at the
Beginning they are everything ever to be and the spirits of broken off
Masses and planets maybe all of spirit is here why is there that
Because there is something we know that by being ourselves
But are future events here there is no such thing as an event
Said the basin to the woman I don't want to know everyone she said
What you might call sky is purple the plain's pale sands
Everyone sees who they are going to be when they learn the lang-
Uage they know it immediately then they forget and no one's
In charge this is the only way it could be the basin said
Many know they won't exist in the stupid life for eons
Whatever they do for eons they forget is this true the woman
Said the only way it could be and for all of eternity after death
They will be working on it too but it might be what they did
Before birth work on the afterwards already there are no past lives
This is just another story the woman said they come and go the basin said

I knew you were my
Dead lover but al-
So my live one
I wonder if my dreams
Are my real
Life
Life so pallid
How did I
Get here
The problem was
That there is
Nothing linear except for
Written
Words
Compressing too all of

Time
Into an
Utterance

Let's try to remember more I say okay Dad says and of the language
You mean he says that time and evolution are only spirits yes

In my first voice I've been working on the universe forever though I seem
To be in this life where you're at anyone truck with headlight eyes
See this winding road it can be ordered and set up anywhere who
Ordered it for me my mother says you can get one in the dark
Let's go back Daddy says in my first voice I've worked on my life for-
Ever in the memory project where even stars recall their fates
And yet here in death they're just spirit another mentality
Wholly intact of exploded matter do you believe do you really
Know this there's all of spirit here he says with dotted-line
Boundaries between entities sending out messages he says
The inanimate one always had a message that it was stuck together a form
You could see it so for one thing remember Spirit Mountain he says

It was at
The beginning its
Structure
Over time called
To it why
And I stood next to
It weeping
For my-
Self
I don't under-
Stand
Nothing is
In charge yet I'm
Fated with a
Ghost wind at
My back
Anyone says

Dad says I remember wanting to be older never got to be old
But at the beginning I sensed poverty that money would
Affect me I would be helpless to aid Dorothy when she be-
Came mentally ill billions of years from then then death
Life an island or story I would return to death with memory

Is this truly being said I said it he says I see your
Mind face but when you're dead it's the same I keep
Losing the language I'm not sure I can show it to you
Once a truck was turned over near the oasis a man had died
Each line lightning fast timeless the minah said or dove
Squish it together until its languageness dissolves
You don't need to do anything today he says you're lucky
Because you need so little you brought me up that way
I'd had so little he says I wanted to give you a lot but I didn't
Even know what it was I'm thankful for that I say how

It wasn't specific sounds so much as what we were
With words I stood on the yellow sands fully realized
You will suffer but you can't break a wiry continuity
Between the events arising from emotional emphasis that
Is anguish the Greeks played it like your stripped spine
But before them I know what they know caught in my chest
To speak in thought so quickly the way it goes conducted
The way it is out in the hall pushing a mop blunt blunt
Against my door I could even dance the language
Sometimes he says we mentally speak standing at
The beginning foreseeing the events of a life not
Caused that's empty I stand there the only way out is to lead
You because I remember and you don't what we have to do

You
Kept
Seeing
The
Destruc-
Tion
Of

The
Record
Of
Our
Love

But I only love the mountains the woman said and the
Woman in the variant he says said I love the deepest blue
Part of my house I love you my brother says for being my
Voice I I say kept seeing the destruction of the record
Of our love does it need to be recorded it can be endlessly thought

We the living universe the record we the dead still recording
Somewhere only in mind without a limit or brainish base
How have you learned to find us in the language of trauma
For there is a break between us and I've always searched for
You I say but what do you see we crowded around you
Last night in your sleep trying to be in your dreams
I am breaking myself again I say to write this
You are doing that for us it's empty I say where the
Living of my planet were I see future emptiness
I have always seen this it's you I'm trying to see we
Aren't sure of ourselves I wonder if we could go a step
Further back I'm depressed
You will just have to see what we need anyway
I have become untrusting but we aren't trustworthy alive
Though the dead can be trusted partly ignorant oh
The spring the basin or oasis of origin offers me nothing
What do you see I see with eyes oh no you don't he says
You see like me a dead man who doesn't wear glasses

Because the word fragmented convulsively I saw it in the
Void that was blue or green it was too big for your eyes but
I was already deceased we bits of logos swarmed the plain
Foreseeing our future battles but first we took pieces of
The word pasted them back together into a made thing
I like that story Dad says the first poem I'm what I know

I'm not sure the word broke apart first somewhere in
Circular time the word would be broken at the end in or-
Der for the world to start again there is no nothing

So I
Keep
Break-
Ing them
Down
The
Mar-
Gin
Of my
Lo-
Ve

But it took a billion billion years for us to stick to-
Gether into our now apparent cohesion did it he says
Only communication or communion not farts under the
Covers but nonetheless as intimate as you can get

I first saw the word or my memory in the light of conflict
There's so much effort to matter learning to crawl
Oh creep on the ground and babble I want you to know me for
This is what I am in the house of molecules no I didn't want that
Every memorable poem knows the body's an insapient
Mess I acquired as one of my words but it's not the only logos

My i-
Conic
Self
Be-
Longs to
You
That's what
It's
For
At the be-

Ginning
We be-
Came what
We could
See
The crows caw
See me
Bellig-
Erent I'm
Watching dead I'm
Watch-
Ing
In the first
Lang-
Uage I'm
Broke-
N word
Watching

They'd still like to cut you in battle if you'd bleed but
Dead you don't and their limbs don't rush them along
They seem to hold up shields but it's a thought pattern
When we stand on the plain before living we're intelligent not
Needing courage for it isn't separate I don't want the
Woman said separate qualities I want control of my form
There's a masterpiece to be lived written by men then what
I am a voice forever firm and elemental you'd think to
Me death alters your prejudice but doesn't heal me
In the epic the real one I walk back across the plain
I stand there Alice speaking now in this forever place
The epic of the dead transpiring at a single point
For do we have to be born to be dead and see mental colors
Both more subtle and intense than the ocular the sub-
Vision of the ungenerous pressing on your heart

I'm afraid of this poem it won't let go of me he came into my
Life the woman said in his view to change it but I am my star
Dead I will not allow another to change me now only I

Can do that one-trillion-and-only-I-one the woman
Said and why would I change he says I like her but all of
Death must change together I'm resting for a moment I
Say in the prow of the ongoing boat or brain there is no
Live lover but I will make up for that by loving anyone I see
Or lead it snowed then afterwards the snow fell dangerous-
Ly from rooftops crashed on the sidewalk we walked in the
Middle of the street I may be leading you to a blank rose
The universe changes and knows its own language
She went out to the grey shore where pieces lie of our epic
And formed them into salt or a savor
Each word was a piece of me the logos I couldn't
Find or say though my mind always the un-
Expected as I hear it my sourceless oneself
There are waves here speaking and shorebirds speaking
The woman said I mean Dad says the variant
The different woman went into her house with the pieces
Tasting of the shore but I still can't remember this lang-
Uage she said to it and it spoke back

You went somewhere
I went somewhere where
I had to be dif-
Ferent like Paris
But these sounds
Call electrically to a
Core of one
Til it re-
Sponds for I'm
The form
I'm the language

I stand on the plain dead not yet born I'm listening for us
Dead unborn and dead after life we also know ourselves
I can't be afraid to know myself don't listen to anyone else
They will mock you trying to destroy your knowledge
Already and for millions of years but the absent timer
Creates an existence rich in sequins or pun

Standing in the memory project then walk across the dark
Of this pointless beauty trying to compose itself
Here are the pre-words grouped like sculptures
They're sounds at the same time as things weird as can be
Maybe me and I'm a magnificent word mouth the mouth's
Alight in darkness purposelessly above the hung coathangers
That are multi-dimensional planar indications shiny
And motile the wiry shapes tingle and I walk I
Walk the mouth tou wou aren't true thou would the
Fire can't burn the shore but I saw boats aflame
No you don't look like that but do you have eyes
I can't see it but I see it like I can't see with my eyes my dreams
And they heard
Them in
Their own
Language
What
Is yours

The song is bending me she hung herself she's hung on
A coathanger on the door hung herself there in this
Language so she could be dead somewhere else
In the dimensions we're in I don't want to keep forgetting
You could smell the honey flowing out of the wall where
The bees lived in the future I can hear them like a quasar
The wires I wear or are keep changing into different letters

In spring now the black owl is mine at source are we
Immaterial can you see what your form is it's vel-
Vet on a twig someone's V the twig someone's Q the
Quasar or quiver I'm trying to find this
Can you understand yourself in your language
My voice mail isn't working so I'll send myself the messages
A carrier pigeon I let loose into the future
You are the owl eyes of a christ my dead friend giggles

We keep creating our world from beginning to end
It happens in this one inflected word broken find you

The big words get smaller in pieces then larger as I reform them
You're not wire words he says you're a gliding over the plain soul
I'm seeing some words I am this way I say the huge story
Walk on the plain until you reach the sea
The story of the dead you don't quite find your-
Selves we find us sadly sometimes
The dead set out the dead set out making art they forget
Poems displays of words like my shapely soul does
I'm going to remember
And I strained my form and shaped it elemental

The se-
Cret
Letters
When-
Ev-
Er you
Move
Car-
Ry you
Carry you
To free-
Dom

THE STORY

I am the story leading you to freedom all one and element
There would be no need if pieces of lake or light hadn't broken off
Plain or what became dumped space orchid bent filled with us litter
I yet being all and stood there beginning destined to lead you
If the god's winds overturned the ships of me they were still lies
There's no dying where I'm leading you is that realization
Thus all your needs are vain you hysterics it takes little to
Feed and house you you see through a millions-of-years smeared
Lens you have no enemies we're from the same and only
Frequencies a visible spectrum including prophecy
Remember seeing it that you'd be born later forgetting
We are what we saw the ones walking fragilely but we aren't fragile
I'm leading you to strength a lake on a hill of insolent pleasures
Blue or green lake red lake I'm leading you to humor your own joke
All of matter has humor planets and galaxies laugh at their
Piecemeal forms their having fallen apart not fallen like angels
But being displaced from their unity their first one as I am laugh
It's not funny that we murder each other we can laugh at it sorrowfully
A convulsion like that's how we became when all exploded all that re-
Vulsion or any language you want we know who we are
In a one first language we've forgotten but ignorantly use
I'm leading you to the lake of un-ignorance on the hill of
Un-folly somewhere you know but never quite remember lovers
Taking it easily not earning money nor buying too much
The place of purple lake and orange calvary I have been there
Have suffered and shaken to lead you through a membrane door towards trans-
Figuration how might you be figured after your complex death
You have never needed objects or this queasiness of products
Your definitions of living kill you into a frenetic boredom
I am leading you I who don't play with you at your trivial ambitions
To a lake colored by memory spreading and deepening
Remember when we first stood here calling to each other where
Have we been or will be but we are what is knowing us as semblants
As souls as the one mind a dovecote a persons a languages
Without any deity but us without any need but to know

Each other's minds again after our presumed deaths reunited
One by one as slowly as we've been alone calmly remember
Why there was matter in the first place why we were there at that shore
Of the lake of space colored with every lake calling spirits I
Have led you back or forward lovers memory is everywhere
The universe being memory trembling our minds creating it grand
Were we never shattered then and what we think we see merest iconography
I remember when the doves were let out grey oh my figures
How have we made us by a liberation in sleep of potency
The air was still at first and we the dead already there want to
Remember hearts voices and a light-mind sourceless us do you remember

I remember the random absolute I'm leading you to
The only thing there is we can't conceive of such explicitness
Entered upon with the foresight of what are we seeing with
Our and it didn't have to be eyes integral seeing
I'm leading you to before I remember the dark desert high-
Way lead you on from the first shabby town where we nonetheless loved
Each other why not tacky lovers a judgment from the later
Self-conscious one I will be leading you to the mountain no imped-
Iment but your friend to slip through the folds of gigantic
Parental I remember immediately that we have memories we
Allow ourselves them I know you're my lovers but what else is there
Others led you to doom I lead you to the casting away of possessions
Like doom like fate like familial indebtedness to a past
One always saw coming and can see as far as you can think
I remember we destroyed things haplessly I'm standing with
You in your deaths you know how you became enmeshed in a game
Of material invention seeing only the bodies you agreed
To see I lead you from that pettiness back to the original past
Into the original future you are beginning to descry
She went there and saw it language and memory pliant
Self at any time how did we make the universe
We pressed on our memories before we had them
I remember going through it saying ah ha ha ha or something so
Obviously who we are even the mountains walking to
And through the eras before I was born do you understand
I to you and now is tiny a part of overarching death

Name of our existence to which I'm leading you the dead talk to us
Saying we need your help for our being is endless we're in this together
We're creating ourselves out of thought and speech I am leading you
To porousness I am destroying politics I remember walk-
Ing on my street thinking I have achieved freedom who else has
It's a state of nonpossession for the universe we are
Possesses itself always releasing itself simultaneously
Through a door of self going on in temporal expansion
It is a miracle she said in the sense that there's no explanation
The miracle lies across the bottom where words support us
And are us my children cry out with me turn on the lights

I am making this it says it this telling you even the body
We're making our body but there's going to be an explosion
At the beginning calling out to them words to shatter into an
Alphabet I don't care if we have an alphabet the woman said
Her name became the alphabet the woman said can I call her Al Dad
Says she walked back to I'm making this should she deny
The explosion she can I say although the scientists will argue
We're making our body why or how is it possible are we possible
I don't have an answer yet the language or miracle's across the bottom
Turn on the lights I can't invent us without it happening
The dead say turn on the lights without calling it an explosion
Matter drifted in it drifted around me was it better this way
I put it in a shelter for I had a fear that it was fragile
More fragile than death or just being I came to inhabit it
Unto every cranny for I can the planet told me not that it spoke
Across or nearby the night is deadly but death is not fear-
Ful and soldiers sing every broken letter sings this is our language

Are you in the night are you in the wind am I running away again
The alphabet the woman said I must find my own words
If I can find thee words she said he says then the primal words are mine
When I was a boy he says I had blond hair then black
How fast did you read and understand that the wind or hear and get it
They think they have more influence because they work in a putrid uni-
Versity but I work in the whole universe wind and night I must find
It the alphabet the dead woman said he says do I have to be nice
No you have to find it it's in the scrolls the Greek boats form in the ty-
Rrhenean sea or in my ears the quasar says pulsates it or they
Each crosstie's a piece a little mark of my way dead or alive
I wanted justice vengeance and never to know the ones who hurt my
Mind anymore I say mind not feelings I say consciousness

If you real-
Ly knew what
Consciousness was
You
With your con-
Sciousness think it's

56

A hoax or
Evolutionary
Cosset
And I
Am leading you to the
Door
Where you are

If it's the only thing you know with how can there be
Another thing for sure well there isn't I'm the alphabet the woman
Said twisting her body into letters there are a billion letters in the
Alphabet and I know them all the grains of sands yellow sands
I know them but I can't seem really to know them

I cried
For you
Now it's
Your turn to
Listen
Language is
Not alien
Nor am
I
Dreaming
Words
And I are
What
Is
And the mount-
Ains
Bizarrely in-
Cite you to
Twist
Your heart
Saying
Find
Me I'm
What any-

One
Says

Razz butt and flash butt he says I don't have to have a butt
There are just a few lights on Yarnell Hill in the night
Really a mountain making sure we don't fall off going
Around a curve traction's good about a car Woody once lived there
Doing road work remember then you let your mind talking
Buzz or flash out memory setting may be more concrete than orig-
Inal happenings are you more there remembering this is
Creating the universe have a thing or point or singleness then talk it
Or remember while misting up or razzing its butt Woody
Could barely read you didn't have to the Greeks and Trojans did
They read Linear B Woody didn't have to read anything
He took us up through the quaking aspen to the tree line
He took us for our first sopapillas he said the best ones he'd had
Were fried in lamb fat on the Navajo reservation
Indigenous because we're this word digging loneliness and sadness
Emotive membranes shining like spiderwebs you get stuck in

If nothing's remembered in order what happens that way she'd
Lost count of the black brown crossties that weren't there any-
Way I mean what's there in the future
Where I am I know without looking the quasar might have
Said that the Greeks knew they would always be tragically there

The point is he says you have to lead them won't let me don't
Even know I exist don't think about the other poets they're non
In poetry there's only what the culture comes to admit
And the quasar some of the stars and many mountains on
Many planets that respond to your tremolo I am reflecting you I say
In the throwback cold it's grey low bulbs coming up I don't
Understand these métro smells stressed bodies geranium
The gypsy playing domino won't you tell me you'll never desert me
Coyote threw the stars up into the heavens now they're there
Mixed as my integrity is and not mine the alphabet the woman said he says

It's a big
Language ev-

Ery letter
Changes
Its mind to
Be in a new
Set-
Ting or brain
Which bog-
Gles I
Love you the
Letter says

The woman in the house variant in one variant he
Says a variant of the her house variant can't find her
Way inside her own house is lost in the house wind
Or mind and if she goes down into the cellar even though
She's dead I don't know I'm trying not to be too col-
Loquial he says why in my our epic I need strength
We must be strong enough to understand ourselves the universe
It takes guts and language she walked down the stairs and it said
It is only your provincial notion of causation that prevents you
From seeing what is for there is but you times the ex-
Act moment of your death lived and modified for-
Ever you chose this you are choosing it first you died

And I saw Dorothy coming towards me forgiving me it was
A forgiving of abandonment the only transgression I know
When rocks are reft and a tree is alone on a prairie
I didn't know you I have always known you whoever you are

The woman said the alphabet the woman said who counted the
Tracks as if to keep death in motion he says but that was at
The beginning of death according to these folktales
And finally she stopped and sat down near the basin of origin
And did nothing further but speak with it
As I have spoken with Dorothy he says and do speak
All the others are around and your brother but I am
Forever near her that I might give her whatever of myself
In healing she needs though this is not our epic is it
Yes I say yes that we must stand forever in juncture with each other

I am heal-
Ing it how
By healing it
And
The quasar sings
Tremu-
Lously
Heal-
Ing

The prescient Al I am sits once again in Paris if that's what you call it
There's someone inside you you haven't been yet who can say so point-
Ing to its or her black rectangular drawer shape in no breeze
No wind of knowing when I found any you as we created us
And she was walking towards her house again also again bade
By all that trembled not to care about it but them
I do I say I guess I have to give away my entirety
You are resting Dad says in a moment between gifts not rifts
We are a town he says not on the edge of anything that's what's
Deceptive differs from another more common way of
Thinking it you or I always already there the bang is mis-
Named the miracle has always already found you so what am I
Doing I say I'm leading you to where you are
In the language in which you created it there are spaces

I'm in one
With my
Knowing it
And the one I
Haven't yet
Been

I was pressed to the escarpment of sand
Near my home before I entered her
And there were roses go in but it's different remember
I go in in the midst of the orange color or fire not the blue
There's no quotidian in death my house birth cries
Out for the explosion in words is a slower singing

It didn't begin without a noise to be heard who
Hears what I say I am the only leader you'll ever
Have your knowing of your own experience lake
Of fire when it comes you disown it your death though it's yours

You keep leaving out evil per se I'm not always interested
The woman said to the fire who had spoken in her variant house
I'm it said the flames arising from your death head
As you try to speak clearly at the first times of which there are none cer-
Tainly you might have been wrong and then the fire said be gone
All but your purest words so we might live again dead or
Alive there's no time a sentenceless collection of acts
The fire in my house said be ragged as flames if thou wouldst
Call words along the bottom or basement or in the attic reaches of the farth-
Est quasar I ask a flame licking what can you mean
And any word is more than it is it says a word is a lockup
Of the address to the universe telepathy we have only and
So I am a word the flame said press thy naked body
To the desert or even oceanic shore that is a word of love
Again calling to heal the division we are born of
This ballad or epic says and I came unto the moment as before

And in the basin of origin sudden tall waves struck at its unsteady
Outlines or along the shore where the variant woman had clung
To white sand for I hope to find power for myself in these
Days of destruction when even those I know are interested only
In their own times and those times' casuistic jargons
I have seized power from you to lead you from my dead house my desert my
Basin of origin I do this for I say you the people have become stupified
That is why we the dead called on you he says on you no other

I saw in
The desert you
Would
Die why
Not see what ev-
Eryone knows
Who sees the

Snake for its
Clothes
Sweetly its
Tongue glides

I see what I'm going to do no one can advise me I myself said
No one's counsel sensible no one thinks beyond evening
I floated up above the river a dried up Colorado or filthy Seine
And went winding til my future home was there below
It was scorched boards of a blackened foundation the def-
Inition of house earth finished and in death your thoughts will
Mutate as the forms of a planet destroy themselves
What will you think I am watching the new blue wish
In chaos heartlessness is possible but not mindlessness
Not to feel the woman sits in rubble forming wor-
Ds I have led you to the apocalyptic scripting
Of me crouching here while our minds blunt and a-
Live call what can be had besides the center of abjection
For my house has burned up in the orange ecstatic flames

It is blue as
It is blue
As
We have lost
The abil-
Ity to
Deliberate
The live
Have
The dead
Face
Bewilder-
Ment you come here
Astonished
At your
Careless-
Ness ignorance
Pained to
Know

You are leading us to freedom he says memory sur-
Rounds interpreted in lost tongues or the first one
I hated to see you go my home or star or eonic fleetingness
The washing machine would stop when it was out of balance
The hummingbirds returned for sugar water the fine
Mesquite leaves fell the ornamental olive bloomed white hap-
Pened one thing crying out in pre-akkadian I don't get it
There are too many versions of her in her house which one
Is eternal that I can identify if it is for me to do
So you are our leader Momma says I don't get it but you are

The woman leaves
Her house carry-
Ing its interior-
Ity with her for-
E'er
That you have
Burned down

I celebrate your viciousness for I can hate while leading you
What is your intention the charge of the dead and of the un-
Iverse material and of the souls of words crying out

How much of it can you see stop doing what the men say
Leave them leave your country it isn't yours it's theirs this plan-
Et is theirs you keep giving it to them you might as well leave
Sky smoke and bombs no one remembers what their religion is
The correction of the correction to the worship of the man god pro-
Phet or buddha it had better be the right one baby leave them where
Shall I go somewhere else one has given away to one's masters it's
Mine no woman's identified with a city or country I say it's mine
The whole damn thing all of it's mine the New York School the Paris School
Mine who is speaking the Damascus School if you choose it's
The bloody female sex the alphabet the woman the de-
Pressed and disaffected deceased woman said I'm so glad you
Said that Dad says in the version that's happening right now

THE LIFE OF THE MIND

Middle of night Ted playing loud music airshaft vibrating
Bartok's quartets I tell him it's too loud louder back there come listen he a-
Grees too loud Eddie and Anselm in nightclothes climb loft go back to
Sleep music turned down I will write a theogony out of chords like Bartok's
Doug and I then the landlord comes in did we forget the rent forgot the
Sandwiches make them now the hand-layered sandwiches for
Everyone way on the top floor the landlord write a theogony is taking photos
Of my mother who's put on makeup and he says to Ted you
Keep wanting to go outside my mother says to me aside he took
Me outside and took my picture she's holding a weak sad carnation
It's beautiful she says like Chopin we start back downstairs on the es-
Calator I'm writing the theogony Columbia let Bartok starve
You're all the same jackals that let starve I'm writing the theogony keep
The academy going at any price fellow poets jackoffs the unstarving
I'm going to write a theogony for each of the chords I first heard as
Words the miraculous that came from nowhere no god spoke
Leading the guilty happening right now to the Place Noctambule I pay the price

Somewhere in the core of death the woman the alphabet Al said
I the primal language must find myself though not an
Alphabet not fractured like that she said Dad says it may e-
Ven be wrong wrongheaded do you know what's out there I say to
Him oh more mind like the quasar or like any old thing it
Doesn't have to be that different when all we do is telepathize to
Hold the thing together the epic must represent it or them too I
Say in my theogony it has to be an epic he says perhaps containing a
Theogony first there were dreams and then they happened or first
Was a sort of nounish presence I was with floatingness fan-
Ciful first there was fancifulness and before that a basin
A small basin large to a bacterium I'm talking my way to
It a language existed before it was said like a dream of it
It was I the name of night or love or force and strife
And the creature was born but I had always been though my
Memory may be faulty much of memory's outside me

Pale or teal blue for reason it is a line I'm trying to prove
For nothing else works the planet isn't working now the universe itself
Doesn't nor anyone's body or brain for long but this line works and remembers
Our energy's different here a dead poet says it's diffused then sudden lightning
                                                              so line's what
I a poet direct to you my thoughts right now in lines through Milton's
Kiss or Whitman's smile a word a whole other this brave language
For I would have loved to play with you more this Al Allen says I was afraid
                                                              cunt fear
I loved your mind and aspect though so forthright and sensitive he
Says is the universe sensitive I say wherever it glistens with capa-
Bility on the brink of mutation gets changed as it were by itself without its
Asking the way your poems change what's permanent then the mind's being is
I'm giving mine to you right now generosity's permanent
Help my mind I say to him and he moves his more for a moment into mine it's
Very fluid he says or is it mine I see a new thing that matter is within
That I knew as words and the language or soul itself's fluidity see it
Yes I see I say I wouldn't mind being that galaxies like mercury
And speaking to you for you lead me says he and lead so gently to amalgamate
The moment so we can see before the bodies broke off it was that fluid sing-

Ing with blue I'm buying all you a blue outfit I say to be reasonable in not chanting super-
Stition like people in the coined street broken desirous wretches pretending to be ef-
Ficient what is that when words tear from my mouth don't you want to
See the grey-yellow rain they're afraid of you he says you're not writing disguised prose
They want to kill me and yet I am leading them sick as a people pretending
Not to be light I can't find it in my pocket one squeals it's in your mouth don't squeal

Maybe I
But it's
You he
Says
Haven't
Been
No you're
Bet-
Ter
You're the
Best
Person to
Do this
Your
Com-
Passion's un-
Con-
Scious

In the leadership procedure I stood on the plain alone as if waiting to
Lead who remember the plain in this version I tell you you are probably cor-
Rupt as soon as shadows you appear or perhaps you are already lazy in
The mind are these the live it is everyone first dead then alive then dead and all at once
And the stiller entities rocks the more supple of fleshless ones rain
In this recombination though you may remember none previous
No one stands out a voice wanders from one to one sound-
Ing different each time this both life and death I say to you

The relevant most relevant sentence states this is where you are no one cares
who you are

Though you are unique and later some will care but then per-
Haps cease to care again anyone is thinking anything
In the voice that binds us that travels from one to one saying virtually nothing
I am your leader because I'm defining this condition
You don't I repeat you don't feel bad at this point
This is point zero for the universe the whole thing we emerged from
Here some once said an explosion of distress but you don't have to remember that
When you are born later try to remember standing here and
After you are dead for at this point you have done nothing do
You really want to act but I've said you're already corrupt be-
Cause you remember your futures try only to remember here
Right now try only to remember here be-
Come in beauty there is no instruction for it we all speak it

PRAGUE

It told me to say it I crossed the white river waving

It's our depression you're feeling it's not quite what
You'd think what they did to us as enduring beyond death and
The reign of the madness to kill us they'd kill
Us again the exact ones would we can't be our feelings
If birds could fly leaving the glass for the mor-
Tuary red crying crystal we're not a
Feeling I'm trying to lead you where to healing
How could you be able to by wanting to so badly as
For myself I'll suffer if you do you weren't there I'm
Becoming inhabited by your urgency
How heal us if you can't touch us I place my fore-
Head against where you face me that I can't see stay a min-
Ute and I'll take you to a beginning with me here
Stay inside my mind all night if you want to
Who are you I don't know right now a poet we can't
Let go of it gradually you will
Gradually you will let go of me exhaust-
Ing the feeling for I took it from you where shall I put
It just here might work or if I put it
In the pendant around my neck I'll wear it
Only for you is it working now it's started to we
Follow you inside if that's all right yes
Come with me and share some of my balance my self my
Place

In this else-
Where this
Hotel room
Light on my
Denim
Knee
Sur-
Rounded by
But so qui-
Et the
Ones
To be
Led

That the entire sea of the beginning had receded so I'd
Lead you across the revealed desert of truth
So it is I and we are going on the flatness of onset our
Universe has no edges nothing different beyond us are we
Going somewhere inside it one asks this is its e-
Pic the information here internal the plain be-
Neath the sea where you knew you would be instead of a
Constant memory of suffering will we forget
The memory's supplanted by your new language
Say my words this you is different
Sublime panting bird I let go of everyone but dark
Dark says the particulars you loved before and may again
But notice here phosphorescent script I'm illiterate one says
Maybe a mountain or former quality of prestige
It's a literal part of your body I mean mine I the leader's keys open it

The key
Is open-
Ing
You
Please re-
Lease me
For I
Am your

Way
Let me
Live
Again

The woman the alphabet Al said Dad says the veri-
Table words lie on my lips like tender spiders for I
Have been opened she said like a drawer and
These words say the new death has arrived it is
Called glimmering or brightness as to be that
Riding on a bus with her across our necropolis
Woman garmented in cloth with sequins and brilliants
They were her words were they Dad says Al's words

I am leading you in words and when I speak our epic
We change the time in death to comprehensible being
The first time you're understanding how you are here
It was always I and when I have no body I move as though
The rays of my limbs the suns of my eyes know no sto-
Ry the mouth of this language opens you are free to go
The first thing I did was call out anything and nothing was
Bound to me no history no indignity no structure of
Molecules or system of thought I would always be at home
The body will show you what the real body is the
Body of the quasar will show it too and the body of
Words show how there's no foresakenness memory
Has taught us how to remember now we will remember really

I lead you to selfsufficiency being your own cause as
The universe so see it a language expressing here
I am leader being self-sufficient I don't need what you
Have unlike most leaders not even needing to lead you
I am your leader because I've been told by you I am
You told me in your sleep when you faced up to your pain
The words for these things are not given to men with their
Pretentious seriality they are given to me in whirlwinds
I am their leader because they want to be leaders so badly
Emotional cowards irrational self-deceiving unab-

Ie to look the stars and planets in the face and call them anyone
Crying out for my leadership all of you stars and men incomplete lan-
Uage the words walk across the purple or yellow or white plain
The plain is crying out for my leadership the sands all the
Heartbeats pulses vocal vibrations and overtones that there are
Face up to your self-sufficiency face up to it
It is the same as your interdependence the same as your heart
The same as that you will have no heart when you are dead

We walked on the
Plain I
Was telling
The King of
Suits
I was telling
Him your
Life is
Shit your mon-
Ey is
You live
In a mansion
Of shit

Last night we made the planets grey spheres with white inner
Crust we made them with our hands at a table
While we were also walking across the plain gliding
How actually had we come there there have always been
Great numbers of us cosmic remnants of a future or past doesn't
Matter are we matter that word anyone might say I'm sick of
My body but not of myself did you do something bad I've
Been asked to lead the dead in fact told that was my fate
It seems to be a universe of fate can we change
That Al my brother asks possibly if we change the
Definition of matter to include spirit for is spirit fated part-
Ly maybe keep walking fated to its body the one we think
We see and its hurtful actions though it flies away at night dream-
Ing of when it fashioned the celestial orbs I'll

Take you to where the grass grows green on the banks of
The salt salt sea you used to play that record he says when
I was matter or when I was spirit which am I I say right
Now we drove past Salton Sea we will drive past Salton Sea when I'm
Your brother he says just follow me now I say I'm leading
All the others are following me I know the way

It is a col-
Umnar carv-
Ing of
Life forms
Mashed to-
Gether
Bodies
In a
Hellhole exist-
Ence
Of no con-
Sequence
Even if
One is a
Boy
Or a
Snouted
Dog the
Universe
Teems
With in-
Consequen-
Tial
Being isn't
That
What
We are ev-
Er told
Af-
Firmed by
Science or

Bud-
Dhism you
Are ran-
Dom you are
Suffering you
Don't ex-
Ist but
As a mo-
Ment
I
Tell
You
You ex-
Ist
There is noth-
Ing
Else
We each are
It I
It is the dis-
Quisition
The dia-
Gram
That is
Illusory
I am lead-
Ing you the
Hellhole
I am lead-
Ing you

No one is elected in death I am leading you away from your
Demeaned lives you thought didn't you to be conscious for one life's sen-
Sations why and do it the way you are told by sex and caste by
Geological age by dead rock positioning in the scorch you
Bit of useless foliage you reptile you ant you dirt everywhere
You are free and they all leave their iconography on the column to follow me

THE WOMAN WHO COUNTED CROSSTIES

I led them O mine the woman the alphabet says to where
The letters writhe like snakes rise up from the groundlike plain ser-
Pentinely forming instantly changeable words for you
I'll lead you to where the butchered and raped lost out you'll
Agree there's nothing more important than opportunity O assholes
Zomboid with anglophone or francophone telephone
Your phone phone computered holdings memorized tellings you have and will
Know how cool O bone tone of the dead oh the dead are here
With you my bone-headed kiss of death emptinesses
Now with me where no one cares what you did or said at that shit-
Mouthed foundation or the bank high on acid I mean death water
Alcohol of silence psychopathic presidents turd diamonds of fecal academic fame
For I am leading to where you are forgotten oblivious un-
Knower so I won't have to remember constantly what you
Did what I saw can't the dead forget themselves everything but themselves
Your real ones or I would see myself three days from giving birth in
Chicago being called snatch out the passing car window
Writhing word treated like an annoying piece of meat in labor later
In a hospital I'm leading you to where there are no events there nev-
Er were I didn't have only 23 dollars no phone or bank account
Twenty of it to take the kitten to the vet when Ted died we must have
Deserved it anyway as I deserve to sit here telling you pen to paper in this age of glass-
Fingered outreach that would make the tinman bleed why I'm leading you
I'm leading you because you know nothing I'm leading you to your origin in nothing that is
                                                beauti-
Ful not like the nothing you know splintered image half-word thought
Throw it away Al alphabet woman no one but I writes here and nothing happened don't
                                you want to be precise was
Ever humiliated are you walking all over us leading us there is something in the wind you
                                        need to know
You need to know it from a woman but you need to know I am learn-
Ing self-respect from the yellow sands up in the no-love
Air proclaiming anything that happens to anyone a lie I'm
Leading you away to a long moment of birth because you are suckers with certificates with
                                degrees with water-

Fall-length scrolls of attestations to honorary idiocy
There is a man here who there is no one of any sex here who
There is no one here with dignity poise or deserving I am leading
You to where as I said the letters do what they want

I am leading you and the mountains you and the nebula and the cowed and gentle whorish
$$\text{bandit liars I know}$$
So well who believe in parties you assholes believe in me
Across the and across the until your past and future corruption is a forgotten stain in a sky
$$\text{taking place a million light years a-}$$
Go who agreed to support one man against another as if to receive his
Kisses my kisses all tell you my love is certainly untrue because you have never de-
Served it why am I leading you someone who doesn't want to manipulate you has to
I'm leading you past the thought shelter containing my nights at the hospital by Doug's
Bed while you were discussing who to call the greatest of bullshit president po-
Ets in the outreach to commoners in politics of the provincial fucking world for you knew
$$\text{every-}$$
Thing and now you are dead little guy what's doing making that list of that this
Running laureate notional senator compiler of the
Best notion or trace or face like a gas mask the diagram of our best body I'd take all of you
$$\text{gladly}$$
To hell but you've ever been it we're leaving it now
You don't need a thing where the grass grows and snakes grow and all the truthful letters
$$\text{of your nightmare to}$$
Be free I'm leading you to freedom you are not imprisoned by your bodies
I'm leading you to freedom you are not imprisoned whatsoever by any beliefs
There is not a thing that is true I'm leading you to
There are words that can sting your stupid ankles words the only real like
Jail and childbirth and cancer and poverty used to be
Learn to speak the new language you former mechanistic liars learn how to talk

It's possible she was leading the crossties to or from the basin of origin I
Say no longer counting them or the pieces of existence or death but
Simply saying you can count with any words as your feet mark off lines I
Am lead leading beyond counting or the manufacture of matter

The woman's heart finally receded for it was a ghost heart or did it Dad says
The Greeks or Achaians rose in my heart to be led to
Tragedy again but I said not again and gave them the shards the
Leftovers from my burnt house to offer up as a sacrifice they keep wanting to sacrifice
And in death someone says I still don't get why I'm here you just are
And so where are you and the epic leading us Dad says it's for those
Words that do what they want to tell us
Growing up from the plain of the capacity to exist

Troubled old
Friend I
Tried
To help
You last
Night you're
Just one of the
Kids
Still
Though you're in
Your forties
And
I gave you some
Tonic but
Then you poured
And spilled it
All o-
Ver be-
Cause your
Mother ar-
Rived and you
Love
And hate

Her so
Much

The heart keeps breaking so what I am leading you to free-
Dom it's easy doesn't cost a slender cent we are going
Where the great words are spreading out all across where
Your thoughts your real ones go as your real body lights up with mentality
I promise you love at the very least that of the great words and me

I am the first words the first language says and the one sound broke or rather it splayed

If our condition's to experience everything at once he says
I can't get through to you except speaking in your head as
Your voice so how I say do I know it's you that time you
Told me to write to Kassie I said to you in my head it's you and
You said in my own mental voice yes but in fact I don't
Know how I knew that was you maybe he says I don't know how either the
Universe doesn't know how to be I'm the only one talk-
Ing to all of you I say who's going to believe me we speak he
Says in a universal tongue of creation that makes
Itself and then my brother says the first language didn't evolve it
Made you love it that's easier than loving people who shrink mentally
We need you you are our ground multiplying sounds you're
Us as you go we have been needing you for a long time
This is what I was always meant to do I say be the voice of you

Objects object light I'm leading you across plains of nowhere to nothing known
So it's patchy you don't the snake twisty lines say know what you're be-
Ing I haven't been it before you don't have to be your-
Self we are different I am different words all the time
I'm telling you as quickly as I was in your head that time Dad
Says what you put into lines crossties molecular insur-
Gencies a lightning bolt is the same thing as a snake
I am leading the real snakes I say and I'm leading Ophiacus

One of the
Things I

Tell you he
Says is we are
Sa-
Piens more
Sapiens
Dead

Leading you to I say a further place of words for the al-
Phabet is enormous and Woody's analphabet the unletters
That the snaky grasses often are any old sounds and in-
Finite overtones their breezes and sudden strict communication

I
Haven't
Been
It
Before

I got the new earrings so I can hear the words they're clipons but don't hurt
It's how we call and help in dreams with pictures to muse on how can this be
If the mind is thee mind it functions to communicate and create I am
Trying to say not everything's a tongue and our vibrations
Are perceived in a different though overlapping world we are dif-
Ferent here who is speaking to me now it doesn't matter
You are healing our countervalent sadness and we are led
It feels like being drawn into a courtly dance
Though we don't that is dance but have been led into the movement of our
Epic our language heard quietly with acute sense next to the railroad tracks
That we know each other's minds listen he says I've seen it all and have come to value an
                                    orderly stillness with a flybuzz inside a tiny
Buzz you feel rather than hear there are flies and gnats anywhere and a vibration in object
                              light makes your noise be patterned with striations
I was wearing the earrings in front of the old civic center across from the railroad tracks

You
Are
Lead-

Ing
Us
Be-
Cause
No
One's
Lead-
Ing
You

Come to my center says blackness it is leading you
It might have been my soul why is it so hidden
We need you to hear us as we proceed on the looking glass plain
The glass grasses the glass snake words there were glass snakes at
Home in my time one approaches the basin of origin Al said Dad
Says I can't hear it she said though I hear what you say it
Says the whole thing's I guess the whole thing we're saying's the sound
You didn't exactly say it she said while the snake was drink-
Ing with its tongue its tongue but you're dead she said to
It I drink of origin it said in order to be glass trans-
Parent as a word or phrase of your always transpiring
I am the glass snake of freedom it says I am leading you I say

A glass
Snake would
Be dead on the
Lawn and then
They seemed
To disap-
Pear from our
Area

I had forgotten about them swatches of glass not looking glass but window glass
The soul isn't a mirror it's dark today it's onyx and jet glass-
Y where are you I see it he says it's you the wind rend-
Ers our wanderings more haphazard by showing an
Indirection or shiftingness for I've never had to go anywhere
And I might follow the wind which is like a glass snake

There's a point zero sound and a glass snake sound I need to hear
If we can hear it I can lead you further I heard it Dad says when you
Said that and then everyone and thing they communicated by being sensed

We enter fate someone shrieks and I say no I don't think so
I mount the platform turn and say
We are under the misapprehension there are strangers in our midst
But all of us are the entity I am leading you from pre-extinction
To initial engenderment and we saw it coming a species life might be put out there is no
Such thing as a species we are one thing we are dead or as good as
Dead but we are always alive and our epic will be known by ev-
Ery animate and inanimate part of us the cosmos
For we have come to this plain to be born and I know I'm born
Yet I am so old that I don't need to learn what we are going to do is stop
Taking orders sit down don't sign up for a course or do what your
Overseer says it's too early in the world for that
So how are we able already to understand each other
There are ideal senses hidden behind our backs I've always known
You as I've said though we were just born the first thing I re-
Member is that I know others we are here to make what we
Have made it's a new version our bodies are ideal even if they break
Down because my body is within myself and if I'm dead it's further in-
Side smeared across the air of my conception and understanding
We are not going to create a society we don't need one
We if we become hungry are going to look upon that as uninteresting
Nothing we thought before is true there is love but it isn't what you
Thought it was if we were god how could we have been wrong you say
You don't know what god and wrong mean they are linguistic errors
We are finally in the area of the first language
But if it is what we are it isn't a category nor need it be
Taught for it is us we don't have to learn to be all of our past ideas
That we are sloughing off into the atmosphere
Any word is its own I have died of you a million times and come back
There is nothing to make of this the wind is our parents and our god but
In death there is no wind this sticky crystalline ether
Do something do anything or don't we don't need to imi-
Tate each other we are the same mind what is and don't need a thing

And the dead still need nothing but the live seem caught just
Have this feeling I say it is happiness attached to nothing do you know it
It is what we are actually composed of my siblings

Like
The milk of
A milk-
Weed the
Stickiness
Of a
Locust
But like
The soft-
Ness of
Gold
But like
Your damp
Fore-
Head in
June

I am the stranger leading you what is this language I
Know I'm a stranger to myself what is this language
There is a story of the dead in which they invent life and death
Will we remember it now I saw yesterday in Paris several of the
Men from the Catholic hostel next door called losers
One alcoholic and depressed has lived there for years one in
Wheelchair oh please take us back to the grace beginning mo-
Ment a voice says no the one in a wheelchair who's cheerful when
Alone but yesterday glum with them a couple more ran-
Dom alcoholics they all sat mute on the sidewalk of rue Mentholon
So last night I dreamed of their escape with a woman and
A dog the dog of death they must have run away from the
Hostel what is the gift of life and death individuality and the one
Who's been there for years says c'est moi I want
The choice of my depression face turned to the wall of the street of
Message boards beer in hand not to look at you he says the
Cripple shakes when he arises from the ground trembles and has to

Carry his beer if he's alone but then makes it into the wheel-
Chair with the woman they manage their escape and
Death do you understand this language death is mine
I take it with me into the field of light away from lofty human en-
Deavor so I can finally try to fucking leave you

But no
One leaves in
Death
No one
Leaves
But I
Leave you
By
Being
Myself
I have
Been con-
Structing
A new
Person
My-
Self
It's
The most
Pain-
Ful thing
I've
Ever done

I'm leading across the dry yellow plain at the be-
Ginning though something is over I am listening
For all the sounds that tell me who you are rustles and coos
Explosions and the stillness of lakes a color
Spreading just outside its outlined shape flower
There had been a night in the old house before it burnt up
Deep in my soul I was also at the same time in my first
House this is an epic of the depression we will remember
All of us at some point in our still journey to be both

The universe all of it and all of death coincident I am ap-
Proaching as your leader the foremost expanse of the inmost
Do we need some pieces of paper we need precision but different-
Ly from the once were that scholars provided not to the un-
Lettered these phrases tell you whispered back from my deep lips
Will we provide for ourselves anyone might but the creat-
Ures ate each other in a frantic psychological reunion
Just be still don't eat all the time it obviously doesn't
Matter if you die and to the dead I say we may need a map

Not referring and no one has mapped I was all scraped out
You want me to refer to those behind me but I see nothing yet only lead
A voice asks me for the rules of our molecules I can barely find these
Words but they're already here each time like in my dreams
Maybe it's the map of forgetting black with almost visible states out-
Lined faintest silver these states we're entering are we in the map or real-
Ity Al I can't remember what I'm for a low voice says
In the sense that I must play my cards right what does that mean
Limousine there were old contortions shadows on the clayey ground
What has been reasonable you are a tense or am I lead-
Ing conjunct our own way listening for no voice outside us
There is nothing anywhere even imagined to advise me
I can't allow an election I just keep on you're back there or not I
Can't remember why I speak the point might be automatic
Thinking for it has no future but to exist are you hidden nothing is
Nothing makes it happen less structure than anarchy implies
Wider calmer and with words the ones not only at
Our feet but minding us so we can stay in tune with them
In these states of forgetting the green wings of our youth
Each forgetting rather than puzzles reinforces a hawk or
Direction the languid yet determined onward of it
That there would be no structure except for consciousness
Singular inward sweetness aren't you there black or yellowed
I can't lack colors to go with the sounds of a mind so steady
There's this body inside me it will be part of it why another
Says the shapes we are must be these states green and blue and
Red ocher motion maps match a song each once knew but
Forgot be tone deaf and still sing it if no one knows it until it's you
Singing crocus or the ear I heard what I wanted to say come from me

POEM OF LEADING

It's like asking how did I wind up in Paris it's just a story
But on the other side of the fabric maybe we aren't friends I
Say to no one in particular I am the soul sheltering poor matter that's
All maybe everyone's just been playing a game with it matter I
Used to be angelic then I decided to be coarse and corpulent
It suited a mood to become ugly rocks it suited you to be seedy

I lead across the glass plain the mass of previous-
Ly pained entity some of the it remembering or bleeding
Do you know how to be different I call without looking
Back because we dreamed everything we once were
And now there may be new shapes to walk into
Tan whirlwinds or doors polished elemental what
Is really there a voice asks all I can remember from
When I was alive is that I was always wrong do you
Remember that it was in pieces or now I'm not
I died because he declaimed to me knew how to I didn't
They all said what everything was I didn't demeaned told
You some image you might recognize for we all tried
To be mirrors everyone does do the dead they see a
Partenariat wherever they look not a parrot they
Hear like this spontaneously to speak and create some being
When I lost my eyes someone says is this a renaissance
I am I say willing to say anything I feel you in
Place and gliding I didn't know how to be it differently for
The adjustments are subtle first don't think except as a
Poem and second it's not that I shouldn't hurt you I don't
Know how to now it's that you're learning the segments
That aren't sentences at all and converse with each other

So does he see you who I can't look back I'm leading you
Words tap me they've always been visual slinky and carven
Somewhere here I walked into it leading where not breaks but bind-
Ing unperfunctorily what does any glyph said sing and the dark
Snakes near the old place into a river or chasm beginning as

Ancient the counterfeit was to see smartly I tell into the flood
Pushed back so we can walk on nothing leave the old past
Take the new past no can't you seeing uncling any story dis-
Appears and the lipstick on judgment's mostly wiped off
Not a face just a mouth and its demolished words I'm swept up in
To here for words rain down without discernment a role they
Say I have to lead I say why fated something was once I
Might lead myself out but I think I'm for you who are
Small in this one you've made so large that is billions and
Billions of light years is it really or is that a definition be-
Gun in the random quarters of a body once I'm vast I
Say leading you away from parochial conceptions of the cosmos
Not that it isn't that big it's that there is no big
Again I love you the arrow bloody heart of my deflection
There isn't anything to call it anymore the snakes in the cave
Utmost speak called in stress like snapping winds we
Found it exactly here in our once variably shaped lengths our
Proneness whipping so stand among the words of your source
This basin near the wild vines is holy nothing made it
The words here are for you and your tired lips
Someone says vanquished by my foul deeds but I am beautiful
Vanquished by our foul deeds but we are what's there
Voice clings across bats squealing brush your face tenderly
Swarmed from caves my loves word howl no fences
And I copped the air a voice says and I copped you if I could
Swearing to make a likeness to my active thought later
The images seared are these images I sealed my eyes extern-
Al and inward memory's only of the words that fly and crawl
I like this storm I like the whirlwind conveying me to the
New justice of origin the beginning will judge what we've done

I'm following the map of forgetting on the other side
Of the memories of the alive I think I know where we are
For I have destroyed scale every part of the cosmos is where-
Ever the same size as one and as everything you think
This epic might be experienced any other way
With matter or image reinstalled as if I were another though
Being myself the observer that anyone has to be

Tell me then voice as I face frontward what can there be
Thought and how can you keep thoughts or voices apart
We martyred ourselves and each other to comparisons
And I told you one said and I told you as if telling were more
Words sudden the only thing of it help me speak them I say
You are there ahead of us in origin a voice behind me cries
They are the phosphenes to be said mother of phosphenes
Alive brutally someone says you can never be dead but
What you did is just a sound phosphene words map of a map
I remember you martyred me where birds crawl and blunt voices
Little nonthoughts scratching together I wanted to be here
Forgot everything to be here I forget where I came from they say
You're rushing towards me for you don't know who you are

Do you understand where we are Daddy says for I do
We are finally on the other side of the story I say speaking unex-
Pectedly but I am still leading without looking behind or at you
Sometimes it's in the pale and sometimes it's in the dark this cut lan-
Guage can bleed though my body has no animal aptitude
Now speaking more and more like the dead transparently

And when the
Language spoke
Saying I
Am your only
True lover
It meant it
Was I
It might
Have been
Ly-
Ing I'm in-
Clined to think
Every-
Thing is a
Lie though
And I
Just can't
Tell if you're
Real I'd
Say to a
Mobbing spar-
Row or a cult-
Ured pearl
Or a power-
Ful man there's some-
Thing wrong with
How you're
Presenting your-
Self

A perception Daddy says of space that isn't one no eye walls sides
But as fast as you can think that to me all at once the words simul-
Taneously there's no cop no syntax cop either pro or against what do
You see space you others I was holding you at the air show be-
Fore you got lost I say I remember shouting my name into the mic
Now thinking all that to each other is slower if you're writing it
But I'm on the plain leading you that too we're arrived at the recognition
Of our constant telepathy I'm in the immense hall of the air
Show in Phoenix the man says say your name into the microphone
I do Libby louder he says I shout it LIBBY everyone in the hall laughs
All of space cradles an airplane and at night the moon hangs out

I am leading you I say not looking back thought-
Fully across the yellow because at the same begins thought
Okay do it I keep finding my mind he says I can't not
Whatever you do are you watching it I'm walking be-
Hind you watching myself maintain contact with my
Past which doesn't exist Dorothy says I lost my mind but
Then they committed me I have my mind now so it's up to
Me to define what a mind is it's the language of your
True self which does at last let go of all the other lan-
Guage can I my brother says both speaking be-
Hind me for I can only lead you the ground is still
But billions of voices are murmuring
And the universe exists by remembering itself

No
One's
Ever
Go-
Ing
To
Leave
Any-
One

Grey to dark now and just here and there a bright image a
Word Daddy says I I say see an imprecise squarish

Shape with several rippled stripes in a corner yellow
Ground there's another one behind it indistinct face disap-
Pears they are communications he says
Wind on it said by a face before she disappears that's a word
He says Momma says because the pictures when you under-
Stand I have been trying to get at for a long time I say though I
Am a world leader a universal one even if we can't write yet it was
Written in eons before and one would write and write again be-
Fore hieroglyphs to move is to write to die is too
Motion and change show things to you and I am writing don't
Look back the first telecommunications from that sparkle our story

Beautiful we keep going and there are more of images on the road
They are words they're only words there is no existence with-
Out or death I'm pressing on here's an antique mirror can
We use it a wooden comb for hair if we have that try-
Ing not to have or remember til it's the right the right one
We are changing our entire structure we must be a-
Ble to if we made us I can't accept any words I'm using
Or seeing the picture on the dark wind of a
Small rose says don't stay still this activity of death
Straining you till we are finally us the soft and snub-nosed black
Mountain glides beside me overtly nothing but itself
This is crucial says my mother's voice that we are in this scene
I call out to everyone we are now the primary word drift-
Ing on and we can't know it the way we used to

Beautiful voices of others any who would like to be
Purposelessness takes you past these old image words
Empty of all but us there being without scale without illusion
I and the dead and live call across all of mind
The true words that you don't have to bet on for one
Opens his mouth and I hear it in my mind I'm a dif-
Ferent the lake of me place this language where your
Body once ailed I took the word coward threw it away
What I'm trying to remember Dad says is how we keep existing
Epic that it's the only thing there is are there any details

Stole
Things to
Give
To you
While
You plot-
Ted to
Kill
Him

That is a word a one and he drove us at top speed to
Get into the correct lane a thing is so intrusive
His face puffy he resembles someone else I have
Stolen so much to give you to bring you here I say
Here I am so different I can't remember who I was
Except that I am your leader I am a world leader
Stole things to give you while you plotted to kill me

I'm stealing everything that you know by knowing more
I stole scale so you wouldn't be bigger than I am
I stole your ability to kill me after we're dead
I stole your wealth and fame which are now irrelevant
I stole your stupid boxes that you call poems and threw them away
I stole your qualities you didn't really have and your
Pills you took to maintain your three-dimensionality
I stole your piddling language and now all there is is the
Freedom I've given you by stealing and destroying an idea of life
There is no moon or sun the only thing that loves you
Is a mountain with a rocky heart of permanence you are stuck with
Do shapes still have to be placed next to each other

Connection already inside me it isn't anywhere dimensional
I don't recognize anything you have made before fools of recog-
Nition it was planned before the time part started I'm
Rejecting that I'm rejecting all but relationship as mind and leading
The kings and queens had money I have knowing what you'll
Do to me if I don't stop it this time you'll enforce me all
Of you I'm leading you before you do your little whore for the group thing

The faux night hates me yellow streaks of pain in the vault over-
Head don't let them break into recognizable daylight
This is your epic freedom of self freedom freedom of thought
Magnetic words this is zero point zero zero infinite

I'm person to destroy human value I say otherwise the new mem-
Ory won't work it's structural a continuation of form
It's just replication that's time but not if you're nowhere
With no values is time a value yes that's what it's been
Was used to define loss and death but now there's no death
Distance but there's no distance we're in each other's minds
Time defined poems and songs but we're not going to do that that
Way as if regularity a cruel exaction held our lips tight do we
Have lips leading do I for you to say you it's your epic

And the images on dark glimpsed begin to gather again
It's going to be the alphabet of the dead we're projecting it any
Voice says from everything we've been and shaken off and who we
Are origination is truly who we are though used once and thrown out

I hovers not on an image banner but cut into the blackness white
Are all of us it this stark I at this moment all of us are I
I am creating the world the I of us cuts my forehead
Opening a thin door out of which slips abhoristic
Letter of revulsion it's a dull green torn square nothing on it
In front of any I horrified that we've begun again
This could be the whole of it but soon comes
A scene that displays a quiet one of what used to be an ex-
Plosion but now dance I began in a dance of Revel-
Ation and all of us I is revealed as orange-black moltenness
Is moltenness a thing and we know this is I us Dad
Says so we have I
                    Revulsion
                    Revelation and
                    Moltenness
The first explosion as alphabetic component is gentle seen
And I place it within my vocabulary as often as
I send you he says a thought quickly plosive accompanied by

A shifting golden diagonal on the field O I
I have to give
Every bit of your time has come for you to take you home
That which but will it have existed rolled up into the cell-like letter
O we called the cell what entrapped I before the new world
The letter or cell can be opened to figurate your death
That of I with scenes from life as defined by a drama-
Tist

You
Are be-
Ing led
By a
New
Kind
Of I

Remember a billion letters as the moltenness sets into forms
We are not remembering in the same way
I mastered memory then I just dreamed it I
Dreamed all interpretation and I dreamed leading
I have nothing further to learn for a long part of memory
Gully a tissue emotion lit by a firefight all this my brother says
Different like it's art not you but it's horrible a fire-
Fight dancing on the molten afterwards of what they
Called the bang all of this played on a banner or flag on
The night I didn't want to begin in like war he says
It was a black word that spit us out here I'm not sure the word dance
Makes it better though I may be remembering without trauma may
Be remembering nothing but articulation all motion articulates my mind moves

Why am I suddenly one says I came to death dead but I'm
More alive than I used to be it's about brackets gently en-
Closed statements of various texture that's the form or
Unit of death mind and matter as we're inventing it and the for-
Merly called nonorganic communicates too in these bare-
Ly shapely mixes all we do is communicate is communi-
Cation the only existent thing besides I

I chose
Not
To ac-
Cept
Any-
Thing I
Dreamed
Last
Night
I was
Simply
In the
Old
The old
Theater
I
Didn't
Need what
You
Who
Said
What it
Said
Said so I
Rejected
It at the
Moment
I
Awoke
Pink
Theater
Like the
Body's in-
Sides I
Re-
Ject
The bod-
Y as the

Ground
Of know-
Ledge it just
Gets old
And I
Don't

I'm marked I say with an X I always am
The ultimate banner of the first tongue ahead of us
At first I think all that's on it are Xs
Momma says I convey an arrangement to you of words and
Scenes I say you say a scene but there's a beautiful ob-
Ject on this projected banner a more beautiful than
In life but I don't sit I won't sit we begin
It conforms to a shape I once was but keep walk-
Ing or moving I as I lead you with our
Motion we're discovering what our language is
One X was that I will she says continue to be your mother
Every object we might see or send in a message of recognition
Of it knows that I am striving to know X another voice
Says I am X I say am I the voice says yes
Every component of us is and every sound we utter
X I am X the stars I am crossed out home my
Name the ultimate word or intersection investigation

Place this
Erasure
Next to my
Heart
With the
Ragged
Roses and the
Ice plant
Is it
Bloom-
Ing
Nothing

Blooms here
It's just a
Thought

The ideal rug stand on it and a bird whistles im-
Practical tree I house it I gather the solar system after
All small into an ideal eye and contain it
It's a question of are you the same as a pebble
Yes you tripped on it but not here or on Jupiter

I enter someone's cave of mind who's not using wit I'm a soul now
I'm it's and he makes the words from a distance different he does
Sound slightly surprised perhaps to be speaking so directly in what
They called English but you are leading me he says
In black rapt contact with another language as I
Was Dad says when I first spoke to you before I remembered
Speaking like a living person can't you teach me I
Say how to speak like a dead one consciously so I can better lead

Once in the territory of ashes

It was where we are now
And you counter with a plan

I am abolishing the political
I am leading without a diagram
The nebulae the galaxy the univers-
Al history do not have a
Though they're melancholy   politics

We have stone and dirt hands holding the old gully open
In this language I
Each time am
Without precedent   each time I

Say
I am leading you to individual moments

Everything depends on how far you're willing to go in your thought
I am leading you surrounded by moments tenses erase fire-
Flies evanescent we did or will do that reject them if you dare
I dare not stop any moment's perceived different-
Ly by anyone yet that one is able to communicate with everyone else
And in this epic that's for everyone how could one
Be in an individual moment I'm in pain I say for
As I'm leading I have been and will be in individual pain per-
Haps pain means time in real life then Daddy says
This is real life that you are leading us in
A place where worn moments flicker and vanish

This language here this
Memory not fractured but a grip
I remember for everyone how to keep
But I have kept my pain heedlessly and then
This gold language will break through being the
Nature we shall have
Everything is sending me its individual moment
We are large enough for each other and for all words

We pour into this area called nowhere this dark plain we are
Erased histories this is my own thought holding my own death and life in place what
Tongue's this poetry it isn't anything like what you think it is
It held me up turning me into steel so I could teach you to speak it

Farther farther the meteor shower gestured
Tell me how this language holds
I'm constructing as I lead a steel-shaped lead-
Er the glyph for which is form-
Ing but essence isn't glyphic the glyph has to move
I'm not sure anyone tells me anything I need to know keep going
A language is what we told us and we moved with it it's
How we move or don't no one has to go with you I'm leading you on
I suffer what is it it fell in battle walk past that and leave
That might have been you I'm different now

You might remember something from
The other side of the universe one day old I remember being here
I hear you I have to keep
On and he comforted his men
I see you words coming towards me
      There's nothing to de-
Fend just keep remembering that you're dead

I grew
Up on
Earth
In an
Area of
Sacred
Rock
Form-
Ations
Glyphs
And
Enorm-
Ous in-
Scriptions
In
The
Earth
Glyphs them-
Selves
Best seen
From air in
Air-
Planes a
Thousand
Years
After they
Were in-
Scribed
Intaglios

One was a
Maze
I grew up
In Ma-
Gic

You can't understand your components you exist and don't have them
I'm not looking for them I'm opening the black drawer
He was the guy who sold us an encyclopedia remember
Looking for a key to the drawer who don't recall his
Name his picture's in our yearbook the Mystic Maze
See the drawer being opened it's black inside

My ones
How our minds breathe is how there is anything so
Be careful in your presentation even in death
Though you have but your mind to present your mind with
Our minds wind throughout the stars our minds we see
Them with that are also our minds the stars are like us
I opened the black drawer that had been locked but now wasn't
Who is this person I say that I inhabit she
Has had too many details in previous imperfect memory
In our new memory of our new soul states she just leads
Walking ahead not looking back but absorbed with your minds
We are searching for the outlines of kinds of words
That tell us how the dead should act they don't act
That will be our new spokenness is it aloud or not
Are there distinctions at all calling out to you if words can call

POEM

To keep from being a stereotype a word cut into air
I am forward instigating a new shape
Imagine the dead man says every impression of image and word
Available to you at once
But I only know things as I was
You were much more than you were aware of
Isn't there a system
                    Imagine you are everything
But in life had been who you thought you were
And also who you didn't even know
She my soul is greater than I but when I become her I don't
Think like that
                    What is your language
The one you have taught me
And the one I already knew

I know you whoever whatever you are
I know you what is there to say and
It isn't about praising
It is the speaking of our structure which is all there is anywhere
Holding us together
Simple I am you simple she says
To me as I say to you I am you simple open this black drawer

We're inside of thinking Dad says words and images faster than light was
Sometimes so fast so fast we're not even thinking
We speak in what the difference between poetry and music
What that is speed and compression of communication faster
Than you are are we in the dimension of no space and time
I'm leading you I say because I have to in which di-
Mension do I do this there's nothing here there's a know-
Ledge of form memory as form and we keep talking I say I'm look-
Ing for language as if it didn't exist yet do I remember anything

There are he says these phosphenes pieces of phosphenes inside one a
Word like her who I don't know but the prismatic gra-
Dations next to it are for fools what's a fool that's part of
The word I see or know this whole display glued on what's
Glued to the night I meet these I meet these words as I lead
We are making with nothing making us with absolutely noth-
Ing speak to each other as if for the first time how
The difference between poetry and music existing everywhere

In pieces of
Making us
And I heard
It the mid-
Dle of a
You said it
You want
To be a-
Ble to
See it micro-
Scopically but
It shimmered a-
Cross the black ex-
Panse I
Heard it when the
Insulators
Touched
Each other as
The freight

Train
Went through
Town

I spoke it called to it beggar but leading
Spill it a little Momma says pour your tea into the sau-
Cer that's Grandma Grandpa's birthday July what
Are these facts out of which we'd build pleasantness
Grandpa says I love you I mean it he says
Walking on the jagged brilliant edge of the difference
Between poetry and music as I lead you away from space

Have I always been you need to keep leading Daddy says
The first issue twigs to us I always do this cold coldly thee
First when I was on the microfilm on the and on
But what was there keep leading there keep lea be-
Ing you're thinking in a line he says there's no first
And then you speak the as if reciting I dreamed
I but there was a different for that a dif-
Ferent mind sound seen thing was there ahead awhile
Leading usury Momma says the dead don't have
Sure you for a while were you I am still
Though I could be anything and not themselves
There is a being next to you that knows good or bad
You barely being bought it don't talk to it yet
Oh to come from and go to what a racket abolish it
Then what of leading only to nowhere along the
Glinting thought from the dark to the opening
Dance it's who am outside and without hope
Do you hear it do you hear who we are everyone's saying
I am your love to do so walk you to freedom
There's a lot of tempus temporary postwar housing
A lot of postwar time with a house and word trees
Walk away you know how to call to anything
I exist I am a world leader I am the cause
No casuistry or pope paper all these words in-
Scribed on rocks in your mind there will be a field guide

I know you all want something else of me like what
You already know you're brainwashed and you're unhappy
Leave it and come back to me a world leader I am leading you

PHOSPHENE ONE

You hear the painful after math the reverb of the primal
Explosion that's what poetry's composed of those vibes sound-
Ing I am your world leader because I know this
You're supposed to view the birds dispassionately
They sing it too but poetry walks it through the edges
Between sounds I am your veritable leader
Thou shalt not commit suicide I said to the planet
Not to you but it its self guts of moltenness there
Is a certain consciousness everywhere it under-
Stands itself you don't please try to comprehend
Nothing dies it is stuck with itself stuck together with you
We keep ourselves going pretending we exist but there is no
Chance or fate I'm leading you to the ripping off of
Bandages you are not wounded I'm ahead
Of you at zero point still what shall we do with it
No one is sick they just can't concentrate
No one is hungry they're unborn not even in the womb
What shall we say you say I can't even tell if I'm talking
These are such plain words who is my heart what am I
Remembering who you are I'm taking care of you relax
Walking relax all we want to find is a truer way to be to-
Gether the music of our thought see this language it has in-
Finite overtones that you speak the composition
Of everything in your these little pieces of us our thought motes
You aren't trying to make money there isn't any
Your biggest problem is that you will never die that's
Why I am your leader here to tell you it's
Just what is you've always been it look at yourself

I speak it when it comes to me already there waiting I say
Compressed glyphs as you'd call them Daddy says are here to
To be you not change you I say I remember when I said to
Momma I'm never going to change did you no I have
Never changed but there is something I need to know now
Whatever you see he says you can read and know
You have led us to the land of our the dead's mind
You are showing it to us being a poet our epic
What we the dead say to each other sometimes seems to
Hold us still but led by you we're moving not in time
I keep calling to the particulars of your language I
Say but not enough's coming clear though it
Must be engraved in me as if it we were one vast
Glyph and that were what I was calling to
In all beauty and tragedy imploring it as itself
To speak as if I could see it from an airplane a little cessna
Why not he says you can see anything you want to

Poets
I do
Not
Ac-
Cept
Your
Version
Of
The World
You are
All
Local
Keep
Walk-
Ing
Your i-
Deas
Are lo-
Cal to

Your mat-
Erial am-
Bitions
Keep
Walk-
Ing
Or
Look
Down
With
Me
At the
One
Im-
Mense
In-
Taglio

If you pause you won't see it but in motion I catch everything

To be the mountain in the glyph shift your heart slight-
Ly I am torso divided into colored irregularly
Shaped areas I have my own heart the mountain
Says or the planet I I say have one too just an idea
I am conveying to you a description of myself the
Mountain says the words exact that in the ab-
Sence of scale I'm not formidable in death you
Don't climb I can't find I say the most beautiful
Words my torso is targeted to be just what it
Is or what I am or it or you are what are
The words you are so literal the mountain says but
The universe the death dimension oh well the idea is
I say to unify my torso dissolving the notion of organs
As I am unified the mountains says this is a dream I say I'm
Always in motion in the previous world there were leaders they were
Trivial and lived as quickly as they could skimming and taking
Asking for love in the form of tributes ask me the moun-

Tain says if I love you I say for a joke I love you it
Says because we're cohering into this new form of form
Form of form there's no vanity in geology though there's been pain

This power I possess is becoming stronger or more obvious
Are you extracting it from others an Al says no from air
Or nowhere it abides in the earth below my Paris building but
I'm with you in death leading the dead and sleeping live

Illuminated if we are it pull it from nothing we exist purely
In power another name for grace or being and not for
Paltry political hierarchs we'll have none of and he
Says the tongues of the previous live crooked were weak
With theft as when you try to steal a soul
The language he says contains a coiling glyph at its
Heart misinterpreted not precisely emergence it's the cell of
Your live life opening or closing and it's the snake of
Language Old Momma tongue words slipping out
To be seerlike any other beings rushing with energy
Your poem he says contains so much power I stop cold
In my death tracks to listen our lines vibrate and shimmer
Electrical cables the insulators the air everything's humming
Hear it it's the glyph the glyph singing itself
I'm leading you I say directly into it

You won't were know known in power the articu-
Lation's dread I'm looking for it like a pigeon with a
Sad eye left all the words they're breaking up
Burn what's left of before and draw the power on it
The words break he had left you had you him
Toes the age of the pharaoh's genital mutilation love
So love it obedient the rocks will melt with the sun
King leave that thought whatever and pilot on in

The verb went with the brève maybe the ankle
Uncle ankh I still have to lead you too and the king
No one knew what they were doing until they came here

Knew what they were you didn't know the one who remem-
Bered brightening the basin dasein these this stick-

Y all over me because feeling who I am of it
Were are leaving where we've been foreign all
That past all of the past and the language of stiff-
Ness and stiffs the school of it everyone

I'm entering this scary scary place for you
I don't have to be here saying your world's a dream
But this isn't so speak without forethought
If he tried to touch you without being kind
Molecules I got new ones and rose above the rape
There is no one here but metal words put your
Nail parings in the container and burn them
Burn your tears and all that of dross

So we talk from and into it this is it and I am
No one made us and we have no shape
The white deer I forget and the sparks spell
World Pieces you have a moth in your mouth
Led her past the unfibulated heart and the junk factory
And then to be here at this all there ever was this is it

SAMSON

This morning everyone dead was in my room why're you all here
Didn't exactly say asleep I saw a book open page of writing I couldn't
Decipher amorphous undelineated they said it said Samson's Divisions
An Erse Book or maybe an Erst Book I understood this im-
Mediately to mean that I am Samson a pedantic voice said there is
Barely a difference he stopped I think it's between matter and soul or
Samson and me or the two pillars when he brought down the house of
The Philistines or between the Philistines and Jews
The book contained a photo of transitional movements a bicycle race
Samson stood between everyone there do I have to die blind when I
Bring down the building we think not just bring it down they
Say it's a rotten organization and intellectual structure one's in
Everywhere divide yourself from it and bring it down now
You can speak the language of origination destroy the state
All governments are decadent destroy their house and goods
Anyone's bring it all down along with their trivial poetics
Their linguistic imbecilities and their cars no doubt you will
Do this topple any man in your way you're blind now so you can't see them

That jars bring you to certainty that we are out-
Side delusion finally is that what you bring down I
Bring down your posessions and ideas if the dead still think they're
Alive oh we don't but the live don't know they're dead

How to
Live
She
Said
Don't
Look at
Me
Look
At these
Words I
Found
Or
If you
Want
Glyphs
Lithic
Hyper-
Regional

Supposing every past action of yours and anyone's trivial why
Were you alive I said I wanted everything I'd done to
Matter I've forgotten just leading why I'm here we all
Have someone says dead I'm simply doing it I say forgetting
You wanted to forget in order to remember he says who
I've been trying to get to you he says can't forget affect
The wind's area spiralling into a glyph like we've al-
Ways known it is the origin of our love he says for
We came out of the darkness for love but were de-
Structive the multitudes believed whatever shapes be-
Fore their senses not remembering they only interpreted another
Do the forms of rocks and gullies believe that they are there
And in this dimension I say I will lead into no belief
There is no sky or ground pillars hold nothing up

Still though and again why do I live and does it matter
It's part of it what we've chosen what is an action pull it down
We're already inside a space with no up or down but I'm also I
Say alive in the space where the building should be torn
Down I'm in both places at once we think you must tear it down

There are symbols always watching waiting to be
Said as they are seen and as quickly so that though you
Are you and remark that I am speaking now you are
No longer who you were though I say I am wist-
Ful for the masterpiece my life I can barely remember
What do I remember instead of war my brother says
You remember your consciousness itself but dif-
Ferently aren't you different I remember when I
Was born I had to cry and noticed that it felt re-
Quired nothing feels required here the language makes
No exaction of you it's important to stay in it I say
The language we're already in it you don't have to react

A man
Showed
Me the
Symbols
For
It in a
Dream
Two
Sets he
Said
Of O-
Void
Pict-
Orial
But
It was
Too
Fast I a-
Woke

And spoke
What have we
Al-
Ready
Been
Doing
I
Ache from
Being
Born

I am concentrating on it Ted says on under-
Standing here so necessary to talk after we matter split
Into loved ones we see each other in pieces of talk or
Else the fly buzzing couldn't land I see you
It is more than beauty that you are I don't re-
Member my brother says how to live anymore we're beginning
We are tearing a building down as you lead us yes

And we stand in the fire and speak one says the universe a memory
Of itself and its beginning that we hold in place I will bring that down I
Say it did not begin nor in blindness proceed there's no fire in this di-
Mension and the words I see and hear that I speak come structured
By a self of chanceless freedom perhaps there is nothing but freedom
Rather than a prison of analysis each word fills the unceilinged expanse
And is it too they are talking to me the words saying notify
For we are the kind of you and you see nothing but us ex-
Tending from your mind voice but we will nev-
Er tell you how to be nor chide you for what you did before
Who was I then once one asks you were an illusion of yourself
Now you can't remember what that was who is speaking
It is I I say leading you and somehow knowing what to say

What we are is revolution we have come back around
And I fully recognize myself this must be the place
Everything else has collapsed including what was called
The body the earth the living the past and future all hierarchy

POEM

May all governments cease and no more men decide for me or
Steal from me I'll happily kill you but you know you've no stren-
Gth someone says oh I'm Samson the blind and just
Scores of pigs run everywhere before the roof collapses
I'm going to live in the gully not needing electricity
I'm going to die there like Marie not in a rehab like my
Mother doctorless and barely allowed after Jerry
Brown refused hospice services to the people in my home town
I don't need him or the president with his urgent vanity
You need a structure but I don't not in our cities of cowards
The problem is everyone's needs dish it out to yourself and tell
Waltons Buffet and Gates you'd just as soon kill them as buy their stuff
I would though I know you want to buy everything slop
Eat porn and communal cream in middleclass fuckit the inter-
Net's not beautiful it's nothing from nit heads incapable and credulous

We are
These
Pri-
Mal
Words I
For-
Get who
I've
Been

Did we make them or were we all made together by each
Other they are our messages to ourselves quick to be
Registered I am the form we made formerly carved
But in this nonspace I am your tongue of discovery
You have I have a spiraling promise in my mouth
We call ourselves the dead who have cut sadness up and
Made it into the symbols never never to be remembered I
No I don't Ted says want to either my new poems are bet-
Ter that I make for the dead with these glyphs of the
Dead with these strangely shaped unheartfelt hearts
It takes the concentration the absorption of an angel to emit a poem
And we try to leave them in the minds of the live asleep but
Keep leading us can remember when you're here that you are here
Otherwise I sometimes search for you in dreams but the
Pain of translation into the living one I was is too forbidding

What if it happens because I am I I am standing here
This is no puzzle Daddy says it isn't a quest you have to lead us yet
Enter my house my mind everyone I say if there is no size or scale
Do you want to be part of me someone must make this first or
Primal gesture of location and openness I'm not afraid
I'm not saying be as I am I'm saying my mind is your place if you want
It though it's still myself and won't cease to be what do we
Do here someone says forgetting who you were and what was
Ceasing to replicate in shadow form how you struggled
Alive to learn to be oh you're so much larger Daddy says in an instant

I have allowed it all in every star and sun what shall we do
Just relax stretch out I think it is a place of forgiveness
How are you leading us now the same way but you
Possess more protection from yourselves I won't let you panic or grieve too
Hard this is how I am changing the universe I am pro-
Viding myself to you as it rather than as just me

I will find a voice says a language for inhabiting you
I can't always be telling you myself but I am agressive he
Says I remember I'm showing you myself I was moneyed the memory
Lost converts to images of falling from pow-
Er to stand on sidewalk you have a nostalgia for me he says
This language tells me that in little scenes like ovals to peer in-
To but there were the sexes and now not you aren't a woman
He says even though you're a live woman the parts of your
Mind that aren't speaking crackle I can't de-
Scribe the language I must learn very raw sore from where
I was filled with another self ripped out my useless story
I was a powerful man now I'm unanticipated words
I say oval I smile at you inside yourself and seeing you
To speak ovals becoming diamonds with bleeding edges
Or overtones for I say and you process a steeliness a stolen
I stole your money I had plenty you had none but now
There's none no one I'm I was very powerful here power's ev-
Erywhere in the words linking all us a substance of word
Pry open for eternity a word I am but it doesn't
Have to be what I haven't ever thought of I'm now with you

I'm
Now
With
You
Every-
One
Says
I'm

Now
With
You

The language a brushed on handwritten script let-
Ters overwhelmed by black thick strokes disguising
All meaning I can't read it and it's black now not white be-
Cause another voice says you let me into yourself it was
Love I smiled fell to the ground dead an official in the last SSR
I'm not a metaphor he says the police will arrest you they
Have to let me read this black writing first I say
Scrawled on cardboard do we have that in the new death
And the daytime square with trees outside the empty
Embassy a flash memory I love you he says but I
Think it's just that I can love unsystematically in-
Side your mind I say I'm afraid I am death
What is the word written Gare de la Mort that's not it
Many many more inside me but I'm still walk-
Ing leading on the plain you're behind me we're inside you too

Maybe it's pretend writing pretend language
Maybe we're only pretending to understand what we say
Or maybe what we're saying is never what we seem to
Maybe something different like what we're really saying un-
Conscious of in the other dimension I'm telling you al-
Ways that I'm leading where there's no scale air or space
To love in a beginning of nothing where you are empty

Everyone's being evacuated from the embassy
You were never safe there or anywhere the over-
Reach governments are elected to power to have all
Of it and tell you you relinquished it at election you have no
Power at all your communications are being mon-
Itored but I have allowed everyone who has ever ex-
Isted inside me you can listen to my mind as you please
You can inhabit my unconscious if you wish

What
Am I
Doing
Momma
Study-
Ing
The lan-
Guage
Of
Acts
Try-
Ing to
Unveil
The
Word
Of
Love
The
World
Is in-
Scrut-
Able
Til
Now
But
That's
Cor-
Inthians

What about but then face to face Momma
Do you see each other's faces do you have them
I saw the face of a star I see the face of anything
Can you see the face of the black word it's
Showing you its face a voice says in the speak angel series

Back on the plain where the black poppies reek instability
Presenting themselves jaggedly a torn petal
Large as my whole eye as I fight to be in the new per-

Ception with the dead while struggling to bring down
The building trying not to see it your way everyone's in-
Side my mind and I'm leading you to freedom any way
What we keep seeing that might be language is it ours
The oval or diamond shaped amalgams of or are
They round what kind of being are you a voice says I've been told
I'm a person I say but I'm not sure then Daddy says
It doesn't matter what do you want it says to lead you where
Your wound doesn't hurt or you are no longer evil
No matter what I did it says I don't want to
Know there are too many stories I'm supposed to believe I say

Just being here there's another hurt word on the road
It's me says a voice it's what I don't want to be any
More become geometry and colors and pronounced danger
There is no longer danger in death don't have to remember
The real words Momma says don't stand for anything
I cry out to them and they say themselves and then me
I can't always remember how to say it for it is an ex-
Perience I saw one and it said something like Hassan's life
Or it says I am what hurt prompting you it says we will find you
In the desert it says your daughter will destroy the haunt of thieves
Yes I say for everyone is a thief in life and steals
Steals the money of others and as much of their souls as
Can be taken it was power over souls that most people wanted
To see in your eyes a register of fear or subjection

For a
Mo-
Ment
I don't
Remem-
Ber
Why I
Came
Here
I
Know

Who I
Am an
Eter-
Nal
One
But
The
Stuff out-
Side
Street
Ci-
Ty does-
N't make
Any
Sense

I am becoming myself by forgetting almost ev-
Erything and will know how to bring down the build-
Ing blind in unknowing who I'm supposed to be
If you forget who they've told you you are you
Can bring it down even in August or Paris as if
Those were things I've always known you without
Your name the voice says for you've always let us
In and you've always been open to our open-
Ing when the world's ways were cold but I've never
Been any way I say all the ways to be were invented

If you
Would
Just
Stop
Your
Chil-
Dren
Don't
Need
Any-
Thing

But
Your
Love
And a
Few
Drops of
Sugar
Water
From
Your
Beak

We are suddenly inside the first glyph or word is it your mind our mind
I slipped into it a voice says always passing through doors my own
Voice here seems to appear in front of me forming designs there is
Red various darks too can you understand me I forget my mean-
Ing as soon as I speak it we are wondering if we need to control it
When do the control and formation start another says
Others speak their words absorbed by darkness and color forgotten
Relentless I have gone on ahead nothing is here but speaking intently

It's your picture you've lost all your pictures cry
Out for this for consciousness vibrates there's no af-
Fect the quasar says I love you though if we're here
There's no one above and there's no reliance or self-
Reliance because after loss of scale there was no need for
Hope what do you think there's no earlier person in my
Forehead always doing this acoustically without
Audition except an internal hearing and seeing with what

And so the patterns I speak have agreed to find me
Where does this come from it properly got here like me
You don't ever have to go I have a meager world
Too you won't always have to be there there keeps be-
Ing a fuschia splash you reckon there was always enough
And no desires before their invention a gold eye I
See it you're seeing with it can be out of whatever there was
Because of no time but everything the words for these

Are inside them no longer lost we will speak from here
The name of revolution's when you come here deserting the world

In your formal or former time when you believed other people
I'm staring out the dirty past muster I can't even recall
For I was weak you'd say and aging but what quali-
Fication can there be now Momma says I'm no longer weak
And I say now that there's no such thing as weakness
You will have forgotten the idea by the time I have seen
The next word drift by strength weakness how awful
There's a mailing tube tube he's trying to get a message through
I want you to know her for I love that is a scar
The dead can no longer name their scars is that it
No but they are letting go everyone needs to let go
Revolution's an odd idea he says I am one a revolution I say but
I never thought to be most people are too fearful
I was he says though I was a big man now there's
No size I'm not afraid either but revolution why
In this one I say we let go of the past as an internal
Hurt it is a mental effort devoid of violence at least for the dead
But you must allow those who've done wrong to let go too
And then there's the part where one must do it even my-
Self and I let go of my story like a life
Somehow it will help everyone if I do this
You're still my daughter Momma says but that's not a story
The memory of suffering's supplanted by our new language

And in the past the men stole from me for they were
The government and taxed me but everyone stole using
Me for culture and paying themselves is that
True Daddy says I am trying to forget my sto-
Ry I say but I'm not dead with my story self ripped
Out almost it's almost gone vulture hovering some-
One some critic will use it for something of hers
I am caught with others constellation pinpoints lead
Us Daddy says further into the heart of glyph
We heard you cry last night others say for we're
Within you but it didn't make us sad it was it-

Self and not for a person or point I had it in my
Purse I had crying in my outfit still like a drunk
Lead us I'm tangled I say in a mark in here that's part
I spell nothing it says just say me to propitiate
The future if you're alive the past if you're dead
Change me it says and I make the letter looser you are
Transfigured I am tearing the building down though
There was no first language there is no
Language at all just us it says we aren't what you
Want us to be you didn't invent us or anything ev-
Er your lives have been dreams if you're to begin a-
Again wake up and tear this building down as you are do-

Ing
In
Sleep
Drift-
Ing a-
Part
The pil-
Lars the
Ceiling and
Floor
Are drift-
Ing

I'm wearing a hat that's a skull a cranium someone put it on
Me last night so I would know what its dead po-
Ssessor knew a shaman a word's so alive it stays in the bone
And once when I was alive I brought word over yellow milk
Lake in a canoe and word was soul like yours to find its way
There is no reason for being this one word sings
You can lead them all and they will follow nowhere to nowhere
No nirvana word no blessing word nothing gets it
Being isn't like anything you thought it was

I have a word in my skull it is tender every-
Thing was malleable and is nothing knows you yet

As I watch matter and words exist don't exist exist again
Where we are here in this glyph that's a word not a word a
Word neon sign flashing on and off though I'm continuous
Within malleability the glyph asks am I a hoax I don't
Know ho ax we are all trying not to be a hoax like a dan-
Gerous stinging is it a bee or a stinging butterfly can't
Kill where the soul and the story on and off merge my sto-
Ry I wouldn't cry for my own trying to smash the
Stinger with striped wings against the wall until I know more
You are writing our epic a story Dad says
It's inside this place now a stasis or near-
Ly stopped pulse glyph it is and if it's on I'm familiar
If off the story's gone I'm still watching I
Don't know what she ever did except for write this
Write this and the letter we're in that I am as I wri-
Te it at this tender beginning of clocks
Kill the bee or not does the bee have to have a nar-
Rative I'm trying to remember what is there how
Much is needed by what or whom here actually
Of what one supposedly did what did you do
What was your body to you with its defects and schemes

As I
Write
I
Hear a
Word
To
Write tow-
Ards
Hoax
Was
One
Clocks
And de-
Fects
Schemes
These

Words
Are
More
Real
Or
Glyphic
They
Ap-
Pear
On the
Road

In a black coat and a red neckerchief with collar-
Length black hair had to wear til it greyed and grew
It depends on whose poems you prefer I prefer mine
And in my story all the terms or constellation points
Have shifted my double did everything for me
While I was acquiring strength I've the force of
All you combined because I was once broken and blind

The wind sustains the shifting of my thought
And the ordinary world you deemed lovable deserts ev-
Eryone I wrote and said what you think I did
But the events that formed me were doubled
By their names in my unconsciousness now arising
Like Scorpion or Orion in the love there was always more
Gold and in devastation more murders so if you
Want to know your real story consider who you are dream-

Ing you will now be helpless to hear me
I was brought forth by the dead for a purpose I
Was born for it saved from death a handful
Of times and taught or taught myself the skills
Of the vocal poem the only weapon that loves

This is the one truth you will hear this decade
The world as you perceive it the flatulence of the scorn-
Ful rich and if I say that over won't you know you're

Lying in your least action find out what happens
I spent the night in New York on the sidewalk
Next to boxes of my manuscripts where were
Of you the body-part ass teaching lines backwards from
Thought to poem to your position prominent fucker
My head is an oval torch and I can burn you up

Then I could never find my documents illicit
My foreigner papers my justification for being
Here anywhere because I wasn't and it wasn't either
Kept in a black drawer all along by the fate that grips everyone
I have leapt out of the microphone into your heart
Rich as a dog now aren't I strong as a disease-bearing insect
Saved for this moment by the weaker one of me
I'm going to let you know who you are
Symbols of everything you hate but symbols wouldn't
You like to be real I am standing there now
I wouldn't want to lose the force of renascence
I am in the light or dark catching on fast I
Can do it wherever I find it the reading
Of what you stand for stop standing in as ideas
Of people I'm here to kill you simulacra I'm tired of
Symbols and weakness and of the prosperity of those who cringe

En-
Vel-
Oped
In
Where
We be-
Gan
To
Speak
Or
Was it
To
Think
What

Do such
Words
Mean
If they're
One
Thing
And
No
Thing
Is
Sep-
Ar-
Ate
Waves
Or
Tears
Who
Are
You
My
Heart
This
Mat-
Ter is
Skep-
Tical
Of
Your
Ab-
Ility
To per-
Form
A named
Act

It doesn't make sense to talk til the words tell me to
The letters segmented stretching floating I was heard and under-
Stood Momma says when I died by whom

And my story left me to become part of this
Primary mixage you've led us to attempt
To call out what do you want to be part of Alice I
Don't want to be a part my whole self unadherent
And the glyphs and scenes we met traveling and the
Script the words of what might stick to-
Gether are my friends out of chaos
A voice says if we have always been in each
Other's minds when we were alone when I
And I remember swimming to shore I was the first
Each one would say and did you already speak
But to yourself as a baby says things in its mind
What did I say I said let's place some next to each
Other or did I say more is that there was once one or
Did I say I am not one of yours or I am one of you
Or I am your heart

And
Here I
Wore
Mirror-
Ing
Dark
Glasses
And slicked
My
Hair
Down
The
Truck
Stop
Was
Closed
Wrecked
And I
Say
Mena-
Cingly

You
Should
Know
Me

VICTORIOUS

Honey leader honey from the lion's body I bring you
A food or mental substance a knowledge from the sup-
Posed realm of wordlessness the opposite of me
Honey leader honey your hair is growing around
Mirrorshades the only thing I see is a vibrant word is it
A word if I know it flash not reading it
Saying it without saying it with lips or brain but
Being honey you should see there's no one here but everyone

I wanted to forget them blindly when the world began again
My double honey stark as a burnt tree when I spoke
Flash and I saw how wrong everybody had been
In the old times when all we created was decorative
If I might destroy the old you I'm extracting power from which
Self in order to stand for a moment above you hold-
Ing my bone club my weapon of greeting hello honey
You will not go on the way you have your tone
Of voice silly and maudlin pompous and demanding
You must now learn from this word wedge your new art

Honey as leader honey I am your mind leading
You can hear me we stand counting nothing not know-
Ing numbers anyone forgot them to beg to be home
Here we are numb for I've destroyed and rebirthed you honey
You have nothing but this vibration we are speaking almost silently
You have nothing but this opposite of what you were this moltenness
None of you my friend but I've led you to your own heart
A place where no one has to know their words or
Counterparts anymore your stories were invented in dreams
Your eyes were full of unsubstantial legends you'd made up
And attributed to the fabricated bastards your heroes of millions
They were just you I've ripped them out your soreness is freedom

Honey leader I'm and learning a language from which you
Can know all others only two native speakers left I and

I and the I that has taken over now shows you the grid of re-
Newal it's a shaky grid the cracked syntax of an earthquake
Honey leader it will slow down and flow like honey
After we agree to speak darkly or densely honey leader grid
This language might tear you but you're already torn
No no overlay all language comes from here
Find it at this time clutching the damage we came from
Its innard strings I pull it apart and it refigures I'm yours
What are your verbs and nouns I am a conglomerate of anything
I speak for a joining of the already continguous I
Am how we cohere mind after death pushing outward honey lava

I am your leader says the language or I the
Quintillionth and first I the verb I the noun the pronominals
My death I honey leader honey calls out silently to
Other honey the grid flows like aftermath
I didn't ask says the universe to be born
And death says I may have asked to die but I can't and we
The dead don't die living on speaking origin that
You'd think of as grid never been such the part of
Speech is to join us in mentality I am the serenest
Samson you might know after I destroy us
Why does it begin in violence because you named it violence
But now you have no nervous system to hurt you

Honey leader honey uncarved again with phantom pain
Today's my brother's birthday do I still remember everything
But it's my day he says I'm finally reborn sis honey
That's an aside or double a twin of telepathy
We have come to the fact of the solution honey leader un-
Named shapes call out that we didn't know everything to see
Now we're inside the words we'd catch hold of
We have never heard of governance I tell us I
The leader the Samson who judged us sad and inept trivial
Washed-up smothered souls groping
You had to follow me past the store of limp spangled dresses limp
Weapons my cudgel is pure like a torch my hair's like grey fire
Inside this honey flow where the language is find-

Ing its nearly unfashioned form its deeper hues
My brother's new peace the source of our plan to go on

Leader my shell is empty or it's all stony dark green
The money was nothing the clothes were vapid the poems of
Others dimming in force the money was nothing a joke
All the money in the world a joke though the sorrow real leader
Honey leader honey power's the only thing we are an ac-
Cumulation of first matter hollow electric and calm
I know what it is I say I know where we are and are going
We are rearranging origin its glyph and its home
We are rearranging the night plan I honey leader honey
Am calling reality now it responds to me

We are calling you to us I and what was once fate the body
But is now my own malleability the light staring
Or is it something I would recognize just who I am
I want you to see it inside the beginning in our
Composite meaning as for the pre-beginning honey
I pulled down the ceiling so we wouldn't have dimensions or scale
Then there was pure action in death which is truth I
Honey and leader am left on the river but I have the boat
Whoever left me for trivia but I have the boat or
Leadership the honey songs beguiling you to start again
Maintaining our connection that is our universe
We are the power we stand in pre-power the whole thing

Before the shell body honey power wouldn't you like to
Act now for the sake of action not knowing why
Without an accrued meaning with words that don't
Drag leavage after them I acted honey leader
Honey without any motive for I was not enacted
And I arrange reality a certain way that's all
With the hands of one of my bodies coincident in me
All night I arrange things without known names or shapes
Put on your irreal shades honey leader be opaque again we are
Ready everyone everything here inside the connection

Last night you were with me because I was broken and good
And you say you are with me because I've got enough honey for you
Matter or mentality becoming words for anyone in any lan-
Guage or stillness we are forming entities for each other
Here in the primal blast moltenness we have arrived at
Hurt from prior eons ready for the mind or dream that acts
I birth new forms hopeless and free any rock
Any rock has a new name and I have one too honey leader honey
What shall we do together with these new minds and have
Accepted nothing have not seen or heard it haven't re-
Acted honey leader haven't judged or been taught
We are making what we are just that

August 20, 2014

POSTSCRIPT : HAPPENED

The language unknown except as a tissue of all sound sight and thought
Dreamed or not the unknown man was killed twice last night and I the observer and
Child awake disgruntled but now I'm not sad Allen you can let go inside of any
Moment let go of sadness I think he was supposed to die per-
Haps I finally killed him as a child as a girl I never say what one expects
So the language of the tissue of us all is now free not to be analyzed by ex-
Perts I am going to smell the language and can the dead smell yes feel it with my
Hands too it's exact it's never left us he says but can't be what you expect
Grass with some gaps there dirt and always a flyer a bug nearby those white fester flow-
Ers too somewhere inside me where all that deadman filth was he isn't
A dead man like you listen everyone the language doesn't need us we are it but not like
                                                                         you'd
Thought not intoning it if you don't have vocal cords dead I don't he says I have great
                                                                         minding
A different it's to activate it in the thought first in zero then with lightning or flash
And I have sent you the color of migrant splendor for it wandered in and like a
Firefly blinked like a quasar rubbed up against what you said but I didn't say a yes
You did you really did kill him when you dream you say something to every-
One's dream mind that's how we know each other's secrets I know all of yours he Al-
Len says that's why I'm letting you lead me next you will speak of leadership once more
I am extracting everyone's sorrow sadness tragedy from their internal haunt I say I am
In here with all of you in this poem where we are zero filling us with flash I am leading you
To freedom for it was specific your sadness but you clung like love to it couldn't function you
Don't have to function inside here everyone you were sad about exists too find his mind
                                                                         we're
Becoming this language I'm leading you to where no one has to behave because we're in
                                                                         the con-
Nection get that we're just here it's just being the language and this power one is auto-

Matically you are power even if you're sick your mind lets it out now here where
Sticky and pliant the unboundaried wants us to glow from zero to the whole ex-
Tent unmeasureable so in your mind and what you might say to me any mental vo-
Cable like yes-it-was-you what what who killed him with white sticky sub-
Stance on one part of his corpse near the waist I think we are seeing that image
In the all-important zero moonlike hiding you a moment nothing has to work
There is no sad necessity there is no necessary don't be a jerk in here come in here and
                                                                    don't bother with

Anything else

And in it she left me the other one I was but I still remember some of her stuff I only be-
Tray her a little near the ocean inside this blackness someone a girl slightly mal-
Odorous left too so I'm left Allen are you there I'm shaking you're not you're your real
One now not microcosmic whose birthday no one's ka-boom after the lightning the
Ka that is another glyph for I I am leading you I soul am bringing you to ful-
Fillment when we change the universe into not a bunch of pieces but who it is
It doesn't tick we don't and we don't have to be flattened cowering overcome by our
Vastness it's us a or the only just is don't reinterpret I know how to be stone and primary
I was told to find you and love you by you all of you heart of it in the recombinatory
Language that makes our transformations possible as we also stay the same thing I am a-
Lone as I write this and I am a soul what is my name at the top of the densely typed letter
                                                                    of an old-
Style typewriter addressed to me I can never see the type never see the writing but I know al-
Most everything it says it just says leader or Samson or and then it says once again forget
                                                                    ev-
Erything and begin your sense of yourself is unremembered I'm talking to you immortal
Flower all in no time it has been no time since we began it just happened nothing happens
                                                                    so what
Barely a form what's a form for I've changed for you can a soul change yes and I speak-
Ing Allen says may I ask a question are you being real or imaginary this is for the
Audience where in the house where they don't understand yet I'm being real
Yes I know thank you I no longer have a house or degree in breath I still breathe
But what I used to know isn't what I now am the stars searching for nothing ray-
Ing from my face but embodied as somehow a further body or seen-by I
Thus lead you so that you'd find you aren't there but here you are not
Maladroit loneliness is not a quality light on the surface of the lamp base gold re-
Flected but I want to remember who I was you say oh I say just try my name is Change

And in my houselessness save for this all-encompassing dark word I change
I name or I none watch the demise of my daily self are you sorry I don't know keep
                                        changing Al-
Len says this is pure word her sister's name is Crystal the older acquaintances want to tell
                                        you some-
Thing all the wives are here but I'm only watching I have so many things to do in the
                                        darkness
Of comprehension or is it disaffection self-contained as a magnet so that you can come to
                                        me like home
Why was everything about finding before listen you don't remember wild what calls you
                                        isn't really other
What elucidates to you in your dreams either he says we're going to finish up today there's
                                        nothing wrong
                                        any-
Where though everything looks terrible it's all so familiar that the dead don't even notice
I I say whoever I am have led you to word of origination uncoiled and unsequential its
                                        roots
Literal and clung to by ideal and unreal dirty saying if you were to have a story now but
You won't you will have something else don't impose on each other don't grasp
What I've led you to vibrates like you do you are inside emptied sore but without care
What was care there is no nurturing I am leading you to perfect sexlessness
I have neither male nor female now there is another neutral crystal and alive
Our language is unqualified what do we speak of we speak I am leading you to
A bizarre loss of identity your primary countenance or calculus for I am neither
Notational nor notional nor polite I am leading to a place in ourselves
I am not leading you home and we will leave this letter word or glyph soon and establish a
Graceful chaos to speak by in both death and life I am after all leading you to
Language that restructures the universe not from an explosion but from its most
Our most salient trait our communicativeness our cohesion then where is freedom ah
And truly to speak to each other what can that be I am leading you to who are you
Because it's on the way in here everything you need to know not how to live it was never
                                        that
We don't have to live we have to be who you are storyless and no one you've met before

II.
OPERA

When you were live like a radio your voice everywhere I
Couldn't get rid of it
But now that we're dead I remember that was like a TRICK
For I had been taught to remember was told WHAT to re-
Member now I say I   am happening

I who lead have a long black cape trailing behind that spirits ride
Decorated with black sequins WHERE TO
We have waited the dead say in this long instant to be over life
Within the old e-   pic so come along

I AM THE LEADER OF THE ENTIRE FREE WILL

I lead you if you remember I remember says one it's frozen ground
I broke open and stars came out says she
Something we made the side of a house is mys-
Terious wallside cerulean tree
                              We have to feed the baby quasar
                                    which mem-
Ory do you
Want I wheel round
So prior and leaves scat-   tered there is a TENT to the right of
My bed with lamp LIT in-   side a

Heart
Surgeon

Gives you a
Bigger
HEART

Take my
Love mind protocol leading now that I
Am
When I am live like a radio before the CREATION

He took a picture of how I was white swirls with eye-
Pits punch your MIND FISTS THROUGH the curtain
We are wrecking physics riding on your cloth cape
How I am in MOTIO in place like a SOUL leave
For I've left it before just in order to see how it was PLACED
I your leader in a body say   I observe who speaks
Say it doesn't MATter   to US IN DEATH I'm say-
Ing SOUL leaves its body I DID a long time ago says she
Since I didn't know I was a Downwinder when I died
AM I one   It   just doesn't we'd say mat-
The man's coming back to fix the lock
Ter   And I know burial it so sweet a sarcasm tele-
Pathic certain uncertain either one
I had always known I would die of what says she

The pronouncement of your shadow outside of Sharlot Hall
You are trying to tell me my life story City Hall
But I am trying to sing that there are two of me
The unearthly one's view cataleptic for a
Long time free of time on these steps outside the drawer
Cede the quotidian rationale of suffering some think they see but
If I died for a long time says she I must remember HOW to
In my autonomous nervous system the frequencies sing of it
Mandolins want to HAVE BEEN with a tumor at the base of my brain

I your leader lead her because I love her
The records of being are what we are why go back on it with SIMPERS
Everyone suffers is it over I don't remember

It was because you ARE it that you couldn't call it
I am here to CALL IT fear raggedy bird has flown
Of the BILLION birds souls I convey that are REALLY birds
Along with others   Can you understand them   what's to you know understand
The SYStems all belong to   the dead YOU honey beans

In place leading I am leading you to the immortal cognition of
                    THEY MOWED US DOWN IN A SICK CHOIR
                    OR CONTAINER of our ethNIcity

                    Apart in the so-thick air of your CAPE
                    Looking for that new way to SING
THERE IS NOTHING BUT US THERE IS ALL THAT THERE IS
Create this instant just create it I mean as instant it
CAN't FLOUNDer I'm leaving it in the ground the pun I walk on
A very long time ago I left it the first instant there wasn't one no
Star has EVer exPLOded it does something ELSE
                    What does it do OUR language says it
                    TransFERS you are not HURT you are not hurt
                    None of you are hurt

141

DeCEMber SUN I am leading the SUN all ENtities same size of GOLD
And COLD if there's no SIZE the UNIVERSE has none
Of borders I am leading to borderless CALM not go to BED
Through the tornup memories LEAD past washboards and mud
The SUN was MUD soft and insubstantial DEAD dreamed it
Was I am leading its SOUL unheard of unkempt
Don't recognize words I am leading you THROUGH THE GHOST WORDS
We're THROUGH WITH

My father says don't bend now
My brother's tears grey I hate them he says lead me
PAST THEM Okay they can be dead REALLY
I said I was busy with memory BECAUSE I am inter-
SECTED by SO MANY TIMES I'd cry if I weren't LEADing
The CAPE is so DENSE it's OSMIUM or iRIDium or NO NAME

I've ceased to see the politicized masses the mediatized pimps and mouths I only
                    see their souls I'm leading you
I'm leading the prison of murders the gangs and pariahs or who WOULD KILL ME
Don't care about the law theirs and yours of retribution I
                am leading you
                WE THE CHORUS OF THE DESPISED DEAD
Alleluia in the empty church I face it and lead it
                Lead us of churches and world reLIGions take the
                    platitudes off our backs
I am leading to the re-creation
You are not a man or mammal that is not a mountain
                Nothing is ours we're free
I'm leading to full-scale humor so your nuance-mad minds can laugh
You were jerks we were asses PAINED
I'm leading you to a town in a country you've never visited
                Where the church is so empty it can hold every
                  soul in the universe
I'm leading you to the farthest crop of stars light years etcetera
But nothing's far or near now vast or petty
                ENTER EMPTY
It's a language train yourselves mentally to sing

I am   I am lead-   leading you to a new s t r u c t u r e
Dream into place each night a fleshly tissue had to be rePLACED
L a s t   n i g h t we have no nights the dead but you are our leader
Never rest I'm leading you on the trail of s i m u l t a n e o u s time
                                        We are happening EVERY time

Newly other the words FALL IN

                                        We are waiting for the CURSED

At City Hall
Part of the CRUX night l e f t   m e
On the floor she was sitting alone
IN the Tales of the Forgetting
Aunt Helen gives me the Chopin bust aGAIN   BUT
She just hands it to me
                                        She didn't do that it was SENT
She just HANDS it to me   and that's MORE TRUE
I have cancer she says and I'm dead you're my CLASSICAL LEADER
                                        WE ALL SAW OUR we our suffering saw
                                        From the beginning most wrong is ORDER
                                        I she said had primary tumors one by one every-
                                        Where
I am leading you to   the new structure we will
Make of all that is you must forGET
In order to know what h a p p e n e d let
Words fall out of order n a t u r a l l y

At storefront version of librairie M. Abdoulaly
Gives me money to go buy ten packs
Of Pall Malls some Luckies and can't remem-
Ber three certificates of worth

I'm leade why am I do this for him I destroy YO-
UR goddam o r d e r when
When different way we needed to
Be we didn't need to   Be honey we are
Reawed No   awe of us   No it's the be-
Ginning of life or death no
Then you can't   you can't not think
No you can't not it's the one thing you
Can't and out of ever infinitely BACK
Where everything already hap-
Pened because the spiral's flattened already GAVE
Me the euros to get luckies at the   beginning of time that
There wasn't and we D I D N ' T be-GIN

I am leading you can't not think
I am leading gridless where everything
I'm leading you climbed on my back any poor soul
I am almost over it   led to this musi-
Cality of the U N I V and disappeared through

Epic loss/ What have you lost/ I don't know/ Where are you/ Here

Moonlight everywhere in the room or onstage no moon
You must present the rationale one says FOR our diminishing sorrow
It isn't precisely that we forget but the lang-
Uage   of memory   can now work truthfully

It is important that there is no hell anywhere

Now I am leading you to   ALL TO   there is no hell
THIS is equality   powerlessness   over each other but
The only thing I am IS power

Why were we when we ARE   the stage has collapsed and in the blue
We are making happen ourselves throw away the ev-
Olutionary it was a line

All at once the chorus   of individ-   ual minds sings
And in my hand-to-be hold a bacterium
Epic lost what have you lost I don't know where are you
Here

I'm leading you to where the humiliating sad
Particulars of your guilt   are just particles particles
It was another blue rectangular   solid framed in blue
In blue I've remade our guilt and I am leading you

If I hand you this   it's a word
If I have no hands dead not needing them think it to you
I DON'T hand it

I remember being eviscerated I remember that that is the
Word for it I remember watching above my body
To know he was mocking me for being a (it's garbled)
I saw the crows they're always in on it wanted to be a lion but
His fierceness mediocre these words come slowly was as-
Sumed   as if an actor even in an African and they sleepwalked
War   I want you to sing anyway   It's not a
False one the memory   Give it to me   How   Give it I'll

And we left it   left it in the canebrake   The true soul hatched
Of you   crosses enferried the night upon me and my cape CLIMB
ON   My memory is I handed you the object
I'm leading you   where you the wrecks play

And if we pause to reflect each other causing
The death of the o r i g i n a l e p i c as you
Were taught the stars made but WE made us

I untape your mouth and open the black drawer
This object jumps out

DEAFENING HEART

I say one says the explosion comes from V O I D
I I say   OPENED   the B L A C K drawer
I am C A U S I N G U S this object
I am causing us   Take off your cape   No

A maximum of cold degrees conversation
Hands me a collage of withered trees or withered planets
Can't you see I've been doing this backwards and forwards eTERnally
I'm looking for an initial relation between all us
The object that you are won't hurt you now

In the black sequence I'm leading I'm leading you PAST s u f f e r a n c e THIS
What the LIVE still think they SEE i s the f o r m e r universe
All of which had interpreted itself WRONGLY for it was FORMED
BY US as if we were a syntax of upHEAVAL when we might d a n c e a t r a n s-
F o r m a t i o n a l occURence back and FORTH through the wall of DEATH

Being the one who HAS broken through I am leading you TO
                         Because we didn't DIE the resumption of our origin
In the black sequence learn you live to speak
                    To US the DEAD in the language we were b o r n i n
Essential and the twigs of trees spell it every SHAPE you make
                    We ARE speaking it memory
CAWS and the more CRYstalline speech of the E u r o p e a n blackbird
                    Anything I HAP-
Lessly say the UNiVERsal MEMORY

I'm leading you to FREEDOM from OLD memory
                    I remember being a FOOL in so many circum-
                    My STANCES were rigid and deSTRUCTive
                    I didn't have to STAND for anyTHING I am the THING
I'm leading YOU LIVE to where you can HEAR the dead in your MINDS call and care
                    Not metaphorical there is no METAPHOR
The sky turns pink and the moon SETS we are D A N C I N G U S

Any rock or bacterium could have taken command but I am leading you
I am leading you to tracks runways and small weeds that
Say MIND through WALL GO and SEE WHO YOU ARE
                    Dead the POWER to hold us t o g e t h e r
I am leading you to power to the WORLD of the DEAD to the OTHer
Half of WHO don't you SEE FEEL a different BLOOD or FORCE IN YOU

I am leading you to the TEMPLE the mind of the universe I AM
And leading the LIVE I will overthrow the moneychangers
                    Tear THIS building down
And leading the DEAD I will erect a new memory for you
                    At the TOP of the mind

We stepped to the fore within and the pieces of
Our brokenness fell away we
Forgot it and what we remember
Is how you put this there the RED ONE goes into
The art US
Here I am leading you to the rest of yourself on the other
SIDE of the WHITE wall MOON in some sign or other I've for-
GOTten leading you to the identity of the MOLECULES of COMMUNICANTS
We are all it the w h i t e n i n g doverush thought you sent
STOOD on the roof along the edge where we speak
Put the WORD t h e r e subSTANCE LESS
And she took the crushed paper FORMS and handed them along in
The GREEN void the t h e a t r i c a l thought of it
I have no OBJECTive I am leading you
To where you won't have THING
It's NOT negation who are we
It's NOT the epic of CURSES
Or the GRADual formation of a MOMentary aCHIEVEment
I am leading you to BILATERAL interSECTION of CHOIRISTIC mentALity
I am leading you to the corner of BROADway and A street MAIN and ROSE
I am leading you to fearlessness to the opening of the BLACK BACK
I am leading you to where you can't see your SKIN any more

How does the universe remember itself
Without human memory it's probably there BUT WHAT is it what
I am I am leading it to freedom
I am leading it manifest in its lingual structure we reveal NOW
She passes through the WALL with an e n v e l o p e divided
Into blocks of written messages from the OUT s i d e
On the inside darkly I am t a r g e t e d by the SINGING
SING THESE LINES   for you will do that HERE
The weather is lousy the envelope says m a n u f a c t u r e d
By us as else and the LIVING try to squeeze me into SAD SHAPE
We on your black back name the NEW SENSES
S l i d i n g n o t e s / FORCE / the counting of deGREES
beTWEEN
WORDS seedpearl-like TONES beTWEEN we ARE
Counting YOU LEADING in your own nuMERical presence
gathering

FOR the particles of ALL US interMINGling THOUGHTS
I'm leading them til the language so slides inTO an EPIC IDEN-
Tity it finally KNOWS I T S E L F
I will let you engulf me tenderly that I lead

Without s o p h i s t i c a t i o n you I lead
With the force of my antidote for the OLD SORROW you I lead
Placing backtracked the bits of our PREVIOUS
ENCOUNTERS you I lead

                    We only count for aMUSEment
                    We ratiocinate for aMUSEment
                    To keep ourselves amused we will create love aGAIN
Does possess a quality contrapuntal but voices are COUNTless
More words THAN you'd conceived diMINISH the conJUNCTIONS
Everything is conjunct to me I who lead you
I'm leading you where I can see in relation to every million glints
Or words a prepositional slant a keen gloss side
Whatever you say goes forth from mind to mind I am leading you
                    You're leading us because you're the ONLY one or thing
                                   who CAN

In the midst of what was wrongly called void I am leading you
Quadrillion sides of thoughts or orbs I am leading you
I'm leading away from order and disorder

I'm leading you for I have no one else in this room but e v e r y o n e
I am leading you to no OAKS no house no CHAIR
The IDEA of the MEMORY p r e s s e s THE idea of MEMory p r e s s e s
                    My SELF but who
                    And the birds sing UNmeekly UNdaunted
                    The way the quasar eMITS
And I eMIT I say I am leading you away

Alone with everyone I am LEADING THEM
This story thRILLS being the in-death VERsion in theaTER you
Have left me / I am leading you
No one has EVER understood anything I have said so I am LEADING YOU
I am leading away from the NACRE SCREEN where you saw YOURSELF
I am leading you TO the INFINITELY layered polyphony of a one's mind
I am leading you to the clarity of playing no r o l e

I am leading you to so much more than duPLICITY
MORE than the theaTER of THOUGHT the polyVAlent buzz
of eXISTing
And if we weren't didn't exist in death WHAT WOULD HOLD
IT UP
The uniVERSE to e x i s t is HELD IN our thought I am leading you
To PEACE we are the automatic BEAUTY of DREAMS
I am PLAYing and I am leading you past tension torture and GRIEVOUS
ExTENded disCOMfort I am leading you aLONG the spiral un-
WINDing of asCENsion no one has EVER
Needed to BETTER ONESELF I am leading you CARRYING YOU
To freedom she who carries you on her BLACK-SEQUINED un-
Sequenced CAPE
I am leading you PAST what you SAID you did
I am leading you to confisCATION and reTRIEVAL of all GOODNESS

So Helen says I know who the killer was so what I mean Angel-Face says
I'm starting to g e t i t   then his voice stops and I SEE his
T H O U G H T a night city slum like my LIFE
Just to get it and BE here not in some self FICTION
That lingers in death he says you lead us FROM that
She was in hell for love was that a LEARNED beHAVior there's NO
Behavior in DEATH

                    You are teaching us HOW TO LIVE again
                    We know how to change your LINE and are conVEYing
                    As we can the arc of c o m m u n i c a t i o n
                    To your heart or CHEST OF DRAWERS pun

Who made you yourselves MADE you in this third part or act I
MAKE MYSELF unlike your exPECTAtion of little nerve I have a BIG nerve

I'm leading you into the ozone area where nothing MEANS you
I mean to BREAK mySELF one final time O zone O a s s u r a n c e
That you can start to sing

I have no pity or compassion I am dead and withOUT
superiority
I don't know ANYthing colLAGE me if you DARE the LIV-
Ing don't dare ANYTHING beLIEVING in their details

I am leading you BACKwards you were TOLD you were BORN
But that was as a BABY   not as E V E R Y T H I N G

I was born in a DRESS born playing POKer born reporting to
an AUTHORity

I am leading you to where you neither read nor hear this but
I nonetheless conVEY it to you your mind is silent enough to com-
MUNicate your chain of teLEpathy holding it toGETHER IT or US
I am leading you to a colLAGE and backwards we BLEN-
DED preserve the situATION of youR WHOLE MEMORY
Wiping OUT the PIECEmeal one you were TAUGHT
I am leading you TO an enormous MEMORY without a nervous system

I reMEMber my VOICE spread aCROSS the sky TELLING it its conSTITuents
What ARE THEY not NECESSarily WHAT YOU've SEEN
I'm leading you to RISK you've never known what it is
It's EVERyTHING you ARE the RISK what can you do about THAT

e beautifully hyper-colored collage the four flo
r you show them to others for me I'm thrilled to
nt to sing but numbers prideful nauseate
NOTES the name is Ruby Blanchette I forgot th
And it would have inspired ME not y

                                                                                                         are the dea

  So she stands t h e r e thirty-five IRRATIONAL
  YEARS AGO
lend it was so red inside it KILLS ME

                                                                                                   mark it a
e says no hands singing enTER no markups her
    ta yo black hand dow Ruby once agai
wanted to RHYME

And we encircled us built our love from the ground
And the souls left my caped back to stand round the rim
Watching our theaTER of communication FORM itself from out dead MINDS
As it told us its forms we told it our THOUGHTS
All in the language that is the GIVEN of our dead exISTence
Known from past and FUTure pasted and COLORED fanTASTically
Enter our city the whole UNIverse that each one or thing in-
CORporates we are building existence aGAIN to love aGAIN

How exist with memory backlog of primal explosions
Broken-off galaxies but it is I who leading you this time
Meditate a new box of memory conTAINing the NEWly GLUED
And this vantage will permit us to exude and soften this COLLAGE
So we know the marine sky better for its gentleness its new size
Only the equal of each of us WHAT is the glue someone says
Mind I say what else is there did I have a life you say but
It wasn't what you thought it was let's find its REAL images

Because what I wanted to see was you you could have been anything
You keep being blue though like a blueprint and I must pace your reality
Out in time to what is said or sung a precisely but not
Traditionally measured poem for our memory's being renovated
Why wasn't it perfect that prior poem tragic like my-
Self but now I am only your leader everyone's leader
Get rid of all the bugs I couldn't they were souls
eardrop could be diamond tears hand me one it's me
e said left over from a pain in abstractio
because that's what it was when it was all ther
n't send you every in my thought MYSTery I'm still mysTERious some dead say

It is BETWEEN all us what we a r e down the street
Where the word Hotel in red neon the pharmacy a
Green neon CROSS tear off the corner of the dark grey for-
M I am seeing from WITHIN

I am pasting ON he my brother says on this open EMPTY MAW
Of a universe black inFINITY surROUNded by cracked
ICE I'm pasting ON the black inFINity a note from mySELF

THERE IS NO CAUSE OF US

That is the first thing

What I am going to remember he says is that I never leave

And with guilt never leave the broken ice WHO BROKE
                              There is no cause who BROKE IT

There is no CAUSE where I I say slipped and broke this I C E
                              We're glad it's B R O K E N
                              We'll remember it's BROken

If you fall in the abyss you still can't leave
                              We have never left
                              We'll paste our dead thoughts
                              ON this abyss

Helen says she's going to cover me   since I your leader am not DEAD AND
Am leading her
Glue on the void the green and white house the black and white tiles
And the railroad tracks next door   she says FOR
My memory holds up this entity
If I don't confuse it with chronology
Yo estoy aqui says Uncle Woody por decir adios
But I see you again at the rim at night the states

We stood at the we will stand at THEE beginning
For thou art that and watch our collaged thinking FORM
The dead society of our twinned individual selves the NIGHT
Where we call to THEE non-violent eMERgence of our map
Nothing HAVE YOU NOTICED has exPLOded
As the previous language told us it did
I am with you in Rockland where the rocks are
They're already here and don't have to eVOLVE for they have come from
FUTURES whence I HAVE LED THEM dead or alive your friends

Beyond glued colors there are the MUSICAL NOTES
The NOTES are GLUEable letTERs and I want to tidy this CHAOS
We have to SING the notes I your LEADER sing to show you
Yes he says one by one   But t h e y a l l have O V E R T O N E S I sing
And UNDERtones says Allen   Paste them on my father Al says
The dead koALa bear pastes ON a e u c a l y p t u s leaf
With its inkpad fingers I am the night your L E A D E R
In death we ARE PROUD   and as we THINK in the time of AT ONCE
We lose the entire chroNOLogy of our SUFfering
It is an image to PASTE ON   purified by new coHERence
IT has its outlines and loves us for our SINS
What does it look like I don't know precisely by SEEing paste it on

So IF in becoming mySELF my LIFE disappears
NO CONnective why HAVE you gotten RID OF IT your life I SHE
Says TRYing so hard to BE an established CHARACTER
How will you REPRESENT yourself now as OUTline of a SHADE

I your LEADER am happy to be ONLY THAT send any CALLS
Of broken ice they said was a FRAGment and I called a N O T E
My ANger or HAtred too becomes so PURE I'M only singing

    Because it DIDN'T come from the BODY
    I SAW what I AM in reLIEF
    It didn't HAVE TO be my PROfile but it was
    And I PASTED IT ON she says you are CRIES and CALLS
    As well as your CHOSEN selfness did I CHOOSE IT

The void is USING me I say   or I it
                        And in the N I G H T no one arRIVED
Paste and paste the VOID don't aVoid it
                        CUTE you aren't aCUTE   paste on perSPECTIVE
Vanishing point a DOOR TO
                        You were asked to aDORE in hierARCH the A R C H
                              in the COUPle or CUPola
I didn't reVERE I am TRYing to perCEIVE
Say, what do ROCKS WANT aLIVE or DEAD CRUMBLED

Another RICH WOman with not enough to THINK
                        USEless chain OF WORDS ACTivists seeking POWer
I your LEADer am SEEKING POWER

The STARS say we reFUSE to be CONstellations BUT you never WERE
I have led you to SPEAK   Are we SPEAKing
YOU ARE VIbrating like a WINDy OR PLECTRUMmED BAND
Isn't it beautiful beautiful beautiful isn't it beautiful

We won't SEE moons we'll be talking to you

MOON: for I a WAYward VIbrant and ALways dead ONE

VOID: I'm TAKing conTROL of your SPEECH and ACTS
For I AM you

I: I am pasting on TORN AMber rays in a SHEAF
In my VOIDed HAND PRESCIENCE transPARent I conVEY
With my mind as I GLUE
You wanted these AMber to be SOMETHING ELSE
                              VOICE: Are they D E A D

TORN amber: I am like YOU torn OUT
                                VOICE: Of what?
TORN AMber: NOTHing ELSE

VOID: I'm in CONtrol of you LEADER as I am you

I: The PHANtom of viBRAtion NO the GHOST vibrates DO I THINK THIS

VOID: There is ALways SOMEthing THERE BUT THIS IS DIFFerent
WE are NOT WHERE KNOWN LIFE IS

Torn AMber: I am Y O U I am unKNOWN

All the souls that we ARE being MEMORY

AWAREness and communication BEING our MODE
                         AND nothing else BEING
For WE the UNIverse are an ORganism much or MANY of it DEAD
                         A state not underSTOOD by the LIVing
I the LEADER OF it WELcome to the COLLAGE SITE of its renov-
Ation upon the CALLED UP VOID OF US features of REASON VISION obserVAtion
and OTHer for there are OTHers who exist in the MORE
                         There is no CAUSE or other SOURCE we repeat
                         There is no CREator there is no ACcident such words dis-
                         grace us
I could have predicted anything for I have known everything

The violence the dead once witnessed that all of us enacted AS
Our idea of a beginning or EXplosion
                         But it has BEEN PROVEn   says a voice
The ONly proof is of MY consciousness
                         It is our job now never to wish
                         Only to PLACE on the colLAGE
HAS BEEN SUPERCEDED the v i o l e n c e by an IMage
Of an immortal BELT of COLOR or SOUND or THOUGHT em-
ANATIONS or WHAT-DOTH-A-ROCK

AND we ARE somewhat that
                         The B O D Y was INSIDE the soul

163

And now say I your leader we're no longer interested in the words
Memory peace intelligence love beauty nor in their opposites
But I will reMEMber says my brother say I no longer call that MEM-
Ory call it what you have made and will glue difFERently FOR
NOTHING'S SAKE

And I your leader SEE that there is no aNATomy
I SEE him he is a S T R E T C H E D   O U T   J E W E L of N O I S E
And what have you ever done to ANY IF THAT is what you ARE
We are PASTing on AMber or eLECTrons or DREAMS of them
You NEVer KILLED for you WEREN'T WHO or WHAT you sup-
POSED
          Have we always been that WRONG he says
We have been NOTHing but deLUSION YET we are OURSELVES
I AM withIN mySELF he SAYS I SEE myself THINK and SEE

Seeing the wind
                    But I am PASTING my old
STILL image on he says and that's MEMory like a
ConstellATION only SEEN by an ANCIENT self

Floating on the black waves out in desert between Needles and
Topock near the airport at night in the hospital Love, Libby
You have to drink from a cracked glass but I'll bring you one less
Cracked Momma as an invisible black wave tolerates us unconvincingly
These ondes want me to see them and so I am leaving in order
To stand on the rim of the most cracked GLASS of all Love,
Libby for the last time   I have a red and a black cloth as in
Roulette but like flags placed over the dead I DON'T GET IT
That will be pasted on or as useful contact lenses
For the dead still sometimes try to work the room
I have to lead them because so many still can't thi-
Nk don't they do something else we THINK in black WAVES
Mages images Daddy always bet double red in
Vegas drinking a bourbon watching people those FOOLS
I want THERE to be something to SEE or BIC PEN SCRIBBLES

                              Why are you telling us I'm saying goodbye
                              And hello as ANOTHER to the BLACK WAVES FORM
                              YOUR LEADER   Love, Libby is GONE
                              Scribbled in BIC PEN to be pasted have you e-
                              MOTION for THAT   the voice that loves the QUAsar
                              OR A MOUNtain Boundary Cone or ANY mountain

Yes because your fate changed we still want the concept AS
That of a wave TOO   because I your leader have FELT it
PULLing from the BOTom of the VOID   my F A T E C H A N G E D

Leaving on a plane in the post office mailing the PROOFS de-
Scending the STAIRS with my dead mother the techNICIAN
Mails them

        We're going down there into it
Or is this just anOTHER PARKing LOT

What are the PRETTIEST PASTED segments of letTERs

So I COulD BE MYSELF F O R C I B L Y
ROses ROses ROses   GLUEd or PASTed preterNATural
BeCAUSE Joe said we the DEAD aren't HAPpy e NOUGH
We NEED you to lead us why me BEcause it's you
Because YOU became EMPty enough a VOIDed BEAUty
Like a f l o w e r UNreal maGENta SMEAR with
A MEMory of TEXture CROSSties on the RAILroad of TOUCH

                A fate is caused by the future's being known
                Though it can only be known in part
                Like the present and this is
                Also memory   the waves pull your
                A N K L E S   it is rife with preMONITION
                AnOTHER WAY in which we had STRUCTURED TIME
                DO we want to DEstructure FATE
                What do we HAVE as we have LESS and LESS and
                        MORE TO PASTE
                I your LEAder have NOTHING touch
                IT with your OLD DEADish HANDS I have AL-
                Ways STARED AT Grandma STUDIED hers said
                I'm studying

Thrice in my HECTIC nerve   FINIsh even if the CUT PAIN
SPARKling SHOTS to the MIND that EACH enLARGEd letTer be GLUED
Why does that HURT   because it's STRANGE to me
BeNEATH where the LETTERS form their LAYer I stand at the
SHORE flirting with the FATE WAVE for YOU

It's for all you so I can't ask you its nature this declamation
Blackness or that absolutely   as I am here I'm pastless and empty
In order to assure you THAT you may be happy
So I can tell you you dead may be happy I   being designated to know

Why were the dead unhappy   they still had a storyteller's memory
I AM TRYING TO TELL YOU YOUR FATE'S CHANGED
Whatever you did THAT no longer e x i s t s the only FACTS newly glued

But I am W R E T C H E D says a man of wrong I did
My AFfect was extreme like the kiss of Charybidis
LET GO OF IT I say you have GHOST eMOtions   But I lived DRUGGED and
Didn't LOVE eNOUGH
Glue on a SHAPE or COLOR an IMAGINATION to be THAT
A new COLOR he says in the BLACK SPECTRUM   and don't try to
Remember you won't   there is no CORRECT figurAtion to recall

Do I I ask the VOID VOICE have to be THIS
We saw it it says for MEMORY PREFIGURES though not exACTly nothing is exACT

You are perfectly formed to call us to order   OH DEAD VOID I say
I have always worked with you it says have always

our fate changed you belong to US
     says a VOIce of ROCK   or I am in demonSTRATION
   f mySELF the vibrant STRETCH or band now DEA
     what we show is for SHOW as obSERVErs choose   I the rock say

  This to be Glued is all B L U E

This to be glued is all A M B E R

   Saturated when you WANT

I your leader dance   around it the FATE CHANGE

  your leader EMPTy lines of force and waves tugged at me

  hile you were gluing and the rock's bandwidth DANCED uPON the RIM of ice

I led you out of the burning house
I say to the NON-existent BLACK waves
And TO my mother and father
I have my narrow FEET   and the NON-WET waves
BEcause I WENT THERE into the EMPtiness and heard its VOICE like MINE
House is there a NEW HOUSE to be PASTED   any of the FOLlowing

I'm at the SHORE but I'M the BLACK VOID

And all the little sounds with which I speak are pasted ON

Anyone you saw DEAD is now aLIVE like HELen aLIVE   You
Can forget how she looked in her COFFIN
Paste on that you have forGOTten   WHAT does that LOOK LIKE a
THOUGHT   a blur flower GREY-BLUE I'm SHOWing YOU
A forGETting   it's just a thing   I thought of YOU of your BODy WHEN
You had left it just a thing   and it wore MAKEUP

Standing on the STRAND alone DOWN HERE list-
Ening to any
                    And the blackness says we begin a new cosmos
They are pasting uPON me a GREEN multiDIMENSIONal roSETTE
They say is AN emotion for the dead called seRENE cogNITION
It is something like FOcus in the proDUCTion of MEN-
Tal converSAtion for that is how we cause to be what THERE IS

They are PASting uPON me WORDS of which none are FROzen
AVID I am diva I AM EVer VOIDed to ALLOW YOU
So you CAN find the space to BE LEADER in mind

                                        without syn-
Tax and let this dissoLUtion be glued on specks of sparks
But I keep SPEAKing   sparks onto the void sparks into the
EMPTY SEA

   there are no PARTS to being DEAD
     so she broke   that I sta
stabat
   it had w once BEEN
  Nd with MEMory to coHERE it

                    STabat in
   edge of the morrow
   I am clair
that I brought H E R E for love it the FORM
   or chaoTIC CLUMP of US
        not a TRIAL
     I AM MORE REAL

   CAN'T do anything but THIS
  clara lucida candida
WE WERE CALLing
  whatever ELSE happened in the BROW

I Alice Notley your leader am seeking POWER
The dead still dice the roll is froZEN
I want something like a NET around ME a SOUL says a VOICE so
It won't SPILL into ALL YOU too much   PASTE IT ON

                    There were so MAny of us on that BATTLEfield spilled
                              W H E R E I don't re M E M B E R

I Alice Notley a SOUL now want P O W E R in-
STEAD of a self
So far away so far aWAY FROM the triumph of a BLUE or GREEN
Self or heather hollow disTRACted by a sound

                    It gets FAINter the self call Allen says
                    You must keep telling us EVerything you KNOW
                    There's no SPACE or SIZE here WE'RE learning NOT to
                                        supPLY it

I want POWer to fill this MY VOID of no size in no space

Where there is ALL of or NO space I am a BROken WINDow

Not in hg th voi
        the void or voic voice
Drea D R E A M you were ARMED to the TEETH
What will you find to STEAL home he said
I am EMPT and FORG T squat here I mean
Within
I invite you all to find more or less as you wish with-
In me as my SPACE en LARGEs you can build SHELVES (joke)
For I am also the one you are pasting upON
He says that he came to death expecting JOY but is sad
I am SAD WHAT do you think that is I ask
An OBject STUCK he says it always is I say
HAND IT TO ME I have no hands I SEE IT
RIP it out where his throat and thorax were
The AXis of SORrow like a roadhouse AND PLACE IT ON
A shelf

THAT is an EXample

And the souls find new colors and tones to inJECT in-
TO me   and the souls of the inORGANIC throb and unfold a-
CROSS a WIDTH of essence
I can abSORB I the void or voice or leader say
All abSURD SIN and HORROR
                                        I have been thus trai-
Ned in the language of abSORPTION to HOUSE those ILLS
Until they BREAK DOWN as you rebuild what
We'll call what we are two blues and a red or E G A B D scale
Who trained you I did rained how and I reMEMbered

EVery time I tried to put the SQUARES
Do you know what I mean by PUT
Where they beLONGED for the NEW one LONGED to BE
SOmething atTACKed ME   Can the DEAD be atTACKED
And I had ONCE lived in a CIty AWED by its INfrastructure
A DIFferent one of my LIVES I want a PURer BEing
As in her LETter to me for SHE letTER is always writing IT

And I came unto a land without understanding who they were
And dwelt there   For I am being this person who DID that
She DID that whether deMENTed or an IMmigrant

And I know not not only who you were but who I AM
And if I am dead the SAME but the POSSIBLES of IDENtities mul-
TIply for they are merely IDENtities we deCIDE which ONES to
PASTE ON and the golden SQUARES like footLIGHTS come ON

Goodbye I said to my niece and nephew embracing them
Don't forget Lela's LETter even if you're our LEADER my
Mother said and I said I WON'T
                              The NEW
LANGUAge TATtooed on the inside of my EYElids
In sets of THREE marks but each yet DIFfers
On the STAGE they never wanted me to exCEL and gave me UNsuitable parts
The people in CHARGE K E E P the best ones F O R themselves

But now I'm free of it for I L E A D
This is the POWER I've assumed S T A N D I N G
You will always be in my heart for you were the first ONE she
Writes this is its own shape that any loves any beFORE
They are supposedly BORN   But I I think an immigrant or al-
WAYS a FOReigner unLOVed was once LOVED reMEMber NO
I must forGET one story for another the WAVES are LONG of
INCOMING POWER all you who seek refuge at the VERY FIRST in the
LANGUAGE of the BLACK cape unto me PASTE YOUR
Sense of self THERE but I you say WATCH MYSELF
THOUGH something has happened as I have died and I am now diRECTly I

In TransfER of POWER
Taking and ceding with each thought
Yet I HOLD the POWER withIN ME so you can HAVE it

AND you use EVERYthing withIN me as you will

Because timeLESS and spaceLESS it's LAYered our TONGUE or MINDSPEAK
Pleasantly hollowed   An amethyst light or proJECT-
Ion I cannot be a TASK FORCE for eTERnity
Since we are all the same SIZE   in the real DEATH or life
And the soul of the EARth the SOUL of the earth SAYS
You can LEAD me NOW and after I burn LEAD the LIVE and
Dead I'm no good with your time Dad says how LONG
It is so my preDICTIONS   will come true but WHEN FOR YOU

 EANwhile torn off e d g e we stand to GLUE spark
NO I glue a spark on the same size as a perCUSSIV
  can you cuss out d e a d Dicky Cussin is dead m
 Mother says
                    blue blue
                         AtTIC se-
DUCED
            That was ONE thought my brother AL says

BUT you're DOWN THERE he says the estuary   Oh I'm anywhere AT ALL I say

This is HOW you   don't GUIDE me I'm NOT suicida
   clip

         I'm a soul trying to escape being
         killed — trapped in a compound mach-
         inery's
         always following me everyone my
         enemy A thought says
         I act perpetually duplicitous try-
         ing to get away from the tracking machines
         THEY'VE GIVEN ME BAD ART AGAIN

The thought is it a MEMory   of a STOry
There is a WOMAN everywhere everywhere no gender in
LED you where
Place the other LAYER looking for CRYstal it's EVery-
WHERE I LEAD

Forget the machinery there's no gend

POEM is a giant robot
The previous uniVERSE a GIANT RObot we were ever in the 19TH century
   hang to change to

I led to the fate wave   that murmurs COME HERE AND THOU
SHALT be reVEALED
                        Who started
                  here who star-
                  ted   eTERnity who star

He says just breathe   the dead DON'T breathe   I see Idahlia
Your MOTHer's on the phone I say to Janet meaning I-
Dahlia just TAKE IT the fate says do it DURing busi-
Ness hours IN the February wind
He was a short guy but now I'm only a mind
                              I think that was Marvin aka Jack

I'VE ALready SAID goodbye   to my shell
                              Was it not possible unless you had been MATERIAL what
                              If you only lived to be one-day old or didn't COME aLIVE
                              I still WAS it says
I'm leading you now that the time and space are GONE
To these OUTERMOST these pieces a tissue of GROWTH
Of spiritual counterpart real
We put THOSE selves THERE and took up THESE
So Idahlia is YOUNG with her DARK her DARK hair

What are we IN   and the fate line or wave along the bottom scrolls
                                        LOOK FOR IT it counters
                              Who you ARE NOW
                              Nobody knew why we were here
You'll have to GIVE UP ON WHY

IDAHLIA was boycrazy Margaret said
                    We were there for beauty perhaps perhaps that FAILED

Remembering a new STOry   as if I had been aNOTHER and didn't
Know YOU   I never knew you I had to LEAVE the ISLE in
ORDER to LEAD and so I left Patmos or Tauros OR Elba
We have DONE THAT   we each live so MANY STORies AND
I ENtered the PLANE I do so a G A I N the STOries rePEAT until you've
COME HERE
                    On Patmos I had reTREated to A CAVE
You keep trying to reTREAT FROM U S
As if you were in your PREvious STOry and HAD a LIVING LIFE
YOU HAVE N O N E N O W B E I N G O U R S I re-
Member for you your aWARD in the FACTory oF FALLOW FACTS and FUSS
TERsely I m e a n t
You don't have to know what you're DOing
LOOK OUT they used to say now you're dead and don't H A V E
T O we are ALready the FARFLUNG FUTURE FEAtures
I see you sitting pasted on like a fruit S T i c K E R
That's my MAGE half of I I remember for you HOW
He needed you   in order to be MORE FAMOUS than you
I your L E A D E R NEED NOTHING   I seem to need NOTHing
P a s t e d on what would I use you for I remember
Another planet the planet says in a grudging whisper
PLANE or PLANET I ask for I got in a plane and LEFT Patmos
So instead of writing Revelation I would L E A D Y O U
I am LEADing you even if you don't know

You will remember it again
                    I had FORgotten
Do you want to BE remembered I don't know he says
I don't KNOW because I'm HERE BEing do you want to re-
MEMber ME I don't know
                         You will remember it
AGAIN   anything but in a different way
We are pasting on a GROUP of SHAPES already GLUED to-
GETHer I don't know if I want to be LIKE THAT I THINK it's
Just a SENtence aGAIN standing in FOR as you
Think it across to my mind like UNpieces there are NO pie-
Ces that the weather once grabbed me like a fallen FATE LINE
It was a STORM   we don't know who's SPEAking
It was a storm and the power LINES DOWN I ASSUME it the
POWEr I am spea it was GREY BLUE with a dirty WI-
ND scraps and grit EVery SHAPE and pressed to-
Gether   L I K E   H E A R T S he was supposed to MARry
I'm dead here and I I say your LEAder DEAdish DON't
I DON'T remember again what I should CARE aBOUT
The POWer of L E A D I N G U S he says remembering aGAIN
ONly THAT you are here for us beGINning to reMEMber
Someone said I BEG OF YOU a long time ago
Did you get MARried that TIME he says NO not as I re-
CALL now there was no EXplanation FOR what I WAS
I remember knowing people had no idea what THEY WERE
I still don't know I say I just have some power

Consider a universe without numbers   perHAPS only HUmans count
But frankly I don't want to be COUNTable composed of the
COUNTLESS as IT IS all of whom self-aWARE in their BLINdingNESS

He stole the lamps for her he didn't NEED to
Steal them from NEIGHBORS WHEN
They were ALready LIGHT I have to THINK

Don't count the lamps
The dead don't need to be COUNT-
Ed
      And RAYS from your WORD
The light doesn't BECKON if you ARE it
Dead   an iDEAL   I DEAL YOU FROM THE BOTTOM
A knockknock joke for Idahlia   WE ARE THE DEALER

There are very MANY and we AREN'T ALWAYS SEPARATE
The
Voices of what   say   And we are gluing on GLUE spark-
Ling

I have led you to this A R T I C U L A T I O N

For the and its thought amassed SERENE CLUMP

No one's SPEAking exACTly   why did you WHY DID I DREAM

I AM GLUING on some MUSIC or some MUSE

buttercup
JUST LOOK AT THOSE

So we were altogether and I in a mass of
he words for it I leader say cliches EN-
    ERGY   LIGHT   music or color languag
 eating at EDGE I see the billion billio
 eloved SOULS   so we were ALtogether cl-
  umped SOUL or SOULS in what lang-
 uage   the uage TRY me it came OUT OF
And there was no never a S I L E N C E so w-
   e were or are   can you HEAR it an
  just to projECT aCROSS but we the Dea
 the all-same-size standing and not COUNT-
 ED as I reFATE   because I am alive so WE
   ENter the saturate FORM ONE IS OF
 s it knowledge or is it turquoise OR
 r e m e m b e r nothing you thought was it was
  REthink the words remember nothing you
 nd thought and was and it   it's a differe
  WAY to SPEak but you can't LIE be-
 cause there's NO USE of anything   a sI-
 GN NOTHing's a sign OR SIGnal babe
   IBIS oh all night all the LONG
 C O S M I C and the words go and return
    reDUN but ter as in ETERnal you
 CAN'T disapPEAR

  It was her EYE sockets   she traces thought
 THOU THOR OUGH it's a SNOW FLAKE

                                        thinking

 EVen asleep
       a slip I NEVer SLIPPED into this COS-
 mic effect in order to reply did I we weren't MA-
 DE it was AT the same TIME unrePETitive
   I LEAD YOU T O this VEry eVENT and thr-
 ow STArs onTO the VOID OF mySELF
   evERy YOU I HEAL by bringing here in de-
 ATH paste ON you are HEALED

And he wished to conSULT with you but he didn't know WHO who he or you WERE or ARE
now Or

Not PASTE a BURNing Ideal unREAL fire on the aVOID FOR the uniVERSE began with
SUCH

PASTE and you were THERE for we were all DEAD at the beginning I reNOUNCE mySELF in
order to LEAD YOU

GLUE or PASTE on the NIGHTingale hour an HOUR as THING as a SYMbol click or SCRatch
pressing me to S O U N -

D these are the N O T E S in order to inCLUDE
AND you will inSULT the living in FA-
CT or FATE I am like a dead ENtity
IS IT The plane TAXIing you aGAIN
For there are always planes LANding DAD
YOU can put yourself ON IT doesn't exIS-
T the planes bring words in and BOOKS OF
THE BOOKS of the DEAD I am R E A D I N G

terrify
terminate
tergiversate   At night the states unfastening me from their edges and I encounter a
At night the states they state that memory's EVerywhere even in the d
At night the states the box of fires opens not greek not ideal but def-

I HAVE renounced mySELF
into DEfinition
At night the states in the SWEET-
ness of this FIre's SINGularity

TERrify OR kill death

We who are being led away from the language of dense matter or LIFE
TO the language of existence

FOR in this depiction of the space of the dead WHERE EVery thing soul
IS the same size the FATE and what about the VOID are they SAME SI-
ZE oh size   or LOVE that's an idea   it was ALL an idea NOW YOU
Aren't but what ARE you I your leader ask we need a lan-
GUAGE in which you aren't deFINED in opPOSITION
TO not exISTing

                    you are my heart's ear we have no heart or ear
                                        I am pasting on a TWIG-SHAPE
            you are in ear's heart's art OR hat   I know it from the past or FUTure
                                    It spells UP   What's UP
                            The dead don't need hats
I'm going to make a corner IN this cornerless space paste it on no-dimensionally
Without the dimensions we are here how the OLD questions don't hold up
                                    What should we DO
                            There is no reflection in the pasted on
                                            WINDow

new space
ead unspace or box
inite this is the most def-
inite state

circling the books like planes or ANYthing you said
no reFLECTion in the fire
                                    This is the most definite state

WHY ARE WE that you have led us here
Of different CULtures and KINGdom PHYlum class
There could be no not-us BUT there was infinite fig-
URATION   And now we NEED NO GROUND
EVerything is CONversation the senSATIONS are reMODeled in-
TO IDEas

I remember how to speak   of WHAT I REMEMBER there is THAT
I DIDNn't first LEARN IT as an INfant but RATHer I GRADually
REMEMBERED IT

I want you to tell me how to act   we AREN'T onSTAGE
We AREn't onstage ANY more like in LIFE

I was ALWAYS TRYing to reMEMBER TO remember WHO to BE

I DON't want to dream about HER me anyMORE
You will never have to aGAIN I say THIS is DIFferent
I am TWISTing TOWARDS and PASTing
PASTING and TWISTING TOWARDS to make the new WORDS

I'm transFORMing you inTO yourSELF you've NEVER KNOWN
That's why I'm HERE
That's why I'm LEADing YOU
Everyone's still missing something you didn't necessarily fill in the blanks by dying

HYjacked the PLANE   BUT the pilot SAYS I can't fly
He is flying it withOUT AERONAUTIcal knowHOW
In a space without air CURrents it CRAshes
Into the airport everyone's still aLIVE
                              DEAD I am still aLIVE
                              Crashed the PLANE into DEATH still alive

I'm telling you what HAPpened you still don't KNOW
YOU don't know how ANything beGAN
But I DO it DIDn't

Warms you for you'd thought you knew how to speak how to think but your LANG-
Uage was a language of desPAIR
Your MEMory FAULty you only remembered what you were taught I remember another
I remember not being her
I remember in primal times when I was minute but conscious I could see everything there was
I swam ashore and became your leader because I knew what you needed
To turn by about a quarter turn inside so you could see without the history you erroneous-
ly Thought you had without the inadequate e-
MOtions you thought were yours the real ones are creation from serene CHAOS
They are the MILD individuation of FORM across a MOUNTAIN or in the midst of your dark
                              night LIGHT clouds
You know it BECAUSE you are fragile Bob says
STILL AWKWARD AND YOUNG
You can HAVE yourself I say to him it isn't what you think it is
It isn't what you think you are it's what thinks

You what thinks it if you can find and you CAN find it
AND I glued mySELF TO the winding waves of fatelessness
We can STAY in the undeFINED universe of TALKing
Dad hands me a CANdle from OVER a CLIFF where he hangs

The bullet nightMARE I'm SQUEamish and take thi-
S such ON the telePHONE to JUdas you can say
I HIT it there says the ONE on the PHONE he SNEEZES

WHO is asPIRing where you think you UNDERstand
You DON'T UNDERstand me I crushed eggshells UNDER foot
The FOOTfall disapPEARed in DEATH rePLACEd by PERcuss-
IVE THINKing in INconsistent PATTERns click
THAT story's a GONE SHAPE winding JUDAS inSISTS

EVeryone who betrayed is HERE at OUR VOID
Pasting ON a ring of TROTH to the process of eTERnity
I can't remember what I DID exactly OR
Did everyone do the S A M E thing as if it would DIS-
Appear and HAS IT it was yourSELF you betrayed
The interSECTION of aWAREness and deSIRE your inVENT-
Ion I can SEE it it's YELLOW a COWard he says on the PHONE

ANOTHER MELody comes on in QUARter-tones while he's on hold
But I killed CLICK S O M E O N E I know click I DID

I WASN'T waiting
For you CYNara
Or was waiting for
Horse and swallowing e-
Vil that lights you up
So you can resist it   Running
                              You have to tell me
                              Where you WENT dead
                              Now we're both here bodi-
                              Less BUT not pre-
                              CISELY without pasts

Each of these squares full of POPPIES
Do you WANT to paste on the words images WHAT
I your LEADer only lead at THIS TIME past-
ING on nothing but my fate FATEfulness
All aROUND my feet shoeless and anTIQUES an-
Tique sensations of HAPpenSTANCE

                              ECHOing beNEATH the poppies are blue SINS but IN
                              OUR language they're not deCLINED like MONey OF
                              Money to or FOR money or accusing instrumentalizing IT
                              THIS with my name at the top and type DEStroys deSTROY
                              TROY an empty site
I wanted you in my love TROY an empty
                              whoever you are
OR NOTHING but my FATE Aeschuylus without reeling from it ANYmore
I opened myself to everything I WAS BESIDES A BODY the old fog of run-
NING from someTHING speCIFIC as bright as poppies can possibly be   NEATH
                              UNDERNEATH
                              I had been the only
                              Drifter in town

T   did you want to k i l l
I ONly wanted him UT TER ly COWED
     until no one could READ IT
   everything   IN or OF   thee dead universe
   can be PUT   it can be PUT in a small box
I am in there Daddy says and I'm pretty BIG
     ReC O M M E N D E D

   I am R E A D I N G it on my BACK

   Where my SECret TROTH is

the white washed the BLEAchers are DOWN
   Memory's unMANaged

   I'm gluing on if I could MAKe it
MEANingLESS an octAVO sliding
     book or SCALE   blue

   You don't have to SEE
   It's because you KNOW it's T H E R E
I'm r e a d i n g it on my BACK
               yr QUAR TERS
          O c t a V O S   NO quarTERs
   An OWN house QUESTIONMARK
Not for ME

Not-dead STAND-
Ing around the ICE EDGE a CRIsis of VISION
WHEN I try to see
Don't know what IT IS how can I SEE
How can I see or NAME the NEW   ASK   IT
IT MERGES
It lives in an unCAUSED house in the cosmos of LIcense
YOU can say anything I AM anything anywhere   ANYTHING DIES
Piled on a dump of carcasses sloughed
WHERE the MASSEd STONE perceive as it or they wish
All in the beauty of chaotic SCANsion

                                        I lost the
NAMES of NAMING what had been pre-
Viously REpresented to ME
                            and your senses
AND your senses SEE us more REALLY

The man tugs on a RING for no REASON
He's not a MAN in death but yet a being   COV-
ERed with SOMber   as if enCLOSED   LIGHT
And a DOOR opens   in the soul BODY
I KNOW that's what it is someone's opeNING ME

In the DEATH universe   remembering THAT'S where we are
OR in the LIVE one I
Who am your leader and my own SOUL don't know what I SEE
The FUNCTION says a voice isn't perhaps neceSSARY as you
Know it STANDING in the STREET would be a MEMory
What am I supPOSED to see SEE ME I am a light no light here
WHAT is the reLATion BEtween vision and OBject it's
COMmuniCAtion
I am so inDOCtrinated STILL I AM
Your leader deSIRous to paste mySTERious beauty on
Which universe am I in WE ARE CREATING IT YOU SAID TO
I will see with all the eyes withIN me anyTHING
In reLAtion is placed by exisTING I remember you it says

The visual can't be ISolated it's composed of EVERYTHING
SEE everything at once
                              YOU ARE NOT A PERSON they
SAY in this colLAGE the whole new UNIverse FACE IT
Immortal like Psyche only BELIEVE YOUR EYES
Ripped out in the mirror

YOU ARE ONE W H E N T H E O T H E R S A L I V E
Are two you came a soul ON-
LY sorry for us Y O U B E C A M E A S O U L
ONLY FOR US don't see what you were taught to
Or speak AS just speak the words are free

And I would rip out my own eyes to be alive like
OTHers oh who can SEE   we the dead see

Look at a T H O U G H T and you will see

WE OUR a voice breaks INto a MULTITUDE are of I I am of those

Is on top of it so I can tell it   the silver become almost black
OF the two dolphins holding the onyx between their SNOUTS
                  I can SEE an onyx to PASTE   it may be a BLACK opal
    So I can SEE your mind
    I your LEADer send the aBOVE
           We can place it in a SENtence
           WE CAN J U S T H A V E I T

           It was once MINE she says I remember
In MEMory you place it on the VOID of memory
           THIS is where we are
                And I WON'T reMEMber the BLOODY WAR
                And I WON'T open to HIS MIND
           Don't you remember what I DID to you
It didn't cost very much I SAY
           And I HOLD it she says to them you can HOLD IT
When I still had two PARTS self and soul
           You were ALways more of a soul than I now I'm a SOUL
           And YOU
I can't reMEMber how to be a SELF

MEMORY faces the wall   if you pass through it
I will PASS THROUGH and the STARS are
           You other memory leading YOU
           OF the DOLphins silver reCALL of the

                F I R S T S O N G
           Trust whom you wish

           trust whom you wish
           UPON the black SAND
           I'll trust your mind
           trust whom you wish

I am leading towards what key you
I am leading the language lets the wall crumble
Leading I place me next to you mind NEXT to you or soul
I am my soul leading you to our originality

I am leading YOU TO a NEW or OTHER origin
In ANY words I'm leading you SOUL to no EDGE or surROUND
It was linGUISTIC we're not inside of any THING unLESS
It's a BLACK OPAL glue on a GLINT I am leading you to
I am LEADING UPON the BLACK EMPTY shore

WE ARE showing you our leader how W E T H I N K

He was on dope you underSTAND so what was I sup-
                    POSED you'll LOSE him if he disapPEARS disappears a-
                    LONE a little play
I think we have to go back for him I WOKE UP
                    The POLICE are looking for you you WENT BACK TO
                                        SLEEP
When you're dead you're not ON anything I've ENTERED the Old City
                    LET'S SPEAK N E W we always do DO YOU HAVE
                                        ENEMIES
            It's loose, off-track, what about s y n t a x in FLECTion
            It's VERTI-
CAL I don't have any enemies   must be losing my touch NO TOUCH
IN DEATH no the man SAYS you have PLENTY OF ENEMIES
For YOU OUR L E A D E R ARE an E N E M Y of all states
                    It is an ACTive TREAson the NEW UNiVERSE is an ACT
                                        OF TREAson

I haven't MET you YET   WHEN IS THIS
                    Before the dawn of clichéd time owned you
                    I live in the driftwind shadowbox self deployed depth
                    I live in the depth
She scribbled silver on paper
                    The leader is the W A L K A B O U T S H A P E
I am asserting my OWN state and YOURS
                    For a long TIME you our LEAder were a SPY
EVery WORD a SPYhole goes both WAYs
                    Life death life death unTIL you TERgiversate TURN
                                        RENEGADE
He was on dope or I WAS ON DOPE you underSTAnd
                    Why shouldn't I be I WAS in fact TRYING TO LIVE
I am LEADING YOU to the LOOSE-TONGUE ACTing in the PLAY where we first CAME
                                        aPART and toGETHER

I AM LEADING YOU
                    You are leading beCAUSE no one's leading YOU

I am a reneGADE STATE in the DARK I your LEADER

And I climb up and DOWN in DARK Until   and walk ACROSS

                    There is no UP or DOWN

                    There is no aCROSS CAN WE still ride your cape YES

I was waiting to be filled with KNOWLEDGE of what we ARE

Some call it ENergy some GRACE some CALL it SUBSTANTIAL

        Do you see how dark opaque blac

        O you not   I REvel in darkn

          NO SONG

         nd then just two or three light s-

        Hapes   TRIADS I think   it is firs

        RouNDed triADIC yellow ma-

            gental AMber   they and they mi-

        Ght be W O R D S take your HAN-

        D DOWN

And then it is all SHEET LIGHTNING susTAINed

                    Minor key OR Lydian or IN the reneGADian MODE

        What do the words S A Y or M E A N

                    Who CARES   Ajax dies when HE SPEAKS in my
                                    EAR

I have come from the throat

I have drifted off the mind of the BLACK aVOID

My pupalike soul finally born in husk
Just SEE it dreamlikely young and longhaired sleeping IMAGO
                    The HUSK is what you need to KNOW to get aROUND
Hear the CRACKLING RAIN
                    Now you are ONE of US Allen says though aLIVE
I am dePENdent on LOVing MY being ABLE to LOVE
There was a SWORDbridge reMEMber the IMAGE of ANguish
                    And what is A N G U I S H an image of
I walked I CRAWLED on the sword it WAS
ABOVE this ABYSS   the ONLY VOID of GRACE
                    When we FOUND ourSELVES on your CAPE DEAD and in
                                need of
                    A further TONGUE   a SPIRITUAL omNIScient
                                LANGUAGE
                    I am pasting on the VOID the sounds and colors of my
                                THOUGHTS
                    Says a voice SAYS a VOICE no one has anyTHING to tell
                                me
                    But you ASSUAGE me   And WE didn't BLEED dead on
                                your CAPE

I can't crawl across the swordbridge another TIME
So I have been REborn as my SOUL
Leading you to LILIES grown from no SKULL   PASTE IT ON
Though I am not dead I am one of you
                    I says a voice paste ON what I'm seeing to say a CAR
                                WIND-
                    OW FLASHING by blue-GREY with a MIND staring out
                    You are the wind the night the rain and all their sounds and
                    Cries their blue charcoal black purple tremulous or forward
                                T O N E S

Oh HAVE you seen the MUFFin man for you have to start SOMEWHERE
He died so he could teach me the language he's a GENius no I'M
The genius

                    I am pasting on his prior djellAba it shapes a person
                    I don't WANT to be a PERson or an ANimal
                    I don't WANT EvoLUtion she says I don't WANT genitals I
                    Want to be DEAD in the new DEATH where is that

                                            LANGUAGE

He's just a TRANSlator one knew
It's keyed into the phantom waves   it used to be eyeLASHES
It's written on the ROCKS at the foot of the STREET on the phan-
Tom wind and BREAKing it down it looks like filiGREE PENdants
                    That's just a message   to let you KNOW
                    I shouldn't have had to pay anyone to learn how to LIVE
                    When I was a LIVE

This THICK navy PLAce
                if you HADN'T been aLIVE
ARE there any who were ALways DEAD
                  I think she says it is a mis-
                  Take to think I was alive
                  DID you have a BOdy
                  COULD you see NAVY BLUE

                  I SAW you but I don't NOW exACTLY
                  Blind aNOTHER was aLIVE
                  SEND OVER THIS
                  I always put GREEN in mine he says
                  I don't reMEMber it green from LIFE
                  WhICH I don't reMEMber any way
Here are some VIOLETS
                  Violence I try to remember beFORE VIOLence
That is NOW I say
The sky can be cream yellow
                  IS EVery thought for pasting ON
Where are the LIVE on EARth
                  Over HEARing

The tranSITIONal WONder of at rest the DEAD creAting Y O U
                                      and your thought tongue inTERnal MUSIC
All of this thus outwardly our inTERnal music
A communiTARian STANDING AROUND ship ship in the MARine WATerless N I G H T

The just let it lightly   YOU
Enter   ARE
Remarkably we ARE   CRIMSON
                                                           mem-
                                                           or-

Y maybe of never withOUT beginnings and ENDings
I never wanted to write like THIS
                                   Because you are LEADING US you ARE
                                   PRACTICALLY singing   you didn't WANT to
                                   SING alMOST in a style
You are reading my mind
                                   The only POSSible DEFinition OF existence:
                                   T E L E P A T H Y built-in memory OR there would
                                   BE no struct-   EVen CHAOS IS STRUCTured
                                   OR at least STICKY   who's SPEA-
                                   King who CARES
All I have ever done is CARE   TER CARES
RETina spelled backwards who CARES
The best minds of my generation are
                                   ROCKS   they're ANcient
                                   calcedony jasper tourmaline garnet
                                   agate opal TURQUOISE the mind OF
It spoke to me of its STILLNESS countervalent to the
ACTIVE nature of my SORrow
                                   But now you lead us to PEACE
It is our S T R U C T U R E peace
It is what the VOID bespeaks
                                   How can you PROVE it
We are here within

You will not SUFfer in THIS mind if I can HELP it

On to PHOEnix
   the PRoblem with a PASTE-on   it might beCOME a PHANTOM
It looked like a LOVEly ABstract CUTout but IT became TROOPS   I
Remember that
I reMEMber your STARE but that was EYES
NO right or wrong PASTE that on
WE are the ones that LEFT YOU   do you reMEMber the STOry NO but
We remember SADNESS at an Alamo WHAT'S THAT
IS there a DICTIONary of ORIGIN   AND the TOPAZ MATRIX seems to say
I DON'T reMEMber ORigin   I your LEAder too beGIN
To DISremember   The waves of void are FRIENDly

Who are you REally a forSAKEr of CANDidaTURE
WE eLECTed you without a VOTE   SPIraling Eons ago
I reMEMber knowing I could only LOVE all of you
PASTE on an ALphabet that DISappears in DOTS then is reBORN
PASTE on the ASHes of DAMASCUS and of TEARS
PASTE on the QUASar's CRUMBling laMENT for ALL EARly STars
LOVEbraid HEIRloom RAVaged PLACEless and free
PASTE ON SATurn   I DISremember AtLANTIS

'm going ther   torn tor or tree   FOR I LEA
nd the BOX of my ARTifac   empty not onl
f GRIEF but ANyTHING   I AM NOT STAR-
ring   TER SIGnals   it is MATterlike but not be-
astlike   In MEMory I'm STARting to reCALL US HERE
orn torn OFF   from FUTures HATEful the win-
d the reMEMbered BLUE trees the BLACK o-
cea   I remember that my INsides were a GO-
    LD TANGLE STRING it was THE INstru-
ment of ME   PLAY it   LEAD us to where w-
e   and stood beginning BEing it the CRE-
ator THE materiALity and the AFTER IT   it was AL-
AYS MADE of WORDS sodden or FAIR   sud-
den or FAR   BUDS that don't have to GROW

I was molEcular told you to join me   R E A C-
H E D   T H O U G H T W I S E for you   aCROSS so
we could hold it together   WHat the VOid
Yes but we were ALready IN IT it ours we its

PASTE ON that I just LEAD so we CAN
AND YOU will hear and see it equivalent to YOU
frayed   to be irREGulars   in BEAUty chaos OURS

This what memory IS that one is here at ALL and ALL IS
Self- inFLICT ed or in FLECT it I your LEADER proCLAIM I
AM THAT because I'm ONly that and have forGOTten else FRILLS
I am your LEADER so you can get to HERE we reMEM
We DEAD reMEMber spHERES as IDEAs I idEa you I say
There has NEVer been a sphere but in a FLAWED eye FLAWED
Because it saw what it was TOLD
$$\text{and RHYMED}$$

To ease the deSIGN

$$\text{There has been nothing but dream and conJECTure}$$
$$\text{The SENses inTERpret HOPEless to know}$$
$$\text{WHY do we NEED a LEADer}$$
BEcause SPENT and possessed of NO thing I am PURE

The INward CURVE of my mind is TATTOOED with the FIRST WORDS WE ever MADE
The FIRST times we were made to play GRUEsome ROLES in bloody FANtasies we deemed
$$\text{REAL}$$
IF WE HAD READ these words of OURS not taken them for someone ELSe's deSIGN on US
God's or a SCIentific PRINciple   I am here to TELL in the FIRST RUSH aGAIN
FoMENTing to be FREE from CRASHing FORMS and TITANS as IF the ord-
Inary ONE were alWAYS SEIZED by FORces when any ONE is that FORCE

That the one   and the third   one music   music of   the word that   that you made
Three stake your heart on the three dice   THREE PLACES at ONCE at LEAST at
$$\text{DAYBREAK}$$

I reMEMber I-voice was willing to atTACK him
  TIred of being LIED to   and if I walk THROUGH his STALL
beat me UP so I THREW the vat of STEW at HIM
It was SQUASH stew and I esCAPEd his STALL
  the STALL of MAN   tired of hanging OUT in a SO-
called SPECIES you named it not me

ecause you didn't learn enough pronto living so
  I have to   lead you I   am now more disPASSion-
ate though I've learned how to ACT theATrically
I WATCH the VIDeos of the PAST and SEE what you THIN-
K you WANT   not in a LEADer I can ONly ap-
  proach that SINCERELy   but in a DREam FO-
R we SHOULDn't PASTE PREvious desiderATA ON and NO-
T anyTHING I'd WANT I can only LEAD

there was always so much PRESsure from within THOS
NIMALS conCEPT like RIDicule OR deSIGN   NO
  CONcepts to p a s t e   I want to p a s t e MORE ru-
bies   in the MIDdle HEAPED
              OR void maTERial HEAPED
              just black just black THE-
              RE or NOT I was SEEing
              the GRAINS of our VAST a-
              ffairs just grains just gra-
              ins

We ARE pasting ON some GRAINS of CHAOS
CHAOS ON CHAOS   QUERY   YES   I we cam-
E FROM

I'm the ONE who spoke in DOOM I've always cried OUT
                                                and DEAD
It's autoMATic we have these REflexes YOU're soothing
I DON'T REmember BUT I was DOOMED

An IMage

The BLACK wings or a BRASS door   I WANT shapes
                                                CHAR-
Treuse rectANGular with STUPid pink VERtical STRIPE
OR a FROSTed BLUE the door sank IN upLIFT it

It's VISualized

                    I don't have eyes

It can disSOLVE as if ONly MORE of OUR chaOTIC MAKEup
I I am aWARE of this UNiVERse's MEMory
As if I were ONE cog I can't be as LARGE as the COS-
Mos beCAUSE I was made to be SMALL living

Did you know

They SOME OTHers made us SMALL
And I KNEW it GROUND a dead GROUND I reMEMber
A ROUND earth as if I could see its CURVE FROM SPACE
It made me NAUseous to be SMALL clung to a SMALL
                                                sphere
I the DON'T have EYES I am now IN a poem inSTEAD of a
                                                DOOM
Yours the POem OR is it MINE

OF and FOR you

When the door disSOLVES I DON'T now unconFINED
I would SPEAK to SOMEone of SEVeral BEAUTIES CLUS-
Tered   it would SHIMmer and she THOUGHT it DID
                                                PURplish
And with three ODDly sounded TONES

If I am aWARE of it MEMory

And IF it were what you ARE
TELL me

Built INto it I'd say   and if I have NEVer been a HOAX
Here to PASTE ON
A TIME   that doubles BACK   or TRIPles

Does it forGET does time FORGET
Or was it TIME we were TALKING aBOUT
I have TOLD you I'm TELLing you EVeryTHING
You DON'T have to know this is HAPPENING that I'm LEADING YOU
                    You're ABle to SOOTHE us but WHY were you TRAINED
You RODE on my cape or TRAIN
                    You are BOUNTIful having NOTHING and you FLOWED
                    Towards us for you SUSTENance AS IF but it is RE-
LATIONship HOLDing the COSMOS toGETHER
                    Without SENSES the heart
Oh HEAR ART

                    We are LOSing the BUILDup of ANTIpathetical CONstruct
                    When MALEVOLANCE SANG us down   that it did I re-
                    MEMber and that I joined it   I remember I will not aGAIN
                    Though there WOULD BE a MOMentary RElease in HATE
                    The LEAVES broken Be B R O K E
I remember wanting to hate but leaving it for a oh a n y t h i n g

The Voices
You have CASH five ten EMPty part and ENDless SEXual CONgress myTHOLOGIZed
That one might KILL for it because of a conCEPTION EVerything conCEIVED only a BAby
A PLANet is seen to GIVE BIRTH to a moon a MEteor exPLODES   EXPLAINED by
Is SOMEone SPEAking   It's WHAT they said I KNEW but I knew ON the HEATH
That SEEN was GREY that SEX a TRIvial event would be forGOTten the dead
HAVE FOR- and we FOREgo FOR WHAT maTERialIZED the CHILD too IS DEAD

On the WIND I say I walked as far as I'd esCAPE I'd leave A N Y T H I N G
HOUSE and FAMily TO pretend I WASn't aLIVE in a SENSEless T R I B E
I acCEPTED NAUGHT YOU TOLD ME of ANimals MAMmals I WASN'T ANyTHING
DO I acCEPT HERE's TELePATHIC conVERSing I'm TERse my SIBlings

HOW do you reMEMber   I'D a VOID HOUses worked the STOCKyards I beLIEVE

I looked into her EYES and didn't FEEL IT   I'M supPOSed to say LOVE to him STILL
Do I STILL have to TELL YOU I LOVE YOU Tell each other a DIFferent THING I BEG you
DRIVen from their MENTal CARD GAME NAMing suits imPORtant like F R I E D E G G S

And THAT I WAS the NEGative I WANTED to be DIFFicult
What do I HAVE NOW it was
An ACT of ELEgant VIOlence not comPLIANCE
You never HAD it

        I KILLED him

                I DON'T have to LISTen to you NOW
LIST list of inTANgibles can you TANGify it not EV-
En a dead rock
Because we HAVE no STANdards or morals   you CAN'T die again
        I was the MORal one I WOULDN't   all I remember OBEY
I your LEADer am GLAD you rode on my BACK
        Do I oBEY YOU
        I DON'T know how to BE now can't foMENT or KILL an
              ENemy
PASTE on a DEATHShead TOMBstone for your old STYLE
        If I KILL him again in my MIND though all I reMEM the
        Memory aGAIN how it DIFfers and that I WANTed to KILL
              HIM BE-
        CAUSE he was supPOSED to give me ORders so I
              ORDered him
You PUT him in ORder
        I THINK THIS to you in bluegrey OVERTIME roun MIDnight
              WE don't have
I only have to lead you to LEAD you I can't care what you DID
ARRAIGNED not THIS supPOSed maJEStic our little COSmic BOX
N E V E R to pity never to be TERrified   RENAME ALL

No one cared we STARved   and the STARS in their
                              GALAXies DIDn't
And I efFECTed NOTHing FOR you but this LEADing
                    TRAPPED we were FAMilies EATing HERBS WHAT is a
                              FAMily HERE
I TALK to my own FATHer or PARtial conDUCTor of my FATE
                    We NEVER TRUSTed our DAUGHters   WHO are now
                                        free SOULS
I was my OWN FATE he says and TAUGHT YOU TO LEAD
By TRUSTing you

If we COULDN'T trust we would colLAPSE but FORtunate the
ROCKS trust each other the PARTS of WAter and FIRE the BAC-
TERia sing toGETHer and the DEAD microbes HUM
                         The WORLD left us to die at the HAND of the FAMisher
                         FAME or famish and that the FAMous WOULD FAMish
                         But they are DEAD   and we can't KILL THEM
I TRUSTed YOU he SAYS   for you were a BOdy in SPACE
AND I trust you NOW in your apPOINTment
                    We should NEVer have had beLIEFS for they were
                              TRANsient
                    And we are NOT   we will forget it all it ALL
                    ExCEPT for GREEN taste an AURa FLATtened and
                              PASTEable
LEAD YOU PAST DEfamation RULES and most of all FEAR
                    iDEa of BITterness
For WE in our enTIREty are as much inANinmate as ANimal
And ALL our souls HOLD US TOGETHer the MINeral wind

nd we didn't know and DON'T   Why should we KNO
   's a FETISH   KNOWledge is FOR the LIV-
E I ASK   THIS LANGUAGE like BEing just comes
    KNOWS EVeryTHING and to SPEak it is to know
WERE DIaspora DICE THEY threw US and our CHIL
ren unSUITa the ROCKS say nothing's UNsuitable
   I'm going to wear my BLACK SUIT to lead for I
have GROWN an AERY disc's exPANDed from m
CHEST the ROCK DRAWER opens periWINKLE souls
AN IDEa of exPANsion   voice reQUESTS and PAST-
ES I am OF the paste aster and COLumbine
  Unbind ANy SCRUples I am DEAD I can S-
AY and my unscrupulous mind WOUND THR-
  OUGH the GALAXY exPANDed SIFTed dandeLION
Yea even though it WAS as SMALL as I'd BEEN

    in dark Until there is no Until

AND she was so ANGuished her FRIENDS did NOT a-
Vail every SELF-CURSE tattooed and my SHAVED head
I reMEMber though DEATH apPEASes me says she
THAT I was covered with INsects BURNED OFF to
ReMOVE them by mySELF thus was I CHARRED

She slept all night in my bed in fetal position

     t burns OFF at the EDg s
   ND the REAL YOU be LEFT bu
    I WASn't STUpid left her
     the place where she was sup-
   OSED to be deLIVERed if
     you went nuts

 killed MYself well that's alright isn't i-
T   No one EVer TOLD me   what I shoul-
D like about LIVing you're supPOSEd
 to FIND SOMEONE   that's not good e-
nough

              PLACE
         what I LOOK
          LIKE   HERE
        A STARfish with EYES
         a green BIRD
        A SOUL   looks like a SOUL

What does a soul LOOK LIKE I wasn't LOOKing my VOICE SEES
                            It's MORE that I KNOW WHO it is and if I don't
                            A WILD print we were WILD disPLACEments beGINning
                            AND your fingerprint FACE smiles YOU ROCK
STAND HERE all together souls
Flesh DNA MAMMAL mobility IS one interpretation of who I AM
                            Do we look like a WRAITH
YOU look like my mind THINKing of you
                            I LEFT her here I LEFT you here the VOCALity cries

    t look lik   I had the hair
    of FANtasy HAD no PROOF
      there WASn't that I ex-
        ISted in whose FAN-
          tasy WHATever
          you THOUGHT I
          am LEADING
            YOU THROU-
              GH

The wilderness of your own delusional OBstinacy
                            ARE you
For you think yourselves
                            We were W I L D   D I S P L A C E M E N T S at the
                                                            beginning
I have led you to GRACE from which your PRINTS
Pull apart and imPRESS yourselves on the VOID
                            STILL
                            Graceful
Have you forGOTten your old face yet HAVE YOU

We reached you by landscape and opposition meaning re-
NUNCIATION Notley leads to strength we reached you by
TELEphone the GHOST phone all the CORDS in your BOdy
ANswered US we needed you to enLIGHTen LIVEN US
WITH LITHE COUNTers to our Evilness we were SAD of
AND you say we NEEDn't let it CLING whoEVer we are
WERE a phantasm proDUCEd by our COMmon UNI-

VERSal MIND the SCRUMPtious light of morning glory enVELops
WE are the ones you LOVE but I COULDn't HELP it you
SOUGHT me WE have sought MANY they were too SYS-
TEMatic creAting more CIRcumstances NOT a RUSH
A CALM MOtion in PLACE you OWN the AIR if you WISH
It I have no WISHes except to LEAD you you NEED ONE
In adVANCE that must be it SALUtary and in LANG-
Uage SO we can ALways coHERE and the souls of trees DARE
VERTicals and horiZONtals on all PLANEts draw near
WE conCEIVE of an emBARKMENT uPON the VOID WE ARE
WhatEVer we THINK is utTERed in words of MULTI-
Ply CHARGED cohesiveness so HOLD THIS perspi-
CACIOUS sentence the deFIant LIGHT in my SPINE
Has brought me to the OUTpost of ouTER WHERE
There is no POLE no BLACK hole and I STAND HERE
We judge you DEFinite and INfinite like US
I am leading you to PASTE like an ABstract FROST
I am leading you TO the inSURgent colLAGE
I am leading you TO cerulean GREEN as menTALITY
I am leading you TO OUR soul and souls
I am leading you to prevalence AND SOUNDness
HEAR it hear the sound of your soul RUSH I'm
LEADing you to PASTING ON of the NEW MEMORY what do
You WANT to reMEMber NOT nouns or verbs but an AG-
GREgate of qualities ROLLING onto and out from
The POWer we the DEAD are the BLACK HOLD of it

YOU are L E A D I N G ME TOO says the Void

We MADE it happen how DID we IF it DID we WERE already
                    There is NO before or after   the beGINning is afFIXed to
                                        the END e-

                MERGES FROM it
                It's ALL figuRAtion a NIGHT TRAIN Allen says
It wanted me to speak in LINear X but I SPOKE in tongues
                    It made SOUND and LIGHT so they say who have SENses
                    OutSIDE of it I'm aWARE that there is FIGuration for FIG-
            Ures their eyes and ears he says BUT I conTAIN time
                The BIG BANG a crystalLINE CLINKing withIN the aVOID
Which is bigGER but I emBRACE
WORMS of light FINGERS of   in the non-sensATional bliss
How do we deCIDE
                    To disCOVEr matTER   we PASTed it ON   GLIB but
                                        founDATional
                    Doing UMPteen THINGS at ONCE   I called to it he says
                                        FROM
                    This SILence   where you HEAR with your MIND YOU
                                        ARE
                    And we were ALL THERE doing THAT

                    Lead us back and forth the one who can
It is COMmuniCATion   PERIOD

PreMONitory adMONition to the MONitor MINE I am LISTENing
And you BADE me lead you CARry you like a CAR
I brought YOU past the ROCKies the MOON the ULTERior MOTive
And the GALAXIES of geoMETRICAL AXes to the FIRST SITE
READying IT with PASTings on in MEMORy of mere MURMURS
WAVElike we are in TRUTH
                              TEN per cent a USED voice
SAYS of national CORNY no I say NONE in the sup-
POSED reallife STATION of POSES I am RIPPED OUT it be-
GINS NOW CARE aBOUT NO FIGUREHEADS EV-
Eryone turns ripped out FAces I mean the aLIVE
Now that you SEE me LEADing you who're no
Longer RIGID the TERpsichore dePICTing MINDS DANC-
Ing I was SHOWing you HOW to GATHer the FABRIC FIRE
PUCKERED puckered MEaning ME and it in a CLUMP-
Y WORD I wanted you to DRAWing that OUT FOUND US
WithOUT heads of STATE they can't MEAN eNOUGH
What do we NEED GET him off the PHONE phoNETically
He must shut UP the CAPital BREAKS in a visio-
NARY reconCILIATION with the GEoloGY beNEATH
TERrain which is LEAKing RAYS CHANge your DEF-
INITION we are not HERE we are GONE and LEAVE them

The enigma D A N C I N G as the A B S O L U T E S

You didn't manage to eRASE it eRASE it I say to my-
SELF or HAVE I eRASed it MYSELF erased mySELF
                And to US
                Night of the GARnet streaks in BLACKness THEY
              ALways come back and the LUNA moth GHOSTS
And MORE OF you poured IN having lost the SHADOW of
                SHADow of the SELF wind what we HAVE is an ALmost
                                  MEM-
              Ory of FEATures NO a REAL MEMory of LOST FUTile
                          FUTures
              I a VOIce DON'T have to BE like that
The SHADows are FLYing aWAY the eRAsure BLENDS into the DARK

But I SEE you baby he says I reMEMber you're my D A U G H T E R
DaughTER I say in the LANguage of the last or lost least or long-
EST to have ROOM for all of YOU so I can LEAD you WHERE
You wouldn't have gone OTHerWISE
              SADness SCAB CRUMBLES we didn't have to inVENT it
                              DID WE
              CHANGE IT to a TEAR in a color porTRAY that thinking ZIP
              OPened and a GEM speaks in PERIDOT
              It's a PLUG where what's that a transient GULP light
                            GREEN
              The light is G R E E N THEY were all the ones that in-
              VENTED a reJECTion well not I THINKing more CLEARly
                            my-
              SELF he says doesn't CLING
I'm leading you no LONGer to think like SPECterS

The VOICE is BLUE and LEADER it's pre-GLUED

What else is pre-GLUED

                VOICE only VOICE you know my ME

                You might be able to SEE it YOU have led me to it

But you were always SPEAking

                A FORest of STARS calls a QUASAR each a MIND VOICE

                                each

I am leading you to ESSence not FORM

                An exIStent each not possessing SIZE

I am leading you to BEing

                What will I be

                The hoTEL of a WORLD so difficult to DEAL WITH

                The RESTaurant CROWDed no SEATing for us

                Who had BUILT IT I don't believe in it or YOU I

                EXist   You the one who already has a TAble

The bellboy took me to the fourth floor

                Fourth ACT

I have BLOTCHes on my face but have no FACE now

I am leading you to BLUE and iDEa of reLATION

                EVerything is reLATed reLATES a tale stranger and

                                STRANGer

                Til it's sounds and COLors in a PASTed arRANGEment our

                                TONGUE

I have led you to communiCATion with every molecule

                AND death moleculE

OF US the uniVERSE I am leading you TO the obVERSE of dePRESSion

I am leading you to the memory of our CONtiguity WHEN

We were STARting to name us and EVer there we SING or FLASH

I am lead you to SINGularity AND COMmunication's cosmic GLUE

RePEATing myself I am leading you children of yourselves fut-

URE anCESTORS of the CYCLIC reCOGnizance I've LED

                I TOLD her I couldn't feel GUILTY any MORE the FEELing

                Had ceased to mean a THING evaporated I

                Couldn't reMEMber how to HAVE it the voice says I'm

                Going to paste on an ELEvator with an atTENdant

                STRAIGHT UP FOURTH FLOOR

In the Fourth Act we will BETter Integrate

The diMENsions LIVING and DEAD

We still need to know why we lived

I'm leading you to KNOWing WHERE you lived

ALways at the void's edge seLECTing what it WEARS

Placing on a lovely STICKer OF an imPOSSIBLE bloom

I am leading you to where what happened WASN'T that

You are telling us aGAIN

It is aGAIN each time I rePEAT it becomes more REAL I am

Leading you to EVER inFLECTed aMUSEment turning in and calling OUT

I am leading you to the bodiless dance of not being dirECTed

I am leading you TO I rePEAT eTERnal AMUSEMENT

And she walked out onTO the VOID and I walked out ONTO
The BLACK VOID the un-terrestrial FOR
There's no DIFFerence beTWEEN mind and matTER or un-matTER
AND I am walking ON it that is liTERally bottomless AS
SPEECH is and my MIND amid the BEAUty of the PASTED-
ON our NOVELTY orGANically non-violent like a BREEZE

In SUDden WINDows to the PRESENT TENSE
My eyes SURvey a mind BLITHE prosperous TAN-
Sy what was THAT yelLOW LOW in death it's exPANsive LOW SOUL
I AM A SOUL the tan wind cries or is it FAR the far win-
D winds aROUND the ideal TANnery when I
The tundra aLIVE sang a NOVel of COMpoSITion mild
MILD or is it deMENted I reMEMber I deNIed your
TALent one says I reMEMber I preFERred my LANDscape

I walk OUT PAST the TALK you CAN come aLONG

        went there with its RAN-
DOM name its hapHAZARD sole BEING
 hat else call thee HEAP'D MEANings SEEN
What else call it and the blossom we AR
 he DEAD the GLOSSY black-bloomed LOV
 dges TORN the better to PASTE it I'
 ORN UP once every WEIRD words SIN-
G to ME OUT HERE of nothing but THIS I-
ENtity

I a NON-PERson can now SAfely SAve the WORL-
D I don't know what you MEan I said as I WROTE IT
They were EVery one WAS in bed with me last night NOT com-
PRESSED or overLAPped not even TERraced I oh CRYstal
Slept BADly for I worried yet of mySELF my IMage THEN
The IMage was DONE
                              In your HEART
CHEEK or FOREHEAD as places of REAson the FOREhead more
OBviously my DAD says I can FIND THOSE OF YOU
Within what would have been a BLINK TO BE non-
PERson as you FOREsaw ENtails STRENuousNESS e-
Ven SUFfering you SUFfered for us you DIDn't get well so now
You're well   he SAYS I SAY EVerything is INside ON or a-
ROUND me I still feel SELFish but have not ACTed thus for my-
SELF who am now a NON-person you say in this ODDly
Tinted greenish LIGHT

WhoEVer I BE I am inTACT there are no PREmises ex-
Cept the UNIverse so-called as if it were a BOX
The LIGHT in my eyes   Some AReas not SUBject
To KNOWledge
                    But SUBject TO pasting on AND
The SORT of memory we have BEEN talking about
My BROTHer says I reMEMber to coHERE   says a QUA-
Sar always SPEAking   there is a LANGUAGE
For STICKing toGETHer BENDS but doesn't BREAK
QUARtertones may S P E L L you my BLACK-
Birds in the PARK of forsythia but NOTHing's for-
SAKEn it has all turned up HERE in the VOID dead or
ALIVE paste on a MAGnificence for ALL US equal-sized
SOULS the lightning bug shouts I LOVE that's eNOUGH
BLIPping it from MARS to C A S S I O P E I A an eTERnity

IN the antiQUArian traits of the OLD universe we were FORMS
Now we have a NEWly found us where forms BLEND

                    And one speaks enHANCED by leaving the FRAME
                    I was framed says one by your KISSes even FRAMED by
                                                            your
          IMiTATive EYES
                    Now the GRASS is perfect the blades TALK to each other
The BLADES in your EYES once surROUNDed me comRADES
The blades in your eyes taught to JUDGE and CUT
Your EYES could have RIPPED me aPART now I'm LEAding you
PASTE SOMETHING ON my DEARS of GANGS my dears of TRIBES
                    I want to be able to say THIS STICKY INTELLECTUAL
                                                    THO-
                    UGHT has juice like a PETal I can TASTE
                    I want to say the form of a KITCHen STOOL
                    I want to paste on a TRIpod but not COUNT IT
                    I want to paste on an OLD-fashioned SWITCHblade
                    I want to paste on the FRIZZY FEEL of MIST on my PEAK
                    I want to PASTE on the smell of a COCKER SPANIEL'S
                                                    HAIR
ARE or IS this MEMory OR is it ANcient OR is it noSTALgia for LIFE
                    It is the BEAUTY we would STAbilize someWHAT
                    My thoughts RIDE they RACE unsaddled MEM
                    NOT MEMory but MIND the mind of a HORse
                    You can now SEE we were all SPEAKing
                    The iDEa of a MOMent is that it GLOWS time here GLOWS
                    And the rock of the thought-to-be LIFEless
                    PLANets has a prolapSARian menTALity
e edg com off seeking esse rememb
e edge there isn before MEMORY

WE WERE ALWAYS STANDING HERE sometimes I found you aloft

                    The rocks slid down my sides I CRUMBLE but STAY
                    I HAVE the focus of STAYing stationARY
                    Red DOTS and FIRE it there wasn't an ELement
                    It TANtalized me paste on HEAT that isn't a BEing
                    It will BURN you it's a THOUGHT am I a T H O U G H T

And if there are thoughts you never LEAVE
And never LEFT it the universe that THOUGHT
                              AND never L E A V i n g didn't b e G I N
No beGINnings leaves or PEND
What LEFT you wasn't you and isn't HERE
MULTtiples do not make us DIFficult the SUNS of our IM-
Agination   No we are NOT iMAGined
STAND here facing each other til SORrow's eRASed because NOTHing can HAPpen
THIS was no creATion we MENtioned ANYthing and you within you
VIBRANT I lay there pulses in the night transFUSED with us unGATHered whole
WE DON'T HAVE TO or stir or sit we were THERE pasting slowly not unhappy

III.
HEALING
MATTER

Inter-   lacings our thoughts   talk to each other
More than one at the   same time   Who says   More than
One measure   quicker sometimes the   thing we are
With-   out a god are its mind   the mind of god

He's walking across   the street   but he could be   a rock
A rock walks   by sitting still Ha ha   He has a gun and
Shoots the lock   to force open   the door   That's me I say
Standing here   with all you none-   theless

At the cracked ice abyss   Where the door opened I'm   listening
The mind's stream-   ing forth to co-   here again   When we're
Here the minds cohere   us all the   universe
The present the   candelabraed   gentle that   we

Are gent-   ly trans-   forming   as us the dead
You are our leader someone says   and healer   meaning sayer
This our practical   collage our   epic   of us

When you wake up someone says I'll do it   This isn't a dream or sleep
Nothing is   Nothing's a dream   Sometimes it's dark here   like an old house
I'm going to wire it when you wake up   It's already   wired   I say I
Can hear everyone   A bird flies overhead   bit-of-chaos it

Sings   Every stage was once an   abyss I say   at the beginning   What
Do you mean   Nothing means much   I don't want it to   And there's no chance
For there's no de-   termination   We would have   determined that
What do I look like   How do I hear you   You are dead where death began

This is the real mind and what we are   Why did we live   I don't know
I've led us here to make the new   universe   already be-   gun as it
Always is   Pasting on the notification   of dawn   which pre-exists
We have changed since we   began to stand here   Less clear   more clear

That this is   your present   whoever's listening or reading

I have come so far with you   that I've lost   my friendships
My relationships   We are now before all commencement
What are you when you're   chaotic   You don't bleed
Into another   What is another   You are a soul   but you have qualities

I'm becoming more   chaotic   each is say-   ing in what tongue
And I recognize what I say   but for an instant   then forget
Do we need a form   of time   we have the right to choose
Don't know what I just   And turn   and pulsate

Time's   rather slow then   there's no then   red and blue
It's one of the substances   In what tongue   Voices   In what
Voice   Each I say   who understands   We need to create it
And yet I'm graced I say   We don't know   what you mean

It's so beautiful   But one says   we don't exist yet or speak
Oh don't you I ask   Or are just dead   All this   without numbers
Where is the soul then   You   within the panic that
You think you feel   And are we   bright globes each

I am going there   going with it a-   while into this cauldron   Down
The stairs into it   I must investigate the abyss   You'll somehow follow

It had to be bro-   ken to need to   be healed   wasn't
Breakable at first   Walk through your   image of you
How can I do that   Behind it walk be-
Hind or through   the set someone says   And I left it

Is it back-   stage or metaphysical   where I go it now a-   lone
For you are torn   you tear yourself out of   previous colors
Words sounds materials   But we're dead   What does that mean
I am receding through   shapelessness to   And there was an image

And you are an image   I a soul within an im-
Age   am not   I go straight into   (so I can lead you)
FIRST WAS CHAOS   I go straight down into chaos the a-
Byss and pene-   trate it   Walk down those dark stairs   into dark

You'll just see   someone you know   a voice says
I know everyone   I say   And walk further

The image of me   dissipated   that was only in your eyes
I'm no longer an ap-   pearance   I'm just   the dark walking
Since I began to lead you   the substance we've dealt in   has been poetry
Words and voice   we've seen each other from   saying words

The universe coheres by communicating   communicating   its form to   itself
Every smallest bit whispers some-   thing   I'm only the dark walk-
Ing I whis-   per into the dark   Where I once had arms and fing-
Ers I have swirl   I embrace swirl with swirl   See with swirled eyes

Can I the soul   speak of myself I say   to who   Can I
Say without an other   And it the   dark rumbles but doesn't   articulate
I know one   is not alone in   death I say   but cha-
Os what is that   Push on through it   is it a def-   inition

All I've known I've seen   if I were blind I'd see it
All I've known I've said   And my mind said its shapes
And I the soul says   is saying now   From what language do   I translate
Do I

You can only   learn it in verse   because it's verse-like
And then who spoke in me   It's this   Destroy what you think you know
About thinking   There's an old   olden one
To enter now in your mind   Buried something there   Still too dark

Piling word on it   Forgot   how to what   spying on myself in
The pool of   distorted images   the school of   the cleaned-up chart
Throw the parts away   the cant trail   you skull
I mean swirl   meandering   you'd   talk to anyone

When I see into   a mind   with mine   you aren't fractured
Or a code   I see your naked thought in   an instant   and before that
I   I don't want   tune it down no   it stands
I got it   Do you get it   We were always once   caught up

And you are nude   you have a bare mind   whatever you think
Just shows   it's no syn-   tax pax romana or repression
It's unnamed   A speaking   that you are

That we have always been   all the force there is   speaking
I'm not leaving   and I can't   shut down

I was yours before   you left me   I am yours and you it
Says   Before gender   and structure   before is when I'm in you in
Foremost dauntingness   always brave the   substance of
Going on   in not time but tone   odors or   hues in quartz

I'm aberrant   because pure   Speaking out of me I say
I or you   came to   all at once   because we split up
Could be in a-   ny part   part of you   could hum or be de-
Tected   tected your windy eyes   winding un-   chronological

I wandered as   the abyss it says   I AM it   If you fall   in-
To it   And I wander I say   as if singing
No-matter-what-I-say   With tattooed words   inside eyelids
My Old Light   I the voice   don't grovel   no cue

The Factory

You can stretch talk   on paper flu flu flute note   stretching out
HOW DOES IT WORK? I say   in actuality   We talk to each other
In the part of the mind   you don't use as much   some mind says
That I say   this I write   is there a difference   Degree of truth un-

Known   I am proceeding   through the chaos   am I really
Do you hear me   Minds say Yes   Are we dreaming   We don't dream
Lizards approach   jump on my shoulder   their tongues flick my ear
I bless them
                    I see   a black factory   in blackness

The scene lightens   I see a simple face   carved into a hill
I don't recognize the style   I see   a faceless mountain that speaks
I don't have my face it says   I have my art my form
You have your voice I say   In *your* mind translated   Who's

Translating it   *All of being*   *spoke freely*   *and understood*   be-
Cause   there is no time   and all that will be known
And has been   is known

We were there   we were always there   we split up and had to speak
We spoke first   before   Did we say we   Try to see it
I was always split off   There isn't   was or is or place
The factory's   made out of chaos   Pretends it makes it   Stop pla-

Cing yourself in time   First I said   first I said
Disassociated brown   vertical line   not on that scrap of   paper
Star shape not on   that scrap of paper   which is torn and close
I'm torn and close   The line means   or does it mean   It isn't on

What do you think   of the factory   It stands in for
What do you think   of the face   Symbolic   What of the
Mountain   That's real   in my heart   So we
In the factory   we were there we were always   There I was

Staring at you   as if I could see   Listening to your voice   as if
I could hear   The line's nowhere at all   if   there's no relation
The line is somewhere   if I exist   In mental   relation   space is destroyed

Memories enter me   from the factory   whose are they
A figure there   can't tell the truth   Her name is not The First
She is a thought   deep in here or me   made   in the factory
Nothing's real   I'm real she says   Abolished borders   between

Thought and memory   Then she says   you can really   have a thought
She walks it back   I walk back into   the factory   Where you came from she
Says   This is your vat   this is your language   these words here
We've just developed them   omphalos   altar   I detest them I say

I want those   You can't choose   Yes I can I want   foresightful
Force I want power   not proserpina   was already   and no prospectus
No prosperity   Never she asks   I'm stirring it up   I'm the words of what
I'm doing   what I do is what   I'm saying   the voice al-

Ready entered me   before the words   There shouldn't be a factory or
Facts   So   I   tear   this   building   down
Irregular cells and swaths of chaos   assimilate   what is torn
Something matters   what   I can't keep track   I can't hold on

But I matter   and am not matter

There is an old She wept   if there's no matter   you won't weep
I open the factory safe   I crack it   in the ruins   The cylinder turns

Across the trail   the harbinger glances   at the house of cards
Called cult   Prenatal   calculator   No   continuation
In chaos   The letters   of the former code   blow away
And the any words   blow into my   mouth of force   of power

Just the wind   just the wind   just it   connects us
Elsewhere it's called mind   Go through the papers
In the safe   stretching a flute note across   the middle of
The clear naught   Languages   include stone

You have no heritage   you don't have to   It can't stick to-
Gether here   Your certainty melting   cer and tain drip with
Bloody wax   I am your friend   says the factory voice   or boss
Sure but I'm your leader   I say   The alternates   are vanishing

The conductors   are crackling   A piece of paper says sham
Take the chamois   and wipe off the   folder   No ditch it
I am now   translating I say   from the   Illiterate

Bend over it the floor under   with whirling winglikes on back
In the night of cutting to pieces   what you thought you thought
Where are when we the   martian rocks   say like geiger-counter clicks
Look a buzzard blustery   walks and a crow caws   I can caw too

What part of cha-   os it's   intermixed
Who's there where some-   one once had a head   or head had one
Head doesn't   have a one   You never thought   with your brain
It was just   organ meat   There's a grinder   pun   in the factory

I walk into   the eye of a   swirling torn   out the back door
It has water and fire pressed to-   gether like   they know each other
You're just a hack identity   Take off   your bandit's bandana
Are you speaking to me   you featureless gravel-bed you sul-

Phured cum adrenaline or imago   I'm a mountebank
With a poignard   nothing to stab   the wind is vicious then lank
Viscous and rank   with urine from no body   Just what do   you think
None of this stuff is stuff   Leftover from a future or a bluff

They keep bumping into each other   Don't get to lie down together
I don't care I'm il-   literate mind of the pre-   and after-
Life in dis-   connection   from how you thought   you thought I
Say   The let-   ters can't blow away   unless you're really

Done with yourself re-   versed and surreptitious
They aren't really there   When I talk in your
Which voice   and the one uncertifiable   I tell it
Who I was   and what I was doing   it says   Enter the Park

Park and Swamp

The word Park might mean anything   I enter anything
I en-   ter any-   thing   a crisis of faith   any phrase at all
What can I be   Leader   I am speaking you   It keeps blowing a-
Part   Kneel in the forest   What forest   the black swirling firs the

Back   of your mind   All the things I gave you   at once
I am trying to learn   I keep trying   to be direct   Is there
Both a chaos   and a stillness   Yes   proscribing time
Difficult   to communicate   We communicate our own selves

Nothing else   Continue to help us change   you don't have to under-
Stand it   Just speak it
                Oh wordlike it
Wants me to   heal you all by find-
Ing in chaos   the wherewithal   so unformed   Or you will al-

Ways be sad   in dissipation   drink up   figuratively   your
Debt   Once again I take the charge   But if this scene
Blows away   will I do it a-   gain and again
And I have   said we are healed   are we not   Not all at once the voice

Says   it comes and goes too   Not yet once and for all not   yet
Not yet in il-   literacy

(Joanne and Bob)

We are the   mind we   know what we say   a grainy quality
What is the grain of death   like a photograph   of air when
I met you   and showed you   some possessions   a box of songs
Near a clock on the bar   I could be clear   with those people

I will perform a mimesis   I said of the poet   It was not as if
I became the first one   Now in the wind   I invoke a qual-
Ity of black corners   when you stick your   photos in an al-
Bum   In the other description   of chaos   they would just float

My perception of   chaos con-   tains all de-   scriptions blown
The grain of sandstone   is mixed with   time floating a cur-
Rent on Tiamat's   sourness   I've exited the whirlingness
Entered   a simple gloom or   gloam   maybe temporary

I'm now illiterate   I grasp for grammar   I remember what it
Was like   to think and talk   with certain of you   as if
Changing   the world's depiction   for the good   This is bigger and
Leading I can only re-   member in the new niche-less way   how I sang

This layer's life   this layer's death   of one layer they're pressed together
Tell me where I am   Is there no one to tell me   You can't know with-
Out speaking the lingo   Draw it out of me   always a voice
Any-   where I'm going   The lock you played the one you shot

Open   Press to your chest   a red spider   the unsyntax can't clear
So go ahead not   seeing the words   they're dislodging slowly
We in-   vented time   to rot   But first   a salamander's trick
Change color   to be near   your lies   meaning *lies still*

I'm trying to pull the connection   No backwards or forwards
No cheats in   the undertow   Just sing a little   dance to it
In which era   or light years   In where we are now stop
You never   skewed   knew   irresistibly enough

That is   crass   So bloom on it   Nothing's   attacking   you
It's really more than   It's really more than a language

(Jim Carroll shot the lock)

Because I'm brave enough to walk ahead of them for eternity
and because I'm guileless

I see   and hear voiced   I see and hear voiced   an inception
Who is seeing   whose ex-   perience   am I having
I see it move   You see climbing out   I see it become I say
Step out of a flat   perhaps pond under   pink sky

She's you arriving   Don't speak for me I   become her or it
In warm image pond and   walk out   Am I walking   Where were you be-
Fore the echoing voice   says wait for him   No   I I say
Have no twin   nor mammalian   form   See   this spirit

You aren't visible   You can see it I say   And begin   to speak it
I'm acquiring   a trust in you   whom too I only hear
Is it dawn   Which one   Of non-matter I say   I stop antici-
Pating speaking   You see color   It hasn't to do   with light which

I see separately   In chaos   nothing's attached   You didn't wait for him
I lift it and hold it   a swirled flower   still but made of swirl

Stand I there   Is motion sepal   separate too   It's
Timed to body   If I move   If I think is that   different
I'm untimed   standing   if you forgot   there was time
Pale violet   hue signals   that this line   though broken

Thinks   I wept for you   not   this beginning when I
Left the odd   water   Did you   I was intentional at that
Point I   intended strength I   know what it is   my thought
My thought in-   forming a hue or   sound   previously dis-

Located   This creates language   instantaneously there are
Elemental   presences sudden-   ly we   will keep creating ourselves
Is there al-   ready some-   one who'd destroy   my influence
Over the elements   Pray you you war-   rior know your craft

Briny aquatic   a hat for the   drowned or birthed
I don't know who   I am only   my conscious effectiveness
Showing us what   to do

The thing I am   that will do   to have qualities   to sign for
No meaning   Remember   what I'll always recall   But I am
Memory   Walking out of the   swamp   I'll attempt to
Get to it   What   What we were doing here   case by case

Sit down on that   chaotic stump   yellowing sky

So that these words   don't make   too much sense   they have a tune
Say the beginning is tuned to C   Then everything's   torn out of their cases
This frail you are   I know   She said to me I hate you   in any lang-
Uage here somewhere   And sadness like on a   periodic table

I stand up I re-   member I'm your leader   Why I can do it
Remember breakdowns   Is chaos one   It keeps things safe   fluid
I let them out of   it they're safer   are they   A rock walks with me
Footloose   What do you say   It says   I'd let them tear out

Case after case   Are they still chaotic   You mean we   Yes
Something's hap-   pening   but I can't follow   the narrative
That's because you don't follow   The wind's   from the shore
It isn't death or life   it's something else   a score or script

If you perform it   you're otherwise   There's the wind   mind of glass
I think I know   how   to make the score

Let them out of their cases

I de-   cided to make my works each   different   their beauty
Comes   from the thoughtful glistens   I'll show you pieces unplanet-
Ary   identityless   trees or lamps   with gigantesque pearls be-
Fore   or after I suc-   ceed with my strength   In what language

Do you bring them   back from the abyss   I am it   soldering elements
After you kill the   he's-dead-he wanted-to-kill-me   culture hero   How
Did Chaos   how was it formed   who I am before   So this part's curved
All these thoughts   sculptures   or mobiles   often painted

I carried the words   in my head   all the way to Wetmore's
And beyond   But that was time   which is a swath here   time
Something   you can use or not   Let's not   sounds are im-
Pregnated everywhere   Is there   a point outside   I'd say yes

Dust devils   in what tongue   a wind of coraline ar-
Rows   all different lengths and   thicknesses showing   you to go

(An enormous room of a "collage" by me every-
thing beautiful and different   sculptures and
'things' metal and paint   pearls   everything
exquisite and a different shape)

I'm trying to find sadness   so I can destroy it   I'm trying to
Find a blessing   That's how you'll get somewhere here
But the arrows blow around and point somewhere   else again
I need   to know how   I make this   the universe   as well   as

Well my friends   do   only everyone   There's one light in
Myself   I sit back down on the stump   hold onto this nar-
Rative bit   who's providing   The light's on my forehead
Paths everywhere   Sit   We find you restful   all of your friends

Within you talking and keeping track   We dead and we asleep   un-
Conscious are within   For whatever you do   is guileless and for us
Perhaps we are healing as   you go on for us   I'm sitting I say
On a stump   enjoying the light   from my head lamp

One arrow now says sad   momentarily   another says syn-
Tax I have to choose one   Choose sad the voices say
Syntax comes anyway   like a tune   or a hatchet job
We'll be telling it   to you   And we   we bless you

I am making you we are making us   back at the   Anytime you're   It's slack
And clack she tightens   But why do a thing   That way's sadness
First get dusted   in the flour   We were running out   of flour
Whose thoughts and memories   whose beauty whose standards whose ideas

And I keep bumping into   and go   For immortal you are weird
Cool it kid   Remarked like moonstones   The thought balloon over
The quasar group   LOVE it said LOVE   I remember you
Walk on   Cities desertified   deserts   of broken buildings   deserts and

Swamps blended   Red desert nowhere unplanetary   escarpments
Curled over   spacious infinities with stardots   You are a chump
You rocks and gravel   faces newt features   or a stance torso disap-
Pears mistward   but I killed you   in my last vision   the lo-

Cal hero says   Walk on full of voices unresemblant   cracks   pipes   wind-
Roar   wolf and bear   rockslide   rustle of known dead grasses
Bad herbs and good   to smell without noseholes   in your mind sucker
You were never anything but your soul   It watched you choose once

But   and the phrases   stop coming   from nowhere   There's the river
The River Nothing   There's the river of nothing

Remembering Everything

The   look down at it   river   and the sun   Sometimes I'm in the river
The look down from the es-   carpment river with sun   on it
What were you doing   what were   you I remember
Now things that   I wasn't aware were   happening I   remember new

Things   as if the sun found them too   in the water   I remember
That that man is evil   I'll handle it I say   Experience was thicker
Than you thought   as thick as thought   the fish were hiding
Because I am your leader   he can be evil   but   he can't hurt a

Dead person   Every time I remember more   you are allowed by
The language of death to   remember it all even   sad that's the
Trouble   I thought it would fade   danger everywhere   I'm try-
Ing to remember   though I don't   want to comes at me   Don't

Tell us it's   too fast to tell   she said I hate you   remember
I fell in love with him then forgot   now I I don't want to tell
Because it wasn't then   it was yesterday   the def-
Initive   I'm just walking a-   head   we didn't have time or

Circumstances made   light and dark bumps   on the river more of those

Memory real memory   I say then see a page before me in unknown   Voice says
My lady my past lady   my most interrupted   lady wind
And she went   went past her   her great-grandmother   into the trees
O Jim and Rachel   it wasn't the wind you knew   it was mind

And then I was in sadness   I enter   in chaos   the part that's all sadness
Sad of what I ask   as my pace slows   You can't outspeed this melan-
Choly   Or would I go on living   or would I go on dead
We told you we were of-   ten sad my   father says

It is of what we would be healed   And of what   are you sad
Your own deeds still I ask   And of aggression   prevailing   in our origin our
Primal blast   You have spoken of changing that de-
Scription but have you   I am doing so now   I am close to it I say

To it   as event   here   But the sadness pervades me   I'm in trouble to
Get to it the X-marked   Can there be such   Won't be well-
Defined   in chaos   I must lose more   of my own
Articulate   phrasing   in order to get to it which denies me

Sadder slowly on   Pass through one's pain's recall   was it real   Jorie or John

The hospital zone the mortuary tree   Bullhead and Saint Louis
There are other words   One is Iron Mountain mount it one
The rehab attendant deaf   that mountain is deaf   and the word the
Sit or stand for a chaotic   time   stand a veritable debacle

Go to the hos-   pital come back to   the apartment   where you are apart
The complex-   ity of situation blows up   singularly   so someone pays
Or the geologic layer   by blowing up   lies down again
Blow it big   We're all the same size remember   minds or souls

Blow them up it says   Blow it all up   Does it hurt
Does the origin of   hurt   What is the origin of   the universe the
Origin of   Are there origin and of   of course not
There is no of course   He   is speaking to you   I'm not re-

Plying   No words mean a thing   Your description is failing
Here where we're supposed to   before or after   blow up
I think it was before   Before has no meaning   memory   Time you know
What else blew up   Was it your liver   or your kidneys

I am in the box of the universe   the box of souls   of the universe
The drawer of it the fanning out   the collapse   of an idea
The equations work   like ants   I am at the   heart of   your wrongheadedness
About to pull the plug   press the red   hit you as   in blackjack   you're

About to lose   Why   Because this is what really   I'm here like a spell
Matter's breaking up just breaking up   like lovers   at the speed of nothing
Proceeding   backwards   lovers at the speed of   nothing

What or who keeps testing me   what are these demonic   faces scratched on air
In red and black stylus-drawn   motile   begging me to despair of
Myself or them   Do you merit scrutiny   Does anything here
Press it try to push   me aside it says so   I can cry mistreatment

It has hair dark blue   and no skin but   black air   it's fanged
Do you know who I am   I backed you   in the brush fires   it says
Dead man coming apart other side   each of my two eyes see-
Ing separately   illusion   or fusion of rushing   you are an image   faces

I backed you it says   when you were   broke   I'm still broke
When strengthless you felt   the habit rain   I'm looking for I say
Not you but the phrases   revolutionary war   behind my plague eyes
Of the river nothing and inter-   ruptive sing my   way past you

Mounted the fallen and grasped   the handrail hearing now lin-
Go I can't understand   Something like curra the black suit worn   wasn't just us
Justice breaks mirror   at the first at the first   so you couldna on-
Ly see init   One of no initials   of the fouled   lake   trying to get to

Time as Substance

It's only a substance   on the way to   I've forgotten what
Have to cross the swath   coiling and uncurling   in mind wind so
How can you cross it   How does it *work*   Nothing works chickie
Green like mine water   chartreuse bile streaks or black like equip-

Ment liqui-   dated mashed   in   when the future hits town
And I circumcise it   the way you would a woman   I mean circum-
Scribe it   scribbling all around   enscribbles the scrounging
Vercingetorix   spoken hiero-   glyphics   Ahknaten   Discordia

Nothing but mountains of Mars   who was one I   was a mountain
You're not remembering   I have never   not   remembered
The mountain shrieks memory's   not education   or guitar riffs   no it's
That anything is   Quasar riffs   You cross the room   I cross the sad river

I have to keep   because it's so bent   crossing it baby don't I
It's a substance   like everything why   sticky   and im-
Maculately complete   Remember how you had to   filthy   yell
Remember bark eyes glare in forest   Remember the heavy again

That there is no song   Remember the obvious culture of
Ocular organization in-   to the shapes of the cosmos via telescope
Everyone now knows re-   member   I go into your eyes and see
Pictures of the sadness I   projected you thought who   The lives of lepidoptera

Billions dead   of   monarch butterflies

Then   *Rosetta healed you*   *that's in the future*   How can you cross it
Cross can mean ass   cross can mean anything
Greetings   elliptical she said   Rosetta can heal you   you've got that stone
One third of it's crystal   just like sadness   Isolate   sadness she says

Just a voice she   saying anything's crystal   Isolate it she says
I never wanted to   be in the future   Didn't want to   leave chaos she says
Time can be used   Why use   something   Sadness adulterated
In that river   find sadness's pure source   and demolish it   How

In the lang-   uage before Greek and   Egyptian   don't talk in a
Timely fashion   I put the beginning last I'd   just remembered
How cold it was to be alone   and how much I liked that
Now I have to tol-   erate the other   aspects   of the divine

How can I heal you   with a clear language   of thieves
Everything was stolen   from where   from somewhere in here

The Villain Poet

You've got that polish it   What   And the poet   tries to steal it
Of whatever persua-   sion race or project   Does that matter   re-
Member there's none   of the usual   matter   here where   or is there alive
Someone doesn't want   me to lead   Who   How can he interfere in formlessness

I'll get lost in it   Wants to choose   another   to lead   Get lost in it   chaos's
Cold driz-   zle per-   son are you a person   Unhappiness of mortals   says
Flickering   dreamy voice   Balder-   dash cant   tragic bleck of those
Who repeat others' words   You don't own me   Philemon   To the Hebrews or Sut-

Ra   of smugness   Wants to kill me as   force or power
The color of sadness   becoming purer   for this   My syllables
Pieces pale   Destroy her he says   meaning bow to him
Block him I say   entering forest of phrases   I've got to find what I need   though I

Can't need   Why won't the sto-   ry come clear   No story   this is real
No outlines   But it's a kill-   ing you say   That's not a story   that's a killing

And one turned un-   constrained like a mobile   or stayed mountainous
I stay   and stay consistent   I'm just walking   and staying phrased
The clung-to symbolism   will you vanish   and only a collage hesitant
Of the unknown re-   main   in the thistles   made of steel

Illiterately   through the parts   walk away reborn renée
So I call so I call un-   filtered   hatrack   trees let me through
I never *see* you anymore   I can only see in dreams   no dreams
I'm watching for watched   when I'll be allowed to   speak it you

Know   what I mean   But you *do*   I don't *know* that
They are so beautiful the   one   that holds up a pearl   tall
Smoothly spiraling metal   the encrusted   with glued-on
Paste jewels   big   Faux rubies big   These works are phrases or

Whole poems or   thought-poems   Because I   have to think it
Because that is what   I came here   to do   that   which I came to
For I have *come* to   among psychic   dissertations   of timelessness
So beaux   like long crooked rays   but steely   solid painted

Crystals in Boxes

I see   that they broke off   the rays or thoughts   then
In   some pointless era or   before the dawn   or now
It's just an image   so's the primal blast   Broke off
Into corpse-sized   crystals in long boxes   One talks   then others

And I'm one   yes   in a box   Bright   well that box thought-
Ful   I'd like to   This isn't my first   site   Isn't it
First   site squall   um hum   What is a squall   Static
Do you like these   sounds   I'm e-   mitting   I don't know

Where they come from   Me   yours you   static   what is e-
Nunci-   ating   Nothing   It's in the static   comes out of
Pris-   tine my form   long but I'm   emitting it
We're in boxes   Cardboard maybe   Carpe   Carpe what

Everything's passing   through   me   sound or   the depths
And the si-   lence won't dawn   There never was one
Everything will   pass through me   Ignore it   Everything
Will be ignorant   They won't know   how to think   or that they

Pass through crystals   No crystals   no us   No   I exist

Something passes through us   in the past   while I'm passing
Through   Heal it   Heal the primal blast   It exists in our cog-
Nition   It has its   in this universe   of complicity   the self-
Recognition   in everything   Heal it   But we've as good

As seen the bang   Heal it anyway   Which voice   is mine which
Memories   I never have to have   a body   I submitted to your
Dream   Where are my memories memories   Strewn over bitter water or
Flying everywhere   tornout bats   We are bats   bat voices say

Nor your memories   If nothing's here   your equations aren't
Whose   Find out how we spoke it at the first   lying in cof-
Fins like crystals   I took it out   the light and sound   and held it up I
Separated   The wind stops   Mindless what   Do you have

Not being   as you'd thought   For when you dream
What is there there   Not a   phenomenon   Do I remember
Do I mind   Say grace   But there's no food   Are you
Starved   in the orphanage   Did you drown   in the font

In proper scale the explosion was not an explosion

I'm standing ex-   hausted   tau crosses   random in air
Before my sight   But it's to hear   it not see   Let me hear
Priceless   a voice said   Can't pay to know   But I've suffered
Barriers down   Breaking again   Wing   I think it whirrs

And so I know you   you know what I know   They fall and rain
What you see is the product of your eyes   And I hear what-
Ever the whirr   To see and hear like us   There are no of bodies to
Perceive   So who I saw   clacked its wings   at some first

It didn't ex-   plode   a wing ex-   panded   and opened
For we called it or ours   our   the view covered with   clabbered
Downy marbled   extension unmattering   a bird breast
Don't know bird   *I want to speak*   *in extension*

Fellowed why   I see   in a different way   Speaking extend
And I here do   You wrongly heard it   wasn't a blast but a
Whisper   if you're as   large   as large as I am
In a language you can never   get over   Heard by the whole   entity

The words were simply too large for you   seemed so
At the time   simply   too loud   Even when soft

So you aren't who   No   Something not so intended   speaks
But how you hear depends on the ear   Dis-   torted   too swirls
Like what's said's a static rose   *I came out of it*   Say it fast
Out of the blast or bleached foot-   long seizure   It was

Only the size of a word/blot/sound   that explosion
Are we still in chaos   There's never been   successive or-   der
I don't know where I   am I say   and I'm still   sad though this
Begins   You must   but I have done so   enlarge

I am the size of   a quasar I   say   roaring delicately
It happens whenever   I know it does but   I have to know   It just does

Any old time   through a vast megaphone   why can't others
Hear   our end-   less existence   why can't you hear it
The dead quasar's aria   why can't you see   Joe's new work
Or touch a mordant-tongued   petal   a dead   one

The present is   to be here   unformed   Someone who wants to harm me
And my own sadness   reminding me to heal yours   amid bewild-
Ering torrential phrases or   what would there be   I
Am almost unimagined as form   Gigantic though   as a mind   oblit-

Erating the famous ex-   plosion   our supposed beginning pose so
We could be a violent cosmos   not this silken whisper   large body of in-
Dividually interpretable   design   *as the stars see themselves*   He still
Wants to kill me   And can enlarge too   in his mind   can

Find phrases   booming across skies   cracked open by a zigzag
I might have caressed you   into submission   But I have grown too tall
My melancholy's bigger too   but expansive   begins to thin out
And escape   Did I have to have it or any   qualities   You have them he lies

Heal us now the dead beg   we must return   to constructing our
Mass   our collaged by us universe   of differences   Heal us   into a new
Sensibility   I am almost unimagined   Can I imagine   what we'll be
Is it like me   Heal us   heal all us   Let's just see it   He's pursuing me

Wants to harm me   in instants of time   when   doesn't matter
Matters   It has always been   Doesn't matter what he's like
Phrases   Someone wants to hurt   my face   On the way to heal
Hurt it a-   gain   Alive or dead

                                            If I heal you   I heal him
Of sadness   Heal myself of   knowing it   The explosive first
Of mal-   feasance   Where is the language   Kill you   before we'd
Know it   I'd rather he says   have the power to kill you   than be healed

By you he says   The language   is gold   like a sourceless light I say
If I heal you I say   is that aggressive   First   I'll watch the first light
Which has no source   but us for we have   no source   I will kill your
Great-   ness he says   In what language   I say the dead   won't let you

Harm me   and I won't   I am greater than you if I heal you
And after you're healed you won't care   You'll be glad I healed you   So I
Must kill you he says

Hurt it again he says   I want to   hurt you down   he said I
Want you to go back to   wherever you came from

And I slip away   vanish into a black swirl   ingenious chaos
I keep my stamina   followed by hollow tones   But he can he
Derail or kill me   You are our leader   voices murmuring our on-
Ly sage or salve   For we think   only you   will be able to

Heal us of the   night factory   of explosives   change our per-
Ception   of force   Find the lang-   uage tell me the   It's
Phrases   It's just phrases   Let it break up   Get fast-
Er   It's thought you know   Or one   flute stretch tone in

An in-   stant   in it   forev-   er   Faster in one slow
Forever   Because a sur-   face broke   remember   Then you
Heal it   Pieces   no longer a-   part   It is a universe
Of art   If you know this   why sad   We're caught

Between the words

260

The Spigot

He's proclaiming   himself   Keep moving the voi-
Ces say   He's then proclaimed   in the daily world   I'm in danger in
The day world   Stay in motion towards   And as I
Walk towards   with ever-   lengthening   strides   am imbued

With such a con-   centrated sadness   I must deliberate to
Keep going   thinking will each step   The   chaotic fringes
Of sorrow's shawl spark into   the realm's normal mixity
And I am in a pure   swirl melan-   cholic

Every ex-   piration cor-   poreal finality   death I've ever
Witnessed   presses on my neck and back   as if this mood be finality
And there was never a   triumph   only failure and grief
Hated   who was hated   who was cho-   sen who was dis-

Carded   Who was left in the shadows with shadows   now un-
Speaking   But we   speak to you   we the dead   voices say   So
Keep going   It's like a spigot I say   It can't be   that simple
When I turn it off I still   have to change you   A silver spigot I see

It's an image   it's not it   It concentrates me   now as it does
I'm about to under-   stand   the disconnection of what's seen
From the flow of   mentality   Turn it off   I turn it off but I'm
Sad   For I made it   we made it with   minds of fate

Had to have it   I turn it off   but we still have it   You have to
Heal us   with words   It was just   a spigot   was on
It had once appeared   Was turned on we   did that
Why did we   It came to visit   on its own   On our own

Images   from where   They said our   crowded senses per-
Ceived   But we're dead   Is there such a thing   as
This image chaos   I see I say   a walking   or instrumented   force-
Ful language   I see what   I or we say   say that movement is

Is that good enough   I see a phrase   thin fibers   either side of a
Small spheroid why   I don't want it do I   Discovered
The drum set did I   Babbling   I have to lead you I
Have to find out everything   images and sounds   for the sense-

Less dead   Still sad   diminishing   What is between these
Phrases   between the percussive bites   between the walking let-
Ters   ambulatory   images images   I see a landscape
With a baby's head that   disattached   floats   above it

It's its head   See faces everywhere   faces of souls of   the matter of death
Faces of dead geology   of nebulae   of my   beloved rocks
All of your   faces   for me to see that's all   Can't you
Change the senses   a voice says   What is a memory   of what a

Face is   to you I say   We are just talking   I'm talking   to you
Our sense   is voices

There are no qual-   ities   Let's go there an in-   stant   Is it before a word
Is the surface   tranquil   then bro-   ken wounded   by a voice   mine
In what tongue   We can bare-   ly under-   stand you   Behind this image
Or backdrop   look   Do you know how to   look at it

It's just an expanse   it keeps being   yellow   floor or stage
I am walking   on it   which doesn't exist   to call to you
I once   saw a be-   ing that was on-   ly black lines   An in-
Scription   walked   No before that   were we hidden   We were hid-

Den   from each other   You will   I already know   you will
Say what you said   You had forbidden me   to exist   a-
Part from the yel-   low void   I will have to   make my-
Self there's still no   language   Every-   thing's in   my mind

If you make your-   self   can you   Yes I can   heal you
But we're not   sad yet are we   Yes   we brought it   in the cir-
Cular route   had we al-   ways gone through this   Once
You were or are   no longer hid-   den un-   made   the fa-

Mous un-   created standing there on the   uncreated   stage
Pre-   tending   We are almost the un-   created dead   You will be healed

Where was I   when I thought   I was on earth   a voice mutters
There and   between the phrases with   no sensual cues   In chaos one
Asks   Where are we now   Almost home   I must remember my pro-
Mises I say   For this is   the truth   and this is   the real   He still

Wants to kill you   Is that in the   partial world   or only this one
The idea of   the virtuoso   It's obvious if one is that   But is there
Only one kind   Nothing's acknowledged   between the phrases
That limn the world whose   outlines   we have praised   I could kill

Him be-   tween the phra-   ses the words   but I must heal him

Three times came to me   in dreams   to explain   the arts
But my affection isn't for   the enlightened artistic   It is for us
Terran dust and   dishevelled   stellar cloud   for the dead not

The smug live   I can lead you   The live   don't want me to   don't want me
To know you   Everything's between   Behind their backs   I'll heal them
Behind their backs   What will we make from chaos   Everything your winds sing

I'll yank out of their heads   the first shudder   I'll yank out of his head
My rival's and your de-   ceiver's   the first dream   Is he live or dead
Who makes such   distinctions now   Where is he in relation to
Where we are   There is no re-   lation in the mind   Abolished space re-

Member   Chaos is our   mother mind   as I am   your leader
What is   the first dream   An experience of   division   as between his
Expertise   and mine   That the mind   is divided   That the worth
Of the re-   warded is apparent   I saw his glove   I saw his

Fingers   What divided them   was the illusion   of utility   and ele-
Gance   I'm finding what I need   without partisans or   book of
Judges   I enjoyed my lonelinesses   and the distance
Between leading   and those who cleave to-   gether   But I must

Divest you   of your raincoats   and hungry oracles   There are no se-
Crets   Everything's intermixed   even the jealousies   of wings
Stepping just ahead   listening   I can heal you   We don't have to need

Tell him   what he left out   as I leap into   the space between

It isn't a trick in here   I am so close   to the sourceless   No tricks
Wash it   What   So you can reuse it   And entered in back   a dark self
We called on   magnification   Now call on   the fair   or is it unfair
They the po-   ets sit there   I will go   detain myself

South of Salton Sea   My shadow I'm becoming   follows me
It was a book fair   I swore at them   Can't I read   the crystal
Through it hear trem-   ble some words   Hear true
You are the voyage   of a tone   across the sky   And then inhabits

Between phrases   Binders fly away   Smell of crystal
When air's scraped   Hear it   south and west but   spaceless
Clear molecules   She's selling her old   pamphlets   I don't have one
I have a page extending   beyond dimensions   I can't read it

Can you hear between   the phrases   Suddenly   the gaps pal-
Pitate   That's just me   offering stories   of the clarities   Or greetings
I promise to use   what's singing   in the thorax   of semblant hill
A little ringing   a painless gesture   fine drawn lines

We are pilgrims   of a painted   beauty   voices say and I   see their forms
We who travel   at night   between the phases   You are so beauti-
Ful I say   that I can't see your de-   tails   We are following you our
Leader   You don't have to see   use other senses

They are in clusters   the pilgrim voices   like the phrases colored complexes
Inks but   I move fast past   them to take   my position
Train me a voice says   I am reason   the new reason   in my dirty
Blue coat   I proceed   hearing the clusters   feeling their presence

What you hold   that is ransomed by you   must be given back

To those from whom   first taken   I suppose but we   took from
Ourselves   *Don't fall in love   with me   It will distract me*
I turned off the   spigot remember   But what I do
Must be more   Listen   The words push together   See the fig-

Ures   I can't   alizarin   blue lake   and gold
I have almost   forgotten   how I was mistreated   though I still
Strove to please   him or them   I am training you to think
Who is speaking   Can't I have one says   vengeance   Don't love me

In this death   The spirits lose   what faces I might find
If they were hu-   man   Retaining   the coloration   of saints
I know this from say-   ing it   I know you from speaking

(dream of Dante's pilgrims climbing Mount Purgatory)

267

It is a network of pain   well-made   that is all of us   nerves   Mountains
Aren't   Do we have to have more   The sun sinks where I feel   I feel everywhere
Oh these voices   Phantom pain   Everyone speaking in   musical
Groups   like singing   My own pain still   I say considerable   for

I've lost my home   and have no place   but this one in front leading   Trying
Something's trying   to tell me what it is   if it came from the future   like a language
Because it has al-   ways al-   ready   I am here but have never   been healed
This unit we are the uni-   verse has nev-   er been healed   Did it come to be

Who knows   The forms are making   their own   brilliant showings
For Dante or whoever   made them   I'm making   myself   I say
Is it out of pain   Any cry or posture   from that then under-   stood I
Don't know   if I want to   engage with you in form   or understand

We're just on our way   Let's walk right through   the crystal here   part of that
Rosetta Stone   Rosetta Stones are everywhere   Did you make your-
Self   out of glass or light   I can't show it to anyone   Because I don't`
Believe you   so I'm leading   to the healing point   exactly at the so-

Called first   when sounds rang out   and were mistaken   for blows   not words

Other side of fab-   ric can you read them   I'm illiterate   Can
You hear   other side of light which light   If love communi-
Cation and mem-   ory be the same   I wound-   ed seeking to exist
For I   wound-   ed myself I said   But there's   bright heat on me

Adjust to   true justice   the com-   plex paint-   ed linguist-
Ic entities sing   That you will do good to   yourself
And change   what to say   until sadness fades   I couldn't
Really go home   But I could go   here   Feel the sourceless

Light feel it   tones and the   in-between   sounding
Where the crys-   tal both vi-   brates and   lights through   An image
I am an en-   tity   And the sep-   arate lights beckoning   to each
Other   I am those   What else would we be when   we came here

Is it chao-   tic inchoate it is   what I remember that I am
True   Generous   lights   dimensionless   I remember this pleasure
And are you real or in-   vented   I am beyond the small tunes
But we have always   been connected   As we made   light speaking

You have to die   Some part of you has to die   So you can cre-
Ate yourself   then heal us   Haven't I died enough   Enough times
Divided into parts   One of them dies   In what language   it
Isn't the unknown   woman any more   It's me   Eat ceremony food

Can I go back to   after the lockdown   my hotel?   Too chaotic
This lang-   uage   has to get home   She dies   on the way to
Necrotic   And I postulate   that I am the first   to find out
What you'll know   that I can die without   anything   and

Come back   It's the part of me that sleeps   I see the in-
Tensification   of shadows   where there's nothing   It says'
Say it   And mountains say Not a mal-   interpretation
Take away my oth-   er speaking parts   all but lead-

Er   I'm trying not to see what   anyone said   The lights of
Rare gases   Street lanterns   the first display   of our kind
Dream or drama   I am leading   rip out the   depiction and re-
Place it with   what is now   said when   she's gone

What are we going   to say   I will tell you   what to say
None of the others are part   It seems to be my-   self   As I lie here
I will tell you   who is left of me   No one else will be al-
Lowed to say   Who is it who are you   The one that gets up

A long in-   cision right side of me   Paul swept up cry-   stal remnants
Did I die   Stay and re-   cover don't run   Who is it   who are
You did you bleed   is there a scar   The right side aches
Most im-   portantly   the toppling of   an internal hierarchy

Signaling there's no   allegiance you must be a-   ble to live with-
Out it   And forgiveness   if I were to forgive   why would I
If I were a   deity of compassion   I wouldn't be   a particular my-
Self so   recognize me at your own   risk   And don't

Claim me   for your party   There is a blue deer   in the thicket
Not yet   Yes yet   Enter the sourceless light and   let that speak
You can't be big-   ger than the whole cosmos   As your own be-
Gin   my relation to force and   materiality   or image

Say there is a first   occurrence   It is extending   active but
Not destructive   Light and shadows   Presences half-spoken   half-
Thought already   But who are you   There isn't that   exactly

In the dead vers-   in the dead matter version   Of   speech or matter
Just because we were   are   dead   that doesn't mean   we don't have our
Own kind of   materiality   Space and time   al-   ways unnecess-
Ary   Be-   cause the language he's saying   gets whatever   you are who's

Say-   ing   So what he some-   one   says   was ripped out of you
You'd made   you   out of what other-   ers seemed   I'm no
Longer semblant   The doctor comes he's   a doctor of dancers
Do I need a doctor   Meet him in the Y   I don't know O why   For the med-

Icine you take be-   tween those oth-   er phrases   where we were
Have to dance the new   Sunlike with red band-   widths crack-
Ling   Inter-   pellate   All of   I was   listen   and the shapes of my-
Self   in motion   causative   It or I lets me   go   I become yours

Simply your   leader   healer   systemically   glue   I am cre-
Ating to hold this to-   gether   I mean real
In the con-   centration   involved I   cannot be sad   Sadness
Can't be anywhere   I am   holding you up   like dancing

Do you see what   I'm saying   Hold-   ing you to-   gether
Healing you sav-   ing you   Follow me now   So you can be
I'm keeping you   with me   Listen to it   Forget or   remember
The doc-   tor heals me   so I can heal you   between this the

Seeking out of   how to   form it   Have never stopped making it
Between what was   crazy emphasized   Any old   as long as
Can or can't   see me   No pre-   tense of   petiteness   No scale
The dance   can keep   the change

It d red one idn't depend   or end   No lace   thing depended   hung
Lace   if blind to   touch   I could   do you   touch it with
My   mind like it   textured   ecru   Not made at this
Time   a voice   But I say   different-   ly for we have   differed

And between us   I am   here   a power   structure expon-
Ential-   ly imagined   with red   stove its   rim lit   red
Saw it with-   out entity   mine or its   Was in   dream
What p permit arts   or parts   of my   previous   life

Did I dream   Here ere a nex-   us   some unre-   ality will be
Ours you know   How   do we enter   it the real en-   tity ex-
Isting   as I am most   real think-   ing   and lead-   ing but
This ri-   diculous   it sort of walks in   body   body

You are my bo-   dy   I'm back here   a lot pre-   tended
The soft   men-   tally the s   it lies oft   I could be   anything
That's ridic-   between the   ulous forms we   say we   see
Warm   against the hill   Could be   buried there   The hill's   in me

273

Backing a-   way from my   life   Photos on   backed
Away from   wall   If I could show you   I thought
All the ways I   felt then   Which she died   The operation was
A success   patient sur-   vived only part of   her died   If I

Could feel for   be   the feelings for every-   one you wouldn't have
To   Do we have t   back away o   from your wall   have them now
And then what   happened   to the wall   I who
Sur-   vived d   you o   remember be-   fore the op-

Eration   al-   lowed someone to   operate op-   erate on you
I've backed away from   the photos de-   picting   What do they
Depict   My fig-   ure   In   order to   lead you   Heal you if I
Could   feel everything for you   Or if I have have I   Did it h

And so   all the feelings   yours mine   in me died
Did it help   that she died   Who operated   Why   I did
I do every-   thing I al-   ways do   everything   Be-
Cause you can't   or understand me   Displace   sequins   in your ear

Stand I'm standing   before a black cave   I enter   solid black-
Ness   As black as I've ever   Need a light   Just a little
One   And as I'm thinking that   what light I need   before I
Finish the thought   am handed a light   Just a light so hold it up

There's a wall   a wall of   portraits in front of me   One is my-
Self I guess   She must be   Stands in front of me   Then dies
I know she's dead   What am I now   Which one has died
Dis-   solved   like an image   on the ground   Where were

We standing   Just out-   side   the cave its wall   of photos
She's gone   the image is gone   Which part of me's dead
I'm sha-   ky empty   What do I know now   I know how
To be   who I was but   something's gone   some one of me

A net of silk threads   a nexus   intricate   immaterial
Did I need her   I am your leader   no self a poet   that's all

The Target Sadness

I see it sad-   ness like a target   but massive   of mass
Like a hawk's wound   a creator   bird's severed-   wing wound
Like what-   ever a foolish mind   like what-   ever you
Like what sad you see   fool   like a wound your-   self me

They are re-   covering her body-   y from the pond   I still don't
Know   who of me   pond of chaos   as shal-   low imag-
Inary   nullity   is that   what it is   don't know   who of
Me it is   I forget   the re-   lation   of chaos to   the death-

World death-mass   There's any   relation you want   voices say

I want to see   it isolated sad-   ness   is it her body   They bring
It up   they who   they're not there   im-   ages but this is
How you think here   Who are you addressing   The wind
With no address   She's me she's sad-   ness is she or   something

More trivial I   can't   seem to know   who I am   And sad-
Ness   mounts in the no-sky   How do you know   A black mem-
Brane over   What else can it be   Destroy it   How   With your
Voice   That is   all I have   Sing it   talk it   to death

What was the i-   dea   Trying to figure out   Make fig-
Ures was that   it why   Why would that   be a universe   why
Even   is that a death   where we are   What else would we be
Sadness   though you of-   ten envelop me   you're a

Creation and I'm not   Wants us to be-   lieve in it   The wind
Will blow it away   Blow it ragged once   and for all away
Time's asleep   Memory's asleep   Communication   is not
At the beginning   was imagined   that there would be   oh some-

Thing   And Something rebelled im-   agining differently   Chaos
What you would see   if you could   and ceased to measure it
Chaos and the wind or mind to-   gether   can expel sadness
It is too real now   Nothing is *too real*   And there is no nerv-

Ous system in death   Ex-   pel the linger-   ing tonal mad-
Ness   We've made it too real   Let it join you   as a dead one
Let it have its own   outlines as a   shade   Let it be dead
We dead aren't dead though   Let it have outlines and skulk   powerless

It is an ef-   fluvium   the rain comes   pluvia and   demolishes it
What in cha-   os is demolished   Trans-   formed more like
And I will talk   and heal us how and will   In what language
All language is   within all us   twisting the wind and its   swaying lumina

I am gone from the   sky   From the mountain   sadness says
I am lost to the   forest of   made things   of yours
I am gone from the mountains   of the mixup   after the explosion
I am lost to your   dreams   your tonal   vocab-   ulary if

You have suc-   ceeded in   subduing me   slaying creature in the
Old way   you may have little to say   The dead and I   will always
Know what to   say it   will begin   I now begin   the
Sanatio   healing   fluminis ostium   aperire   germinare

Would the shapeliness of mind   now own me   Would the
Particulars   of the knowing   of death now   enter me

Every-   thing be-   ing the same size every-   thing's   each's soul
Being the   same size   who are you   I didn't   you say   have to
Ask that quest-   ion   did I e-   ver   I once asked   you
If you knew me I   say to any-   thing   And ask   you now do

You know me   Vast as an ar-   row star-tipped   What
Will you do with   who   eternity   It's   the same size too
These meet me   as I ar-   rive   this time   Voice   and think-
Ing pro-   duced from an a-   perture of   no dimensions

We do on-   ly e-   volve if we con-   sider time long-   er than an
Instant   Other-   wise all at   once knowing   what comes and
Goes   meet me at the met   singing gloria   or praetorian
Guard   this once   the nights   are   finished   di-

Visions   divisions into day and night   are done   I am curing
You   by dissolving ex-   ternal dis-   tinction   and every other
Linguistic   illusion   You don't know your uni-   verse   until now
It is   as we are being here   beginning   What   is it   Us

Do you   know me   I be-   lieve I know   all of you

I was just murdered sudden voice   you must heal *me*   As I say   all notion
That violence is   intrinsic to us   or the making of a star   is dead
Had not occurred to me   the star said   that fire hurt   or that I am large
I was murdered!   he says   And now come into   the privilege   of death I say

Why was I born he says   Were you I say   Or is   there a fan-
Tasy   that we are physi-   cal   And if I scream   with pain   is it be-
Cause I have   long been told to   or because I'm   in a dream
Are we dreaming   our existences   who did you   submit to

And could you never have   left   the dream   Do humans and planets
Fear lone-   liness is loneliness   a thing   Are you a thing   My
Dear were you an object   Who now will find   you ob-
Jective to   senses   We are thought   by ourselves   We are

The thinkers   We   made us   We will   make us   again
I am sorry for you   and glad to see you   you of all people   welcome

I was shot   repeated-   ly he says shot a number   of times
I didn't do   anything   but be stupid   I acted   my size
Thought I was big   roughed him up   tell no lies
I still wasn't   shot for any   reason   who is   and I

Want the rain   to fill the holes in my   body   But now I'm
Here   Healing be-   tween the syllables   Mastery will un-
Originate you I say   The first phrase that came into   my head
Empty firewood   The rains   of nothing here   make the holes

In my bo-   dy steam clear he says   clean I'm start-   ing to be here
I'm starting to be   here and   I'm satisfied   unoriginated
That's a funny one   and I have all   these words I   don't know
Starting   to clear me   like rain   Starting to clear

I did every-   thing every-   one ever did   That's what I
Did   That's all   pouring down   like nothing or   like love

What happened to   you   will be part of   the healing

Give each oth-   er grace   the lang-   uage   has effects on you   It is
Everywhere   under-   and overground of you   Fills you with e-
Ruptive   jewels   you can see with   your void senses   the wherewithal
To heal   the dest-   iny of being   healed by   our more than words

The language be-   cause our   minds are is   everywhere
I touch   you with   it but you are it   are/am I   or I be-
Tween it galleons   of time-   worn babes sailing   the red-black sea
The yellow   then em-   purpled sea   sounds postures   you danced it

We do every-   thing I know   holding a bowl of in-   ception
You al-   ready know it   I'm fateless a-   gain   bowl of ocean
Bowl of chaos   See its al-   phabet swimming   Just use it
Laid in they will ad-   here to us   being us those   letters

Don't put them in   your clos-   et let them live
In the epic the blinds raised   suite of books the old   come with me

He's There To Kill Me Again

Rosetta heals you   We're uncreated   Man wants to kill   me between
The phrases   Because you don't know this language   Puts on   binoculars
Tear them off   Do you fol-   low   You don't need eyes   I want to
Win in   as it was   But you're just dying   I want   to win he says

Covered with kaleidoscopic   gems   I don't care   What do you
Mean   Push him away   I want the world we   knew he says
Pilot my own   guide me   Everything you   say hurts in
The wound   It's shrinking   I shrink it   going on   you'll just have

To he says   break the mem-   brane again to start   Star start
Idlers imagine things   Distraught amber you don't ev-   er
Have to star   start judge or try   Do you want an   idea   No
I'm covered in sudden   I'm covered   shower of   glyphs or limp-

Id what we are   Sourceless glyph light   The refraction   commences where
We once made   it start by   pushing   him out   of the way
Already future and came back and   No promontories   Already a babe
Pick it up   It's a little   It plays with you   That's something

Shake all those   letters off your cape   They'll fly away and   start us

This is the most   healing moment   Every-   thing at   the same time
For I was sud-   denly sick as death   And I   am sick now
And I am heal-   ing us ag-   glomerative   sphere of   accretions and powers
The wound of sad-   ness the black   baiting hole imag-   inary shrinks

To death   Part of me that part of me   still dying   And you near
Healed   Lying on cha-   otic bed I close   my eyes   in which reality
My bedroom wall   in which chaos   the long wall   of a tunnel
Dark and rough   as if used   by an engine   and all along   where feet fall

Candles a line of cand-   les of uneven heights   lovely   of uneven
Heights   all the   candles   you'll need   in your transit
Follow me   I'm your lead-   er   The bedroom's crowded
With my dead friends everyone   What dies in me I say and who

Am I now   Michael   the murdered man says   you're kinder   you won't be mean
Follow me   along the cand-   les I say   I'm   no longer   sick or sad
When we ex-   it the   old glyph   flat   yellow   field   We
Are that   I'm healed   says the killer too   I just am it   the exact change

The words   don't have   to go with   any more   Don't have to
Go with   what one said was   each other   That's one thing I
Am heal-   I am the heal-   er of rigidity   Love   isn't ri-
Gid you know   Have chaos for   And   if it hard-   ens it can't

It musn't hurt   For the living   Do you know   why we lived
That di-   mension   might be an   experiment   But the dead
Live   rocks live   And I a-   live am   dead   talking to you   in and
Between   the phrases to   heal in the poetry we   are structurally

Smallest pieces I   heal   Are there pieces   There's a bird on my hand
Sparrow soul   I heal its fleas   and their bacteria   I still don't
Have to   see you   except as a bird does   cyn-   ically it says
Ate my pastry   on the table   I am heal-   ing you   to freedom

Do I have to re-   member   Only our struc-   ture of   floating dice
We are al-   ways throw-   ing   How are we like   this
I'm healing you   to know that   Are   some things just   are
Are they   I'm healing you so you can   be   You weren't before   were you

If I could pr-   ove I say   that we make physical   changes with
Our minds   how we began or   didn't   In-   iniated the mat-
Ter we   know alive   Back into a sing-   le cell can you   There
Black and be-   fore   It was a chance   wasn't it   I deny chance

I am heal-   ing chance and lead-   ing you   I remember   being a speck
On the ocean   And be-   fore   But there's no chance when   the fut-
Ure's known   It isn't e-   ven the future   Hidden behind each   set of let-
Ters I see   something bothers me   Have to heal it   I remember

Speaking the hidden   Whatever I say is the hid-   den lang-
Uage behind   It's before I   remembered   Can you remember before
Memory   And I made it   How   The hugeness   for I
Different   definition   heal into it   Hidden behind   it I am

Heal-   ing you the word I   isn't bothersome   Lead-   ing you
Step behind   Everything there   uncreated   as we are   I know what
I'm doing I   always have   you don't have to   lose it
Between or be-   hind before   the speck I was   to make

I'm spea-   king to ev-   eryone in this ca-   thedral   Do you remem-
Ber   The cathedral's   so long so   many souls who   are they ev-
Eryone   Remember be-   fore memory   when we created
The cosmos I stand there   I say I love to   stand here   before you

I love you   I love   to be in my   words the hidden   words be-
Hind the writ-   ten strokes   I love them my words   If I forget
You the   audience the   vast oth-   er while I'm in the words   per-
Forming them   that's all right be-   cause I love   all three ele-

Ments   you the   words and stand-   ing before you   So it's
All love   isn't it   But I get   lost in my   words   the hid-
Den   as we were once   hidden behind ourselves   I am de-
Scribing to you   where we are the   cathedral of chaos   though

It seems gothic-   ally tough   as well   It is clear   and I am here
To perform to   you ours   our creation   of the hidden   which
Will soon be   all we are

If it is like this   I am not placed   I am what o-   pens
You are   what o-   pens   This is the   black   vowel
Didn't hear   it with ears   Was an-   other sense   not a
Sense   The jur-   y is out   The judge has a tremor   That's all

No gui-   lt no sad-   ness   The tre-   mor results in a click
Dropped her pen   My cof-   fee's clouds dis-   solve
Into a   fract-   ure of a   second   I per-   ceived as the on-
Slaught   of a   new mind   It came with   matter

That's the part I   It's not there   if it's ag-   ing   Mat-
Ters not there   The judge   can't find   the crime   it would
Be in your   heart that's al-   ways moving   I was so
Moved   by your change that   I   disband-   ed the off-

Ices   of ven-   geance   the bureau   of definitions   this
Small   lang-   uage with-   out organs of   tax-
Onomy   with-   out rules   This body un-   ruled
To suf-   fice for now   The memory   of   the next mo-   ment

It's the small-   est one   Greasy-   haired he hands   me a bit
Make a smallest hole   Go into   There was a   place in   my mind
N o n o t   o r   So I'm in be-   tween squee-   zed but   where
Is it dif-   ferent   Slip through the   ti-   niest   place to e-

Merge   As between r   and g in merge   It was un-   der a   counter
In a dream   I mean   I slipped through   a crack   in some wood
Be-   cause   you are in-   side matter   you could be in-
Side oth-   er matter   If   you're mat-   ter say what   it is you say

So I'm in my-   self   Wind up where   The white   beach of
A dead ocean   But was in-   side or be-   tween wood   A beach
I come   out at there   through the crack   below the coun-   ter
In   my   old   house full of   silver-framed   por-   traits

If you   squeeze be-   tween the   a and i   in portrait   also you
Can get there   This   is my sermon   We have   inside the
Turquoise   or coral   a small bit   of the lang-   uage
Between   tur and q   or and al   I live   I lead   I heal   I have to

Al Allen   has put a crown   on my head   invisible to you

289

You could   kill me by   inserting   an icepick   within a mass of my
Molecules   It has to   be the right   molecules   someone says
Have you e-   ver left your   well I've left my   bod-   y   Pro-
Bably a   fan-   tasy   another voice   Did you   rise up be-

Tween molecules   I arose   and saw myself   From   between the
Letters   I mean mole-   cules or cells   It wasn't much
In a car lost   on a dirt road   moonlight   wanted to be   If
You can get lost   you might make it   Every-   thing has always

Happened   in dream on the road to Topock   Lost walking   too
Far   finding in the des-   ert mountains an   industrialized

City lit   Asleep in my bo-   dy you'd say
                                                I slip out
Between some or-   gans of mine   in the guise of   myself
Are you lead-   ing us   Yes this is   one way I   join you
We can go anywhere be-   cause anywhere's   us   Now fol-

Low me   all trillions of you souls   down be-   tween those two
Pieces of sand in-   to a wormhole   so to speak   speak like a worm

The wormhole bursts

In this hole   all of   us   talk   I'm addressing   vast you
Again   We are not tribes   Between r and i   or i and b   of
Rib   in tribes   we'll slip through to   what we are that
I've nearly healed   We are   the grace between   every-

Thing we   think ex-   ists that   you know doesn't
You weren't hurt   your memories   are all   superficial
You can re-   member better   than that   Remember
A better universe   with me   In this   wormhole

Between   vermillion grains   I see opals   I see into
Your   iris   or   if you're a rock   your unaccountable
Like-an-eye   I see that you make the   slick   milky striae
After   the wormhole   bursts   with fiery pendants

Be-   tween which let-   ters you ask   Someone says   in
The length of my cancered   spine   beauty sang   inside the y

Are you leading   patterns   of spirit   This the primal use
Of poetry   the or-   ganizing principle   of spirit   This was and is
Our true primal be-   ing   We are patterned like   these
Words   Are we   Yes   but faster   fast flash of light

Then we   won't read this poem   but will be it   You
Can read   it or are we il-   literate   as you once said   of yourself
I'm not illiterate   I will be light   what I read or say   now
Go with Siber-   ian sha-   man in sleigh to night   then light

He shows me pages   the pages   without figures   figuration
For what I'm lead-   ing is still   unfigured   but beautiful
Abstracted you'd   say   the pages have   colored bor-
Ders   magenta   and on the page   inside the page

A yellow   palely lit ex-   panse   Or does   my poem   di-
Vide   into minutes   not pages   minutes   of a cir-
Cumference   notes of the music   I mean of words
The music of words   between the phrases   where we give off light

Organ-   izing princ-   iple of spirit   in a literal   measuring way
We were littoral   standing round   an abyss   Going there now
Traced phrases   my phrases   as if drawn   are more than   wo-
Rds   Drawings   the word   that we are   For I was made flesh

The word made flesh they say   drawn into this   unconceivable   bod-
Y   What kind of drawn   How are your phra-   ses con-
Nected   By the sound   The word is   its   image   or angel   Colors vi-
Vid now   not pen-   cil traced figures   Are the   figures

Matter   traced among   molecules   and singing   come one
Follow me I say   follow me   I was made flesh   and still am that
The pattern of my   spirit cells   isn't visible   to mat-
Erial eyes   only to   you the dead

Follow me
Stand at   the abyss again   we understand now where we   are coming to be

IV.
TO PASTE ON

MALORUM SANATIO

The century or year or night one might bloom a miracle
A night-blooming cereus white   this could heal you
Or decorate the new abyss turn the year backwards un-
Fasten its manacles we have a different year on Jupiter
These transgressions in their authentic beauty digress
Like a pasted-on feather I want to know if I'm healing
Him oh so talented dead man illiterate unlettered I say
In the dark club playing his unlettered guitar as I stand on
This corner I've got two containers you've got two dogs
I'm supposed to know why in order to heal you or him am I
Let's not concentrate on what it means dead guys with
Past to be unpasted pressed over with letters who can
Read them and random sequins mounted whole pet-
Ite you are blocking the way of the killer I'm dead now you
Say to your harmless dogs in the halogen faintness of my
Thought have I healed you yet I'll continue to try
On the street corner behind broken ice whatever planet

If it's a feeling I have to heal or if it's a disease
If it's the torpid depths of your eyes you don't have here
If it's your loss of self-location the safe house I counter
With an electric provocation my own talent the
Speech of a riff or bladed number like thirteen blue
Paste that on if I can enter our mind and stay just a-
While to tell you you don't need what happened on the pla-
Net of brutal futile actions throw them away the dust-risen
Thinking of illusorily-limbed bodies half-
Erased creatured of woe we lumber
And I left home oh and stumbled over tragedy a sack of in-
Edible pebbles I'm sorry you have some hurt throw it away
We call guilt up every morning one says put it there and let
It be there let it follow you until it's gone grief
I can heal you illiterate reader the night is my eye

Is the healing a thing can you see or listen to as whispering
Allowed in at the universal we're all the abyss all there

Crowded staircase could be descended to dark grace no
Someone pleading for comment on her poem on shiny paper with
Rosette sticker paste it on the void I said I've been given the
Rosetta Stone stolen the secret crystal you are a pun and I too
Thus healable manu à manuscript fiery about your invisible head it
Off I am healing you with paste it on the collage danger
Anger'd backwards frightened till he as if menial
Tried to slip away crowded as if he could be forgotten
No one will be and you must exist dead or alive
I stole healing slab of crystal kept in a grey pouch don't
Come in here a voice said but I have brought back every dimen-
Sion that I am mentioning till I find the one in the pun you are
No one gets out of here unhealed
                                        The force of the rosette
Or any cheap posy or portrait of a being paste
It on the healing and project all your old identities as if
One of them might be you project the one with unkempt hair
And the one punk where authoritative with a knife or
The one of you softened I put it on the one with no one gets
Out of here unhealed battered by grief bastard you're rife
With spirits of the murdered or dread like a capo everyone's
No one gets out of here a fake was everyone and caped I'm
Healing you of all your fakery burden of that
Which one was the real and is it re I Al or is it you or
Oo the two empty eyes I pun till it's genuine
For I can heal any rag of soul slime cloth
A bucket-headed dunce of a dancing jackass confidential
Here you are don't any person planet cloud or sublimation of a one
                                        try to slip away

It comes from the dissolution of action what happened you were ineffectual
Incapable inasmuch as an abyss with old images gliding over you
I murdered and harmed you say   Stupid your victims are all alive here
I had vile motives   There is no such thing as a motive you were
As you see an empty snakeskin a hack's diary lived
The account of your deeds virtuous or ruffianly is boring
Your attempts at constructing a character have failed likeness non-
Existent there is nothing established consider yourself ethereal

And if the stars melt could they call out heal me of my
Bulk and burning heal me of my properties punned my
Light you who suppose I have never thought or knew I was on fire

You who are dead here I say forget all but new memory
Remember from now remember from nothing to recall
While I walk on faux tiles of Paris my mind glides
The nothing that loves me grins like a bat I am healing you
Terrapin shell heartless non-one the shoals of hypochondria
Only beauty never tepid always neutral lives at the first
I claim everything as my abyss in order to heal you
I haven't any idea who you are praying mantis paramecium
Faces or fecal in the heavens orange choral shouts
I don't care what you did or have I search for the one lang-
Uage to heal in which infants recognize when anyone sings
The terpsichorean weeps from raging as another
Is that it an act yes tears chrysalises of graced
Thing which comes in the aftermath but this is only
What we are creating and you who still live are here
Too in the part of your mind you're unconscious of
Beyond the old words this collage pun re-cognates
What you once knew starting now tipped to a reconnaissance
Like fingertips or pebbled surface knowing a mirror's essence
Because we've all always known each other shudder at the moon
You have to be here lily-breathed or punctual
Projecting the fungal or fiery with what sounds or
Thought I've always heard you blackness speaking

And I go in there abyss or us and paste on a heart for it
After I see it or rosette or transfusion any red word
What do you care you aren't your forms
What do you care if you dreamed your enactment or life
After I see and after I see it so I can heal you the universe
The imagery we'd made of origin had been catastrophic
But what I enter is a pearl a round chamber of whiteness
I alive can only see as if I were in perfect luminescence
I mean I am in it or am it nothing happens in the void
Nothing ever happened except in your dream of a creation

I sit in this pun and I touch its curved wall speaking
I sit in origin not an explosion but tthisss

It didn't have to be or did it out of this chamber if I'm telling
A myth or truth only a point of origination you can't break
Me I'd say then words materialize on the white wall
Do you hear what the voice says they say it's my voice
Oozed out in faintness then healed what is heal to come back
To this hole I was in it I changed her diaper pun and gave her back to you
Each one was one and I can understand whatever you say or think
Because I don't have to the waves aren't water
His eyes closed when he talks to me could be a word from any language
You have come here to heal where nothing happened except for a voice
                                        a perfect quality you are

One says it might be you healing between the syllables
Abacus with segmental notions would one need
Would one need to flower flow or congeal like a rock
One need to be in layers or sparkling clusters unseen
Would one need to be seen or unseen heard or unheard
Touched or left solid and still inside a cloud red for no one
You know you can never die   that doesn't heal
And you have loved many times   that doesn't heal
You have an identity apart from your loves that might heal
That in its vastness connects with theirs again
The vastness can you touch it without skin or organ
Why are you living what other and the waves again of no water
Simple each line in beauty though the rubies be hemoglobic
Not every entity bleeds and the scratched excrescences
Of words from the inner surface of the pearl return
The first healing first heal the first to be is first to heal
The first rupture it doesn't say that it says I break through
A free black slick-coated prairie dog running in boundlessness

Spidery or unilinear like scabs of scratched drawings
Healed as soon as they're born sores or breaks in nacre I'm
Healing you leading you and healing almost the same word
Breaking open with something vulnerable to know

To memorize a motion a structure I am healing you
Inside the whiteness of your eyes a thing blazes known
Torn admired those can be rot maddened ever in
Principle quality-less you hear my heart of figures
There is nothing there but a sound for what ears
There is nothing there but smoothness for whose fingertips
Mental for a mind I am healing you a mind
What did you think the mind was another thought 'oral cult'
The overriding impressed so that you forgot going west
I qualify Elijah as a train break enter like light
There can't be any real light what would be real light
The airplanes in the letters spelling pick up the receiver
I am trying to reach appeal to you I am healing you
Across your dusky chest with all these words in it
Knitted together like a better flesh I am healing you
There's the unfindable waving how many fingers
I'm told the language I seek is hidden where I am

At the point where in a forest you became flesh the words ap-
Peared back and forth between skin and words sound and
Air your body transport remember there was no environment
It was green stagelike a void and one was a knight with a k
And one was a night with an n I am a knight or night
Come to meet you unpressed for time perhaps wrinkled or winks
We were images of people you were painted I was eyes
In the forest of void near the winkles near the coast
Everything washes over some seeps in purificatory
My words keep coming towards your pain until it's an il-
Lusion break into your heart scab over and are written
Are you literate does your memory read I will never be bet-
Ter if I can't remember who I was before I was written on
Marked and erased me my heart made so narrow
I remember these old old words to who soul pierce
The sound of where one sat near the waterless sea
All of us call come here and be healed of displeasure
Healed of extreme distress of disease imbalance and fit-
Fulness healed of every mark that hasn't a source in your
Spirit healed of ruptures between substances these words

Are pure without cynical precedent or calculation
I obtain for you the blessing of others we heal and holding are you
Falling away so you can remember all words ever spo-
Ken in any language remember thoughts all thoughts
For you can in one instant be healed knowing everything
Remembering everyone and finally remembering who you are

My Address

My address still the auto supply Broadway he takes me into office
Show me the language   Xs it's Xs   I don't know to explain
Like a dream and into the black   rip in the back store air
Each X see it and you'll know   You have to see each one a different X
Do you paste them onto the abyss or are we them standing
A word here doesn't mean anything or propound
Prompt annoyed alone in a blue marine void so young again
Are you reading this from Xs   it is how we proceed
And saying from it almost written inside me that
There were the Xs all over so what I said didn't matter
Now on escarpment they are throughout being thought to
You adequately visual so we can form us not out of mass
Why did we each become or was it becoming without a mech-
Anism as we've been taught sets going on an evolving course
Fitful or tragic it was only some Xs masked like raptors
So am I an X or what it is that can be seen by the dead
You are our leader Alice Notley c/o Needles Auto Supply 419
Broadway Needles California without for many years a zip code
But what was I behind that X how do we materialize
Standing where I was without my looks in the bleakèd dark
Not a science narration or quasi-myth I'm not as you proposed
The only thing that happens behind the screen being an X
I let myself happen did I spiraling backwards comet
Of Xs and jet bead dashes no not the further identity he says
You stood in for you he says   oh I've said that before I say
But when I suffered I was buffeted oh X X X and space winds
You can see what they are to say in this suppressed tongue

303

Torn Petal Orange and Crimson

Torn petal orange and crimson rag twists with blue bursts
Connected by a new memory web a sticky relation
Squawks and whistled squawks by the airy pond
Cosmos we can't *see* soul-extensive and nonetheless hued
Heron slender the slender foggy grey farthing far-strung
Perception sure but paste it on the new abyss the roseate
It's getting cloudier all around my forthright mind
With void thoughts raven-feather texture it's just *your*
Object as I led us through the tunnel of candles
To astral foam white known to constellations' tinted velocity
Yellow permanent or terra cotta plastic recall others conceived
Longer and longer the tunnel to the healing station
Unseen love and green so dark it almost chokes the chest
Heal all thy selves every light for I was leading the candles too

The Raggedy Shiny Black Place

the raggedy shiny black place a voice says go in
shiny woven irregularly edged puckered
unwelcoming attractive unwelcoming black do
you remember how you arrived at the festival
there may have been an earlier paradise be-
fore we thought like this even we dead alive
fly buzzing bothersome turns into story
drunk man then mean woman finds him puke-sick
drunk in relationship to avenge themselves on us
for abolishing sadness from prior arrangements
we were watching they got ready to kill us
we're not going to remember what to recall is
how we hold this new one together let go of the
but I don't know when time is when is time
this new one therefore they can't kill us

I AM THE MEMBRANE BETWEEN
THE DEAD AND LIVING
I AM THE CROSSROADS

Tell me what you want there to be

I want my hands to be clean kid says
even if I'm dead   if I come to you with dirty hands
they might always be dirty   We don't have them
in this   time   layered   In dif-
ferent times at once   I didn't have different
ones   I had a cat one cat

Promise me corners   You want a corner to be in
I want to back away

They aren't eyes   So what can we as if visual do
If I name what you used to see   the way you'd
see in your mind because memory im-
plants the real thing inside you   How   It
merges with it   Where does it come from
The lady in the lake

And I promised him a ventilator   He could just stab
grace   I like that word grace you said

I have no language   You said that

They put us there in that jail   some are here
they raped our children   I don't have to
remember   the child says   Memory's a word
It's a demon   It's in your pocket

I remember deep space with candles

The rain is a memory   Turquoise is for you and itself
I don't see you when I don't want to now   I might peek

These forces that they are   that they used to be
violence thought out first   then vicious done
Did they use me to be mean   yes I did that
it all seems like things   but I can't blink
I can't blink here   You don't have eyes   I still can't

Equal

Equal   we are all equal   in a miraculous   language
I have called you here to continue to   convince you
And I was the water   and I was the land   voices say
And I was objective and   sacrificed
I vibrate messages outward   in complex tonal sequences
How small I was you say the same size as you
I floated like scum on an ocean   how did I have qualities
When why did we split up   why did we focus in   upon ourselves
Did we and darkness and suns   why did we qualify ourselves
There are relatively few mammals in   this universe
Do you know that   But innumerable souls   or
This one vast one   I have led you into our vast room
What world of death do you want   Not this fragment   I
Haven't allowed   myself   a big enough   form   or space

Do You Really Want Me To Change Him

Do you really want me to change him   Yes he needs to
Change   If he reads you and not the novels   He's dreaming
There's a girl in profile against the black room   In red
What are you telling him   That you are our leader and
There is no story   I tell him all night to read yours   and change
Because you were fiercer for the words and he could be too
Everyone wanting to exist in time like a tick   your blood
There's no blood   until you're an animal   dress of blood
Why did you get up   To see where I was   where you aren't
I can't ask   Tell him   I'll help him save books be-
Cause   the storytellers won't in their vests of checks
Are not inside tragic fate   as I was   the eras of rock were
Those who fleeing   were cut or starved   and the burning
All the forests along the border   But then there is   Yes no border
You're dead and in shock   though I'm making that better by
Helping anyone to find its soul   will not be overpowered
As mine leading you is invincible   Tell him   that my words in your
Book our book   that they are his   Can he have them
I see minds coming to meet me for their healing
And I'll make you better for all your history   your tim-
Idity forlornness disappearing   so come into my mind
Enter here awhile   there are parts I still don't know there's space
Let them all in   Are you letting him in   Yes he should come in

Fragmenta

There it large night burns I remember always projected
Let me heal how there is nowhere else and memory's different
It's locating you where we stand that's I'm your core an in-
Stant your soul an instant take mine calmly and you I'll be
Empty singer because mine's over its worst I'm better it says
Where's mine gone I see her in someone's dream the rest of us
Summit of moonstone or ice we on it surround a black voice
Gigantic or somewhat small or not of a size at all
There is no size I say I characterize myself as a mys-
Tery to me and who surveys the mystery I do obviously
I'm fissured striated worn and shiny in the ebony hues
None of them were what they were the people's bodies
Showed where they were it isn't a body it so change-
Ably unstably unnameable
                              Am I looking for the rest of my substance
Fragmenta we're attracted and there would be one in agony
But I'm the black door to myself have come here in curious love
We are all the thoughts that any of us might have now hovering here

We will have texture the only time will be texture
Lately saw a lovely small lumped up hill of cement on the
Floor beige or pale or something's pocked
Gratuitous air holes like word fuss old darkmouth a door

Souls of children between life and death of ebola
Came to my bed last night to rest waiting
As if peopleless   When I got up most of the children's
Souls had left

The texture of this new not time from behind the Xs
We explain our matter it isn't material
Behind each X the counterpart   a ceremony of reconciliation
Between the speech of the dead   and that of the live
I keep seeing it feeling it but it won't stay
A forthright brilliant instant vanishing because it
Can't be corrupted   spoken once or thought to one
And remembered in the memory that holds us here

In bathtub with hammerhead shark
I begin to scratch its head whenever it
attacks me and it wants that: *how hands
are invented* floats by on a placard.
  In a house with Jim Carroll and Ted
There are both fish and fish-like turds
swimming in watery air. We're in
kitchen. Jim says he doesn't like the
more brightly colored fish. Can I wash my
feet? he asks. Yes I say.

What are you trying to tell me?   But I get it.
This is ours   Because we're one thing   we try to be
Together   Because we're the same   thing and if you're
Not a fish or a rock and if you prefer feet   Or if we what-
Ever   What goes here in death is whatever

I didn't find   searching don't find   quickly looking for
Down around me   against grey wall   Trying to explain this
Language   It shoots out fast   Making a world   Of what textures
And so place it how   Place what there   some colors

———————————————————————————

And he came to see me last night   I realized he was dy-
Ing   the Dallas man (Thomas)

———————————————————————————

Join us a fraction of an instant   to place on void   the green rush
Texture   Framed by death   If a guy's mind's murky
It won't be later   Paste your old hat   on the cosmic col-
Lage   It had held my head together   Yes whatever and the mats
To stand on in space   Which isn't there

I heard one   with checkers   What do you mean   Clack
On the board that   sound and texture clack   Talking too fast
The rug's dull   A shower   of black sequins down   a waterfall of
What we don't know   Poor the Lesser   Poor the madwoman

Or making   Hold it   We're going to make   optimo
Rocks optimo   geo-   logical mind too do you know   And musical sliding

When words   came apart   And then in your   mind they
Spread out   or rain down   Do they   have identity
It's the decomposition of   Antigone   Or any other
And the word *instance*   dissolved   and reentered   primacy

And now not dis-   tinctive   can we talk
The sounds   husky and sullen   or tense   Then who
Who describes then   A leader walks ahead
I am pulling   apart from   this first mass   to lead

I would not suf-   focate   in the tomb of   our oneness
And I   it must have been I   pulled away
Have the let-   ters come back to-   gether   Somewhat
But I know who they are   and know who you are

They fall down the   integral   page   Held
As I am al-   ways somewhere   being part   of
What is   What do you see   Drifters   dust devils
A drifting abyss   the start   Only the dead create

————————————————————————

That one me said something to another me
grouchily   I was divided

————————————————————————

Only we dead can create   And out of the shattered
Letters   And out of the first finally   we see what we want
We who were al-   ways here   shap-   ing it   As the letters
Of the words   the letters   rain down and swirl

All of us   We are throughout it each   equal-sized souls

———————————————————————————

In the park keeps being a glitch in time
Some small event happens wrongly, or
Something's not here this *time*. Sup-
Posed to be here—should or shouldn't
Be happening, the spirit of daily life
Says, but I don't care   if the surface
Of time gets all puckered   Let it now

———————————————————————————

And so to make   a no time   The col-
Laged time of   superimposed   thought   in the park
The crumpled   brown bag   was or wasn't there   either one

Came to be   out of shifting   meters

I Want You To See

I want you to see   what you are   the heavens   in a new form
Think of no space as when you   think and everything's there
In your thought   in the order or simul-   taneity things come
So there were no edges   was no outer   except as exotic reaches

The voice said and   Ed took off his shirt   to reveal   his   soul
It joyously was the same   shirt   floral   print   so
See it   as it swirls   as he turns to take it off   or reveal it
Blue   with small florettes pale   outside of town

I like to take a ride outside of town   one says   and
Since I had done it once   I had always done it in

Some way   no complete description   joyously
Faster in ours   take me down   Take my down showering
Letters   sequins   blades of made grass   metallic   lakes of
Blades   of flash you say   A reflection on a wide   silver bracelet

(Ed Dorn was wearing his shirt under his shirt)

Twice Imprisoned

twice imprisoned have recertified kept fore'er pro-
bable linguistic demarcation where you are my shell

       sequin
  sequin

shower of green the rushing storms time's all bunched up
a tweaked fabric see   push the phrases   well   hu-
morless one   quietly inside me all night a pos-
sibly embroiling un-   catalogued   notes on
a brain produces notes on   a mind   makes poems
constantly   I favored you I forget who dead
and the winds cover us in transparence   I re-
member   that the new universe
        that the new universe

He had a gun but everyone did
Because he had   a gun he thought origin had one
After he died and was thinking around anywhere
Soul of a volcano   ask it if it explodes erupts whatever
It *was* my version now I'm   the same size as a rabbit
What language a form of Later from near Antares
It floated   it floated in space   like a plasmic unit like
A song floats after   being sung   and came   here and there no
Way   I see it and there were spores   clung to you Numa Pompilius

Why Can I Only Imagine

Why can I only imagine   a prior world   Break everything
Imagine   Break it   And wear dark mouths   dark minds
Not a mammal   There was a mind I   Knowing
Falls to the side   All but   the gentlest of pyrotechnics
And This ad-   vances   And This sways   And This shapeless
Or is it motile   The shape of a motion   in place
Or is it the motion   of mind   I saw   myself come down
From the hillish parts   to town   I saw myself

As a self   a limpid mind motion   I saw it with the
Mind I was seeing   First division   There's a tangle
Of mental extensions   Let's not be   animals again
Or geophysical   formations   How are we   able to

Talk   I'm myself   I tell in myself it   to move
Or just   I am implicated   in the air-swish
What's air   And I float   Can't speak   And I'm speak-
Ing because it tells itself   that it is   But didn't start

Michael's Poem

I love Ferguson for its dream to communicate
It has together its starry wind starring wind
You are mine eternal I like these words
I Michael 19 and forever at the same time
I don't want you to fight because you don't have to
Alice care for me rockets of decent space nearby

No one's too big here dead
And the ones I miss be here soon

I find out how to love and how I loved it was hidden
Sparrows everywhere silver bits I was well brought up
I told the cop he wasn't big enough and I meant it
My Mom needs space and I myself having so much
Bequeath it to her ringed around her rings of space
In the roundness of a new time like mine
Everybody be peaceful it's your nature

YOU'RE SICK AT THE FILLING STATION

I want the new universe to have no homes but be a home
I want to step out on the air of home edge of home abyss
The dead don't cry but I feel my curling down tear ghost white
It may be the last tear so save it a thought to glue down
We want you not to be sick again don't be sick the dead aren't
Watch where you're going or stand where we have no location
I want it to be so clear that our souls are the same size we don't look
        up or down
What's overhead where you are the abyss more of same white the deep
Remember white the edge of the deep it's a memory
Remember us into cohering what do we want to be
All us souls stuck together small parts and large the whole thing
I am your friend the fire's ghost says can't burn you any more
What are you for then souls of every fire they were like songs alive
Is that what I was am I a logical fallacy I am existing
And fire made all the fires or became it their souls are here
Are they yes warmths you could list them all and I was there
Am here everything is there's no space it's friendly and dense
Not dense really and my own soul presses you with colors
The new universe will have colors of spectral ends where you couldn't see
So it was so red you couldn't see it is it a quality or a soul
This is only naming but the talking is becoming cells broken wavelets an ocean

We are connected through the vowels in all our names
We are an effluvium of vowel-connected words a skein of names
The vowel in your name to that in mine is that what you want
The net of names of everything floats sparkling on the abyss
At rue des Messageries I lost my carte d'identité do I want it back
Heart of vowels and eleventh-hour heart medications do you hear
It was roselike the rose's soul whether you conceive it small or large
Your rendezvous with Dr. Chibrard is at her mother's house in the 11th
The only remaining illness would be a dream of it or body
We had bodies of creatures of fire of metamorphic rocks of rain
We had them and now we have their images how do we think how do you think
I am the choir thinking or I was an appointment only that

I now remember every type of thing as if the whole effluvium
As if the whole of depth's delicious soundings uncraved and bare
I went to the rendezvous carrying the rose I had the disease of revelation
Every moment or vowel split open in a cry of its reality
Every moment burst now pasted on the deep so it can glow
Does it have a soul it contains them I went there or here it says
I came unto the city of the fallen an appointment
And you were appointed doctor of the night and eleventh hour
We leave it and come back to it or them as souls suffered did they
Do you remember which of your memories do you want now they can be endless
Moments can be endless the story's not stable Aldebaran's not heard of
Story not heard of heard of you who are one of my Als adrift in death calmly
Looped into a crocheted shawl or blanketing enormity of names
We're connected by a new memory web a sticky relation

Who will mind the drunk woman's child did she herself want to be mine
My child the tall drunk blonde this does or doesn't belong
And he left me again for death or even in death these songs say
If you have a thought it might float here forever but it doesn't have to be
        a thing
I want the matter of us to be known as timeless and free
Calling it to order concentrating on a just or fine creation
I never told anybody how I was at my exact innermost point
And that I am now it has gold torn edges where it hurts from shining
I am being it or observing it I am tending to it
As if it were I but I am I pasting it repeatedly along the folds of the abyss
The abyss is chaos and itself and myself are we pasting our images all over
        it again
Yes but we can be different a different language or structural lace
I was and am lace if you look at me right or cloud of same cloth
I step out ahead and say I can't be with you though I am with you
This is what happens again but differently for the fabric allows it
It gives itself to stretching without wounding breaks without pain
Clouds blow to pieces without getting hurt after all
Are we going to be clouds or cloudlike I want to paste on a lake
I want to be electricity I want to be a new electricity
All of the thought like that without pain seeking gold
That has no quality but goldenness a girl that isn't girlish

A rock that isn't so cold to itself it doesn't play
All of our structure will play we won't have a sou but soul
Paste on what you think or energy inserted from nowhere
From nowhere to nothing no it's something isn't anything something

I know all the language I'll ever need's inside me
That I am literally a speaking and that I speak myself
You turn this way and that and say the forms of the abyss or new us
Are we pasting it all on or being it what's the difference
N is for springtime and L is for combing your hair
But that is only this time I want Various written in my eyes
I'd want you to see my face as all that can be held here
In an intersection with yours and all others an accordian
I will meet you at the top of the stairs that spell acuity
I will meet your body spelling the nations of anywhere
I will meet your words your words from faint teeth spelling apostate
The nations and states of life after death spelling oracular vistas
Oracles and earrings of words toppling the master fake
We didn't need to be freed only needed to free ourselves
We shouldn't have believed the language as marks of separation
The marks are all ours made by us in dazzling origination
We were sifting out and stood there we sifted ourselves out to stand uncrowded
The crowd is uncrowded souls of the blossoming letters
I have never been apart from my language or my thought or my soul
When it's mute it's just quiet and I spell quiet with my long ghosted limbs
I spell limbs showing you colors and the sound of a throat
Or a lute I'm not dancing standing here a lack of enforcement
No one makes you speak or sing or appear even appear
I will not appear in this instance in the dead's thinking arena
Where cavorting of torches as burning thoughts as lumped flame letters
        takes place
Someone says go home but I'm home everywhere pasting home on
Pasting home on the abyss to hold with no arms but words
Within myself I hold the home of where I've gone or am going
The form of a sphere if you like but there is no 'this planet'
All the past imagined as histories and maps and customs
Count on nothing these are the words of a primal stir

Do we now feel that we're creating the cosmos and are it
There's no sword bridge over the abyss when one's the abyss traversed
And as I venture once or ever into the abyss I paste over it
Paste it on itself in its continuously various beauty is it dangerous
There is no danger in death but danger might be a seductive word
And in danger I was as a body and I hold it close as a word
As if it were a painting or an arete of an actual mountain
Are we not actual here speaking surrounded by collage
Memory glue are you of us do you love us I'm not apart it says
I want to glue on a new shape the inhuman ghost of a fetus
I wasn't human yet when I died it says I was pure
I was essence and the multiplication of my jewels belies all but
          communication
I want to glue down the glints of my thoughts it says as they're stroked
I'm gluing on a tinted square barely green with a central black dot
I want to glue on the letters like sadtracks or disrue
I don't want ever to have to do or think anything glue that down
We are the sands of a planet somewhere their spirits glue us or love us
Is there a difference between the gluer and the glued
There is a pang or pitch in sadness as a black stab I'd like to preserve
I want to glue on a new shape from chaos a shaded messed-up throttle
The word or image either I want it disedged and enlightened
I will reside beneath it all within the abyss's slipperiness
Within the bits of its cogency dispersed dashes and mad florettes
In the middle of a microdot a giant stands not having smashed it

What was once how I was I want to be some of it's a language
I'm combining units to convey to you the art of living here dead
When we paste them on the kaleidoscope flashes red glass breaks wavelike
Our components are no longer hidden I flex them and slither
I'm speaking a saffron length called ray or a word show
I'm not at one with anything just gluing emeraldine flower shapes
I am the memory of every universal fact to expand as a hue
I am the memory of when I was another and am of myself memorial
I am the memory of my escarpment overhung form or mesa
I am the memory of speaking now speaking in xylaphonic taps
I am the memory of the chorus left alone to prosper
I am the memory of an atonal aria once or a bear's grunt

All pasted on in the form of a new language segments recoupled
When the cars of the train touched starting into expansion
I am the memory of being dirt of being timeless and across the bridge
The train crosses the river I remember how to sing like a comet
Quickly in an arc traumatizing any guidance
I am remembering how to exist or be dead or both

I am the memory of finding you I am the memory of origin
The origin is to remember itself we glue that memory on the abyss
And it tells us it is the memory of becoming itself over and over
Do I remember erasing all other accounts of how to be
I have pasted you on though you float as I float on the deep
I am conscious of floating on the deep and being the deep
You are lucky for knowing all us and all of every entity's art
The mountain's art the comet's as you can see and the nebula's
I am the nebula's art cast a mist across the strains of the abyss's song pasted
I want somebody to see me song of my extension scattering and core
The core of me nebula is like a thought of yours but entreatyless
I am the memory of subtlety a violet selection of the spectrum
We want to paste on a spectrum non-finite and rippling
I am the memory of when I came here and of leading
I am remembering how to speak and sing speaking and singing
I am remembering how time was coiled back into its cell
I am the memory of the idea of ice colorless and glued
See the glue but not the ice see wind and sound almost white
See the glue or paste so clear and our own ghostly reputations
As in the fame of dirt and were ground into it become it we sing
I am the memory of my disease one says what shape is a memory now
Everything looks as if I said it and saw it later
I am remembering your own song your form or containment
I am remembering that the soul is more vivid than the body
That unveiled or free it is all memory the force of gravity connective love
Do you know not-sensation being colors as Saturn is
I want non-sensation glued onto the shifting floating collage
We remember we had no sensations I had one thought the thought of my form
This net of language Xs is enough I am coverage diamantine
The abyss says the collage is construed to be throughout it floating
The abyss says my leader your name is Abyss

We know it wasn't sensation until we called it sensation

Are we pasting the word I remember your kind someone says to another

We are pasting on forms for ourselves but we are ourselves

I found my thought in the old dime store someone whispers

I am the memory we are the memory of non-visual or non-auditory existence

I am the memory of all the ages of my body

I am the memory of endings as I have known them when I called them endings

I am the memory of slanted or crisscrossed lines or texture of lineation

I am the memory of stratification of layers of thoughtfulness or amassing

I am the memory pasted on of hardness and color combinatory red

I am glued on the memory I am the memory of gluing down remembrance

I am the memory of a wall made by others or having made itself organically

I remember any word you can think of any word is a memory

The cosmos held together by memory the nothing the not-memory that is not held
        together

I am not held together I am gluing on the held together for amusement and
        experience

I don't want to glue you on and yet I want to see and hear you

I remember shores I remember I'm standing on a shore

I remember alongness we many stand along the abyss

We have been led by you to perfect communication

We have been led to the shore it's any shore the edge of pleasure

Pleasure is no word for it you have led us to and then we must pause

We remember where we are and have always remembered it

I remember peace at leading you I remember a simple lead

We are being formed having formed ourselves we have pasted on no structure

And I have glued this instant on the abyss I have led it and glued it

And I will do so again oh just a little ahead

Martin

I just want to anyone next to you gray
Next to you last night or this morning after I died
It's frightening then not you my crossover point
You led me to where you slept just ahead of me a green light
I think green or moving though you slept
You want better language it's going to come forth
And then I lay next to you Alice having died
You have no character you reach out to us
This is to specify a non-racial arrival last night
I am reading you how to say no upheaval no place
But you   'I'm in an airplane now'   Anyone follows you
We want new thing natural prosperous structure
'Prospero's' keeps coming up   Can I stay with you awhile
'I guess that's what I'm for until you've adjusted'

Thomas

Many of us have entered this plane with your or to you
I keep coming to you because my own are grieving for me
They're acting and they're like actors but I'm no longer like that
Are you   'Sometimes but I keep trying to take you with me'
You're going to Paris we go to you that's funny
And the babies are different they seem to float off quickly
They don't talk I think they're here they're very free
They died and then floated like free lights the older kids
Are near you needing more of language like me

'You must stay press alongside the words which are drawings
See and you have the names for them already'
Can you explain it better   'They're coming alive
Or you are   from getting to know the words of being here
The babies too   it's this word teach them to talk

I'm tangled and alongside loops and vowels each soul touching
We're essential in that we're all of it touching
Touch it says   the first word so you can know you're you
It's a drawing   T O U C H   is the first'

Who Had Ebola

Proximate or intimate bitten by a grueling pain
Later   As if I had the teeth marks   To leave by
You move along Xed a process by crossing
To be pulled gently by you Alice what was true
The gray wind pain around my organs I
Turn gray   'I see you Thomas'   Bring me no name
Not yet   And so we meet in the pasty air
'I'm helping paste it down not air but word'
It was word that called me to its changeable
Formation or lineation   don't even say those
The blood I lost wasn't precisely mine
I'm coming across to you and I left my sweat
And the liquids of my unreal blood
This isn't a story   I'm something better than that   I know

WE THE DEAD I MEAN I WITH THE DEAD

We the dead I mean I with the dead who have led them this far

Are standing on a universal escarpment a white ledge ice or mist around the all abyss.
     This is happening as I also appear to lead a mundane or mondial life in Paris. But I am your leader, always ahead, have led you here but always ahead. We are choosing the details of the new cosmos we the dead including me the not-quite-dead, in the sense that we are resaying us. But we are the dead the dead make up much or most of what this is, as much of the universe is undetected scientists agree. But they do not know what we the dead know, that all our carefully measured physical structures our sense of scale our presumptions signaled by time and space collapse in timeless and spaceless death. Where we just are.

If I can help you restart and recall us as we were or are though we are dead but I don't mean as alive I mean as we the dead will be for we are more alive than thee. We are your longer-lastingness
                    And the dead have often called out to me. I am telling the truth this is not just literary. We as the most prevalent and the most knowing having gone beyond you stand here at this abyss of what there is remaking it and you and revealing it and you essential. Sizeless. Unviolent. Death inflicted is no weapon if you don't die and we didn't. You will continue to kill each other on your pitiful ground but you will not die or be extinguished. You are making yourselves up though materially I don't understand how we do this create delusion and pretense on one tiny locality and casting this story all across the night sky as if it ruled it too.
     I was called upon by the dead to lead them to oh memory reseen for they are or were sad and haunted by their prior lives. I am leading them from sadness to revelation and re-creation. We are and have made everything there is if by we I include what we understand to be the forms of other planets and orbs nebulas quasars suns etc with their geologies rockinesses fierinesses and etc the we. We are cast as dead or living all here one and many I am leading you to freedom I say.
     For everything says things vibrating held cohesive by what. Is it gravity or memory a remembering how to hold together. Words exist for everything what are they. Is there throughout an articulating mind I am yes I think so but don't know consciously its basic language there are no pieces in mind. So I must look for an unpiecemeal idiom you can't take apart or separate from anything else. Have we no taxonomy? We are changing you at this moment we the dead and you are with us as you will. The unconscious living.

I repeat this is not a fiction you are undergoing change and certainly need it as you know.

We are standing above the white-rimmed abyss or chaos recollaging upon it what we choose. Being dead we cannot force each other's choices having no hold or threat. We are thoughts perhaps and our choices are thoughts perhaps and chaos or abyss which is perforce us that being all there is admits what we say we give it in the form of forms and pieces but there are no pieces. It eats them with its or our mind but we we are probably making a thing of beauty in a no-time or no-space but a oneness of plasticity mental of course. We are *choosing* us. Though I alive am merely leading a few feet ahead as I have always been in my life.

Most of what you would choose you don't have to choose having realized you are dead and empowered only by what we are which is what is and that is real not a conception of nothing. I am trying to let others speak most as I tend to choose words or colors or tones or interesting adjacencies. But, for example, you don't have to choose hope. Or any special kind of love, which seems to be the same as gravity memory mind communication. Yes we are forms but what are they as I even now continue to be myself a dead person says. And the universe itself us says I have to get better.

This is a long thought or speaking in one language but underneath it maybe everything understands it.

We are making us. We are making you. You will not continue the same.

All time is available to us in no time circularly so we can't start clean but have the future to choose from or everything that's why sadness or tragedy or personal evil lingered and I led us from that but then there is the beauty of an image. Or edges or portions of it or something unforgettable so you might paste that on too along with whatever you say in your mind making. We are making our beauty we the dead are changing the world of you the living this is more real than your doings of wars environmental manipulations and assertions of power among yourselves. We see that the origin of materiality as an explosion in vastness a terrifying vastness to you was no vaster than my or a fly's soul.

We have abolished scale for we are all equally sized in no space and no time there is no scale here so what can we paste on the abyss that we understand in sizelessness? I saw it one says and can only do so in contrasting qualities such as height mass even color extends across or up and then stops. There is I say the memory of qualities alive in mind and you will paste a memory upon with your mind and there will be no size of a thing for the thing will waiver like a dream change as in a dream be as it needs to be in meaning which now faces you as words do said in dreams coming from nowhere. But everything comes from you are you not more fortunate than you ever thought more real and full of original power to make beautiful our death in existence?

I am pasting on lightbursts and ancient earthly architecture oh but that was made to scale but it only has the scale of my mind. And I pasted it on in our mind it has no height relative to anything but within itself maybe but that changes as I think upon the lovely building up close to the bonnets of its roof.

Inside the dune on Venus it is textured grainy sanded does not does not. Does not seeketh not what were your rules and how do I find you conglomerate in death or any even earthly mountainous conglomerate for we are all a mind? My language is . . . collaged and recollaged upon our heart abyss or oneness but without the petite and local notions of a force to destroy or kill. That as merely linguistic as I change you into the dancer you always were the singer and poet. It is a collage for there is glue or force of soul and there are drifting surfaces of mine eyes. They are the words of and they are the chosen of our us the one. Come to this reality now don't linger where fragmentary personal projections tell you to buy and work and want. The great collage of rose light and storm love the gentle crumpling of blue sky paper contemplating the sentence structure of eroded landmass glides beneath my view. Your trauma light that is it is now a quality of light though there is no light but thought.

Your thought has changed. Hasn't your thought changed?

Beams

Beams for building   Abyss is one   its denizens   constituent shreds
Its fish   These are my fish from the play-   ful depths
These phrases maybe   And so there were in-   finite metaphors
Superimposed   instead of one   Babies   Standing for what

Paste on everything I   say someone says   Even if it's wicked
It's just some more me   What about this form I   say
It's particles it's   part-thoughts   fishes I mean   planets or
Meteoric   populous sounds un-   til another tongue

Studying the   instructions   But   we already started
It's not in order   No order or   plan to   paste or glue
I'm leading you to   And the torn   the torn indifferent edges
And the choices   winged glued on   a metaphor too and you

And the beams   stretched across   and the in-   structions
Glue on a shaft of   light with fish   in and out   or meteors

Stigmatized

I walk into   I see it the living   room it will be   with beams
Or it is   the universe   gigantic   you work on it   in it
These words tell you to   with wooden beams   I'm bleeding
From my forehead   hands and feet   Stigmatized   From my chest

Shallowly   I'm being sentenced   Or am I leaking self
It's me not you   in the sacral room   under the floor of it
Not leading   in this instance   but bleeding   They are committed
To me I see   See them as   geometric shapes   triangle head or cir-

Cle because I   don't know to see you yet   Will all this
Be glued onto   all living   lost causes   like   lost wellsprings
Be glued onto   I wanted to see   my interior   my fatedness
Did I   A crown of phrases   I don't need one   You have phrases

Composed of   whatever we are   the one says   bows his triangle head
Sweetly   Anything   might happen or be   coming near   come clear

Lotus

Vision of lotus   imaginary   how explain its   ecstasy of petals
That there were so many   as phrases of   an infinite poem   Didn't think that then
But that as many as   there were   each was more of us   or it as pleasure
An infinite surface   I felt it   not in selfhood   but in   recognition

As many of our souls   as there are   Splendor   No one in charge of it
And on each you sat   or I sat   on each there was   a soul
This seen   beneath my eyelids   without colors or   much designation
Not dreamed but known   The abyss is thus   this is it

And can wear anything   for eyes say and   can wear anything

And so I see   and so I am   each phrase of us   seraphic
Let them make their way   Paste on manifold   phrases or   paper stand-in
Is it a stand-in   I had said Collage   so casually   in the beginning
Everything I do   preordained   though I am leading you   preordained by who

All of us and the lotus   the color of thoughts   I mean sentient   collage

WHAT IS THE FORM? LOVE IS THE FORM

One says flee the beginning it's too frightening
You don't know what you look like or whose thoughts you're thinking
I'm convinced I've come from nowhere an inhuman soul
One says look at me and what shall I look with
The voices in my head translated into plain or alien phrases
That I see and feel with I don't know what you're saying
Mobbing it's called and the wind when the phrases run wild
I draw them on the page I inscribe you at the beginning
I can't seem to remember what I'm doing here or where I was
I may be in a state of insane premonition because I'm leading
I'm leading you or saving you having pre-seen the moment
When you might be violent I smiled and instead you smiled back
The dead aren't violent whom I am with who go with me
Skilled at being dead they continue to invent the diction of the dead
The collage of the new death made of the known but now different
Though I can't remember where I've been where I'm going
I'll try to change every moment I'm in if I must
I will change your sense of the beautiful and elegant I insist
Calling back steps ahead that what now comes is not future
But a collage of pressed colored winds the vocalese we are
I've told you I'm changing it advancing into enlightenment changing
How you were once a universe and now you are what what's a soul
What's anything this language will resist us is it even ours or us

And must turn to face you suddenly I know I must turn and say
In this place of our room of all on the escarpment of ice and lights
It has also been given to me to be your I-know-no-other-term Savior
I don't know what it means but I face you I couldn't turn round before
Though I knew it would come to this as if harsh light on a desert tree
As if I would leave my home forever or my former interior
As if you would mock me sweetheart with your deadwood eyes
As if the solar winds parched my face and my mind though I bled
From my forehead and the wound between thumb and forefinger
Didn't I previously deal with our sorrow isn't this an ancient film
Shone over the new creation who are you you say but do I know

Yes this is what I do there was nothing left for it you have found me
What does it mean whatever happens you aren't sad because of this
Remember there is one alive carries it with her the web of misfortune
The desiccating veil it's just a trick of your own eye perhaps
I've signed up for everything now I turn and paste it on stumbling
Stand upright with the glue of it slightly pink affix it
Wearing my remarkable crown that's transformed repeatedly thorns
To ribbon to slender coronet I never wanted try to end it can't
In Paris or St. Mark's and First or on the star Alphard
I am nothing but invisible essence my first kiss

I was only what we are then I became less didn't I
From spirit become flesh then degraded into suffering
I abased and strange here I who identify with no one
Have no verb now but lead paste or save save everyone
What is save then of the others who love each other corporeally
The blessing must be death no there should be another one
For in this earth life I pass through I'm transported mid-moment
Any moment to death's grace or saved thus you are too
How embarrassed you must be you say to speak like this
It's when I'm embarrassed that I know I've arrived
Where I lead you what our paste is and what we paste on are one
But now that's the dead pasting no the live too how muscular I sound
The tripartite leading of those who can follow the snowed-down upon
The rained on the perpetually discovered by other substance
Love falls on you wherever you are if you can perceive it
I stand where the language envelops me true I bleed for it
Yes I give up to you the fact that I've bled for it and so for you anyone
Animals suffer among a universe of apparent unsimilars
Perhaps we are sacrificial sacramental purposed
And if there was first chaos it accepts us as its most abused children
But you are everything the soul you were at first and are ever
I remember before I was an animal I remember before blood

There is only one paste one convergence one connection of us
The fearful began where we were I am remembering the blue-green
The blue-green-black or pale-blue-white was it the glyph's core
When was I first your savior you had died the sky not colored in

Was divided into paint-by-numbers pieces near the old shortcut
Where we were first tortured that's not a true word now which now
I have brought purest clearest essence or soul to my suffering
I mean yours divided into scourges oh when was that done
I was getting ready for war and before that left you your blame
I mean you left me with it I've forgotten how to remember
Because of the savior I am I can lose everything I was again
Come up with me to the cross or crossroads or connection
You have stretched my memory until my guilt's edges frayed hum
I hear it it was the first thing I heard when I was young
And we drove over to it wherever that was calling Last Stars
In the first language for the whole universe hath suffered as a wilde Deare
And my soul then broke into me and cried out good morrow I am thee
So you will know how to save all others remembering completely
So abject you could heal ones of being gruesome firelike suns in their dreary orbits
And the atmosphere but the air of a morbid old mind be healed of its gloom
All across roads was memory thankfully accepted of is it how to become
That would require but we have left requirements along this bloody old trail

I am yours who led you past requirement to true perception
Having suffered alone until I became my soul I have shown you what a soul is
I have shone on yours until your eyes being blinded could see
I'd stood between the worlds life and death so many times I could have no lover
Other who keeps one mammalian steady I'm unstable as a vocal cord or tone
Hum for you almost cries of hum the word red at the crossroads of but you know what of
What a bizarre word did it come intact what are these that move and sound
Am I saving them I am saving you from your war-haunt your panic
Which in death would become a simple moan I'm now saving them from
Did mammals invent the fear I save you from de-invent it
Paste it with a bit of fur next to the words Sweet Recollection of Infancy
I am saving you from guilt for I have bled it so much you don't have to
I did this out of our mutual distress though I really only wanted to be alone
And now I'm the soul red-tinged transparency I've lost my inheritance
Just humming call until you get here so I can bless you the new universe
Of criminals soldiers fallen meteors viruses their souls everything ever a remembered
        existence

If I could find oh am finding how the mind of us and did it just
Make appear once more the specious item matter all at once and forever differently
The simultaneous mold of eons pressed into a flattened round of evolution like an
        ammonite paste it on
As the one moment keeps happening one is changing from within
I am changing it saving you paste that on with what my new eyes see
That we are at this instant splitting off amoebal into cells decorated soul matter the art
And I saw it and made it until it would devour me and I fought it
But it was you and thus I fought you oxblood and indigo arms and emotion
Becoming what was now us whose first nature I now suffer to reclaim
Having embedded in my memory the mosaic events with no borders on the timeline
Crowded onto my specifically thought-out self as I'd shriek let me purify us
I can do nothing without you and bleeding out all but the memory of base and beautiful
        existing
I save you like any bodhisattva who couldn't get out of the house I've gotten you out from
        the burning lumber
I'm not a coward and can save you by speaking until you see correctly the winds along
        the escarpment
Soul-blown the thought that your new mentality is seeking and can see that all exists
        within your mind
Crystal red pointsettia red ruby the gloves of fire tamed given back to a gem given back
        to clear thought

Alice's Soul

I entered where I was sent wearing small earrings
don't know if these are the right words from your mind
syntax gold that there was a glyph the universe I'm reading its mind
but I'm reading yours reading mine whenever we are somewhat enmeshed
I entered where I was sent to spy for the system I had come from
I had no form before I was madly born but I was there then who I am
the one you to make make others listen I know I suffered with you
there are red stripes across my unhappy face as you describe your calvaries
and then from as if afar I say or am I she to become you or am I you
so serene again I remember being this soul the spy and savior you are
it hurt you too to be neglected because you know too much so skilled
do skills have merit or does suffering do you now deserve to be me your soul
I don't know if this is time but you have never been a piece of meat
resplendent from ashes grown tall we are ready to name ourselves

Alice's Soul 2

It was because no one cared what is care across the universe
That I chose to care fell into it landed unequivocal care
For anyone as Alice's soul that perhaps needs no name
So since she and I are now consciously one in what language she'd say
And I'd say there's no linguistic thing about us as us
In fact I'm her now and she isn't here transmuted
I am calling to all of the outer universe to see itself rightly
I Alice's soul or I say simply to see what you are changes everything
Can you see how things move across themselves in grace even if factory made
Can you see that whatever you touch or even think of you're part of
For visible connection contiguity all artists prove such communication
And I don't know you but I mostly don't disrupt you now I should
The planet is too hot and violent but more the universe is melancholy
I know this by knowing it as any soul must know everything
I now realize I've imagined nothing that only the soul's visions are true
Clashing with the collective dullard mind mine calls to you to change
And leave your old self in some office or truck like a locust husk
Come here I Alice's soul say to join in remodeling this pliant chaos
The world the universe we knew now a fossil of our former thought we must change

Souls On Métro

No one could stand it the métro was so slow later halted a man started
Strumming a guitar making patter I couldn't hear how could
There be room for a guitar I should be like him tell you things I'm
Shy tried remembering a dream of a language of spontaneous irregular spirals
Did I even see anyone our ridiculous eyes I remember when my vision started to
      blur at age six
I thought I was effecting this change deliberately I still wonder
Why would I have done that pushing mentally at my eyes as they worsened
Maybe they hadn't seen right was I asking them to see more not less
The new sight would be subtly different as you joined with what you saw
My sight blurred more I felt my way more and with glasses then contacts read
      constantly
When I was in my thirties my retina detached I began to see street lamps as crooked
We didn't have any money then I wasn't examined for three weeks
Waiting for the street lamps to straighten up why not
After the surgery in the hospital I gathered my wits to go on seeing
With a worsened left eye I still find street lamps crooked
I don't know what's really out there I'm still working on how to see
I'm tired of having separate senses though or of the idea of senses
I wasn't really looking this morning in the métro adorable Jewish child
Alone glasses and Orthodox hat dark coat bewildered by the train's refusal
Ladies in skirts and weirdly toed stilettos I'm always looking at the feet
Greying men wearing dignity the train wouldn't run for them though we all saw it the same
      way it wasn't working
It's just a train you'd say ephemeral I'd say I'd say souls riding nothing much
In no real clothes blurs on their way to some imagined location anyway

Transcript

There may be a film

     it's on this mind

    there

so I can hide some- thing From yourself

Nothing we did was important in life the activities activists

The Hungarians beat you up you lie contracted they kick your head

We're all here now dead together life lasted a minute he says

I didn't know how different the time would be dead

Michael says he can't explain it I say He can't talk in it yet he says

You talk without time here I'm translating now

Simultaneously You'll have to and being here's

More like your phrases The film's so you'll hide yourself

Hide how sincere a savior I am Of progenitors

Possibly the previous savior is replaced No that's not it

This time no one will grovel The dead still do he says A bit

To each other Here's an ace here's your ace he says

You keep showing the way Take off the film

Just say it he says I follow you too I want to be saved

I've always been this I know they beat me up

So I could marry you and die They changed me

So I could die in comprehension Then you'd find out who you

Were Take off more film he says It's just a film

The movie version is time the activist or atavist

Miser warden cocksure asshole he says

Follow me I say I will make you pasters-on of souls

But there under the film it's body parts then soul

You're right he says Life is pornography

Follow Leave slave and follow me

THIS SPEECH IS A SPIRAL

Where we are I can tell you   in this spiral tell it's you
It's so peaceful in chaos   don't want to change much
Let what's said   appear by itself   like this   flying over the void
Then resting upon   If anyone told me   anything I'd leave but
You want to be told   sitting almost in front   These bleachers
Are olden   I want them in our collage   What about the oversized
Pill I swallowed last night   How do you go about   doing wrong in life
How   being dead do you   get over it   Where is beauty to walk in
To cast on   the void that   just won't swallow you
Don't you want to know me   Who   but no   Though I'm speak-
Ing to you   You go about doing wrong   by doing anything
We know this   No you don't you are   constantly in action
We   are in action if   we invent the universe   again I
Am slowing that down   by talking   The pill I believe
Was to help me better   as a soul   occupy   the identity you see
This speech   is a spiral   handwritten or spoken   galactic
It curves   in black   like a new kind of   formula or score
Chaos's formula for us   Words of us   my flesh   So sit within it
And remember   that you weren't born   have always been
I sometimes think I re-   member being in   my mother's womb
I'm sure I remember   before then   and that that's a future from now
I remember being let out of prison   which one the womb the body
The body's mind   not the same as the mind   Do I really re-
Member such things   If you're shocked enough I'm satisfied
And the dead say   we aren't free enough we're   listening too

Because I called it to me   the apparent self   I would be
At the beginning or   when I was born   Because I
Saw the future   and acquiesced to its outline   without details per-
Haps   Because I saw I would be necessary   to you as this one
Because I saw that   a massive will   as it mattered becoming
What we touch and smell   what we cohere as   would force the future
Oh it was what I couldn't pre-   vent but I   could oppose   with
A more loving mind   Because of that   And to deal with your so-named
Development   evolution   would take in your   time sense so long

It appears that I have waited   But in the real time   this is just
The next instant   and I say No   Now   we'll do this my way
Evolution uni-   versal is an iota   You're listenIng because you've had it
Those bodies those actions   what seemed to be   massive painful
Blows   by selves or the natural   the difficulty of living
In that body you willed   telling the story   of bleak night and its children
Until that was what you saw   You see forms you invented   incised   in an
Air   also named by you   seen and approved   real
We swear we   see ourselves the same   The lie that can be stroked
Scientifically measured   even loved and murdered

You see in a wave or a heartbeat   your ability to measure   I
See adjacencies neighbors   part of the rain or nebular consist-
Ency of   my own mind   I may be born again   tonight
Who have never been   born I said   even then with a lost
Sense of   self like words like   cunning   peaceful   boring
I used to think everyone   I used to think I   resembled everyone
The purpose of my appearance here   contrariwise proves I'm not
Keep trying   Humans say things   like You were depressed
And There's a rumble tonight   I hardly talk now except on the page
But I know I can save you   I see how it's come round again
We are standing   on the escarpment and   nowhere else
Beneath stars more brilliant than   any you've imagined
And then I finally speak   Have you seen this   these
Had you seen that there is no size   that street life flowed river-like
That the velocity of footsteps changes   as you concentrate on gait
That colors brighten or dull as you stare   that there are no outlines
And we'd said everything was fixed   Yes in the sense we'd
Fixed it with City Hall   I went down into the void for you
I suffered for you I now know not myself   The story changed
The phrases changed   I fell to the floor   in depression and fear   did I
Because all shifted   the floor   the ability   of my body to have posture
In front of you   Who would always say   the universe outside me
Was there   and as everyone saw it   It is not   We are on this white
Escarpment   and I say unto you   Do nothing   Allow the collapse
Of all you're told to hold standing   Let others kill you if they
Must but   Let's remake the real   And in this country
Where I stand   are we able   to crush inculcation   and begin

Again with the first words   absolute   absolute spray
And the white and dark wings counter with   I'm examining matter
It's the same as my thinking   and has the movement of a song

Can you see me I'm different   I'm an appearance seeping through
That I'm what I'm saying   the mist of thought   makes my face more intangible
It's the new memory showing itself   of how I a soul   am
But do you need a memory to cohere   do you need something to remember
As if you look at a screen or monitor   What was the first one   And I remember
Watching you put on your form   cells then minnow then baby
I remember seeing your eyes grow though   I could already see
I only have photographic memory   it has to remember a *thing*
I remember watching you all of you   know what to do   as if you'd
Lived before   I was just a soul   but the stars recognized me
Everyone everything grew   while I waited   and continued to remember
If you would only see   that the house is on fire   I remember
Nothing further for the nonce   spiraling fast Antonio   love of proper names
I don't remember the word loser   and I love you I'm bleeding too
The factories are on the East Coast   and in the Midwest   I resolved
When I was first a bacterium   never to work in one I
Would only be a soul   You've grown so old the dream says but
You're a soul   don't you have experiences back home
We are counting on you all the dead   voices say just a few more drops of blood
Red rain on the thorny wreath   because I kept calling   suffering to me
As if I were doing that for everyone   so you would know the crown of thorns a spiral
And that all your interconnections   all your races and rock and water
Are as twisted as a soul is throughout oneself   You are all the same thing
You are all the same race   You are all the   same memory
You remember   one drop of liquid then another on gray   You remember
You were smarter than your body   You remember there was a room
You had to enter   You remember compulsion though secretly you
Didn't feel compelled   You remember that there was love and I would love you
You would feel loveless then I would love you   whoever I am

I enter a room because I must   with bloody beads on my forehead
I have a compulsion to climb down from our summit   on a rickety ladder
And enter an earthen room   I have two more things to find out
And in grace I enter   with love I enter   What language do we speak I ask the room

345

Soul speak   the gospel blend   of kindness   you could call it
Said without a mouth   we are one cord   Yes but   Try it   more deliberately
And your banishment   or mine   you need not work too hard   to speak
And my exile an act of love   and my loving   exile over me
Hangs here and my ex   -halation of stars   starts   stops
Not working   It doesn't have to work   It doesn't have any thing
Don't wear a belt with words on it   I have always   loved you
For your art   the second thing   when you began to matter
But having never understood what you make   it robotically took you
All soul receded but thine   and thine any word oh any word
With the grammar of no one   with in you its exertion blood drops calling
Each word or phrase blood   crosses the cross and the X
What you say will never stay   Blood dries   soul   and it soul
In your drying-up body is called to love   like never before

Called to love like never before   to speak as I never have
To know everything   and truly   to stand at the beginning
Saving you with my life's blood   my mammal's experience
I throw away my last envies   you too know them intimately
I can't have them even to save you   the success that would make you listen
And so can only with love   can barely speak this   all so to you
Hear without knowing it   As we are one   Stand now face-to-
Face that I may ab-   sorb from your forehead   yours
As I did with my brother   take on your mind-wounds your flames of ob-
Sessive guilt   your resentments your deadly urges   your
Having been mocked your screams   become a quiet bleed
Pressed against my head   Because I can take it   Finally
I will cure you of sadness   before or after where time
Loses its direction   between words or steps   or motion whatsoever
I am here and it's before   evolution   the only wind our mind
We're bloodless ground   about to break apart are we
We are re-creating our demeanor   though you don't know do you
Stood   in an endless line   in an endless cathedral of selves
Each of you presses   to me your forehead   in between the smallest
Motions of sound and spin   where there is room   in between everything else

No Jury Trials

It's always dark there no jury trials   like on the cross
I was someone I didn't want to be   Sure I would have
Killed him   If I knew how   Do you remember this shiny ribbon
You were wearing it   I wasn't that person I was only a shaft   of light
Story's going crazy   Just a motion of mind you should know that
By now   that's a story   You agree on it   to condemn me
Because there's too much to remember   I tried to get past
I wanted to go home   Then he hit me   That's not in your deposition
It may be different   story of the same   The syntax was odd you'd say
Burningly   not   he was on fire   Wasn't he   That time may-
Be I was   This is why I can lead you or save you   But not
Relate   Relate to or a story   Nothing you've asked me makes sense
I never go to parties   of stammering crows   Walk past
Walk past the librarian's desk   and re-invent the book

Michael

I had a beautiful thing in my room   a red scrap
She gave it to me a girl   Now try remembering things
To go in there and hold it   a scrap of cloth   I was stay-
Ing with my grandmother   on Bentley or is that a street
Parents didn't get along   a child a kid   but so big
We had some coffee   I didn't like coffee that much
Felt older holding the cup   Grandma her bathrobe you
Say and she cared   about me   I didn't mean to mess with them
I lost control   With how big I was   I didn't want
Anything much   I think I knew I was heading here
Like wound-up to   that I would   And I messed with everyone
To get it over with   Like that   I didn't know
I was alive alive   until I was dying from the shots
No one helped me   to do what   but who wants
To do what   But I like this to   paste on   Alice okay?

It's Mild Here

It's mild here she I one says   palms a yellow sky nowhere   Caribbean
Or Camargue   Another planet   She approaches low buildings I'm told this
And I blew it up she says   but *he*   tells me she says it
I'm not a bad person Monsieur   she says to him   The waves would be
Correct   For political reasons   I had to rob the gas station   it blew up
With shapes in it   I'm being told this   as if I'm in love
After I leave   because I'm broke   I remember   how to *have this*
Meaning three things   at each outburst   There's no meaning
On Mars   except she said Chiron   I said Medulla oblongata
Where Helen's tumor was   It's the past   and her clothes
I remember you   Can you hear it   remember how   to be free
As if Free   weren't attached   to anything   one knows about and
Now I'm free   there isn't any   thing left to   attach to

Screams

Screaming no sense but a round or gathered thing
There may be what left exponential caw or what throat
Mine and the throat gathers you who desertingly keen
So I bent there then lay on green making this unpopular
Noise was quiet made it again expressively meaningless
Obdurate yes but curving not regularly I feed you
Because I am the oldest bird in terms of experience
They are bursts but is this real grass or even glass
Wouldn't matter what on this stage if I felt trapped enough
They began to relax and hear that I sang in a manner of threes
Clusters of words meaning several things not importantly
And I couldn't keep the count I just called out
You must hear it it must exist we will not have to grovel
To something said a long time ago and then adored

I Can Take It

No one was really there but me I can take it
Why do you want devices when you can have everything
I would stare at his window he had once been there
Then never was again I can take it there must be factors
A postman delivering nothing as if he were smart
I don't want a number can you understand I want to be
There are three because it sounds good do the dead count
Reverberant who counts who matters to you dead stuff
There's this new kind of matter at the corner of Hurt and Decay
I named those streets did you want me what for to tutoyer
I want to enter the beginning repeatedly in case there's love
What can you understand who stayed on the right path
All of you who stay on the right path of the right righteousness
The poets of the dead letter as delivered too late

Jan 6

I could never know myself and so am eternal
Adding and adding to your heart   We have arrived dead
From the Syrian War disheveled in every part shocked
So enter me I say and rest   We are changing refuse to recognize
Sapience your presumptions even the idea of knowing
Don't want to know except in your sounds those gathered screams
You can lead us if you continue to perform them in the way no one liked
No one liked us   that's why we're dead

There is a sound rumbling in an abrasive black core paste it on
Why are we near   you   Sometimes you have to come in here
Searching for tones I will hang them about your ghostly necks

These are my friends now   others don't have to believe in
She told me her one miniature thought to print in a small book
That there is only resilience   and that's what power is

Jan 8

Because you too came in here bloody and torn up still shocked from your death
All on the same battlefield   Why bother to live anywhere
Because all of you came here bloody and torn up in my unbeliever's bedroom
Where I your savior say things and sleep   Will my blood stain
Your bed you asked   You're dead I said your blood's dead
Your blood's a spirit   You were very brave Charlie
Though we don't know if we'll need courage in the new universe
Courage implying its opposite and also brutality   Impiety does that go you ask
Grace is almost all   you won't have to take a position   though you can
Almost sticky grace envelops you   I'm sorry you're so devastated
Now vast-stated free eyes wide open dead the shocked can
See everything   Isn't there blood on your duvet   Across my live eyes I say
Crying again for people whom I didn't know before

Green and Gold

Green and gold
        These love you   green gold
        Fish or rock
        with a lacy or un-
        even edge

Because green and gold I am uneven   I told the murderers
To come in but not   talk to me   not talk in repose for eons
        This hole or
        window   has some red intermixed
Who you were   and now it's eternity   you live in
Taught one nothing   nothing but ciphers can be taught or for-
Gotten   I can a savior save you collage of fishers
Whose eyes are   outer space   magenta fiery for
        Green gold cerise
I am just saving   And I said bring forth a newly
Appellate firmament   glued with ages of mobile lumin-
Ous lumens   sliding across the foil of sky   I remember
Try to remember be-   ing here before   at the beginning
Of iridescence   the only time you knew how   to speak green and gold

Hope Salome Seligman Ashfork

We are beautiful   the images you see   correspond you write letters
In red and her smile   You have led us to   the white boulder of
The inscription   And one hath wrought the eyes   breaking your
Does it have to say heart   core   breaking your core   The air is better

A ferry station to take the ferry   to the island   and learn how to paint
The dead world   at the edge of   like where we are draw in lines
You can learn to draw a line   But there aren't   any straight lines
This is the rogue me your savior   And I paint you   my image
It's wrinkled or scored   my face a score   We nod know
This silver part and the wave   percussive unscrolls   epistolary
To my sisters and brothers   bismuth gneiss and coral   you are well I hope
In your color glinting   deep bonneted remember   Hope, Arizona
And the aviary at Salome   the Avi Casino   Seligman   Ash Fork
Engraved   Any word's picture   glyph   Mind traces still   Love, Libby

Molten Flower

Molten flower   this white or flower   with center of smooth
White fire *the core of my eye*   original   chalky first substance
Radio active   that I'm given   having godlike achieved my eyes
A chalky   first sub-   stance in   my hand radio active

It has sometimes been proposed that soul is struct-
Ured according to threes as if it were a poem
A thin sheet of soul this would be the realest substance
Perhaps affected by stretching something that glows sounds
I noticed last night that in a fact my eye was
The first eye I had returned to its inception in
A burning lotus in a fact I was existing first with it
This was a fact I was god would I need another fact

We want a dark purple stain   over words but they must be legi-
Ble   beneath the weather   When we will break the weather

No One In Charge But Myself

No one in charge but myself   She wanted to change me   Said we'll get you at sea
Rocks and magma and the sea it-   self Yes I was once an infant   each allows
These thoughts of mine can be seen   no one in charge but   they want to change
Me not rocks and magma or the   deep who were all once   were we children

Were we children with   gold glitter sing   no one in charge but wants
To change me   I'm sad he said in a way   because it isn't like buddhism to
Be dead   It isn't a way I say   Hold onto the sounds of words between words and
You'll sing   We'll get you at   No you won't though   I'm your sav-

Ior   Where did those first children come from   was it me
In the collage effect anywhere   they slid out of my mind   while no one's in charge
And now they're fossils   In the future howling back   your tears at
Not being comprehended   No one understood   the infants of chaos

Recitative: Not having needed anything for eons can begin the universal voice
The new tense or torso as you go in transfiguration who else will love them but me

Crucify me at sea
Gold and red

X

Its primary torsolike pillars support naughts
As if each held up a zero   Your incomplete torse   Whose
It is holding my cruciform punishment for
Loving my mind   What do I look like mind
Thoughts played across at angles to each concentrated other
Your real world an infection of dislike and fear
I am god disillusioned of respectability decency laws and attainment
Only I love without bothering about who
The children with ebola hovering in fevers still send
Their souls to me to cuddle   The Syrians sit across the room
On the floor with their new nothing   certainly better than
The old   and the Charlies rearranged into Cubist bloody trauma
Ask if they can spend awhile here   I told
Their killers to stay in the kitchen   night-
Blooming cereus white around the foam upon
How we are making   new matter   becoming it
Out of my crucifixion   being this X

Cannot Slide Away

Cannot slide away   Force being of the mind   weaker might be strong can
Not slide   I am stronger larger   without a body I
Michael I don't want you to   you to what   don't mean nothing
Mean-ing-less   It was a mean   ingless: a joke   The

Ingless meaner than I was   Alice I'm learning to talk it
Here   Silly coot the wave   of sound   It waves a claw there
But   I can *be in*   a wave of sound   talking   say to you
And I remember   I remember niceness   like a sponge

Like I sponged   it up alive   When I   when I died I was
Terrorized   I'm still   like I'm scared of so many   shots ripped
And I can do that   But then   remember a paper auto-
Graph   name in year-   book like a whole   your name's a lang-

Uage Shawna may-   be I'm remembering   that thought not
Having it   Memory's holding me up   I have a held together me

Undo

If there isn't time, but only change, what changes? I mean there isn't time. The orbits of planets as words do not equal as word time as word. My wrinkling skin is just that. There is no passage no of no time.

I'm going to undo every story but not every image. I am your savior, you need me, for I am an unorganized religion. You are too dumb for organized religions; you actually believe them, gullible and controllable. I see you as fools, but that's only one thing.

To recite beautiful lines of poetry is healing and power-imbuing, physically transformational. To let poetry inhabit your body is to heal yourself.

I see that your black hair ragged fades as you lose all but
A certain representation your eyes show your location
And that once tragic now rescued by death you have force.

Some people terrified at finding themselves conscious in bodies invent a religion compelling everyone else too to worship so it will be true.

There is no god but us; it's a good thing we die. But we aren't extinguished. In death we're better, powerless over others without bodies, but still hapless, too hapless. This must be where I come in.

See from the inside out without story edges I'm not a leader or savior I'm leading and saving you within seemingly alien moments.

She says if you'll put the gold glitter on all, every last one of, my words I'll give you all the money the gold is worth. No I say. She repeats the question, I repeat my answer.

A crucified savior is not a victim. I am actively saving you so that alive you will refuse the gold of victimhood and dead you will be smarter in a different universe.

See here, I don't need anything you have. And I don't need your aid or friendship. Or influence. I don't need to be alive though I seem to be so fated as if I were needed, so who am I in better words?

Wanted me because I would not remember. That everything, every individual shitty thing they do, and think, and show as themselves, is supposed to be important.

The universe a sad affair. Half-realized? Or do we have no knowledge but our false measurements? I am tiny as well it the universe says. All of me can be compressed and seen on your thumbnail.

I went through it all and I say what was worth it but to continue to have force in my soul for no especial reason. No said anything I needed, but then I had no need. I had no value either. I rejected every part of your definition of living and so saved you.

Michael

Mom it's okay
I lived long enough because
I'm still alive

As our savior   Rene says   you must amuse us

In days of Bush or Obama? She's such a queen he says
You did it to me again and you're dead!
As faggots or dead we're all equal he says
The year you were on crack and slept on the D train I say
Another learning experience he says   I didn't want you to
Ring my buzzer but you were still always worth it
And you burned up my copy of Eliade's *Shamanism*
In the fire you set at four three seven   But I brought you
Beautiful flowers he says   in a vase of red Bavarian cut glass
No one's like us alive   though some of the dead are pretty good
Do you know I ask even more than you used to   I mean from being dead
I don't have to make remarks he says   though I always do
So you'll know it's me   But I don't have to fight   use words to fight
Mightier than the pen or penis   my mind is

(Rene Ricard)

Let Her

There is a   Memory starts with a   Across the first you saw
Across the first one I saw   water and sky   did I really   Firmament and sea
Climbing down wearing black   enter the kiva-   like room
It's empty and black   I can see   I sit down on a chair

Can you ever ev-   er see yourself   Can I   from within
Remember nothing   Can you do that   I re-
Remember painted lines   unevenly latticed   brown on blue
Oh do you   I don't want to live   through that again

What   Anything   Parts of things maybe   There's a fireplace
In the black wall   I wear the crown of thorns   blood droplets
Memory's blood   not real   This is the language
A convex cell gold   not like the one in which   time is coiled

It explodes gently   into letters   All of us   I and all of us
So we could separate   and cohere   Let TER speak
My wings are eyes   I was the first one   to see it
How   the sky and water   met   without a cross

Your eyes are lateral   and infinite   a bit of red
My eyes are round scopes   without perimeters   Let her speak

In the lib-   lilacs last   brary   or some classroom crass
I'm not there now   in the dooryard   placed the letters   bloomed in myself
Don't teach any-   thing to the   dead we're going   to read
It   Keep going at the let-   ters I'm   the leader   savior and president

I place   the let-   ters that let me   And I am sav-   ing you from wor-
Ship   These letters signify their ap-   proval   our intelligence
And my friends the let-   ters held me back   from the mayhem of
A literarily   self-absorbed and clumsi-   ly choreographed

Exploration by the cri-   tically con-   cerned   that is some po-
Ets dead and   dying   downward   growing and dying down-
Ward like trees   I like someone said that line: Clean leaning trees
It's not in Li-   lacs I thought   Don't   but get up and go back-

Wards again   I am placing these let-   ters in my-   self as at the
First   when lilacs first   and the letters said   leader for you
Had held your-   self back   before you knew   that the fool-
Ish were that   Can you lead them   Oh come to me   we will

Read   the poem of the dead   Collage in No One's Time Sig-
Nature   These beadlets   of blood   I'm thinking for you

When Lilacs First in the Dooryard Bloomed

Take These Letters

And it was because there were as many as or more than you of
Painted lines appearing I could identify as anything a pen or brush stroke
Still I say it is better to have nothing for as nothing yourself you are most
Intelligent   Purchase nothing and owe nothing to anyone recognize nothing

During the cruciform memory a wintry dark blue sky with low orange bar
I am told I will be crucified once more either in memory or real memory to be en-
Dured retroactively again in counters a drawer in which a black box
You haven't yet opened this box of cross

I was to carry it up there for they forced me to
At the beginning of splitting into many was there al-
Ready such sadism   The planets weep for the
Brutality of their formation   At the very least you are con-
Veying yourself as if you have to are forced in any instance
Nothing you do makes sense but this this torture
Had they nothing else planned   I had been brought be-
Fore the magistrate and told I was guilty of this pre-
Cise blasphemy I enact now oh for the third memory
I push the cart with my cross in it up Montmartre
Then they affix me to it because and there I fail
It is always for your talent artistic iconoclastic
Why did I bother to walk across the void and create them
My crucifiers by placing in mind or page their own letters
The words of their substance creating the happiness they dis-
Dain for money toys   I have messed with their games again
I attempt to escape within thinking   Open the black
Drawer now   And in this memory   where is localized in pain
The knowledge of all poetry that which we are made of
And from the cross I thus speak as it was spoken to me
By my first self

        Take these letters
From my lips and invent with them your-
Selves again   And paste them on the very abyss

As much as you're alone but not alone the crucifixion proceeds
There is peace in such a finality of other's judgment your name
Lucidity as in the first black box you step out of the grave
Grave Alice who never slept but watched over her dreams
Who owns poetry who owns politics who owns your eyes?
I was surrounded by the pernicious ownership of one
Academy or another throughout my times my honey
You *were* malicious those *were* your races souls cried
And when you die you are welcome in the bedroom of this
One sick last night amid ruffians or archangels I am fight-
Ing not to detest the mediocrities damaging sound
And laughter in the most essential art it isn't about you
You don't know who you are or what you are really enacting

Crucifixion'stissueofinterconnectionsthatarenotonlywords
Seepsthroughcorporatelytomakequiverfeverouslikeabody
Wordscomprisingafabricalsobetweenvowelsverticallysideways
Thisfromtheblackboxthefirstsubstanceresemblantofanore
Thesubstantialpredictionofmydiscoveryistelepathy
Evidentlywhenindivisionwewillstillbeofthisinitialcommunicative
Edgelessimmaterialitythisconsistencethatwearetwinnedto
Withnoorthodoxybuttheevidenceofyoureveryone'sandthing'spresence
DoyoudowithitwhatitgrowsusbutIwasalreadyhere
Towatchnothingwaseverlostorisandbatteryself-mockery
Strikingeachotherwhetherrockfireorfleshwhensohookedandone

I was looking for an active and complete
Love—what we are—
I had to be broken to release it
The Crucifixion Rumble

Green Grow

When the letters began to appear   or whatever you'd call it   no one
Sounded them or   called them a thing   I saw and heard you
Is this right   When the letters begin to appear   we glue them into
The collage   that is simultan-   eously forming

They might be gold   green grow the lilacs   Do I press against
Or am I part of it   The letters   sounds   come out of
My mouth but I for-   get what I've said   any old
And change   the green lilacs   for the red white and blue

I could paint them   gold and paste them to the   language I
Learn   indomitable   And he who would   For I suddenly
Know   the language   He who would betray me
Call him forth for I would say something   to him face to face

Would it matter what   it might be   and the letters of the sounds
The sounds of the frag-   ments of the collage   make the collage
Do you think that   by being crucified I   will not gain power
And the cos-   mic wind from my mouth   sings To the Extent That

To the extent that   I be hurt   letters more   letters sounds

Honor

I was still discarding her   and that world last night   dark cloths flowed
Down my body-like form   And I was beset   The wounds are ment-
Al but not imagined   The wounds are purpose-   ful red
A physician cleansed them   said he'd not seen them   the previous night

Why anymore   I have separated   myself from   my last community
Someone said   was it I   We must now   paste on more red sequins
Every particle of you   divorced from my last   true community
For   and for which you   do I have to   do this without naming you

And I would fly up   above the   anticipatable mockery
It was about Honors or honored   or without honor in
The word disappears into its letters   dis-
Honorably or not the letters glisten like a body's   particles
Silver not red and I bled for you who or for what
You bled airy blood and from it I grew someone says
The lethalness of this situation lies where you exclude your-
Self because you cannot bear falsity though you are the dreamer
I saw them or it I suffered then saw all of them
Who are you telling this to I am telling it to no one

The Poem

They leave you up there he said calling you names
As it gets dark remember for you've had the experience
Retaining barely a consciousness the body'd shrink away
But there's only exposure the necessary fasting you are seen
They want to watch you all humans being empathic predators

And then I said when there is no conventional body
And little recognition of forms as in a violently painful half-sleep
You become your other after they have had you like a feast
This is done everywhere in many ways often subtly in an instant

You may so be done away with I had seen the impossibility
Of living with others yet loving for that was my condition
At the crossroads when they asked me to partake of rules as in
A commune of pretension I left unruly
Who stands by me now he or I say and I said last night
Holding the world together by my total recall
At anyone's distress they are so sorry sounding like pigeons
They who call themselves poets and have no letters

Run With Your Children To The Border

How far away   is the farthest reach   Here the farthest beauty sequins

Side bar the idea
Of putting all your evil
Into an object or
Figure
Give it to a bad person a dream   Smear your dirt on it

I think this is Legba   a faceless voodoo
                         doll
                         Ever at
Ever at   the crossroads
                              I'm still covered with the filth
Of war she says   I like the sequins but I'm dirty   unhealed
My city's become   instead of quartiers   camps of factions
Men dirty-faced   Run with your children   to the border
Put all your evil in an object   I was their object
At the crossroads   shot and I sent my children   on with another
Fell on my leg across the cross-   roads became the sun
How it blazes   in your eye   Die for the idea some-
One's shit's superior   smeared on written
Scroll   The words of the superior   belief
Belief   Am I a   participant in   your dream
Who said he loved me he's dead   mercurially like a bul-
Let   No one aims   they just project them-   selves towards
Any   for movement's a lure child
                              You're dead now
I need to know about my children I can't be here
                              Help us I say change everything
                              I want my children

                         Paste   the let-
Ters of no belief   sequins   Just paste on the sequins   to soothe you

Declassify

The forms   Who respected me she screams   Everything reduced to
Essential sequins
                Stay with red awhile
These sequins
These   No all the colors   have to come into it
Not just the blood I
                shed for you last week I say and the
                              room's enlarged
A long table's set   with the candles lit I led here
We don't eat the dead say   But still the table's set
We are expecting   more revelation   Please join us no
Matter   how bad you feel
And the brilliant souls   of the planets and stars   will sit next to you
What will you cook for them   and unanticipated   shapes of
The collage   you rhomboid you A
Any old thing
                I am a mass of sequins
Sitting at   the head   Was there just one sequin
At the beginning   Sweet words to eat   and long   healing   lines

Popped out of   a hole   in nothing   like a poppy
I saw it I was   already there   My dear Coquelicot sit down
Elijah's brows are scowly   and his lips so   tight he can't
Yes you will I say   You will   witness

And where the smooth scarlet lake   or petal parted the dark
I saw my own mind open   its only task
                        outward
                        further
The molten sequins of the Word   poured forth   from the poppy's
Mouth   into me   They were not the form   of a body but
Were its existent   nature
                my nature
Paste it here   I want that one   the dead woman says   I want that word
I want that   an operatic scream   or is it a poppy

Old Fish

They wouldn't let me go or let go of me   I'm little   or I was
They take us with them make us listen handle us
Did you have what did I ever   have to look   forward to
There's no forward here the sequins are broken   broken up
What should I what should I know   Teaching you a language
There that enormous prehistoric fish

My power shoots through my limbs like sparklers
Morphish in quadrilaterals   to a quattrocento peculiar red
Take two more Ts and put them somewhere with snow
I'm taking the charge again   I was asleep   You don't

Know me that well take charge of yourselves
Perverse sequins the chartreuse ones are a fume
I'm countering with thought   arrowing towards   slice no
Slice   The man used to hit me   when I didn't say the right
I you stand up to it
                                    Your intelligence
Does not come from   Because when time's abolished
Backwards and forwards you are seeing   what's going on

the fish the language slimy and anguished
big-mouthed and -eyed   scale-sequined against glass
wants to speak   and approached the maker
in myself you could be anything   but already seeing the
future which has now been so long an old
fish   everything speaks the fish says   I everything speaking
huge full moon of some planet   there's a firecracker tree
the fish says none of this ancient religious talk of
anyone   contains what I know   I know there's no
water where I'm dead yet I'm older   than all the breath
and the fish says my language is so old   you can under-
stand it in your violent   looking back and forth until your
body loses its tense   remember I followed you with my eyes
from my tank   in the aquarium   at porte de Vincennes

for you are   my leader   I will come with
you to stay at the first where you'll learn the   poetry of the dead

The Language Says It

did the mountain have qualities without the means to perceive them
so the red is unadulterated or adulterous it blurs out smudges un-
controllably or is it the sequins   encrusted then transformed substantially
when I leave time I almost see how we could have created everything
did the mountain who says huzzah or I know you

if you glue more sequins and more and more soon your children will be here
for we do not indulge measurement or time   I am an old fish it says
old is a quality not of measurement   where do we find our own
language within what is being recorded   it is soul-like too

you must let me love you I say even if you don't resort to sequins
it is of my mind and will help you by justifying your worth alone
I don't want any worth it might be like freedom or another mind
I don't deserve not to be sad   the language says you will no longer
be sad   the language says it it's what knows right now it's red

Only the Language Knows

Fathomed I led her to still place ablind and in the caul
Paste that texture she was sinking unwet of course which is
And nothing is determined or anything be the ancient old
Fish nudges her she's replying again hoopla
Doesn't try to know why to me says it aren't you in
Crucifixion yes still but escaping in moments like a mesh
A ruby mesh pulled out to come lead her for we're simultaneous
I think I might be always old it says no young you no none
All one old again maintaining the constance of love or word
Woman says do I dead do whatever I do just that familiar
Or vermillion she cuddles near it we're perceiving a beaut the
Old fish says doing that for everything I'm beginning to go
Along she says this ripples with saying and we paste it on
Only the language knows what we do glue's made out of
Fishes others fish says fish glue snail goo slime only ideally
And says halloo and I say I'm trying to figure out where it
Goes as figures sliding in and out of sequence for you laugh
The woman's in infinity finally diverted and I'm buoyant

Here is some tornoff window on Paris arrondissement
Apartment outside opaqued here is your square mind
Dispossession by how they walk out in their normals
Why do you do and say all these like containers who wa-
Nted to be and I never did contained on the moisture in the beak
I'm leading and saving you to form of no they want to con-
Fer like conferring experts of the po- phratry etry whistle
I'm the best whistler the whistler said in the dark radio
He knew the fish and also smooth mountain with P for Parker
Because I parked there the mountain whistles to me
She said she was sapphire in the night that says it all old
Fish not king push words more so hey they
You young each scale or sequin on fish connects
I get to connect blue widening the scourge possibility
Cross intrusion scourge spear I was way far away
I am way far away each glint asteroids of tears
If they're beautiful agonites or other jewels from other planets

Agonites

We'll help we'll help in the night   we'll blues in the night   help in the night
It is another instance   of the black rainbow   a linguistic device
For we are speaking thinking   in onyx blacks and pearlized   grey-black blacks
You don't under-   stand it retain it for   long you don't have to

There's some deep dark blue   in the black rainbow too   Do you
Remember making sense   just in the moment   the moment
And I was welcomed to the thrall   of this kind of   speaking in tongues
Without too much fuss   or rehab of the spirit   no one's guilty

So we stand gleefully talking   or even singing   I your leader
Do not lead here   for we enter   our identities
Into the music without minding   speak-   ing what comes up
And I told you   with a musical ur-   gency that I was yours

Again yours and yours   And we automatically   thriced our lines
At least for awhile   In this dark depth   A subtle pride to paste

Michael Brown

Exactly he says   I can say it exactly   for just a little moment
And it doesn't matter   But it's all I'm doing   Wipes memory but
I keep remembering   how to do it   He hears me two three times
Who   I don't know don't have to   Haven't eaten food in months is it

My eyes all over me seeing   I get to be everywhere   And I look for Mom
I find her in some air   But she doesn't know it   Talk to her
I can find a place in her   like a little microphone   Talk in the language
I think it makes her   dream of me   She's still sad

I don't know how to make her   see me right   in the dreams
But I'm finding that love   is what I'm in   The language says it
Making me feel good   when I say things   I can't remember
Alice can you   talk that   way our way   I don't know

I always make sense that lasts   Tell my mom I miss her   I don't know
Her   And I'm thousands of miles away from her   Though so close to you

All The Souls In The Cigar Box

You can put the universe   and all the souls that exist   in a cigar box
It's all in my two-room apartment   everyone seems to   need me
Not for a specialized reason   but because I   open out to them
To explain it or try to   is painful   Do I believe it

Yes afraid I do   How literally   Are you literal my
Reader   I mean not to me   But you're there aren't you
They're   perhaps more real   than you when they cry out
And I just let them   we're compressed on   my old same bed

Or sometimes one's   more important   or is a mountain
They don't all love me   they're here to breathe   that's figuratively
I accept all their experience   always tangled   and partly un-
Known even to them   Why do we go through it   Why be a mountain

And we're all   poetry because   we're compressed and lyrical
Or vast   I'm full of their endless lines   they're full of my care

And If I Bleed Enough Rubies For You

in this kind of space both compressed and airy Michael said his
watch was hungry he didn't know what he meant and laughed upset
about his Mom but I understand we're in the future too he says she isn't
here doesn't know I'm okay   she may know that I said   but I saw
this was last night that the Japanese man had been decapitated
he held his head that is as an image and could not be convinced we
saw him whole I do hate explaining this he still has it today that's
all I seem to remember of the night
                                        I've been grieving for my brother again
dead twenty-seven years though I talk to him frequently the parts of time
cut up and encircling me as vapors
                                        I went running in the park at dawn

This death language he Michael says   it might in-   clude other people's
Their languages   because we're in each others'   minds so there may not
Be just a pure one   If time's mixed up   and the future's now

It was a beautiful thought and it's keeping me going Michael
Do you think when I write a poem   my thoughts might be yours or anyone's
Yes Alice when you write a poem you're wide open   I'm glad I died young
So I could know these things now   whenever it is whatever time it is
There is so much thinking that there's nothing but   thinking talking thinking

When I awoke I saw in the news on my iPad that IS had
executed the Japanese man so I am not a lunatic
I mean after I saw him in the middle of the night with his head
You have a job to do for us my brother says please do it
You are interpreting us he says leading and loving us please
Just continue it's very important why I ask so we can
Understand what's been going on in this long moment of forever
You are part of this forever he says have been and will be there is
a way you have already made us free before you were born
every part forever how can I get rid of having been a sniper
for forever he says   I am crucified for that I say in an eternal
cycle of making you well he says it doesn't balance does it

at a certain point I say you have done nothing any bird
sings that nothing nothing has been done the dream
our actions are gone and if I bleed enough rubies for all of you
our actions of the human dream and the dream of the universe's
origin in violence are gone

I AM LARGE ENOUGH TO SPEAK
IN THIS CATHEDRAL OF OUR SOULS

I spoke to everyone existent at various points in the night
Anyone seemed to be waiting   none of us arrived exactly
There is probably no reason to dislike anyone though I could
Rain it's raining this is the army Mr. Jones my soul said
I wasted some time disliking someone then appeared before you
The dead poets who know that what we are is lines of poetry with both
Vertical and horizontal focus and a sweet compression a control
Of our own elements for its own sake it's a self-evident goodness
Or bounty the old fish who is the ancient of language understands
It floats behind the window with its eyes seeking and liking me
As I explain to the poets this that they know though forget
It doesn't matter who you get the information from
I myself am not reading anyone at the moment and
I have no formal plans I only ever wanted to be a poet
But that now seems to be literally infinitely complex
Everything I say refracting so many times or ways I'm dazzled
Rather than speaking in tongues I'm speaking in planes of light
And the murky old fish projects to me the phrase As you wish
We are not speaking vocally to each other or are we translat-
Ing I don't follow one says and another wonders at the double verticals
And two circles in 'follow' no that one says not saying I am a-
Lone among many   We taught you to see yourself as certain
Are you   And I never was my uncertainty has been steadying
Is that true I don't know I only know that I make poems
I exist and when I'm dead like you I will do something equivalent
So far no one can tell me what that is   only that I know how already

In the part I say then where spirit and matter are the same thing
We of us the universe were the only ones so to emphasize materiality
That with our eyes we see and only what is seen exists heard or felt
And so trying not to see I see too much even that's not there
Dissolving grey peripheral scurries shadows that aren't at last dirt the red glints
The red phenomenally not there that's seen sometimes beneath the lids

Oh nothing I Alice believe in most exists can a scientific tech-
Nician measure sorrow or define its source in a cosmos of elements
These others you speak to they say called the dead or even your
Poetry audience are invisible to you non-existent what is that lovely
Latin rhetorical figure joining two words that mean the same thing
Chiasmus no that's X the letter crossroads I'm distracted
But not distraught are you in my audience Quintilian
We of us so many of whom cannot be measured now why
Did you call to me as if there were hearing without sound
Presence without sight why do we speak without marks on
Paper or even birdcall-like pattern but rather in mental immediacy
Yes you are suddenly within me helping me to speak to you
All of us comprise us but what I seem to know is new even to you
A gentleness defined by the absence of the violence we thought we knew
And if the Syrian woman now dead says *I* know it
It was for me to acknowledge that so but not its weight
Figurative compared to the existence of all our minds including hers
Should she continue in death to suffer and I say our mind can assuage her
For it becomes the whole cathedral and a planet's wars are twig scratches against a window
Yet she is shocked and I am giving her all I think not as particulars but as effort and energy

I am not dead I am alive and know more than most what that is
Grey-blue the window of my apartment golden-lit within our cathedral
Same-time chalice to drink from without taste buds drink to
The diffusion of story in particles faintly sparkling throughout the fabric
Of our body in this grand room losing its invention at last
Story did us in but we have broken and scattered it like poor old time
What you thought you were who as an urgent continuity no
And I wrestled with it as if I jesused were a tale not a love
You are crucified at any time or maybe even brave was I brave
To learn not to want a quality would be mature enough no bond
I stopped wanting you myself or you and lost my formation
I gave up my heart I let an old-fashioned orchestra play it elsewhere
Abstractedly and fetishize the melody sung in the middle by the vocalist
Purist in the instant of the white petal soared with
Freedom of thought have you ever experienced freedom of thought
Who would know outside of you have ever thought some-

Thing you were certain no one you knew had thought or no one ever
Now dead we are within each other's minds but alive we are childish
Know not where the new place is the dazzling anything the freak
I will say anything to all thee for I am thinking it and so fast
That my alive hand writing can't keep up O forsythia O organum
O Lampedusa O name that simply wanted to be said
And it will always tell you what you need to know the language
Of poetry you'll never hide from it though dissolve the story of
Your guilt into small molecules that appear periodically the let-
Ters said as you're overtaken by the thought that must be thought the words
The new story spelled out in bits from eon to eon is only
A scrolling pattern an outer-space flower a three-note motif

I was born to be like this so I could give you my mind old fish
Corvid black or blunt green whatever color for what senses it knows
Me get on the bus and I was working all along or here perversely
To be harmed as in the music overtaken by an ominous tritone
A fish scale or mixolydian the red sequins or sequence of lin-
Guistic sounds written in what original but we are that mind
The language though telepathic and instantaneous can be drawn out
In a history enacting not a predestiny but a foreknowledge
If we're each part or all knowing everything though gloved and cloaked
In the way this description comes to me partial like a wing hidden
By night the beautiful and deceptive lover of either abstraction or protoplasm
What I've always meant is that the singular moments were more than the fate
I attained you all you dead poets and the other fiercely-souled dead beings
Of my loving acquaintance and the attainment foreshadowed was nurtured
By a parental future and an ungerminating past I was not
Created by others but I was loved as we all love each other's curve
Of mind and gesturing stance more than the plan unconsciously crafted
That we would be now impatterned in a crisis even
You but it's obvious that such a fraught mentality a sadness
Must be corrigible if it's a thought thing my people
And as we are one we change it caring for each drop of sorrow each grief
For we are a massive consciousness and we have crafted it
And we and we or I and I have always especially the poets known
That each line is a feature of our sapience but also our composition

Our elegance in essence our wish and that even of light to be efficient
Efficacious making ourselves more of beauty in this actual collage
We place each other alongside ourselves brilliant and enmeshed

V.

OUT OF ORDER

I am savior/leader   As a substance of that
A blue wavery badge inside me impersonal that I "got"
"At the beginning"   Impersonally I   lead and save
From now   Remaking the universe
"dirt and air glued together"
And then there's the dimension of death mixed in

This is how many souls there are on the ice at the beginning
As many as   you can't draw or paint   So glue that on
It's just a number   Like X as any   this is how many
souls or minds   casually turning towards an X

Whatever else remember you are standing here dead or alive
trying to change the universe begging to be changed itself begging
turning towards an X
                              the original crucifixion being
the intersection of   soul and matter   it's where you bleed
no one or I right there either on it or   in motion
X walks across   what do you remember
every one of the infinite number   of infinite souls

that taking on a form was not my choice   or saving you by going along
so why have I done this though   I wasn't asked   I must have chosen

Weren't you there   We happened to be   Happened to
Be formed   Orbs formed were they   And you cooled per-
Haps   The only thing that there ever was   was
Describing ourselves   rippling across all area
Rippling across all a-   rea the mind   of one
It's still like that   And when I was born   tried to remember (describe)

You make images out of   what you've already known
A childbirth a hole (black)   But I knew   I'd been dead first
To speak of   rippling across galaxies   or in other words
Something vi-   brating said   sang or heard just seen

                                        How do you remember to hold
Death together since I know it's there
It may be by virtue   of the crucifixion   the cross or crossroads
Its intensity   engenders the crackling   the rippling
Effect of us   where life and death   intersect sapiently

An X or T would hold us together   I am holding us together
You chose me   to crucify   in order   to hold us   together

It should be so perfect it doesn't bleed immutable
Red soul sequins I say
I carry red flash in mind   we all know red and black
Stand up to it   These words   pucker here and push stars
I star or is my name Bruise   re-   do you have to   -member
I don't use you   this word precipice   I caught
I remember your mind   This first one word BRUISE
Dead like light is   here it's only a soul   I'm not just go-
Ing to love BRUCE   how frail are we ceramics
A cream ceramic   more glued together DIRT
Perfect   Am I before I was bruised yet   If I can
Get there   Love me until I'm there   colors be-
Fore flesh   and rock   this so com-   plex gradient greens a
Magenta then white trace   At the X crossroads
I remember how to be here   Near the station

The crossroads   went down to the X   where life and death met
You don't have to do it   the expanse of its   traction X
Behind it the sluggard words   caught up with my
Thought and me   Because it strobe-flashed   the whole

Freak uni-   verse in front of my   eyes black-&-silver
The molten stuff   the nascent language   the SHIT
That's when you wrote it that   Because spoken
But still not as fast as   the thought of us   unborn unmade the dead

Unmade the dead I   —who are you—
The eyes on the ends of their stalks   The head or mind at-
Tached to wire limbs   But my

In-di-vid-u-al-it-y moved me   The wires or lines the kind
That vibrate that sing and carry   your mind out-
Ward   Why?

PASTE ABOVE RUMBLE

In the first instance there is a worm of light   It isn't light
Did you see it   I pass through it it's a passageway   to the cross-
Roads   How soon   How soon does anything happen   Crucifixion
Two rails or stripes planed   passing through each
Other   X or T   It's important that you not   be a person
Meat not meat   but noise not noise but I'm try-
Ing to understand the terms of another dimension
Place the comas in a row   erase that   Tell me Cross
Tell me the truth cross that I'm nailed   at the ware-
House
              We are near you   because of the swift air
I'm translating so you understand   you can get it
At cross   Every we need you   at crossroads all of us
A near-cliché   but resilient   Behind the cross
The source of   coherence   though those hills be wild
I had no animal intention I was free   Within the split-
Second history   of your planet   trapped in an end-
Less dot   That was my   And then it my life is
The dreams here fractured   But first or now   admit that I exist this one

I'm your leader and savior be-
cause I have this mark inside
of wavy blue lines vertical with
some yellow

        Cure us
you must remake the universe producing new elements

I am memorizing your universal heart

Black velvet rectangles   *someone with sword*

I fight going towards an edge in the past
I could be a thing   in yours   a panic or theodicy
A diaspora of molecular lusts or chasms
Or futile   digging what thought out of   you
Fought an array   of days edged
Gem sword one-ray pulling-self away to my
Bliss   is it like yours   You are calling me barren
Asteroid   you see a push thingness away
I have a habit even dead   of   self
Not to be rid   but still to trans-   form
And transform   There were four of us pieces
                                 Can you see us in biz-
                                 Arre orbit rocks
                                 Fighting the atmosphere
I'm aware dif-   ferently trans-   lating myself
In an aftermind

Fighting not to be a rock

Agonites the new rocks I found

In those days even the bitumen had volition
But any days are first   Will   something sparkling and abundant
To paste on   (perhaps I was a pebble on Mars . . .)

They were eating cirrhotic flesh
Near the ceramics studio   I can't hear your language
Bruise was trying to drive but was too pained
I was Bruise really   the first real I remember
This soul is shrouded from field of battle
Where I had gone I only knew war now I'm un-
Justified   I remember I will be dead I am start-
Ing to remember my moments dead   Tell me
I want to put a path through the collage
Can you move on it   My mind will go there at peace
Flashing slow   and it will take over   my real mind will

_____

We take this and this and make of them this
And a bird-soul swooped down of a red-wing
with in its beak a tiny diamond
And pasted it next to the so-called point of density
Which it covered with its soul-wings until it didn't explode
this version is possible as well as I the X though I know
I am Xed

        to make you live   dead or alive
        how that works that I ab-
        sorb all the pain of beginning a-
        gain

Does the collage need motion   from where   Does it have to come
From the Cross   This memory   of light encircling blackness
Am I stretched across that   X on O   Do we break up that glyph

And every start is my own story voice says   But we have re-
Turned   all to fluidity   I circled the blackness like a . . .
For I didn't dare   be the one   placed across it says

Who are you   Pressed
for gladness it says   I am trying to create hap-
piness   don't you want it it says   I don't think so it's too
thing-like though could be pasted onto the collage . . . frayed
after all the molten-ness   it that is I   could be tectonic
I want to be tonic   the other sound says   maybe there's a chord
already   Who has ears for it   or are we one ear
hearing changes   That's motion   and you the X are
turning too   Does it have to be like torture or night

They came for me   There is no you or they   They come for me
Can no longer ig-   nore me so they've come   Aren't you proud
I am either im-   passive or fearful   but not my
Mime   my impersonation   of myself   At the very beginning?   That's now
Can you hear the chord   Can you remember

Folded over pale fabric green blue in three sections of soft form
Like wrinkled mushroom effect or creaturely the small slit made
Could be an eye against white line edge of cut wall plane
There darker bluer blue and a dark and a pink lump of fabric

The eye says I saw you but I don't move yet   no a voice says sup-
Posed to move first   three slats and two gridded circular fans

Can we paste it   It may not be rigid enough at this time
He says the sheer beauty of death   almost makes up for his
Mother's lingering sadness   huge nebular with fireflies
We're at the beginning it comes backwards and around I always say
And I heal you and it comes back I'm healing you here day one
To see the day one and the founded upon beauty who can't see
But sees   that we become in one sole   moment as one thing
The clouds interstellar look like cloths mine the bluesier

---

arrowheads   but they didn't   have a word for their shape
I'm becoming harder in substance hard air so you could chip it
the alliance always progresses towards doom then we are loosely or-
ganized on the principle that I am open 24/24   that's all

He was wearing a nylon parka   No postal code
Slanted eyes light brown   round face light skin   a boy
An adolescent   Takes off jacket   I've come to meet you
Teach you a language   Which one   I guess I'm dead he says

This quaint one   this quick   Can you see my mind
Fast inside   no bother   that's the language
Just look in   my mind quick   Transparently
And if you know me   nothing happened   just an accident

The lake ice broke cold   Was it quick   Instant cold through
Couldn't climb out   The dogs couldn't help   You're really telling me
That's what I think and now the pattern broken ice is part of
Ice trees burn   The ice is burning   It's about my mind

So one time   Everyone knows   the ice burned but
Where I'm dead   in your apartment   I speak all at once
The point of the life   the point of disaster   the point of you
The point   no point in separating out   the words

The history I hold   is also in the stars   I hear it

I don't believe you   the dead often said   I can't see you
so my perception   he dead says   of what you're doing is that
you're unclear   believing yourselves clear   with excellent eyes
I deal with shapes in your mind   in a part of   your mind that
often you can't get to   but I can he says   because I'm dead
it's where you dream   it's where the world   is beginning
it's your crucifixion   and more   where you welcome us in but
you're seeing the mirror-image consciously   like any scientist
that's why that first time I spoke to you   years ago
you answered me from there   and heard yourself talking to me
otherwise you can have   that experience   writing poems

To be here   it has to slide
                slide
                            not explode and take place
It happens forgotten happens   We already know   what we're doing
Forget it   Doing   I can't do damage if there's no   lasting moment
Can this be good   We want a bit of memory twins   or twinge

Duplicates I might not   like it that much   Describes
Memory de-   scribes and what is said   is happening
Even if   I'm recalling what   occurred first in the wings
Remember a   geranium sky   I step out onstage

With my   This isn't right   With my speech unmemorized
Whatever I say   it's whatever I say   like now   in this poem
You want to de-   stroy me   There's a cold mist in our area
I never   let you down if   you weren't tense to prevail

Can you teach me your diction   diction   No I can't
Teach you me   With my ger-   anium memory   You assailed me
Clashing   When I was a hit   Omaha Beach   Where
I came here   at the beginning   to liberate my-   self from the foe

You don't have to spell it out or do you do you   he
Puts the appurtenance on the foam   to float
Is it the mechanism of evolution what a joke
I'm standing on the corner   wearing the stigmata
The corner of DNA and Alphabet   Out of which pour
Letters   There are so many more of what-
Ever we are than you   climbing up the hill
To elementary school being smarter than the teachers
My knee was bleeding in a long line down   I remember
When the Pledge of Allegiance was ruined poetically by
The insertion of the phrase "under god"   It
Doesn't sound right I kept saying I was seven years old
We can't spell it for example allegiance and republic
What it felt like to speak when I couldn't yet write well
It's all arranged we learn it from the sun heat and air
We learn it from animals I watch my mother's tongue
Inside the singular density of nothing concentrating
Around sound does it think the washboard remember and
Expected to cry didn't like expectation I still detest it
You have to save us right now the dead say I'm trying to

And so in order to experience pain they had to watch you
In order to experience anything they had to watch first
As one volunteered to be the leader in living and loving
                                                                    I'm
Seeing flashing but geometric forms along the periphery
Of my visionary experience   it is part of being on the cross

                                    So the first thing was
That you experienced it   the crucifixion so you could
Remember memory   Trying to lead you out of the burn-
Ing house where you dallied   I have the blue wavy swatch
Inside me a touch of yellow I just have it so follow

In this dialogue we will learn why we were born in or-
Der to remember   so you would be able to lead us all
Out of the burning earth after you were crucified
By the intersection of   time and space which weren't necessary
You have to lead us out of the heat in one part of the collage
Where we all explain to you who we are anyway

     life and death or space and mind

that I will the crucified poet of the universal poem said or read

Someone climbs out of the   or maybe as molten   at first
Pasting on collage   with either molten paste or ore
Oh yes I'm yours   no difference between words and stuff
The president shouldn't make his own coffee   a voice said   What
Can that mean in this cafe   I to the film   'Tear it off'
I pull the caul down   This that I'm calling   I can do thing pure
The tiniest swims out   has a soul big as yours   what is swims
Mr. Sims sweeps the store floor before the creation
With coffee-grounds-like cleaning compound   I watch him
The Roman soldier climbs up the terraced hillside stair-
Case   Nobody knows this   history of rough hallucination
That he'll kill who   on what minor planet   speaking the language of
Decapitated orators   Cicero's hands and head that hated Antony
What hated who   which matter disintegrates
Thinking it once spoke   now speaks to me in a mixture of tongues
Patch or botch of mental   An installment of early cel
But I'm dead and it's moving on its own   What's that

(Michael Brown)

I want you to see me he says take my hands
Don't know what to write   It's a long shot
I show you   he dances a little   I'm making matter
The fate of it comes from   that I'm making it

Get it   I can only make it the way I am   Which is
What are you like   Alive I am maybe a caricature   What
You'd expect   so you can talk to me   But
Dead   I'm thinking   I play and then something arrives

But it's not like what you know about   Look
It's rolled up   cloth-like   It isn't for any rea-
Son he says   I think about it like it's . . .   it's there
Pale pink or orange-pink I say   I just kind of do

Things he says   Why   I don't think why   I go find
People but   I don't need anything   I like all this being

Does death matter look like what does mind look like knowing what
You're or it's like how does it know as flat cloth or spirally lump
I'm crucified again at a gathering to find out why the cross is necessary
So I can tell you so I can tell you from it what the matter is
Blue pages of cutouts we've been cut out of that ethically excised she says
Me I'm up on the cross again creating an equanimous death world
At the intersection point not an explosion but balance I'd say
My figurine is missing someone says it's just a symbol
Did the world of matter only symbolize us us exquisite figurines
Now starting again a chaotic crucifixion I'm losing my shape
Still tacked up here becoming stretched fabric windblown undelineated
I'm not losing my mind but something unethical's emerging
Unsystematic blue and purple unreflecting but madly smart
Pained pinwheeling almost around the so-called navel
Trying to invent trying to invent this wholly new stuff
Don't call it a thing can't see it but it's there I scream
It's us we've always used the wrong matter use this one now

I'M MAKING IT NOT DISCOVERING IT I'M MAKING IT

I made this other matter

THIS DEATH MATTER WHAT CAN YOU DO WITH IT

(I never did what you wanted me to do
with my prior matter)

I keep being I making our substance

throw away your ethics and start   no one understands
your ethics do no one good   no one understands
have nothing instead and stay away from people
or knock them down   but you were with a band of men I
couldn't stay away   I joined the molten sea didn't
you   it was only hot if you   if one was sensed and
not just a soul   the soul slept   the soul flew in the black
other world   like the one we're in now   the real world with-
out nerves   the real world without nerves   I went against
my will   and was born into   prison of the world I went against my-
self it was grotesque   another says I was following love
why   because I already loved them seeing the future how
it's very tender   like listening   like listening to the dead Afri-
can on your bed   and you're a dead African too   And I'm listening
it's very tender   it's irresistible to listen   listening is first

Not unless you're wearing the gracious dress can you be death matter she says
But I am shown it of me my fingers on stomach become white touches
Simple whites on it dark   The soul matter or universal
Matter not always a light   I am dark ethereal matter
And if I'm taking it around   with me   or am I making it
As I go   Can you or I know it as I make it   if I am

I'm sure this is true but can I control even see it again
Come back to us a woman in a headdress says   keep coming back
Are you the world no the dead so I returned fealty
Temporarily relocated in the daily supposed-to-be
To my internal all-encompassing beauties of the unseen

Where I am crux and wound but also the nothing what-there-is substance
Anyone can make nothing   At the beginning a voice says
What you was made   the photo you see backwards was really
Figurines   You can buy some more   in the store
Pressed for more living I I say the crucified am creating
Memory memory and memory cross-hatched dark matter

The grey light stream or cosmic alien daub click light
I was X of the crown of thorns again X ter pate in argot
Of patterns of forsakenness or coming to life to paste
I made a torn thing it said but if I paste it on it's no long-
Er torn it being a vocal or tonal complexity you catch
In the new tongue of the northernmost pate of my head mind
And I go to Jerusalem or quiver like a weakened knight
Morning fracture of the salient I am will make us better
In the stars where you are and can collage without tearing
Though I'm roughly stretched along the cross of creation
Some besides space time to elicit from myself or crest of fate
Using fate to destroy fate for forever change self blows to
It's only these words I folded up their clothes and handed them back
Black socks with like sequins gave them back to the Sadducees

He was wearing a nylon parka. This is not an experiment.
All of us in the same room who'd forever be in the same room at
The same time. This is my mind he says. I am showing you my mind.
Do you want to look into mine I say. I'm cold from drowning be-
Neath the ice sometimes he says though I'm dead remembering how
To be cold. Looking in your mind he says I can show you a white-on-black
Word   like a touch or camouflage for it   BIDE   a simple one.
I'm tired of biding I say. Already he says. The dear says it
Knows who I'll marry. Of course. You used to marry he says.
Do you think there was a reindeer I say at the heart at
The heart of the beginning? The deer loved you and you bled it
He says. Or I bled I say in example these words so true.
I am warm in your mind he says though I am drowning
And I wheel I say always on the cross emitting care to save
Your mind. The others in the room   have crowded around just us.
And so each of us exactly. If you save me not from dying
But from a petrified sorrow using somehow your crucifixion.
Your endless in-place anguished love what can it be.
Where is it from do you make it. And in his parka the boy
Says my language Ter Sami died but I didn't   even here
In the black garment graciousness of the language of us
We who aren't figures   the language before my language is
What I am teaching you. That we are grouped. And remember
That language he says as the rocks and fire change. Nothing same
Memory. That I remember it is language of each.
And can each one speak as one would and be understood
If so I am not the one native speaker always remaining.
So in the mind of understand everyone we speak and make
Our dark matter words of anyone's night unpressed for time.

So you're saying   the beginning was   inside one
As or not   catastrophe   Yes when they crucified you
You lie across it   They're stretching you   It's rigged
It was supposed to be   your story I say why is it mine

There may be no differentiation   And no measure
But I can't be telling the truth   Concede that you are this voice says
You are the X   No one else is willing   I went to the cross-
Roads to hitch a ride I say   Then we had to watch

You follow you watch you suffer   Teach me your language you
Know it   It's the fabric   So he'd come up to you said it
Will now be me again   And then I killed him?   For which you
Were Xed   That could be it   he says I   just don't know

The plasticity   of the beginning   is too . . .   chaotic? he says
I kill love in order to love I say   The night rains down again

The eyes that evolved later   But in compressed time didn't
I have none you   defined them not I
                                        Calling out
But I lived through what happened
She fell down started to slip down the terraced slope
And I pulled her up but she   was dying   Why is she so small
Who is she I don't know   Or I do   but won't tell you
Change the meaning of the crucifixion a voice said   Or its tone
Michael says I'm sorry I'm just sorry   archangel's plight
It's occurring again right now I say   I'm becoming an X am I
Will be destroyed again   though I am glorious matter
Are we really letters   As much as we can't see a thing
What I see here   Michael says   is the inside of stuff
I see *stuff*   I Alice say   that what will now create you
Is an opening onto   a dimension   that so slows beginnings
They crumble as they form   The X might disconnect

I may have killed him but did more important things   nobody said that
The moment had a circumference   If I were inside you not me
Maybe even the mountain   it said it you don't know if it's only
In the close-by dimension now I do   Once there were the they crashed through
Like warriors   with their crashing music   I am standing at origin
A moment like a tear- or dew- drop could be like a planetary ring or mist lit
A sense that periphery subtly ex-   pands and I feel the   for growing a mind or
Developmental the progression round grew out around as in a life

We are a listening as if to ourselves speaking in crystal
Crystal   Someone said there was a grid for this lang-
Uage I say no   It can't be measured   I stand at the be-
Ginning to say that the new universe cannot be measured or monitored
We will let ourselves happen in life as in the death world where
No one can be killed   We speak because we are speaking   You can't tighten it

The shadows against the wall indistinguishable the loft wall lofty
Is it order or mass of radio-static   every thing projecting
I said I saw you   want to change or rearrange
You were twinned to measurable stuff once
I converted   from impressions   I-conversion
From doubt to a sense of the moment
Is it temporal   help me then I pulled her   through the air wall
I'm agitated   are you electrified   AGON

What are you   not an image or shade of former
A holy ghost?   insides woven   of?
Rounded but can slide through   body was a mold?
No depravity   lights inside me whole planets

I can read so faint this dust   you are what I was   which one says
Stars or is it honey   It ran out of the wall or barrier   Smelled it
The first honey smell   of bees lingering   We travel across cosmos
Even mountains and seas do

The sea of war   then silence   The sea of cogitation and debt to you
I tried to find a home   last night but found a room con-
Taining a heavy brown diagonal and some magenta red   Paste it on
Beside the sea   the deco salt shaker will there be motion

Now read the knobs   inclusive of the stranger   my voice a
Widespread stain within me   all they had left to start with
This is a company remember
                              some of us asteroids
Or asters   fought off whatever came towards us   paste on its
Diasporic wake
                of spores I guess a question mark
Truth shifted and shifted   what a nut   Drums   erupt so lost
We have always been slightly lost that's our story
It doesn't glue   *It had to be you*

Could you become too empty   to crucify   you must know you die of
The burden of being up on the cross   not of anything exactly
You are letting life and death transfix you at an exact point you
Say and it's . . .   difficult or autonomous within   myself going on
That I feel it that I'm doing it for you . . .   or everything

And then so to hear you in the front of my head

That smart like us one says but out of sequence
Instead of trapping time and space   to make ongoingness
You have trapped life and death   to create . . .   let's call it
Communication   We are trying to find an order to our . . .
Emotiveness   A patchy but searing memory not a
Memorial but a gasp of   stabbing recollection
I remember it I'm inside it do I have to go there in the air
You should be taking on our sins for us   Oh I am
All I do now is absorb them in the night beneath silly dreams
I am doing everything everything   making   the tongue of it

Are you agonized or if that was spoke   in cult I
Measure its or your   your band of vibrations purling
Becoming in dolorous extent is there always ceiling or cessation
I climb onto the ceiling the new bare floor of mine but this be thine
And in that only era says a voice was nothing but a band
Communication the so-called words interconnected stretch in-
Finitely were what there was   Your precious mountain was of it
They were not just words they were matter were they not
This voice I speak says the voice is a congealing from that voice
Which is but the reality of death and what is cloaked
So it speaks in your limbs when you are living *when I*
Was alive   and in the perceived structure of granite
What has it to do with my crucifixion I demand
That you are the place of congealing of translated rupture into event
But now am I above that or not to my new height climbed
Poem would be redefined   a message or is it then gone

I paste fog and a tree or upright with white twisted or spiral flower
I paste an irregularly rimmed pond torn against a thought of a whooping crane
Is the thought flat nothing's flat   I paste pinwheeling sparks
I paste some feeling I used to like   which one   of sitting still alone un-
Thoughtfully   Possible?   I don't like your heart full of guile   Paste?
I still want to paste on that I saw what you were like, do I?
That's worthless   Paste on worthlessness   it's got grey taint frayed and with dirt
Paste on cool hardness exterior and through until the cave
Paste on the heart was a cavern a chamber of crystal giants
In those ancient days there were crystal giants everywhere paste that on
How about indifference   how about a cloaked scorn for the death I'm in
Paste on a cloak round shouldered but inhabited by emptiness
Mental molecules death matter thinking the image of a cover
I'm covered with the thorns of last night paste it on next to paper doily
A rhinestone greeting in my mind to yours hello silly-ass former one
Paste on that the dead neither sleep nor are awake but are cognizant
I see your stream of thought spoken by your image paste it on
The image I am thinking paste on of you   Know you're there
And with its eyes closed hands clasped it projects raptness
Paste on the rapture of our deaths and their knowing particles which may be pasted on

Whispered out the crab nebula you crab you tentacular wispy limbed
Whispering your oration along flickery expanse the counter-
Dimensional anti-crab I am whispery gas and mist-pebbles
The dirt of prepubescent oh very and ever pre   non-organic mind babe
Just please yourself selfless non-creatura hatless
This kind of thought crabs sideways to mammals and their thumbs
I am so big I just do that don't even have a tone-of-voice sister
Only ever possible tone as I make it playing the ghost celeste all across
Whispered to you beyond my comprehension the all I was
Whisper that I'm place these breeze words in your mind the way *you*
Need them I don't need and go on to become king crab soft scuttle
Of the directionless anyone of sea of space dust white like
Aren't you rich not to exist and to paste abstruse realities here
Whispering back to me is so canny low sound so smart

I was so large a whisper
that everything I said
at the same time hap-
pened though I'd never
seen a thing
                              Do you see it become itself
In the instant now when everything already is
First it's shaded by an ecru shade with a pull loop
Keep off the heat after dawn
We cross the sky in order to show ourselves
To who   Now I'm dead but first I was dead
So large a whisper that what would come about
Had already   My consciousness shading the dead heat
On D Street   had already   You had already been dead
Have already that everything I said crosses the sky mind
I wonder what's going to happen   can the dead be surprised
I told myself it was worth it whatever I did
Was it   Or that my impulse would be correct
Spent a lot of time on impulses   often wrong
Pulse pulse   Each pulsation momentary jeweled
Is there failing   No   It is my first time in the sky
When   With a stage whisper conquer the universe
But this was how we were not are
Is anyone thinking our thoughts it whispers to me
Do you want me to   think for you   But how will you
Know yourself   I will recognize my thoughts
Emitted   from the sky point   where the cross is you

Recapitulation

We are walking on the night sky   what you'd call that
This is a memory if we have memories   But I one voice
Am telling you   We walked out of nothing in the sense
We didn't walk out of anything that made sense
There are moving mutational upright forms
There are orange sea-like expanses   We're supposed to
Think there's been an explosion well we don't
We're not interested in what the live want us to think
We are the ones thinking we aren't precisely thinking thoughts
We just think consciousness mashed together pearls
We aren't going anywhere the sky's a black tundra
We remember the previous instant nothing happened
I awoke next to a lake and I was pleased   morning
You remember it in death without being it but it's
More real than a memory in life   We walk across the air
You are leading us we remember our minds we remember
Consciousness we remember that the universe is consciousness
Or is it a remembered consciousness are we now elsewhere
Are we in the silver other part ourselves but more
Did I finally leave the labyrinth that was ancient and beautiful
Did I leave it when we arrived at the escarpment and collage
Did I leave consciousness and have I finally arrived

a peaceful crucifixion in soft brownish wood
I had gone to sleep   my face lit by sleep I saw
I didn't have flesh   I had wood   or rather I
had a depiction have always had a depiction the
senses depict us to us and these words do I had
suffered   but now we existed in an even more mat-
erial dimension   in life that would not be robbed
from us in death where we knew a language of
spiritual imagery   my olive skin and crown of thorns
that crown's better than the gold coronet but it hurts
it isn't I say Christ it's   I who have lived and writ-
ten in poverty for you in the language of gracefulness
and now I have led all the dead to where we stand
in this cathedral of frost and deep night but at the
same time I am wooden with flecks of red paint

stay in this spirit the practical world go to hell

*

She steps across the gap of space   skirt in hand
I'm on the threshold
                         The light of day rings up
It didn't have anything to do with
                                   Was just being itself
Is just re-   fracted order

                    She stepped across the threshold
Remembering her poem   Composed but not written down
The hour / sustains me   Caught in any / time

There was no black hole   there was a failure
Of your subsequent equipment I simply   she stepped
Across / I was crucified   having no gender or hour

Until that moment   when fate was spoken not   written down

*

in the small house in the black night lit where everyone is
she/I steps out of shell body leaving crown of thorns and coronet
(transfigured)

if the light my light encircles my jet blackness then
but there's no then   I was as vast as that I said when
vast was what one thought one saw   I saw luminosity
embracing infinity   and I who glitter and light   a swath of universe
if I burn you what is that   but I don't for   scientists imagine me
I that steps out   of the darkness surrounded by brilliance
and am neither dark or burning   obscure or jewel-like

Here's the black hole no that's just a photo here's the real one
That's just a word I saw it you're dead you've no eyes   It passed by
There's something dark somewhere someone can see   Is there
I came to my senses   From where   They used to be fractions of themselves
The first thing was this speak Did the hole speak It said pro-
Bably something will happen You're joking Yes The best bet

I went with it
                    Let's talk about the creation of the dimension
Of death that envelops life and is enmeshed with that ab-
Straction they both are
And I went there
                    Supposed to be negation so
Didn't start we all came from there not the frig-
Ging hole
I went to it and called out
For I didn't know this
Language yet   And now
I don't know what I called

But I've never been too dead to communicate with you
Each one enacts the beginning of death at some point
It razors out a small hole in a black container
Which is not death but universal ignorance
I seem to have control over a lot of what I do
Through the hole calling out whatever with no vocal cords

Cross tau or chi   X or word crucifixion   My hands' wounds
Have I wounds now   my old hands to see   Born from a wound
Planets pour out   Comets fly out you can see
See in my mind   a voice says   I see you seeing me

Stars for wounds or eyes   remember   I see you too   trying to
Heal us   by suffering   You are projecting   electrical thought at me
From your oldest mind it says   lines of flash voice
Too many images   and your flashing words   curl around us

This is how I make it   make and heal it from a sort   of cross
Sort is a lot or fate   cross crosses   What do you see your mind and
Is your glue blood voice says   My glue blood is voice I say
Voice of mind   electrical line   words or images   words flame

Everything hurts me   words or pictures
Catastrophic action   if it hurts me won't hurt you

citadel of rock forms city of stasis historical course shown e-
rodes to unknown mass words move can you can't can almost
that is read it at beginning not a full form try to form he says
I'm literal rock prairie flat across under geologic sans mouth
you're writing scribing across from who I am at Frailey's cer-
amic shop where you bake the clay but glyphs are near
rock mouth glyph stiff sound for igneous ears hear here
I'm lurking written on that boulder myself tonally inert
then there's a long musical scale the notes are soldiers I'm
not consider a long scale as a row of soldiers in blue
as who or what already wants to use it for power a struc-
ture I'm just a rock if they can extract your spirit who
I don't have I'm a glyph they'll turn you into life I'm alive
read me spoken in that story unelaborate stranger I can be

we were all in your room last night dense as old stars ev-
erything together nearly unmoving even in mind yet
comfortable what were you thinking I thought I had wounds
was still puzzling how this was I had stigmata for you
every time to find you can love the totality of ones and
even embrace poor evil having no power over me now
but last night I was careful so many there I was
set like a jewel wounds on my hands could I still
write like this I thought and at one point I was col-
laged I saw myself patched together not ugly
but not seamless pieces of anything I was does this
apply now everyone needed me needed this bizarre
acceptance of mine fulsome letting you in in your
shock and your dragged along stories of the wars

memory as a universe

trees could be clouds composites composers effigies
I saw it the statue there   but not that one Pallas
then if it were a world of   and will be   statues you are one
but I'm not I have to keep you from being that
enter woods or clouds fleeing from statue
we are in front of house can't see it   no we
in front with invisible statues   go on in it's
light brown   it's just a body   a soul goes to you
I don't want to sit down!   I have to give this
soul my memories   I don't want any of this
leave the little house   we now have no more memories
you can have mine the house was a mess   keep
yours out!   I will reinvent what memory is
do you remember how to get here   leave leave!
red of who doesn't know   the magellanic
the magellanic clouds pulsate with consciousness
very tender   but it isn't money   you don't know
about it I do   promise no more humiliation
start to cloister and putting in but these are strange
items when we rip open the lining soul and I
I meant lent I correction at the heart of it
where you're tiny sarcophagi in the stratospheric
wind   I was putting on my clean voice doubled
my brother spoke with me from I until clean
treachery was once liturgy and assailant I cruci-
crux in the form or former the weather cranks
you're complete their voices are statues   keep them away!
I don't want to know what happened double voice
everyone's voices were statues once I remember but
my isn't I can't hold it wind concerto and the singular
of majesty tell me your uncontrolled finally voices
I'm told you can possess me for vibrating instant   you or me

In my own method of transport feet or knobs
In my I can read any knobs or feet speak your aspect
I can speak already speak your aspect anyone says
We are saying these things as well as screaming You Don't Know Me
The first words ever spoken were You Don't Know Me

In my way of transport whispering feet or knobs
I read the obscure You Don't Know Me writing when I first spoke
Remember someone had already left that screaming message on a rock
Then the table is set with crystal dishes that chant You know me
The food's on invisible dishes made of invisible molecules that are them-
Selves made of invisible syllables the famous poet is cutting up pieces of
Buddhism signed by the author to put in our fabulous collage
Put glitter on your face or aspect and shout Don't Think
I prefer You Don't Know Me

—————————————————————

The people by which I mean anything are standing near the foam again
Anything at all is standing near the abysmal foam asking me to write
Down write or memorize or sing or know or already know its story
We walked across the heavens to here and you led us same as before ex-
Cept it was really the first time and we got caught got stuck in our own matter
Or upended on us turned insideout or we were thrown out of the hole
Anything we might say is it can we stand that speaking the first
Language which was itself what happened and what the matter was

I was to find you   How can you speak
I have no net I understand (ken) almost everything
Who or what are you   I'm from there   transpiercing into yours
Are you material   I am an old cloak   with the sun inside

Body?
        mind. Let's say I'm some of mind

What's your problem
              The universe is holding me back
              I'm faster   even than speech
              I think so fast I'm in motion

              Too fast to run . . . becoming a sun
              Don't want to
Whose rules are you following
              Got to spread myself so thin I can't compress

Are you hot
              Yes I'm too hot   can't ex-
              plore explain   Bad weather
Love?
              No   it's to play with time
              That's all we did there
You're dead?
              I don't know   I'm frustrated
              I don't know where the rules come from
              Notions like gravity get rid of cast-
              ing myself off from self off from

the point where you   it didn't explode   it was my mind
and I arrive from   you don't look like you now   I arrived
that is as the one point I   what they erroneously   try to divorce
I feel I was there too Michael says   puzzled   without remem-

brance I see now   keep going with that   I'll always remember
the only thing I was until I woke up
gem microphone   jet dot   I don't remember you
it was a black tear (wept)   I'm not here   where you see me

we left the tight place where we were   but it was a floating
you don't know time   let's call it something else   let's call it float
or hawk floats   until you're seized
every time I was seized   did you burst and expand

the so-called it   roiled out pain   from my X
maybe the dots where they cross over   if I'm in this poem
I'm safe but if I'm outside it I'm not   so we are creating this poem
the universe created from my crucifixion I believe

because there is a "doing"   speak through the gem microphone now

to orate   how you'd need that   what I'd say
And if you think you have a temperament you don't
Your qualities not so easily named like patches on
            the collage of you
might be modesty and obedience but what good are they?
And if you think you are affected by the stars
please cease to think until you learn how your
            syntax or line in-
habiting your body or site fills it with ever more
spirit than a constellation could
                              I come down from the cross
to say that only eloquence will recreate the universe
though not being as you thought it eloquence it is
continuity and the speaking as your spirit seizes the verse
that sometimes at odds finds the only words others will hear
For I came to you and then to them as in a soft rapid whirlwind
We will understand from what is spoken that we too are
speakers in these earliest times of the language that's
sound and movement and delight in logic, that is three things

death is logical being continuous; life shatters death
that gives it no superiority   why strive to remain
in it which is a rudely colored dragging out of a
set of sensations   All of real power rests in the death world
I the crucified am its supreme embodier

We adherent there are steps even footless rock
The transparent part of the foot telling the truth
We who at first would surround the black hole or cross
Make our entire home out of transcendent memories
So if you slide halted you find we're precise here
Already we moved like retired warriors gracefully
We moved like a new kind of wisdom clothed unsqueamishly
In satinate changeable colors with silver or gold
We remembered violent in what tongue monast-
Ically as what had once fed us and stripped of the old
Force the new one turned conquest into that dying
Thought how to cover what's over not relive even sin
Though it had seemed to saturate you came with an-
Guish we are proceeding through the Galactic Pass
As bodiless almost aimless wandering habits
We have a new tale and standard that bravery is tonal
And grace the gold note catches the riverbank sky mark or
Mottle we complexly followed you as you led
But sometimes you rested up on the cross watching us
And sometimes with us you are arranging new clauses
Torn and tinted out of what memories that no one knew

I don't think you want orders   suggestions?
to forget your tradition   there are all these ones here with their fabric
you keep finding traces of chaos   who did does nothing
think I know more than you   sentenced me but I didn't serve
I want you to know what I know   various soldiers say
my mind is open so you'll know   I met the comet too
you were carrying on lamenting in a corner of death last night
I'm busier than that   it's right here where the crucifixion's lost in tides
I'm transparent   close to the street   and into my
chest thinking   I stepped into her   I remember that
pushing away her fear an element like stray matter
all you have to do is go somewhere and then somewhere else
comes backwards I remember the route   where it's good
I left some stuff over there   a pile of hurt and bad acts   if I have to
I just left them but kept my sense of my own expertise he says
I want my flamboyance she says I want my treachery
everything in flux   you didn't do it now I say to her
she says I want to again   go away   go in the kitchen with daech
I say   I remember the creation
it happened in my kitchen lower back carry-on stay out
I said but then okay come in I'm in control of your death vibe
whatever you did at some point in cosmic blindingness
enter this other   it's just a dimension I keep going there
well tell us   and I put it there too   ignore what you don't like visage

We who of speaking are the interior masters ask
What our anger reflects once was it yours too
Sun or moon whose words steal across my back
Dedicatedly old hat the time come to explain my speech
I come from a long way off translated
Late fracture into all made me   I am in-
Separable
                    Pressed in   are you   what difference
In parka says you didn't need to separate it out
Or try to   language

                    They left moodily anything
That could be the inception of ours our epic
We followed you moodily and all our winds clung
They will always   It doesn't want an ethic
The universe or a description   it does
Want this epic   The battle of my moods
Shade fell on me and became my skin or rock layer
Once once and a petroglyph incised and what was scraped
Away called itself the rejected but is part
We are now different and the memory shifts
We can only remember in terms of what we are now
Makers collagers an epic in motion but not in time
A wide green rectangle attached to lightning bolts

A lot of us aren't sure that we want to be related now
Not if of fate and the Erinyes come over and over as if I
Had to be some myth I don't remember he says never knew
I worked for you someone says but I don't know you any more
I still want to be related to you I say to my brother
I don't care how many people you killed as a sniper
They are all in my apartment or on this escarpment
We're all related but we can break up memories and enactments
Into citrine-colored facets pasteable   I think a low voice says
That big bang was now exactly now when we're breaking them up
This is our narrative and if I remember a piece I'll put it there
But it is no longer a piece of a trauma but of a story we're making
An untimed story we've never lived in and don't have to be
So some point explodes so what it was our dark minds fed up
And what it made wasn't time and space because we're dead where are we
I can have fiery-faceted citrine mind if I'm a dead mountain

We are the live-in-darkness ones the other matter where we start
And come to us like gentle knights on steeds the pieces of explosion
As if dancing slowly   I saw your mesh armor instead of element
Me I saw element like bismuthine pulled apart into lines or was it congealed
Was that in the dead or live reality I see voices come apart a black voice not void voice

We never needed to say "matter" you know

PATH THROUGH COLLAGE

The ways through intersect at me my mind or body

the peaceful wounded   caring for you but
that's not care it's a gathering to me of the fallen
silver souls   And we rock this noplace death
with voices not describing us

PATH THROUGH COLLAGE

the only revolution rough paste
to create any memories   I remember
holding the universe together again and again
by not being what you wanted then you wanted it

And of the beautiful recollection   as if impressed in wax
The knights who are I   gather to praise a new kind of matter
Of we dead will be the malleable but   everlasting fact a hypostasis
Dark or light   and we have recognized that we just are unsolved
And my hands or thoughts of hands   in the highest apartment placed
Upon this matter to feel if it would   already need to be healed
I can heal what I make I say can't I   hast thou wrought this you say
More: can there be words and then that thing of it so dar-
Ling

        take the fingered wedge   and sense of unworthiness
        take the old air overbreathed and inspire it
        take lumps and long unfoldings
        of selfish material

                    and glue it on
               inform a new matter

the reason she was still sad dead erased in this new mixing
because the molecules of sorrow might themselves be broken down
into their infinitesimal sub-parts until this black and light spiritual clay
invests us with clear grey pink and inner curve of a bubble do you follow
inner curve of the mind that forgot itself in this discussion that is palpable
dead-thing and existence you will have to let go of what was done to you
as much was done to me Xed in perpetuity to stand for what happened
to anyone or -thing but we are reassembling our thingness
into spirit matter we do this again and ever lacking nothing for re-
newel   And a voice says you must continue to reassure us in your way
you are all that we have reminding us of our sole lonely claim
to be the stars and suns and expanse that was once time
can you see it can you glue it   as spirit we will now transcend spirit
you will always be my love you must say into the wind you are reinventing

I was sad and frayed said the voice   though not alive
Why do I keep having to take care of everything
Even though I'm dead and though you say we're beginning

In the language if you killed someone   dead you are
Not that   your title might be not-as-formerly   not mister
Even your world you killed in no longer existing
Who are you   I ask myself on the cross who did I be-
Come   All of this and us we are pasting yellow dust devils
Ripped in half or whole   You became who wrote for us
You became crossed on the cross   by time and space dissolving in-
To you out of whom sprang the supple language of quiddity

We of the past Sami languages walk with all you dead
Paste with you black burnt siena and neon crayola hearts

We give ourselves to what is not a wind but a memory
Of wind that is anterior to it memory's structural ideal
It blows   The words come to be said   You are on the cross
Calling to us to paste down the word for hypertrophy
It is hypertrophy no it's inclamation I called upon
Everything we say's another kind of living or fate a fabrication of voice

Lying next to me late last night another killer/soldier
Just lying there absorbing the shock of his death vestigial disgust
What is disgust when you can't open your mouth to talk through
You're talking   We latch onto something in your mind that trans-
Lates   Translates what   He says even my thinking's changing
Huge swathes of thought I don't know how to have   Bigger than
My head he says   flowing out of it into the whole of the sky
Why am I lying down   when it's pointless to rest   I want to
Be next to you but why   I came naturally to this bed
I never rested   when I was a warrior   What am I now
What am I for   This is a coming to be of what you are
Nothing I recognize   Flowing in and out   of me   I was pro-
Mised glory and goods   I don't understand this flow
Of different me   Because it's me   Searching for my violence
I need IT   my belief   I need to intimidate you don't I
That need's seeping out   how rough on me   to lose it
I can't do anything to you   Just talking   without a mouth
Later I see he looks Asian   young   has a sparse pointed beard

I made it honey I lost everything
isn't that marvelous   I remem-
ber   us   without hating you
I remember your companion the
leech no longer red-black no long-
er valent   Only polyphonic minds
words like light wraps where one
had shoulders   I remember you
were in a vicious dream I had I'd
known you for seven years   in an
apartment on third street   you
wanted to slap me around   But that
wasn't me   though I wore the inveterate
sign of the grey-black dove ruby blood
and had already been slapped by a sonof-
abitch   I'm mindless now except for bat-flit
rumors and happy to be so gone I just talk
words come from nowhere to be said

We go to the rim of the abyss or margin of Lake
Unconscious   That's where I live that's where
The cross is   whatever tells me what to do or
Vice-versa   I'm asking it things is it just me
We are asking it to know more if we can that is
Articulate our infinity   continue to collage our colors

I left you for
Articulation   Why
I have such thoughts and words the silver fabric beaded
Shivering

On the cross of thwartedness watch my mind despairing
Metallic late-day gold weight so you can know
How you feel   I was just up there part of my juju
I remember how you had wanted me to believe
That everything is regulated well it isn't it's created
right now

At the lake you have depassed Devil's Elbow and dived in
help me know   you ask it
but all knowledge comes from me the crucial phantom
directing the collage

the path through not for physical walking but a tracer
or more than one   this is the path through or one

the path swirls sometimes like a ribbon   what is it for   nowhere to go

a glimpse of it sometimes   paste on glimpses

you led us Alice across the plain to here to create new beauty
but we are have been and will do so in no particular order of tense
it is now the past some past one says and I'm alone in a cloak
a mute cloak of the impossibility of intention or procedure
I don't want to go on and when I followed you Alice
I wasn't sure I wanted to futility didn't matter either
this is no story it's a cloak it's my beloved listless aimlessness
shall we paste it on the abyss it's still mine and I don't want a thing
even to paste even to paste with a voice what color is your cloak
darker than a witch's mind and I want to stay like that

The broken line diagonal light raygun sparking down
I sat in the airplane being transformed in spasms of color-
Less blank it is something for which none   A mass of words
A heap glued and the image file burning revives for you see this
I crux who save by creating a new X intersection that of
Not image and breath but light and death   every bit of
Word moves and gesticulates like a thing in the res fate to be

In the plane night they pull out the last of it in me

(Michael)

I'm finding my way around   It's a maze you can get
Once you learn to move in it   Never to the right or left like that

All at once you're there   No sense of getting there either
You don't take a trip and be between stops   You don't have to walk

Yet it's not as if you don't know how   to walk
People and places beautiful in a   heightened way
They're more than normal   perfect
Like a painting and photo combined   I've never seen them

Before like that   Have I seen them at all the people from my fam-
Ily my ancestors   have smooth brown-black skin
There are clouds up that don't move   Or I go somewhere else
A place where I'm thinking   Like I talk aloud standing

In the words of my thought   Words are like a making up of
Music sometimes   I find out what everything's about   then forget

It was amended   so scorpion   that   this is blank
if you read this hobnail   why do I have to know this one
in knowing   Slip in through aperture be-   ween bicamera
who has photos
                    no one knows but me
                    because I don't speak your
I brought these early rocks   in my capacity
I change your sore   they aided me   by being brave
they are the same as words   was the hole between di-

mensions a wound   yes death is a wound of that kind
the people   if you consider   every identity as   part of the people
they follow   stepping on words   to get to our new
at night I am holding some close   even killers

We are losing things   photos and copies   we go out into the
abyss at any   time then return   my apartment the escarpment
I can hold   any dead   person or thing   close
and words I don't know   shaped like spiders and spirals   dots

or thirteen dimensions of   a wavy line   Strip off your
bad thing   and throw it   like a peel or scum   away

We of the heavens burn in tune to each other verbatim
I was in someone else's dream all night can't remember it
Sometimes it's like that   it was okay though I myself
was just looking at it   it didn't really matter
two guys try to resolve small problems I sit here breath-
ing now   What of consequence even if I lead you re-
peatedly die for   burning   in tune to you verbatim

We went down to the sea of agape to lethe to consolation
but I couldn't forget ev-   erything I remember you're my
sister she said do you have children   a simple dementia
we went down to the wall between something and nothing what a joke
nothing is always something   no one can win
we keep burning in the same key I mean noisily vibrating
if you get away you're still with them the jetsam still knows you

Could you say the cosmos is consistent   Its in-
consistency frightens some   the meds are dreadful you
always break through them   That was a long time ago
when you couldn't remember you'd become more real eventually
Like now you can't help it   even if you do nothing to better yourself

I stand here and know they're letters how know that because I'm ev-
Erything though with partial occluded   recognition
So tall and twisty sculptural but moving   pale blue then
You can turn black   I stand here and know you're a letter

Though you can change your shape   even cactuses and Joshua trees
Can't   Let-   ters letters   can if they want   to asking to be
Seen   Prophetically   I am in or am   your face
It has a stem   and smooth limbs metallic   blue now

I can be anything anywhere   The lis-   some letter or
Litigious   order in the   letter court here   are all the others
Swaying dancing in place   This old dress I say I
Can wear this old dress   of what al-   phabet I

Taught you says   the blue-black   letter come to
Me in the tone of voice   of hesitation   wonderment and   chance

but what of the texture of memory to learn to project
fortunate or unfortunate replay of badly loved tunes
so you used to do that now you do it dead no sensory input
you do it dead without what matter you were what mirror
no one loved me couldn't get out of the house war wouldn't end
wasn't supposed to be a mirror here of you to me it's just old
it's old words you blur them until they're pale blue swirls
everywhere not to remember but have a little how I
remember quickly freezing when they came to arrest me
for heat I had to freeze so quick I couldn't plan to freeze
these are our sketched across epic in the war of blue swirls
I remember hatred a cage for your face when you wanted to get back
I remember having to be hated I remember scarecrows melt into glue
or any no structure of recall my shoes or pants just texture

Who or what would broadcast these are its outer soundings
It too itself or I-voice   there's no space   red of my mind
Around and the sheered-off the crimson as if it were an energy
Tearing the story a physics of sorrow or fate in cochineal
These dolorous   no you are already interpreting one voice says
I am simply making something to paste on says another
Out of whatever   She weeping lay down in the bed of first night
Near me long face and a scarf for it wasn't over though she be dead
And the moment of living violence bled into the long death moment
So its cog teeth passed over continually where she had no
Skin for she was now an image but what first could there be
In the scream you ignore momentarily tearingly and red or
Purple it was fistful the men said no other game in town
To all the stars and planets to be the black hole said that we
For this is our narrative are stopping breaking up with defunct
Gearwork ancient the red streams out again I thrust my body in
So nothing would be born but the elemental crackle or is this
A collage   Some of us move quietly around the new lofty room
There's a reindeer's heart or there's mine stop leading us on
I'm quiet after this crucifixion where's my noise sassafras

It was a dried dust-color spiral I pasted on in a cut-glass dimension
You don't have to say anything you are being said and edgeless
Orator's memory will hold it the new universe from now
Or other discolored spirit like some other imprecise element

You were the words so the planes landed
we give you our energy now from this point
how can you we can without compromise
you are though the one who knows says heals
am I forgetting any memorial thing here
and in the stars . . . and in the stars the first were
the first now we're headed home to the first
there is no destruction when you are the only
unit

I bring prolix my brow shapes we haven't
chosen those shapes   choose shapes here in the
hotel   on the ice. Casually   that the universe we
had curtailed with formulas pulled back from
our dream and changed its shape where we stood.
And if I said I formed you out of my very suf-
fering, you or it said I struggle with the form.
That we in every part articulate another
when we know we are one. But I say to it we
are finally so many we can't see you as one,
though you are us and we must be one one
body or mind even I the poet/orator/savior/
crucified perceive so in my torture. And
I perceive that I would be wrung dry
of suffering to produce form. That being
my point says the universe but yes there
are so many of us and to return to the most
prior beginning all of us must return not
as one thing but as each. And, it the uni-
verse says, *you* have made your one self be
so many forms you can't keep track.
True, and it is wearying. But I can't begin
yet again, in this same again moment; I am
my mutational form. We are changing
and when we know we are changed we will
feel peaceful. Blood on your forehead it says.
I am thinking. Is this my epic too, says
the universe as one. What else would it be?

Why should I want it   when you don't have anything
He says I want to paste on the image   that you touched
Mine with your bloody forehead
I had been blind and dead am still technically sight-
Less for I have not known that meeting of eye to object vibration
But I see that our thoughts are mingling and the touch
Of the foreheads will always exist I don't care if you a-
Live are singled out you singled me out
He I see as an albino with crisp hair freckles shut eyes
What you see I always saw   sound making relations in shapes
But I saw your love's sudden concentration on my mind
It wasn't because I was blind he said I didn't if that were
Real now I say I'm trying to find a light in you that tells me
To go on as I do and ignore the part of shades the buyers
And sellers of live drama

On the part of speech but there isn't that without verbs or much pronoun
Flashing across the reds of night or those white featherlike strokes
So that is how your momentary boxes were found worthwhile
Although somewhat makerless scraped off or scraping the walls
A loss of self-consciousness as pun you're too old stranger

I still didn't want you to forget me though I danced without you

The man of death's weapon gets scraped white the myth scraped
All that's remembered the strokes of paring then no face that was
One though one is   do you now start to read what you hear

Roger and sense delicately fossilized forms of use

What have I the almost-pronoun brought back from this one

With is there a room or box carried barely personable
You have friends you have to give things to of yourself do you
I don't want it back I don't want to be yours

What I across the skyless blood-smeared autonomy
Accept

I saw a principle   I already detested it
the statue   led you to battle   And she hummed
I got up on the cross and it could have been the
same thing as anything   I somehow do it
differently I know I'm changing it I keep
trying to say what it is again nobody tells
me not to be up here I am leading you to
believe in me offering you nothing
though I say I've invented reality and maybe
I have it has to be *for* something you all
keep telling me that is the epic and you come
to be its members arranged so there's substance
and formality I'm leading you and urging you
to love regroup resist definition   healing who am
wearing wounds   let me do this for you
the only one I can

Came towards me said no more projecting just you
he wants you dead from jealousy   so now we'll really give

whatever you say as it is held against you   I prepare a path
through the collage   more   that there is neither life or death without
this mouth unevolved   so she speaks and the staleness flees
but if I but if I speak there will be something   so I made
elements that word means anything in itself or trans-
lation you mutter   I took them to the Terpsichorean and said
death dance please   but souls dance without limbs
saying whatever   comes into its mind like a countertrack
to the skipping pebble   more he says   and I will fast stick

to the wall of words til I've absorbed every keeping-on and turning
I was not meant   and aught I know precise is a reject
seeking flower moments   I will never get out of here
The basic language voice says isn't truncations or cuts
you think you forget it   but whatever you said then exists
everything you say is this made   but how did we
start doing this   I think you did it he says   but comes
with memory and then something remembers everything for you
I'm holding the memory flat against the wall   I hold the memory

but I can't remember what I remember oh somewhere you do
on the westbound say you're not on   the languages just trans-
late themselves to pieces like that thing I'm saying you learned I
taught but what did it mean a thing   but we don't know
how to be without   it's just   you caught it   but if I'm the mem-
ory because he says you're the memory why am I each thing
ringing so you're remembering   he says because the dead
the words have to already   be but they remember the scribble of it
I know he says you want to know a straightforward path
that's a trick of the forest none here   lead be crucified heal others re-
member   no one else can they hadn't already arrived
in this place before as they say the beginning he says   then
who am I   oh you know if you're anyone or not
I remember less and less oh you'll remember everything with your back
against the wall

the memory   and it isn't in a line you don't remember a line of remembers
but the pieces of one you might   what's the scribble of it then
not straight obviously   and they come to you not all at once
even if you're head   because you he says you're always remem-
bering something   the dead might get stuck on a guilt
but if I'm on the cross   that's the memory and everyone's re-
living their despicable parts   always remember and the first
we're going through that again   no I'm changing it

and a group of real uninstitutional crystal along the path
dead crystal of anything she leadeth me you can sing lock to be
picked no hair these in the ruby lines fossilized like flesh world
deeply below it unjudging all the way to no bottom to time's
body see the twisting shelter of it or death as a shrine electrified
here on this road after exhaust the work on it or the railroad
with many africans have lost identity none of us cured or ghastly
we could kill me a voice says then I spiral into beginning
having betrayed people the which you remember for me
I remember consciously I say in me searing my duped patience
telepathy with cat or that's dangerous mountain a youth
dead mount to be smeared with its thoughts in a lipstick vacuum
backs all raw from hatred as an element cosmic no word order
the deadly night in the eye but we are voting beneath a green light
do you want to stay or go is there a choice after my demise
are there choices in the night something to choose to refuse
your golden apple your precious exquisite multiplying thought
shaped in everywhere I want it to be mine not yours
facts or you plot or am in   I am losing it again my ID
DO YOU WANT TO STAY OR GO   IS THAT   IN TIME

It's not difficult   but the sadness being lengthy
And was it ever warranted   never arrested yet
You are muffled   and the statues appear imagistically when I'm sad
The white smooth one of me or we   who needed to stand here
Dreaming of better than eyes I don't know if you need me
Pertains and he wonders why he had to drown white in his
Jacket just to be here where he used to be   I have more thickness
And definition he says   perhaps I'm supposed to shed it
Useless process   and if you once had to do wrong you get sadder
I'm not sure I had to one says   but what is that   we were so dumb
Tragic but I didn't   I was almost looking for it   but I didn't
Have to be compulsive or impulsive   hard-pulsed or walk on edge
I too remember   so many say to me   then supposed to balance
It with joy as if there were these   inventiveness   out of messages
From others on how to be and destroy   the protean hands or rays
Do it   your mind does it   filling in gaps between the calm

I was dead yeah but I was something somewhere
Blown across everything in the nowhere dimension
With some energy I can give you some if you deserve it
I'm only going to help you in a pure way like
If you're sick I'll give you some electric juice can't do
Everything   But where I am exactly where you
Are but not like a ghost in my own simultaneous
Dimension   because we're both part of everything
You don't get it   I'm articulating within you though
Use your brain to help you write our epic   I'm
Always whispering in you the world's full of imagistic
Shit   I can only say I don't really remember it
I remember it's all scurriers with hard-shell tensions
Trying to kill you but then you're dead waiting for more
Change   the epic of changing death the poem of touch-
Ing us with a lie-detector then a point explodes again
Not really we aren't pictures in anyone's eyes and we are
Evidently the ghost dance   what is a ghost you'll find out
But not in time but in time for something like our
Salvation what you're here for no one knows why so tell us

a lake
a green lake of
a lake of ice
a piece of snow
the escarpment overhung
the chaotic abyss beneath
remembering
forgetting
forgetting what you cared about
not caring about   not caring
loss
loss of a name for the seer
loss of a name for the conscious one
loss of a name for the extent of everything
a creation a making
a creation without logic
a creation without a purpose
a creation not yet knowing its parts
not yet knowing what there might be
a non-creation a sitting still until it happens
there is nothing that can happen there is mind
of mind I would be
crumbling no scraped walls
as a concept you would already   have to have known it
not a concept not matter
not a concept not matter but remembering
I am loss or I am lost
with   for   or not   not a verb
a piece of static

because beautiful   nor healthy we don't need to know
the rains bent   so forth   and then we each have to remember
I don't take it there   wider and written or drawn not legibly
can you tell me what's clear   there   and the static   feel hobnails to know
it was about static that might burst out at you
there was more   a sort of story the girl   you could see it at once
in my mind   a sort of red-brown backdrop or surround'
she doesn't do anything   it doesn't signify   is it clear
I rode horse all the way to   and partial seeing   of the ride   and at the
same time elsewhere the girl   I saw the horse before I saw
the painting of it white brush   you have to go get   your clothes

You have to key it in she can't but I can the wires are naked
In this factory-like room he's so impatient that I do err but
I am doing it she was too timid   We will now cross the bridge
A different man and I are stopped by cops but on the other side
I have identification he says a blunt instrument wrapped up in
A white handkerchief   You are a recovering addict the cop says
                                        OK go on
There was but one substance perhaps it was mind
Or there were two that were essentially the same thing as essence is
Any of us can identify with that it didn't have to have an origin
Or was it   Can there be one   or is that just linguistic
The way "nothing" is   And then we did it all in compressed heart-
Beat instantaneously though you can unwind it in an
Evolutionary line like a scientist wistful for time
It rolls up when you die but you are not dissolved
You are unified spiral as art the ammonite I will
Remember it all in a new way tell me again

Weave the hand no ditch it long rays for fingers long beams
you will sing a low penetrant not penitent   not a penetrant
that is the meaningless word trilled   not meaningless
they still didn't SAY who was supposed to hear it with what ears

I am following you everywhere for I am you my heart   .
I am your love I am your purpose though I follow
Thrice came judah to the wrack or wreck in the ice-tinged
Wake the curse of any ship in any space   not judah any name
As foreseen for there had never been action only renewal
Of old sick light emitted eons ago   until now don't
Name them stars   And wandered from each other still pulled backwards

The voice in the night said 'pledge to use old signs'
But I must find them and will they be old   Make them
Myself at the first invention and was there that interpretative senses was there

I is invincible especially on the cross of whatever design as long as it por-
Trays an intersection. At the point of intersection I was born. But to con-
Tinue to be born I will then transcend that point

I stand at the beginning   One does not have to have legs
to say that the new uni-   Not necessarily aloud
verse cannot be monitored   There is no one outside it
We will let ourselves hap-   We being it must go on
pen as in the death world   There are also living the dead
where no one can be killed   They cannot be killed again

This verse declares my opening to causal light a phrase that
Doesn't make sense though you know what I mean. I
Have uncovered this lux within myself. I am rumbling as
Golgotha did   and the dimensions are disconnecting in purple
Shapes of cross   the place of experience as consciousness
Memory condensed into   is it radio or transmission
Where did it come from   nowhere or some other kind of
Moment   Not an agon no dimension wins   I   do   I
Am not a dimension

Whatever space you want then vast or imprecise floats on or in or as abyss
Whatever you say comports with the chosen space the sounds but I'm
Thinking really not speaking it what says thought normally ex-
Isting in a head space that's no space it says who are you a light
Are you sure a light in a thin space of no extent to speak of a lit what
A lit crucifix maybe light of torture or contortion or sound so in-
Tense the fire of it bursts seen Romantic   Not in that kind of head for
I a voice was once notorious and now experiment with thought or soul paste
Unreal unreal you can make it out of groundup premonitory
Whites where pictures are cast of what happens to us dead
The soul of a firefly that's what you are   tried to speak to me here
Because once thought he or it was love wants me near I slip away
Everything slips away or pastes down a will or form is it
Form thin or vast it might be far the new space   And the tiny
Color I'm still a crucifix floating and sleep brown like wren the

Letter or language   your memory of your old wingform paste
And the word crepuscule curves around a hat what's a hat
I tear off love as some aqua-green for no eyes   Are we perhaps all memory
Weren't we always so of form seethe and prevaricate like you used to
We could paste on a huge memory castle squares sockets stairs
Don't have to walk climb be sheltered   do we have to love   *I can bear*
my pain not yours

YOU CAN'T COME IN   I already did
You won't get it   I'm in I don't have to get it
You can't speak this language yes I can
  We bid you   you came in in between
the words right?
  We bid you   bring nothing just lose it
Okay
        I remember loving you   Don't
  love me or I won't come in   You're in
  Won't stay   This kind of place you
                don't go back on
In my life went back on nothing
  The guys swung over for a sec
I said no
  I went to Loss - - - - -
That's how I got here   at what time
No time   You made it   What a river
  Don't AnyOne press on me

                                    .

He's lying on the bed   your dreams are he says about people who say things
I kill   But you're now killed   At the beginning of the world he says
Something was killed   Not at this beginning I say   and you can't kill anyone now
I've killed enough for ten twenty lifetimes   it was Africa   Are you proud
I'm sick I can't get up off your bed   You're dead   you can get up
In the first world he says we   killed the first air and stars   We turned every-
Thing we could to stone   I wanted to change what I saw   And Allah
A pre-   sumption I always thought wrong   but I like to be clear about
I wanted to say a reason   What are you going to do now?   Lie
On your bed   are you disgusted   I'm trying to make sure
I get your words right   Why   I don't know how I hear and under-
Stand you   It's because I'm so near   even in you thought dead
He's whispering another   man says   Is that how it's done   You figure it out he says

if you let us see the signs in your head a voice says
expressly that we see them in your head is that the
same as seeing my voice I ask expressly it says this
is the science of what one will hold in one's mind
a picture or   vocation an interrogation a drawing

I saw a face with a mask of light   a rectangle e-
mitting light and was examining   the darkness of a dark wall
her mask was light   I mean my mask is light exploring
leading or crucified you see with it with a mask

the mark on the dark is in my mind I examine
lately I saw her or it who's myself   'pledge to use old signs'
they may leak from the stigmatic wounds on your left hand
Praise X I have never known why I did anything
the explosion is only a lento   the pain is only phantasmagoric
detritus of way-station light there are no thorns only the engraving

I left you to go home but then you were there
all of signs in my head the old signs on the windshield
on the black windshield on wall will there be severance
there is no windshield or face but a rectangular light mask

there isn't anyone here I see everyone but they're not here
at the start who is it just this sound there isn't any
thing static vibrations wind chimes rustlings buzz or
is that me you are on the cross I am vibrating why why
are you you aren't here night or day pure air trembles
I hear it with what with it I'm of it whatever it is I am
so you are master of your own quintessentiality baby I'm
just shaking hearing myself shake til it's these words like
even on the cross or in this instant across I'm leading the
universe to timbres and tones we are and making do you want
formal as in what I say language they all get set off
and touch each other the glass air pushes into wordings so
what you want to call it's all in your mind you say to
me hear it I say with whatever this is that we are all of it

If you made it because you did that with your senses sorting
Didn't have to sort says a voice   If everything you see is a leftover
Images says another   What's an image   I brought it here
Who are you image   What are we remaking out of what it says
I left by my door and   what say the commentaries is my door
created the world   I meant that literally tomorrow now it is
Just a door   I meant that everything would be larger unsorted
And would paste down figmental shadows that pleased
But in death itself is all equal   The trouble has been the
Drag into it from the sensory life invented at the crossroads
Of sorrow   You were going to fix it for us one says

Once one says I had no fingers   then had them   Now I have
The image of fingers   Did you really not have them be-
Ginning I I say am begging and am leaving via door

You are always crossing that line   and we have not seen yet
I had no eyes for days   and dwelt in the embrace of mind
It was all consciousness   every shadow of potentiality
And that there would be no history   now I brought you
This accord my brother   we will be parties to
That any shade speak without a   story without   a mouth or vocality

cannot be named as
before if ever   We
are taking part the
forms withdrawn from old matter

Reject your previous attachments
What you now attach to the moment round
Whatever you discern without knowing I am pon-
Dering undidactically

Press the knot and glue it down on the former I'm the form-er
Why knot these pictures that were taken of the past
Only stand in for being there the stand-in the big-banger or ore pay
I'm paying for your identity   Xed in to cover whose losses
This part's positive remember plus what do you no I now do
Paste to without recall what arrives this matter pretty
The jolly this torn half   gluing all the dirt together

I have no heart saith the universe yet   and Lost
You're only an abyss and us saith I the ever Xed
This heart dot conception this cell which story disappears
Ravels into or then you burst again as if existing
That's only if you are but we dead the most of you know
That probable dream of your origin is now covered over
With to heal the tear the X of my half-life and
The other half is now being pasted on

Grasp the small knobs to read   no to have memory of the words
feel them what you say and remember the epistle at the beginning or
is it oration I have come here to tell what I know for I remember it
when we were younger we were perhaps in more beauty but didn't know
now when all seems flawed and corrupt do we know how to find beauty
I'm speaking to the live of their worlds but to the dead of their minds
that are sullied by turpitude for if one is impure or hurt everyone is
and the very stars are why are you sorrowful I can't forget the wrong
the knobs I am touching are the wounds on my own small hands
for I have been on the cross again pondering if pain is of the nerves or mind
I would try not to paste myself on the new collage as this but I'm yet this
I have so far been enabling creation only stasis is produced by happiness
but there must be other mind surely we don't know every way to see or feel
whatever beauty I thought I had perceived I'd myself made
and I made my pain for I allowed myself to feel as one expected me to
then at last the long moments I found between the throbs or beats of sensation
that had a different source in myself where I didn't precisely exist
I rested in those I who didn't exist then but knew I rested
I had found what endures outside of qualities within me
and I bring it to you here take it the end of straining clarity yourself
try to memorize it but differently from before it might be in these words
or anywhere though you have no location and it doesn't somewhere in-between
the knobs

Sooth or balcony of ash I destroy
sooth the spouse of commencements
hygienic or hyperthermic as an old sign
you are just an old sign   the way back grabbed
my wilderness we they trow but old signatures
and as this corps came together I chose it
in the wode or in the plain of astrality the whirl-
pools where genuflect late hieroglyphs who walk
move or flete like dragonflys do I sing
forsekying from before or after skylines
you mite fabricate thy flesh or flash exist
and if enacting is trusted as if with a mind
I enact myself that is a wold mass or chi walketh

Go back before the wedge
                            edge of alkalinity or salinity
there ys a voice of no marks and it is mine
that breatheth earth or roils the waters you'd say
I'd say that make matere where
as if the iotas of that flew about in blind
and my own voice likewise particular in piece
and where do these particles come from our one mind
but without shape of thot without skewer
why wood ther ever be change or e'en a now
why wold any *thing* and you are singled
tentatively armed like a bear or a god one
like a ringe oneself cercling one's own self
lyk a magistrate at once a magus lynx
an owly face a starhapped blandishment to live
as if that were a word   and then there be one with
if a word is inbound and cognate as thee universe
know its verse and do I know from here
pledge to use the old signs oh what are they

and they bring me to safety softly like of mine
hart of an axe   that signifies my acuity
the very chi that cut chaos shortly a myth
but y seke the truth in its roodness for thee

I do al *for* you as you have bidden and in pain I
close upon the centered fact or bee or unbenight
twist at once to evolve in an instant flat into you
but seedlessly sweet and thyme pored so to smother firstness
that it ys dead and e'en its ghost live only the old signs
thruout the spirit of mine thruout the shar-
pening witt and the first arrowe shot to stiffen
and the fyrst hole blown open for only action
so wede move acrost fyre and we dyd but I
was up on the cross or rood in yet the first stage
in simultaneity of atomic parts of grete us
greter the night unblinded by its lights   and urge
its pulsations each an olde signe as it would be
and this pulsates without counting or wind-carriage

I see but in your mind wher you speke freely
I see what you and I know and how to go about
you see with your voyce but there is a mentall voyce
calling on up and it says the one who speaks
I see in your heed the old signes a maze of sounding
and I read how you told me of an instant that hystory
of the universe that in a meer second all of it happed
and yet were you living out your wee bit of yt

The signs for it *are* it   for as I see them in mind
I am that telling all at once   the signes themselves
and though I eye- and lip- read them I'd still be them
as if stolen away or are they the stolen by mee

that canna be systematized   and I saw and see the round maze
in thy spirit from about as to how to follow and get out

––

it didn't matter which tongue she spoke she was an old signe

––

I contain the maze   of old signs: alpha, fever, victory;
and before that stillness and reed; and before that the crachat;
before that flower petals shaped like wedges in ombrils
and I was a woman and before that an age a rock and fossil
and before that a sign ever a sign for the signs of eyes
and before words I was a word and crucified before I was born
stretched on a tau and before broken open to create you
I was whatever sign eternity *is*   spoken by the wall

we moved over the deep with our own minds and force
we quietly broke open and at once there was now   the measured time
     some knew but
irrelevant to others   we quietly break being you who were pieced
to break   a composite of signs which have the only meaning
I myself watch I mean we in the only laboratory
we move across the laboratory   calling it the sign of thought
we had tried to order ourselves over and over   alive dead or other
I am other   I am calling us to order   across the marine dark signs of it
I will let no one go unforgiven   untouched to my forehead
but it is I who do this and beseech you to follow the maze
in your own mind I bequeath you you need nothing but
an amazed spirit and a life eternal among the glittering signs of it
to be amazed seeking nothing for you know the way
it requires no thing or victual shelter or cloth
you don't need to be alive or dead you are simply other
aren't you and you are not in pain   that is a sign
the old signs are other now they are not signs

Breaking you to engender by stabbing in eye
Dying loved one wants to stab me in the eye
From the earlier eons a death of one despised I counsel a merci-
Ful tolerance   If these dreams mean something, do they have to?
It was about static that might burst out of you at you
Electric warriors for no reason and the whomping music of that
Speak to me   two kinds of duration one is a hollow dome of moment
One is almost like that static   event-crackles or phrases
I'm standing in a darkness shaped like a meñinas wedge of a skirt
Nothing occurs I remember sense of misbehavior then loss intent
On destroying me my eye but that's just loss itself not a
Person   I see you I say to the bedaggered   He of course blind
The other might be someone else why not

I'm starting to accept the cross   this is our story the dead say   that's
The cross   Want it to be like something you'd say but it's my cross
How am I helping I don't know   That you are singeing us
Until new thing even in death for we invented all this you say
Lonely-making death   Unperceived universe   Call forth
Reality   a tiny life whatever you didn't have to believe
In it the shape   believe in don't believe in   the construct
It's some blips someone says   yet no one can leave
Not so bad   Make a start   as in start-le and she sings
They pulled sounds from me translating them frugally
Paste on the new collage every disordered dot real now

you must have learned how to save yourself
somewhere in your substantial intelligent life
or was that necessary I climb down rung ladder
cliff wallside and slide through round hole
it isn't well lit they're shades against the light
and my head's open they are looking inside I watch

placement portentous of calling forms small
we need you to tell us . . . it starts . . . but
the meaningless terms . . . stentorian and your
voice or sound . . . mine resounds all out

into the canyon . . . at each place where it pools . . .
a beauteous or cursed . . . not cursed . . . in
the tide of it collecting . . . an invincible presence . . .

for you see . . . like street lamps . . . or striations

_____

why is your head open
to hear and talk to you   to press to yours my thought

Memorial Day I remember the first onset of the universe
I was told someone was dead but there was no one
To die or to tell me is it the river or air or other element
Surrounding me you must cross the Sky River
Its language already provokes fear and beauty I speak from
And if you live here follow me it's you I myself will die for
And I died for the wilderness of it and the planets I didn't know
For every voice I had remembered and recorded
You who are listening   we the ones who listen to what
We say   there are twisted pieces of disintegrating stars about
Dirty planet-dissolved dust long-lost light in pools
Space collapses for it's just an idea but we souls abound
And I call to you at the first   I am the most light years away
But I am everywhere there is nowhere my voice is everywhere

VI.
THE POEM

OTHER SIDE OF FABRIC

Pay no attention to this world   Stop doing it   Stop doing this world
And *I* say that   I say I'm ageless   and effectively   on the other side
Of the fabric you call this world   also known as   'the labyrinth I left'
I'm mocking it   I'm offering   the healing of words   other side of words

'I was born dead'   says an old punk song   Come to life now I say
'Born dead   born dead   I'm walkin thru   this world born
Dead'   Come to life I   the formerly crucified   woman tat-
Tooed with the Labyrinth   say   I who converse with the dead

I who embrace ev-   ery soul of the real   dead at night in my
Room   who heal the very dead   say   Pay   no attention to
This world of de-   faults of elections   and crass men of the
Accepted fab-   ric   I'm creating   another element   Come to

Life with me   Ig-   nore the United States the   European Union
China Russia India Is-   lamic fuss   I'll accept you however sha-
Dy you were   I embrace the slaughtered slaughtering dead   but also
The alive   Leave whatever   you're doing   just listen   Listen to me

What I sing   and what the dead say   The very dead say

This I know   that the dead are   still alive   without poss-
Essions   or the power to kill   each other: power-   less that is you
Who will die   are then alive eternally   without any   others over you
There is no god except   all of us dead, as we've   always secretly known

And in the death world you   gigantic you a soul e-   qual to   any
Soul in the u-   niverse   not the planet   but all there is   And this
That you have   everything!   set against   some candy floss   Your
Accomplishments born of crass urges   I'm walkin thru this world   born dead

Robot with a gun   what else are you   bank accounts   praise online when
You have instead   the true everything   and you can't keep   any-
Thing but it   Don't you want to know what I'm telling you   nothing you do
Makes sense   unless   you're a bum on the street   but he's

Not even happy   Rocks make more sense than you   And they're not happy
So they tell me   You're alive   forever   with equality without power
Over others   What are you going to do   Just what   are you going to do
With equality   without power   without   someone   over you

And then am I   and then am I   who am I really   Am I a healer
Can you need to be healed   And yes for yes   this gap be-
Tween what you know   and what you are is   still a gross wound
The dead themselves   only partly   understand   They call me up

And ask for help   You don't believe me, you   I'll heal you anyway
And lead you   and suffer for you anyway   Here on the page? you laugh
Here in any   real space   What do you think   you see   high
Rises and cars   stale air?   I see shiftingness   I hear worms call to

Each other   I hear the hills settle   I hear my lines   heal the stars
Which are frantic too   from being thrown into space   eons ago
And no   isn't this fanciful   Not as fanciful   as the trappings
Of your life   are stupid   But I can't only   address you:

I am *for* the dead   I mediate for them   I hear them talk
Singing   manipulating   their frequencies   soft under-whines
Like fingers sliding   down a guitar neck   I hear my mind
Call what   do you wish   And they say   Write this

The newest dead   and the oldest dead   of people animals plants the inorganic
Join me at night   Sometimes I'm just asleep   They join me anyway
Somewhere inside me   talking   The very newly dead   poet was there
Last night   said something like   he wasn't   a good enough poet   too con-

Stricted   Kind of late for saying that I say   Though the dead still write poems (Note
I'm speaking in flashes   like the dead)   Now you'll learn to be dead   and you'll
Know what you did   maybe   I try to help with that . . .   Once I dreamed that we
I think we were the dead   in farthest out-   er space   sat   about to sing

Choir-like   And would be led by—   our choir master was—
A young re-   tarded stuttering boy   That's the point of   everything, I say
And when you sang   and when I sang   I simply sang   without being myself
When I sang   being was   not being myself   I was finally able to . . .   do that

But I said I   heal the dead   of their sadness   Yes they're still
Somewhat sad   And I'm helping them   re-create us   You'll join them I say

He followed me around   all day like they do   Your poems written here still might be . . .
Slight I say   I kept staring at him   in my mind   He was vacuous
Why are you looking at me   I'm trying to find you   Why is it *you*? he asks
Why am I here   I say Why anything   But his problem's   an emptiness

You fill it with success   or other stuff   just stuff   Political righteous-
Ness is good   The poetics of whatever   or sensations floating by   any-
Thing floats   to be had   Any-   thing might do   Or your
Usual tone of voice   He hears me think that   Looks almost hurt

Whatever I think is heard   by the dead   And I'm careful with my
Thoughts   An interesting   kind of discipline   not to hurt the Universe
What have you   missed out on   so far I say   you're almost but not
Quite substantial — but   what is that?   Just a thing   another thing

We weren't meant to be   these things   substantial   insubstantial poli-
Tical apolitical   racist or not   Nor animals   mammals   or not   some stu-
Pid category   natural unnatural —   he's still in shock of death   I'm going to write
Now   I say   Hang around here with   all the others   Or find your loved ones

In another part of town

The dead think so   quickly their thoughts flash   Syntax of
The instantaneous   I'm trying to write   three or four flashes per line
But I'm only alive   and am my own guide   Actually their guide
How did that come about   It's on the other side   in every way   under the

Pun is the real   Sequins/sequence or   I've got a pain in my side
No sides in death   no stances you've   stopped believing   Still that
Affect though   Cure you of sadness   How   I don't know but I'm
Doing it   *Why shouldn't it be me?*   I call out   after the vacuous   poet as

He vanishes—   Dignified sad dead Syrian couple   enter heavily he's
Mustached   She's scarved in muted red   Oh sit wherever   I
Say   And a woman in blue cloak   still running   runs into my arms
Looks back at   pursuing men fade   Oh en-   ter I say Sit down and rest be-

Fore you join your relatives   they   who have cavern faces dark
Receding with   shut eyes   And still need to be healed
Of sadness   Still need to know what we are   Mountains cry
In modal grating tunes   Whole planets   collapse softly wail

This is my life now   not a dream   It's as real as this city of Paris

GOLDEN GRID

I keep seeing a   golden grid   a pale gold square of squares   almost re-
Ticently gold   What is this golden grid these pages?   But let me show you how
I healed my father: Quote   (last week)   (these lines   are they a grid?):

The suffering of it   *leave behind*   *just do it* . . .   Heal me, he says   Finally
I open my mind   or is it my chest   heart   I open and it
Absorbs all his bad stuff   Because we don't have to   name the stuff now

If you make it   into a thing   I deal with it   *heal heal!*   tone doesn't matter
I hear a lot of sirens   but I'm jerking about   absorbing your baggage
I'm better, he says   what will I be   without it   Calm maybe . . .
What about you he says   Oh you're not   supposed to ask

I might get confused   that was too easy—heal heal   tell me some more

I'm just seeing he says   not feeling   I'm pretty wide   like there's a lake
But if I see Dorothy   I might not be healed   No   stop and think I say
You're clean   I think so he says   I had to fracture   it I say
I broke it into   small pieces   they got smaller and smaller

I'll do that with guilt   when I take it in   but   where have I put it

Why is there a world
I don't know yet
Haven't the others told you
They've all been waiting for you to find out
　　When you do I'll have
　　always known
　　and everything
　　will be different

I see myself pushing the frag-　　ments of my father's guilt　　through the grid
The square spaces in the　　golden grid　　hovering gracefully in air
With its pale gold inter-　　secting　　Why each intersection is a cross!
Is the cross where one hung　　I mean in image but　　real anguish　　for

Anguish al-　　ways permeated me　　like an element　　or bodily substance
Nor can I tell　　the difference be-　　tween what I write　　and what I live
Do you believe some　　*thing?*　　I believe that I am crucified　　for you to perceive
This is the epic of the dead　　It proposes as measure a　　grid of gold

A voice had said to me　　in my mind　　'Pledge to use old signs'　　Did I pledge or just
Listen　　I must have pledged　　The cross is an old sign　　I am of old
Use to you　　though I will continue to be born　　from moment to moment de-
Fying　　evolution's line　　In this moment and in　　this very one

I am thrusting guilt　　others' guilt　　I've been given and　　accumulated
Through　　the grid windows　　It is bad　　opaque stuff　　unwanted stuff

Take my stuff everyone says   They clamor to trans-   fer their stuff to me now
But why do you have it   Why this system   It's stupid isn't it   The
Newly dead poet drops by   If I give you my inability   to write better . . .
That's not   the name of it I say   Perhaps my vision failed   Perhaps you

Let it fail   But you have to know what it is, I   can't take it with-
Out its shape   Shapes! he exclaims   I didn't   know enough of those
But you're a shape   he says to me   On this side   of the elements
Not a shade but . . .   dark and smiling yet   receding into

A vastness   Your diction's chang-   ing I say   I sound like you he says
I was a mimic   Like any poet   No my guilt is   My . . .   Oh I say
Just give it to me . . .   He hands me   a vague parcel   It isn't
All of it I say   You didn't give your-   self away   I mean give it away

Is that a sin he screams   Are we talking   Continue to heal I'll
Continue to heal you   What am I doing here   Why is there a world
Tell us just tell us that   we dead all say to you   You were born to tell
Us that   Do you need a   new memory   that would be a   new truth

Do the dead need   a new memory   a new kind   of memory

Yes the collage   Oh yes the collage   Well this is it isn't it   that you're always in
In the part where I was crucified   Yes the patchwork collage   and the subtly
Subjoined seam-   less collage   that on the other side of   I'm an important
                                                                    shadow
And in the part where   I was crucified   to create you   or is it to heal you

Out of my almost dying   first of sorrow then   of disease   always saved   I
Have always been saved   in order to do it again   on the collage cruci-
Fix part   No we're collaging the   new universe   into existence   the dead say
And I was up on that god-   dammed chi cross or is it tau rho   with my head

My head softly to the side   How can you be all these different —   It's a collage —
Because I   was the inter-   section point for   death and life having
Stood there with-   out a god so many goddamned times   Was there . . .
So burst through   and now on this   or in this side   I am the one

Healing you   and we will paste that on   Having been healed   with rubies
From the dime store maybe   My bled-for-you   beautiful rubies
Do we need a plan   No we paste it on   as it comes   Continuing to
Be born   moment to moment   in the new epic   creating the

New moment-to-moment   memory   You'll get it   eventually

The new memory   the memory structure   is who are you of course
It floated to   us for it is us   I say to the dead   in my Paris room
And if its walls were black   like lace or it   was made of cells be-
Fore   we imagined cells   Its walls weren't lace the memory was

Lacy you say   A mournful sexual orgy   an elegy put away
By someone named For-Lorn   In what language   Memory's tongue

Nothing's separate

We have a memory from space   from outer   space the dead voice says
And I will remember   what happens   in moments almost sealed
With a different structure   for each moment   For I've destroyed
My own character   You are healing   me of sorrow   And I'm

Dead I have no brain   What do you have   I have   what the en-
Tity called Everything-including-Death has   Everything-cum-Death
It doesn't have   just your old matter   It has its
All the thoughts   there have been   still exist in it some-

Where   from moment to moment   remaking its mind   or collage
But how does it do that   To ask how   is a linguistic trick   Which one of us
Is speaking   I don't know

There were so many   in my room last   so bloody all of us   The young
Muslim   his victims marines   some of whom had killed before   And I
Saw myself   in the hidden cache   of my own mind   my
Hiddenness   Saw me crying   twisted-bodied   come down from the cross a-

Gain   bloody   to greet this violence   Are you still insane I asked the killer
How am I *here* he said   You will never be   where you expected
Expectation's for human fools   I don't know why he said   I was ex-
Pected   to kill them   I mean I expected to   His bearded   oval face

What do I look like   You're losing image   Your face crisscrossed with shady bars
I said or she said   Give me some of your guilt   No it's mine he said   .
You can't die again   You can't carry it all   He's crying   holds out
His hands that are losing image   I take them   air I hold them

The marines silent   columnar stoic   Images   image blood sticks to them
Doesn't flow   And my image blood   flows   as I am used to it
You fools I   am this one and no one else is   You readers   I do
This   Dissolve your world dear images   which is an

Image too   with my disastrous blood   I am the one who heals you
(Last night I   was healing them)

EMBRACE THE EVIL

Because I am a shape   What shape are you   Because I   am a shape
Not embodiment not make-up   But on the other   side of what you saw
Not fabric   or perceptual ab-   straction   the form instructed
The shape is mine   yet the shape is yours   I am   for you

Shadowy moves across—   sense of limbs—   or is a cross, stationary
For suffering or cipher of welcoming?   open-armed   For both and more   I'm calling
The word *I* reflects   my location   like a source of   pulsation
And they come with   their filthy crimes   and I embrace them

More easily than   the trivial buyers of goods   or of current schoolish words
Taught by professors   imams   mediated presences

But they come from the aery reaches   who has ever seen

And shape says to shape   shape to my shape   Heal me

"I'm healing you   by saying so   I am healing you"

Michael Brown continues to talk to me   You think you own him?   No one's
An ownable image   He complains about   someone I'll leave unnamed
She shouldn't   talk about me   Lament my death doesn't feel it   She didn't live
Where we . . .   doesn't know . . .   How much now   do you recall?

. . . I mess around . . . guy in the store . . .   You see I'm high   I'm big
Suddenly   this is . . .   ridiculous   that there's store   and
This stuff and   he isn't high   so it's funny I   mess him around
Can't help myself   It wasn't me . . .   Now dead I'm me   Then later there's

The cop   he's scared too, it was you know   funny at first   Now I'm thinking
He was just scared   I could see that   he's stupid   I don't do this stuff much
Is this what you really think?   No I don't exactly . . .   Then he's shooting me
No one knows why they   do something   all of a sudden . . .   You can't do

Things like that here . . .   I have to talk slow   Alice   so you can hear

To the dead I talk as fast as thinking   It's like sound   just sounding
But something else is   that you're not using me   like all of them   I'm using you!
I'm laughing   But you're teaching me I say   how to talk like the dead
Fast and blunt   Sometimes it's different from   that he says I'm   finding out

Memory's everywhere

Last unclear night   I think to you all   And muslim killer   and his victims are
There again   in hazy bloodiness   Who can act now   confront the other
The oldest marine   solemn accepting   as if he'd always foreseen my room
And his face hovered but   his body   was blue   shadowy limbs

The killer faces me then   in gauze version of hysteria   a leftover mime
Because he's losing it   like in a slow hiss   a deflation
You're here and not here he says   we are dead   and you're not
In alternate tiny   points of time   I'm dead I say   I'm both dead and alive

I've al-   ways been able to   know it when I wished . . .   You've committed this hor-
Rendous crime   Your victims stare   at your unreal face   I'm pushing out a
Face he says   Trying to be   what I was used to   Trying to find what
I should be   I thought if I   shot them   if I could place   myself on a

Holy *side*   I would be someone else   than me . . .   Are there any ones here
Like me   Who's here   Or are they   the privileged   Are they that
More privileged than me   not just money but affection?   Never I say   though the
Illusion was perfect . . .   illusion of privilege   We're all illusionists   As if we pulled

Each other out of a hat   I don't get it he says   What can I have   Is this dishonor?
No the marine   says it's   Something   after   Nothing
It's what I was   waiting for   you kill some   then you're a killer
Then you wait   I'm waiting he says   for death to change me   Am I changed

You are chang-   ing I say to the marine   I see it   but I see image
There can be pure image   somehow pure image   You're located aren't you
I'm still myself   though more spread out   like a bigger mind
And one part of me   one place   is shocked and wounded

Or remembers it was   And I talk   as if I have a mouth but
I don't   My talking knows this   It isn't really   being shaped
By a mouth   And I hear that my voice   doesn't really   sound like me
Or even sound   I hear you I say   in my mind   and I speak to you mentally

What is my   equipment he says   I don't know   I see you in uniform
In my mind a thin   layer of you   You're   whatever a soul is
A resonance and concentration   What do you mean   You really were you
And now too but . . .   What do you sense?   I sense you he says the

Part of you like me now   There's no description   It probably has mass . . .
I encounter you your mind   and it helps me talk   it's like a wind
But there are dots or marks   that let out what you say   and some-
Thing like a face sometimes   I   love to hear you   for no reason

I seem to   hear your whole mind   (Then I Alice   come to alone)

I have no rest a   young woman enters who's   died hanging in   a jail cell
Somewhere   But we dead don't have where says   a Syrian I don't have   Syria but
We can have you as   locality and   you have your room   So this woman enters
Dead and aftermathed   aura of hurt   gone eyes sunken eyes   the hurt   purifies

Into the contemplation of it   a transitional wash   Almost visible   She's chang-
Ing   They told me to come here she says   if I'm not ready   Can rest and feel
Something of you — Why?   I'm not sure I say   I'm just open space   and I heal
I don't   want to   remember   she says   Why aren't I   dead?

You are dead   Well I feel different   I don't want to   remember!   It
Won't hurt you now   And you don't have to   recall   specifically
In order to be healed   Hurt and guilt's just a package   You're   something other
You're you but other   Hand me the horrible resi-   due the package when you

Can and I'll   put it somewhere   She her image   lies on my bed
For hours of mine   She's in the other time   I didn't   really want to die
But I'm better   Why should I be   better what's   happening? I don't think I
Did anything   Killed myself   for nothing   I killed myself   Why?

It was this noise in the   car she says   Just this hornety   buzzing of us
Traffic cop and me   We buzz each other   as bad as you   can be in sounds
How did I get   to the jail   Get out of this car I'm   too shaky
It's like I'm working up   to dead   In a rage   My head my face won't stop

Pauses   Why am I in this stupid cell   Long time   between things
Time's a long space   a small space that's   long and   I call people up
No one comes for me   I say things on the phone   Nothing happens
Can this be a   life   in jail for not   signaling   a lane change

If I don't sig-   nal that I change   can't change   Never got to change
Where are my people my anyone   my family   my anyone for me
What's the   point of being   inside me   why be in side me
And I'm in-   side me that's the only one   EVERYONE leaves me there

And I hang my-   self with a stu-   pid plastic   bag just to
Get out   I don't want   to remember   that would be   another cell

I'm going to   heal you I say   You're dead it's over   Just
Lie here stay here   You're inside me   I'm not a cell   I'm vast

Later

Inside me Alice   I call out to all   what is it like for you   inside my mind
We don't always   know where you go   or what you're doing   in the world
Light it's light   without a source   thought has light   and patterns colors
But we're some-   times below where you're   consciously thinking

And there are dreams here   but they're not really   dreams be-
Cause we're in them   You're dreaming with me not dreaming   the suicide says
You're awake but   unconsciously dreaming of me   That's how you   take me
With you   like reading minds   Where's my baby dead baby my unborn she

Says   Yes I'm there I've entered that place I say   Can I find   my baby
It won't know me she says   And I was always   thinking of   that baby
They must be evident somewhere I say   the unborn   Oh do I hold
Them within   We should find them   I'd like to know   what they are

I'd like to know   are they conscious now   as others are in death
Do they have anything   to remember   Then a voice says   going back to what it
Looks like   in you   it's like soft shifting   vocal patterns   Your
Voice and mind are one   But it's not always words   it's the shapes you say

Violet and white moving say   or dark   and it moves through us   to heal
No matter what you say   I'd like   to find the   unborn I say

Walk down within yourself   below dreams   someone says
Oh you know descend the stairs   like you always do   And so I count back-
Wards descending stairs   with the suicide, Sandra   in my mind my enormous mind
At the bottom   they are in darkish waves   as if playing to-

Gether the unborn   Image closed eyes   yet they splash and sway as if in
Placental waters   Beauty I say but   what is   this mind like
I can find mine Sandra says   Our minds are more   connected
Contiguous I say   And she holds it   It's pure soul but

What is that?   What is not that?   Are you mine Sandra asks
I am mine it says   And I hear it —   You don't be-   lieve me who cares

This mind peace-   ful un-   bothered by us   Then whispers in my ear
Be gentle I'm not born yet   Do you want to be   Don't need . . .
Sandra gives it back   to the small waves   How do you know
How to speak to me   From memory it says   The only thing

Is memory perhaps   the golden grid?   As I've specu-   lated doesn't the
Universe need to re-   member to be?   It holds it-   self together . . . from
Moment   to moment   And the death   part of it   where my old
Friends largely exist   And the souls of   past geo-   logical form-

Ations   And former planets   And their materia their matter
Remembering within the uni-   verse's memory   as I do   the-at-
Each-intersection-of-   I-hung-on-a-cross golden grid
So I could en-   ter my soul consciously   my death-to-be . . .

Once I led a life of   anthro-   pological interest   in modern cities
With their cares   their usages and social classes   their smothering self-
Centeredness   Now I'm everyone and everything   was   and to be
It flows in and out goldenly   of me the inter-   section   So

Am I memory?   Is memory   the grief-catcher   sticky mesh

Sandra ever with me says   Memory killed me   This I say
Is the memory   that you co-   here   And you still cohere
Stick together she says   And I'm not crazed   anymore she says
It's just gone   That's death I guess   This is a moment   how does it last

It has no length   it keeps remembering   what it is

Sandra's with me everyone's with me   as they wish   Let's go on
And the dead pour in   from Syria   Let's go on   in my room below dreams
Or wherever these moments are   wet as tears and grace
Let's go on   How are we making the new col-   lage   Gluing it down by

Listening remembering   How does anything work   Well maybe it doesn't
We were a culture cultures you scream   We were a country   Let's go on
Shocked and precipitate   in red garments   losing sense of life yet living
A battleground for nothing   against nothing   ours became

Let's go on with tears and grace   I see I'm dead   a man says
De-   capitated   and yet I have my mind   Who am I now some-
Where else mocked   for staying   or for fleeing   Where is my god
He isn't here   You knew that   It was a story   He says what isn't

Do I have to be   in one now   Maybe in yours   I'm never sure
I'm not making it up   but it's happening   if you're here
Who am I now he says   in tears torn   You are yourself I
Say   No one can kill you   or rule over you   you are safe and in-   tact   Study it

Everything was in place in my head   Now I don't have it
I knew what I fought for   Now the symbols the   words for my
Righteousness are lost   Yet   I still have a mind   I don't know if to fight for
The illusions we love   against a rule he   doesn't deserve

Is worth it and to die for it   and not die   Who am I   with my memories retreat-
Ing   I see they exist but aren't in me   There were so many factions it
Was said   no one could be a true thing   only a splinter in Assad's foot
Go to hell the world said   Who can make sense of your fight

Though his men massacre   rape and imprison hundreds of thousands   Remember
This talk lady?   I remember everything   I say though not   all the time
Memories have their own lives   even though ours is a tiny   parochial
Planet   But a new universe   from moment to   moment is being in-

Visioned and im-   plemented   You mean in death? he mocks   Yes
Everything you thought   is   still alive   and being refashioned here
We do easy work   Give us a hand   with no hands
Contribute poems and tales   not   written down   in the old way when we

Remembered the world   into existence every day   its framework

And it's the next day in the unreal world   and I've gone jogging   me Alice
Ridden the métro   stared at the others of   the class of ones who ride
Ligne sept change at Gare de l'Est   going to work in their   Frenchness of
Considered clothes   painted toenails   men's lightweight suits

Dark bald heads   brown bald head   a youngish   business man
Women with ear buds—too   late for the ones who   put on their make-
Up   with small mirrors   A baby behind me squealing   at first I thought was
A machine   the train's brakes?   I hear the American R & B that

Guy's listening to   through earphones—And I think it's okay   if I love
Them all   I don't have to tell them you know   they don't have to know

Yesterday in the afternoon I   invisibly healed   an old friend   two years dead
I took his guilt   It was exhausting   quick but entire—You
Don't believe me—   But the dead do the dead saw   And I will heal you
One way   or another

I want to tell you San-   dra says   that the air here   is pure the
Airlessness but am I pure   Do you have to be   It's a very long eter-
Nity   I'd like to be pure   It's not a jail cell I say   It's not a code either
Or an image   We don't speak in code here she says   We speak in

Reality   Tell me about it   It's like light and when I speak it   it's stuff it's
Not like words   It doesn't stand for   There's nothing here for it
To stand for   I'm translating talking to you   You've already learned it
I say   Well it's here   it's just here she says   Like I am

What you say is   what's here   And it bursts or   is longer but
You see I don't have   a body   I have a place I   where I am

And your memories   They're not me but I   still have them
Depriving me   of value   Was I val-   ued did I   try or cry enough
These words come out   automatically or are   they thoughts
I don't want to be   as small as the old I   among a bunch

Of bodies   Can you help me   You're not quite ready
For what I do   Almost   You're moving fast   Too much feeling she says   still

Okay everyone's most precious feelings   their judgments opinions   so memorable
And okay how you feel   resentment and so on   or exhilaration   passionate some-
Thing something   of the parochial human earth . . .   Every thought we have truth
We propound now is archaic   creature   Science that primitive idea   of ideas

The strangely—   and technology—   sewn-up quilt made by planetary impulse from
Where   Why do you parade these scraps of clothing   as if they exist for-
Ever intact   There is no idea no advance   no urgent truth   Have
Lived through   nothing   Yet you feel it   what do you really feel

We must have justice   You died   and came here alive   I know a man
I know who assaulted me in the vestibule   grabbed my crotch on
Avenue B exposed   himself to me   on the Paris métro   I know who beat
Up my relative relatives   raped my mother's elderly friend   I know do I?   and in this

Moment nothing   My job of the moment to   feel nothing at all
So I can heal   every one   of their shitty ways   Feeling nothing
I will feel nothing   for any mongrel   of the race   There is no emo-
Tion   Nor manners culture or information   no ways to follow   No one did anything to

You   We don't live there

I healed my brother   the final coup of heal-   ing for last night
It's now he said I have a lot   and handed me   three bundles I
Took into my heart   or chest   And then I have it all
He became a boy a-   gain for awhile   Ran away to play

I felt sick and be-   came once again as   crucifix crucifixion
(No one knows what   you die of   on the cross   remember?)

Now I'm better am I who   Everyone attending me   lightly within
This will be our epic when   the story is told of you   as the group
You group of dead   Proceed to tell more   can't you say   how it is   what you are
Not necessarily as story   but   who you are is who are we

Including all sub-   stance planetary to speak   elemental or hard
Formed or fiery   I have suffered for you so   tell me
I broke open   broke open   am just frequencies   speaking like you
Tell me who or what   our mind knows of it   our unity   our laby-

Rinthine dissolution

What like me what shape   what speaking   what shape
Saying says   says to me almost blips   because the shape
Is peaked   and its im-   pulses radiant   frequencies
Are making sense   It wants to   be with me

I came to you last night   dead but still   broke it said
I mean like a body hit   You   smeared a mental   leakage
Of mine   on yourself   It wasn't really there I say   You brought the
Image with you   Of my destruction it says   And what or who

Are you I say   But I was a mountain   couldn't you tell   I have points
Hazy shadowed   molded as if touched   I found your mind I say
Or something like   a field of pulsations   I'm on the other side
Of perception now   We are almost   image-free

I can't lose mine yet it says   My image   They blew it up
Bastards   I don't care who   anymore   or
Which is which   Relentless filth   what do I care
Dead you won't care I say   I just heal what-   ever   whatever it's done

I'm trying to sound   like you it says   So you'll understand

I become the grid wind-   ows my chest heart   Become the intersection
Nothing else for it   They all hand me guilt   I let them   press it in-
To me and every-   one wants to speak   The French poet says when he
Gives me his vast crimes   Je parle   pour toi de temps en temps . . .

Because I am bro-   ken I say   I give myself away   inexhaustibly
The universe broke like me   That's what happened at first   It
Breaks again   Tell the truth someone says   We broke into a cha-
Os   then I reclaimed it into cross   When and how   and why all this spo-

Ken how   So many voices   and all the while   I'm receiving their
Bundled sins   Why not say sins just a-   nother word
I am filled with filth and   pressing it through   the grid as fast as I
Can in-   ternally   This is the poem this is   the collage too

This is our hearts   I was a rich one   the mountain says
Rich with stillness   and form   Is my soul thus that
What is a soul I ask   what are the materials   of death or life
What are the words   this speaking when   they aren't signs

Only on the other side of sight   will you see where   we are
I am it speaking   says blank   Yawns   Someone left
There was no place to go but someone left   I left I say
I speak deliberately and leave the   beginning   Yawning

No that's still just a myth   I killed myself says Sandra   Can you say
The beginning   killed itself first   Je me suis suicidée
This wasn't what any-   one meant to say   Is that how we started
The other side of   the fabric now I say   Let me see

It's dark and I can al-   most see you shadows of mind   smiling
We are contained first are we   a silver surface   one is a ripple
I move across it   like a mind   and disturb it   my or your
Mind starts it up   It's nameless   it's us   No we're hovering   Nei-

Ther   And anyone's mind was moving   primal element
Whatever I think starts   I can move it   with my mind   every time

You are watching a ball of light   come out of my chest   it's
Like a bundle of blazing gauze   Out of my chest I think
Or is it my mind   Sit in chair and create it   Not chair not flesh
Telekinetically speaking   you could have   any combinations

Of what of what?   We didn't know what we   were doing   ever
I let the ball of white light hover   my chest the black cavity
Wherein is thrust   all your guilty sadnesses   (all night they . . .)
Has it changed into   this light?   Notice — no explosion

You have to know   how to move things   with your mind

It is a blinding white soul   and it will become   the new us or
Universe   Are we in a   material part   or what?   We are where we
Stand   The mountain says you can trace me   from that soul's
Molten shadow   Can we in plainer words say   what's happening

All I really know   is that a soul or ball of light   has come out of my chest

You are the one that's the   mind   What will you do with it
Sandra and Michael don't know   who they each are   except for now
What is your memory of   Of being the one that's   my mind
Anywhere   in any dream   given whatever it   told me it was *of*—

This can't be   a dream   I have to tell   the truth
I have absorbed your guilt   and sin   am thrusting it out
As a form of light   or new mem-   ory   what holds us together
There was a dream in   which I moved ob-   jects whenever I wished

Where we stand   at these crossroads   is there anything to move
Do we exist without ex-   isting   Voice: there are glints of
Light   shreds of   guilt and sadness   The fabric   of this side's stuck
Together   where we are   and the glints and shreds   fiery figments

Sometimes the fabric's black   like a voice some-   times grey like a moth's wing
I am making it   How   it all comes from me   and my absorption
Of your sadness   Will the fabric set on fire   and in beauty   per-
Haps   like pyrography con-   trolled but then the fab-   ric burns

It's burning the words are   burning   but not burning it away
Not true enough   Yes it's true   These words on fire for you

Do you see how ridi-   culous your real life is /
        <u>*Come back to us*</u>   *Michael says*

It's before you've ever thought of be-   fore even a spark —   where did it come from
My mind knows how to   make it does it   I dreamed I could lift any   thing
With my mind   Why would you want to   Michael's laughing

The chair in the dream won't stay rigid   the wooden back slats
Lengthen and bend   in the unnatural light where   we really are
Though things sort of work   She sat on the chair   though it wasn't there
I wasn't there   I was here inside the cathedral   of selves

If you're all   what effect a change on   and what is there a beginning of?
Are we seeking sep-   aration or   unification   Michael   We're
One thing seeing   each other he says   Like clouds   but better
They're bright as hell lit up   No sparks   More like birds

Angels? I say   Wings he says   I flew over the   time when I died
A year ago   The time   comes back around   But I don't I'm permanent

Last night they were drowned ones   looked wet but weren't
And there were others   He of all people   thrust his guilt at me   casually
(But now   I can't remember who   he was)   Frank said I
Can't do this to you   It's what I'm for I said   besides the poems

There isn't much he   said I've been working on it   awhile

And simultaneously   soothing the drowned   I'm now sup-
Posed to be awake   in what's considered normal   interaction   No?

Who am I   If I could recall really recall   And we are on fire meta-
Phorically with memory the structure   I remember   says the igneous stratum
How to be here   I remember says Saying   And I say I will now
Go back again   backwards and down as if I can al-   most telekinetically

And I crawl down that ladder   Ladder counting   Look like a spider
See myself al-   ways see yourself don't you   And down
Break through the   blue paper sky down there   this these lines aren't writing
You're reading Phantom   I'm standing Woman Nowhere

The original explosion   might be somewhere across paper
There isn't   an explosion   It's all breaking up across paper and I'm   nothing
What this mind did does   this soul . . .   So I'm god okay
I can start it   I have to   you already exist   I

Keep doing everything for you   There is no violence   just a crackup

I think that's right Daddy says   what you're saying   is right
What to do is   already here he says   That's right
This is the epigraph

Escondido   or the wind   Speaking same as reality
It was a proto-mind   wrapped around like arms   a gulf
And hummed or vibrated   I mean started to   But I don't
Want to tell a story   When I start out I   don't have propensities

The gulf is the golden   named of myself   I see it   Who does
It all has to be for you   Still for you you can-   not suffer
Suffer it   What could   you bear   But the words I'm speak-
Ing aren't spoken   They're the same as all   around me an

Element   But not known before   in previous   universes
You don't have to   And so you do   It isn't compelled
Its color range   pearlescent so far   You can hear it tremble
I don't have senses   We are of it   How?   We are mingling   How?

I think I am controlling it   Will it remem-   ber to stay

What is soul what   we're patterned upon   on the showy side
On this side it runs us   talks us   unmemorized but   is it memory
I ask again   or is it poetry or is poetry memory   Or am I
Your body is spir-   it my love you're not   looking at it right

I've caught it drying up   You've caught it changing   but you can't be caught

Can I have a blue skull   painted like an image I mean   choose it that
Steel-blue brush stroke   Anselm Hollo says   only if there's
An angel too   Voice sings I can't get along without   you angel you

Do you accept the angel   The pattern on its wings   caused by speaking
I accept   what I create   as I have created   a moving self
From a distance   with winged feet   whoever
Would've thought   of transporting a soul   thereby en-

Suring long periods   of doing nothing but   getting here   right here
All I'm creating now's perfection   in the angel   where it goes in
Place   I'm not moving   I see that what I see   has its own love
I want you   to be around me   always be around   whoever says

You can be in or out of time
How
In your head   There are openings to slip through

It's like saying I'm   a cut-out of soul   a voice says   of the big one
But I'm bigger   Or soul's all there is   with play against it
And has its own memory   *the* memory   folding over on it-
Self   never cornered   or equated   I am the living self voice says

I'm going to give you my stuff   Sandra says   and does that   It isn't so
Much I say   You're young   and of a   rigorous quality
Do we have the individual   We are creating   our new shapes
Which like the one soul   fold infinitely   never cornered

Is that a shape   It's playing   my brother says   Anything that hap-
Pened   gets stretched turned over   reshaped   And I was a man   Pah!
And I was in time   somewhere bent   I was bent

The poet who died   a few weeks ago says   I've been writing   in my head
'You have to tell the truth dead / Because nothing's not it'
Those are the first two lines   translated   from the Angelic

But I Alice am not dead   trying to tell   the truth
Partially crucified in August   everyone's sadness   flows through me
By my choice   The buck stops here   Am I the only live
Human being   who can say that   Are you listening

Contaminated by Accepting Your Cares

All night I tried to push   my own stuff   through the grid
Like dark mud or shit   But was it mine it was like   mine   yet I thought
This is really   Sandra's or Michael's   or bloody Syrian grief   caused by
Cultural fixity   Can we have no traits now   And felt almost suici-

Dal dead-ended   in a small space   though the just-shot   kids from
Houston wallowed against me   in bed shocked   children die with big eyes
Do they stay children   All souls   are the same size
Like a quasar?   A quasar clanked in and said I   was drawn by your weird-

Ness so like mine   But I still had a tough   what-the-hell-am-I-
Doing night   And Michael calls again   Come Back to us   and I return
Though you don't believe me   Well belief is for fools   though I'm not lying
And how can any-   one live any other way   loving the one soul we are

I'm supposed to   live for all you   and so I will into Part II
I don't know what's   going to happen and nothing's sequential   in this world
The black hole in my   chest yawns accepting   all your bitterness
The air in Paris hot   I will never leave   any of you   I will never leave   any one

YOU FORGOT TO THINK

Our New Soul

It's bric-a-brac of malfeasance   with gold ink   brushed on it
It's evil change   I took it and changed it   into gold light   without think-
Ing   *You forgot to think*   No I was thinking   but on the other
Side   or some underside   of me   So it's our soul   Yes it's our soul

It's changed in-   side me into gold now it's   becoming you
This is how the universe really be-   gan billions of years ago
We put new soul   in us   made of gold and dead   transgressions
The memories are crushed   together and the weight   of their death is

Very light   *That's like a story Alice*   My own new soul-
Suit is actually   pale blue   It was in-   serted in me
A few weeks ago by dead friends   I don't get the gold one   I get this
One to help me   stay alive   long enough   to effect the change

Yours is for light and beauty   But mine is for strength and intelligence
And for eloquence   Whatever   it may now be necessary to say

unconscious

The soul I could say the soul   is like a bright star but   never dies   No not like that
It's in negative   experience   You connect two   planes of experience   alive
Dead you are only one   but knowing about   the other
I'm telling you   from nowhere   I'm about to   introduce you to nowhere

I am unconscious there   the hive's abuzz with   ghosts there
Our energy   is all mental   these words are   no good I
Can see color Red be-   cause I found out about it   when I was alive
I   have a memory   but you don't usually   remember me

Who are you   Can't you go on   I need to change how I
Speak   We are alive where we are   If we aren't there . . .   Yet we al-
Ways are   And the signals continue   I am not   a man
That present-   ly as if on cocaine   knows   Or water too   a different medium

So are you   a different medium   You are always   on my mind
Who are you   just who are you   Don't you understand

It's out of the silent   but it isn't silent   One place a prison which
Is just the going on   of all of us   as shapes or voices broadly

So find yourself here   I am accepting   from serial killers   their foul
Packages   which seem to contain   kicking creatures   You forgot
To think   My new motto: I Forgot To Think   Now I'm pushing through the
Grid   these alive-like shapes   And I push them hard like black stars cold

The killer himself   screams like he's lost   his flesh jacket his skin
But he's doing this   He gave it to me   And I push it through be-
Fore it attaches to me   on this side the death side   When I'm done
There are spots of   black cloth on me   I sit down and peel them off

In the undertaker's   opinion   this is a strange   undertaking   I
Was born to do this I say   Whoever it is that I am   Is this an angel's
Mistaking of bad for good I ask the killer   You forgot to judge   I'm the one walk-
Ing on the edge   of monstrosity   since I'm alive   You're just you know dead

That's mean he says   I'm saving you I say   I wonder what shape I am
He says your jacket's worn out   And you're   kind of   transparent

Crooning   crooning   Or am I keening   Don't want to—yes-he-
Raped-and-tortured-me—   discuss it   because you're strong and you al-
Ready know   Your image has   a sunken look I say
I'm better dead   but if he's dead too   he's here   I can't find my—

You have what you need   Can't find my ring or something   I had a
Here you don't have   You have things don't you   I'm living but I don't
Care about   any body's stupid things!   Why are you yelling   Upset I say
Why are you   Just sit down   I can't sit as a body   as you know

I was sup-   posed   to care about everyone   in a war you
Care and   you   care don't you   I'm doing a different thing
But I'd kill him if I   could   You can't you'll have to put that   broken re-
Flection   in a backpack   and shove it   into my heart

Whhaaat   Do as I say   when you can   he
Has no power   there's no power   in this death   except to
Think   Can't I   help the living   First learn how to think
First forget   Forget to think   Then learn how to think in a new way

It was mine   Why can't I find my   can't I have an   old
To keep me going   You'll never stop   He'll be here soon or sometime   So
What   Is he   going to learn how   to think   Come sit here
Pretend-sit   Let's tell each other   some of what   we know

532

Alice and Kayla

Remember Prescott   Remember Mars   I might as well remember Mars
And I I often went there   to Prescott   I grew up there   did I grow she says
What was that for
                              they pulled out my fingernails
Remember Granite Dells
                    I struggled not   to betray

Myself   having no one else to betray   being   unimportant   but I knew
There was still   betrayal involved   have you ev-
Er be-   trayed yourself   The idea was to be his   sexual victim toy
Well you sub-   mit or struggle   you're his meat

But they are the meat   the lies and the meat   I'm   speaking now
Remember Sharlot   Sharlot Hall Whiskey Row   Sharlot Hall she says they had a
Memorial service for me there   in the square   I remember a store
Near Sharlot Hall I say   where I bought a vase   for my mother   birthday present

Way before you were born   But you're already dead   and I'm still living
I remember one red flower she says   If I con-   trolled myself   and didn't
React to him   even when he was raping me   And will I have to deal with him here
I remember swimming at   Granite Dells I say   I remember an empty lot with

Starlike flowers   I remember playing   *I* can't remember that now   I'll remember it
For you   I wanted to be heroic she says   I remember wanting to be   magnanimous
How can the dead remember I say   Your memory's changing   isn't it
I was trying   to remember   how to live   I have to remember   being dead

Think with this space you're in   a different way   think with space   remember it
Stay with me Kayla   Stay as long as you like   (others   always approach)

Theatrical save the   blood isn't it   I see shad-   ow puppets through
The fabric   on the life side   pretending the importance   of their gestures

That shadow   has a missile gun   that one a grenade belt   that one's the
Pleading woman   All three delicately   cut out of   grievous skin
I remember masks of demons   hair of strung rhinestones   and alternative heads
I remember   my head   a voice says   it wasn't the one   I think with

I arrived here after my   decapitation   holding it like a prop
Most people don't   think much he says   they wouldn't   neces-
Sarily need a head   I remember the silence   before the sword came down
Then I got up unseen   and left the   shadows there   I never stopped thinking

I just died a-   nother voice says   the last premonition   came to get me
That I would wind up here   Is this liberation   I'm sick of everyone's fibs
Is this liberation   I've had enough   of the labyrinth   of opining
And the heavy   kimonos along the way   All the ghosts are on that side

How the Stuff Gets Transformed

How the stuff gets trans-   formed   after it's pressed through the golden
Grid   It comes back as small particles   How   It does   We don't
Have time here   transition   We can just call it   We do it   just do   Be-
Cause I have to   I went to the corner   furniture store   and got a furnishing

How explicit do I   have to be   I have all the in-   formation of the uni-
Verse all it's ever had   available   It's been doing wrong   for an eternity
All the sick junk I've   pressed through the grid   floats back to me
I'm afraid we   know each other now   And if it's particles I know

It's soul particles   Soul has its particles   putting up with all us
And your bad act-   ions were done with   soul intermixed
You didn't say that before   And I have to do   this creating
Of new soul new   memory the col-   lage out of   what there is

What it is   I have within me   magnificence   to crush up with the evil
That was in   the ground of us   but now it's dead crushed and
I'll use it   I'll use anything   These particles   refuse to be
Regular   That's correct for this side   and even the   other they're un-

Anticipatable

I saw this bit of spirit   First I saw Lela my aunt who's just died   she can't talk yet
Her face recedes   pulls back into darkness but   I recognize her old and pretty

Now this   bit of spirit   a streak of it   it's pink and separated   out for me to see to
Know there's that though   everything's that   separated   separating out
You are so separate   I am   Lela I'm here   though not dead
She doesn't know how   to talk here   and she had dementia   will speak in due

Course   Lela I love you   *I love you too*

                                        And now here are two   depictions
From the new universe, friends   First is a woman   in bed   in a room wav-
Ery   wavery because   it's there and not there   The lines that
Mark off the cubicle   roll back and forth   are unfixed   just that much   It's a

Pink room as if daylit it's   beautiful   and   Here's something
My father sent   to explain   our new reality   a blanket
Hung like a tapestry   blue with red roses   the blue changes
From pale to dark-   er as you look at it   and becomes more   translucent

As you   look at it   Does looking   create it   Partly
Let's look at these   particles   together that I   present now mentally
And make trembling a form   and trembling   make it a
Life form that   when it trembles   changes color   or thought   And you can

Hear it tremble

DIFFERENT

Suddenly it was this: that the bone was   pointed at me
And I was sick again   stomach-sick   I am alive   Who is try-
Ing to kill me   That again   someone dead says   Someone
Wants to kill me   I say   Everything in this epic   has to

Be true the voice says   Someone   wants to kill me   How do
You know   I know   Is it the crucifixion   part   Not like that
It's active malice   subtle malice   on the part of   specific parties
Have tried it before   Don't give in   it's psycho-   automatic   They

Made me sick I say   They're afraid I'll change   something any-
Thing   I can hardly   believe it   but I was so   sick last night
And no one will be-   lieve this page   No one wants any-
Thing to change   Or no one wants me   to be the changer

Escape them the voice says   Become waves   instead of particles
When necessary   And I say   It's a dream   maybe   just that
No says another voice   they want to   kill you have always wanted to
Do I need to   be alive   You can change life   alive

But you change death dead too   As long   as it's you
Who am I really   The one we need so   they've pointed the bone at you

LATER THEN

Joe shows me   his new work   the Soul of a Pansy   Dark around a
Pansy shape   inside which it's   white   blank not   paint just white
The work's not two-   dimensional   three? it's thick in a   frame   floats
But it's not virtual   either it's tangi-   ble in a death way   with some blur

What are the materials I ask   I fix the particles   they exist *here*   you see
With your mind   a several—   not sure how many—   dimensional icon
It's partly created   by your seeing it   but that was   always the case
Your mental eyes   help fix it   It comes to let you look   and if you count the

Dimensions   it becomes more   fixed   I prefer it less fixed   that's realer
Is it a thing   It's in my mind   and then yours   Where do you get
The pigment   if that's what it is   From my mind and   I draw   with my mind
More as if   with eyes   than with hands   though I have neither

Everything in the   alive world   was like paint   Everything
In the death world is mind   Is everything   in death that
There is   something like   an object   that can be visualized—I mean
Is everything based on life?   No he says   life is based   on death

The pansy's soul   was here first   not the pansy but   the pansy's soul
I I say   prefer the way it looks here   unfixed as I am except for being

Don't have anything
Don't do much

You should learn how to sing

This torn fabric   dark felt   hides that room from me   That half of it   What
Do you want to   is it see   see   And keep   seeing some ones what   do you
Want   to is it   see   I want to learn   how to sing to   Whom are you ad-
Dressing   This   whatever   They gather close on   either side of the felt

On which side am I   with my long sight obscured   Let's let it be more opaque
This note   is not for ears   all the   senses are one
It is a word felt   the word is the word felt   Opaque opaque
Like a driver's license   sound of wings in   your ears   I hear

Wings Michael says   I open the beginning   of this moment again
I'm leading it   through a new   rip in the felt   Can you feel
It's the most perfect   view I've ever had   Michael says
I see those vib-   rations   like a red sunrise   who's singing them

You can know more than one   of anything   at the same time
I saw her   she was malicious   purporting to   be the
Victim   pointing the bone   She was only a note   Everyone's crowd-
Ing around me   Walk through the tear   everyone or thing that's ever been

PARTICLES

I'm now in this world of   particles   blank-white   like the pansy's soul
Nothing but them here   and I become them   smothered formless   disappearing
Later much later   there are—did I put   them—pink   lines around layers
Of white particles   as if there have to be areas   Finally   particles with more or-

Ganized and   cursive   pink lines become a store front   It may be St. Something's
"A sweeter place you'll   never see"   In this process of   transfiguring

When I forgot to think I just thought
                                        Take whatever's inside
Me that you need   I am mostly the new   particles   She can't
Witch me not knowing   the new particles   I'm still not sure who
She is   There's always been some-   one who wanted   to kill me

Is this real enough some-   one says   In this part it   has to be opaque I
Say   Out of the different medium   out of the dif-   ferent nirvana
We are really doing   this now   Shadow puppets   back away
It's too pure they shout   They are just shadows those people

There is so much uninhabited death
If you're creating that . . .
Do we keep making it though
You are making it   and it isn't dark it's clear
What is its size   It doesn't have a size

Throw the lots now   I don't think I'm sup-   posed to throw   lots I say
That's what we al-   ways did   Saw it through   outer agency
And the one who wants to kill me   I say. . .   casts spells   But she wants

Power   All we are is   power   We need lucidity   Then I entered
A room in mind   and sat down   I do want to know   what hap-
Pens now   But these terms are   inadequate   Did we make or
Are we overwhelmed   by   the particles?   I was once . . .

Must there be amnesia   after all *seeing*?   I saw once

Yes I made it   make it   and it's unknown that I . . .   that part of
Me   divined it   without lots   We conducted   what there—
It's inadequately   termed as *is*—   through or into
Formations I   decided   very particularly   I am watch-

Ing them   becomes my eyes awhile   That's a symbol   We've made
The living world. . .   symbolic   The death world   the death world
Of folded crumpled space   of sizeless capacity   contains our
Tired symbols   to cast off   you cast them   off to me

I am going there   into that fold   that folded-   up place
And I slip in   This could be any   any thought   or thing I say
I have no identification   amnesiac   happy   cold-blooded
It could have been here   where I now make us   I'm making it or

Being it   prevalent   will prevail   It has never   been desperate
Remembering countless   curves and folded-up   experiences
Should I call it   You are calling it   says a wrinkle
I perceive this you that   has no margin   The writing

On you is   the same dark color   you are   and anyway I can't see
These dark words a voice   I can't make   you materialize
Not material it says in   my voice   It says itself   in me
We don't need incidents   or equations . . .   It's all

Coming out of here   in you it says   Do I want something
You are perhaps wanting   in texture   I don't   know I say
I want to know your   dark language   the same as its
Surface   That's the texture   Is there an us-world   Let go it says

How opaque crooked are you   very much so   *they were in zero street*   *now*
They are farther than they were   I'm in zero street   as the song says (there's no
Song)   Tell me, me, what's what   somewhere here   there keeps being I
Mean being's kept   Flatly this particle on death row   that's nev-

Er ex-   ecuted   *I call to all the*   It calls to all the   With no caution
Spooky morning   on which we   didn't come from   anywhere
Glue and mem-   ory   The collage being begs of   you a new
Memory   or is it memorabilia   No it's the whole   cosmic glue

I am holding you to-   gether   For how much longer   The signs
Are breaking   Simply being here there   is nothing else
Where did it come to   you might ask   I was   always in the street
Your scrunched-up night   doesn't know   anything your

Scrunched-up medium   cannot hex me   Your   It's only a spooky
Dead word who you   think you are   Full of shit a
So-called circumstance   There are no   circumstances
This new mem-   ory   dances around your   dead space

The dead dance around and   in between where   your power's shaken
Up   you are annihilated math   the one   going no-
Where   I am the new memory   opaque and crooked   jolie
I don't remember   you   anymore   I've got your dust   to paste down

Flashback Clementa   Do you have to remember   Someone has to still

It's contrary to god's law he says   There is no god   Then how discuss it
That someone shot you?   I've just stepped out of   violent   hatred into an im-
Proper death   You haven't entered its central fact   you're afraid of it
And covered with blood—can you see?   Yes but what am I seeing   with?

You're part of ev-   erything the universe knows   how to do   Life and
Death knows   That's eyes . . .   Later he says   Yes it's irregular
The way I see it and you   I'm still bloody   To be   political here   not ne-
Cessary   We're just minds we're god   It's a rendezvous   with complicity

Still later he says   I see the back of   your head   when you're open
Like a store   I see you at the play   and I see the   part of you on the cross
I see the tangled lines of type and script   and images   liquid light you're
Thinking   So I get in your head and talk   I'm still afraid to be dead

And finally he says   But dead   is what I am   Is it beautiful
I sup-   pose   I'm not conscious but   I know   I talk to you
We're doing something   What are we doing   I'm not afraid now
Let's change the shape of it   Are you sure you're not   conscious I say

I'm in some other category   and I'm not *trying*   to be conscious
And I *am*   talking to you   I remember how to communicate   That holds
                                                                    everything together

I've got to remember what I did I   killed them the new guy says   I shot them on
TV then my —   I shot them and then me   I've got to remember   Am I remem-
Bering wrong   Oh you're here and I   killed your asses   Do you remember
The blonde still can't   speak   There seem to be several   superimposed

Images of   her her mouth's shut   She al-   ready knows she
Doesn't need it   The man beside her's gap-   ing his   mouth's o-   pen wide
They don't want to see you I say   Why aren't we extin-   guished   They
Turn away   They're leaving I say   Can go any-   where in this   death

And now I re-   member   I was in a   call it a   black fold
You'll   if space is that funny   remember irregular   areas of it as if brain-
Less   Your gesture I say to him   was meaningless   That's why you'll
And you for-   get it   having followed   me into   this crinkle I

Want you to leave   me alone for a-   while   He vanishes saying I
Can't remember   the TV station   clearly where   wall the wall flattens out

I myself in this mo-   ment can't   recall who he is
Do I want to   remember some-   thing   Nothing's inscribed
In death   No something must be   Like the most   aboriginal of minds'
Total recall   of the land-   scape's   history

I remember so much that   never happened   and what the living are supposed to do

That people would do   a minimum to survive   And if someone tried to
Take over perhaps they'd kill him . . .   As a deterrent to force   slip away
I'm slipping away   No one can keep track of   my name   Sleep in a rail-
Way station   for a few nights   Sleep in the airport   remember I

Remember I once slept   The dead close down to be alone   It's been a long time
Since I've needed much   some food and repairs   I'm staying thin
I have taken up the magical arts   of slipping away   of scarcely eating
And sleeping   I've taken up the magical art   of not keeping track of the famous

I haven't much of a phone   I mostly telepathize   Media is used to
Fuck with your mind al-   most exclusively   Stay away   from it use
Telepathy   none of this is whimsy   You whom I address are all coward-
Ly   full of flat words you've been   served by robots   The

Powerful are robots   Your reading   material's a robot   Reading it you
Are a guess what   I myself   barely move   but sometimes I run
I don't care   if I die   My children are mutants   like me
Insanely e-   nough you don't need anyone   but me who

Won't do anything   for you   but assert your   existential worth
Each of you is the only   one who matters and you   don't need anything
I am turning into a tall   sheaf of vibrations   again
I can talk to any entity   living or dead   In your mind this instant

It was the warehouse explosion   China? they find their   way to me finally
Quiet to-   gether who ever   needed to be over-   seen by the singular
Powerful I   am powerful   I just touch you   with thought and you say
Maybe it's better to be   here   Our leaders al-   ways fail us

It's better to be   dead where no one   can force me to work
Force me to list-   en and believe   I'd rather be touched   by your
Mild   magnetic   mind   Her face is burned just an   image her
Face is healing   her face is turning into   another   substance

Light or fluid-   ly light   waves or particles or   neither it's a
Third thing soul   My skin is cooler she says   We're all one thing
Silken   I want to be in a play   about a woman   who says
I am free to   turn away   And my silken   column twists

Turns away   She sings   There is no money   There is no way
To follow thing to de-   scribe   Everyone who told   me what to do can shut up

Who you are   what you don't know   that's what I never knew
Wind came I became that   What about nerves and pain   Gone
In an instant   Who you are was what you   never knew

What was this substance   my body I inhabited   my soul in and out of its small-
Est bits in alternance the vibratory act   That I was that   act my unconscious
Who are you I say   What you don't know   that's what   I never knew the
Dead voice says   Wind hurri-   cane came   I became that   As for

Nerves and pain   gone in an instant   Who are you   What you never
Knew   the old folksong   Why did I live   Why was there life
What is this substance   I am now he says   I left that part of me be-
Hind the folk-   song says and   came unto this town   to sing with no mouth

The unconscious my soul   was so united to my flesh   it told it to be
Still so I could sleep   It fought to leave when I died   Now it's con-
Scious I'm the conscious   But I re-   member that life al-
Most as if I   lived it   Were the nerves and pain the   only thing real

In it   Living   establishes memory   That's as far as I can get now
Alice what was the mem-   ory   I removed from my brain   when I left
When I left that self   mired in   group delusion   mass hallucination
I Alice say   the living must know   they are hallucinating   the world the known

That we remember the   fantasy   is all of it we   need to know

C'est très obscure la gaspillage de ma vie   J'étais bon j'étais méchant
J'ai fait mal   pour le faire   Tout que je vois —   ça n'est pas de la vue —   mais
Tout que je vois   est comme une nuit   c'est ça ma   mentalité
Tu es changé?   Comme d'être bon?   Je ne suis pas bon . . .

Parce que j'ai fait mal avec   trop de   délibération   comme un chat
Je la voulais savoir   à savoir la mentalité   pour faire mal
Ça m'infectait   progressivement   pour que   je le sache   C'était
Une forme extrême   de la curiosité   Et puis était-ça *mal*   Finalement oui

Est-ce que le mal est comme . . . mal?   ou comme n'importe quelle   action ou
Une état d'âme   c'est ordinaire   mais c'est   aussi opaque
Il n'existe pas ex-   actement mais   moi j'existais exacte   C'est possible
A être quelqu'un qui   ne prend pas soin   de mots

J'étais poète très tôt   et j'étais toujours dans le mot   le mot mal
Le mal étais mal là   Je pense que . . . puis   le mal est plus que un mot
J'étais un vrai malfaiteur   beaucoup plus qu'un autre   Tu es content de cela?
Je t'ai donné mon colis . . .   Il y a plus je crois   Je ne veux pas être opaque

Pour toujours

Rudy says I   photograph my thoughts I don't just   have them   I look at
Them through a   special lens in my   mind I possess   as if
I brought my camera   as part of my mind   and I take pictures that's
How I think   And I saw it say   Michael Brown's soul

Like a thought it moved like   blown-together pieces   darkish but
Squares and shapes of   fabric that pulsate   something like a face
About or above this form smiling   And I take its picture   It's all in me
Sometimes   the soul is a sound   But I see it   I see its pulses

And hear words I somehow photograph   *I am your change*   Or
The song telepathized   Let me show you each   word in
Several lang-   uages   superimposed   so you see each
You see its mo-   tion   How   My mind sees   what one says

Because that's what's here   And if illiterate   you see and hear ondular lines
And flashes   of light   images you re-   call from life   with small dif-
Ferences now   Part of the wind-   ow I   remember it but several
Blurred ones   on top of each other   or is it a   rolling blur

There was someone   leaning on the sill   elbow forearm hand   cheek to palm

We're supposed to be touching each other   and holding each other's babies

What do you need to   remember from life?   That you cared   Allen says
As for the bone-   pointing the bewitching he   says it's   part of the larger
Pattern   of your fate or role in uni-   versal history   It the bones or spells
The primitive ag-   gression against you by peers   was foreseen

By the dead though not arranged   This negative energy   has made you strong
Against it   but they could still kill   you   Do they know they want to
Not precisely   They like their silky malice but   never   think it's that
But what pre-   cisely are they   doing I say   Allen says

They each   there are several sep-   arate people   think uncon-
Sciously that they'd like   you to be dead   not knowing you're al-
Ways half here and em-   powered by us   But they do also want to
Strip you   of all semblance of   genius and virtue   They don't want

You to be who you are and will be   Many of the   sorrowful e-
Vents in your life   are connected to the bad   mind of others
Others did not want   you specifically   to succeed   at your art or love
The poison be-   comes stronger   You live in i-   solation you

Become sick   Or your beloveds die   Or your esthetic is
Derided   The bone was pointed long ago   By more than one
Not paranoia but how earth is run   The identities of the
Malefactors   can change   There are several living   people who wish you dead

I don't want to lie

Rimbaud says   this translated in-   to English I   can do the spells
Too I remember   But from here . . .   I remember   people fucked with
Each other's minds   as you would say   out in the sticks
I think I am as soul   too objective   I have ob-   served my life

Found it wanting al-   most forgotten . . .   I don't want though
Your so paltry enemies   to win   Am I childish   We could cast more
Spells   Or strengthen you   strengthen your . . .   position   Do I
Have one   I'm trying still   to get rid of some   things from my

Life he says   I don't remember   my crime but its inten-   sity hurts
Like a malignancy   with sharp nails in me   I pull it out
There   because I have a   purpose for it   Eat a little raw image
Shove the rest   through the grid   And you will! defeat them

Will I know I've defeated them   I don't know   Hands me the writhing image
I don't want to lie   I don't!   This is happening some-   how   I bite
Down on it   Tastes like coffee   saliva   mine   and maybe
Insect carapace   I know the spells he says they   are ment-

Al   You've given me a   hint of malice?   No be-   cause it's you I've
Given you a certain sight   a second sight   so you can see your enemies
As they are   Give them nothing   until they are dead
Believe that they are malefi-   cent friends   and colleagues

Is this true   And I am freed of that demon he says   I thought I still needed it

Memory   "why did I live"   Do you remember   what you did
My memory's flat on my   soul one says   Is your soul flat   My soul has no
Exterior dimensions   Before I was born . . .   there was a base   it was green air
There are tiny   memory packets   black   in my transparence

I could extend myself   was not finite   or tangible   imagine air extensions
Ripples   Did I interact   Everyone was there I remember   Daddy says like flying
An airplane   The sensitivity to the infinite   inside pieces of air
That was you maybe   Others   might be anything   Did you need to

Remember then   Maybe maybe my identity   What were the memory packets
They help you   They come from where   They come from yourself   How
You seem to have the option   But I didn't have any   options I say
I don't have that   particular memory   In life I remember   semblance

That I am to seem   like something   Before birth you don't   have to seem
At death you   are different from before   I reached out   and touched the face he
Says   It wasn't god it was my   soul—me   I don't remember you a voice says
To me   But I don't have to   In life you have to   remember   how to get around

If you're dead you   remember how to be   The part of first
Mind that was trapped in your   body   soul your   soul I
I can't remember it another   voice a bad man says   I don't have   that
Yes you do I say   you're being it   But I'm not happy yet he says

The way I was happy being bad   Why didn't you have   any options he
Asks me   I've always been the same thing   I don't have to remember it
I'm not sure I have   the memory packets   I'm not sure I believe   in them
I've never forgotten who I was   Walk on pale water   without options

Le quartier, c'est mon ami

I could see he'd   had a stroke   walking misshapenly   to le point de presse
I'll do anything rather than   face it   that I need to take
Charge of the world   in its state of emergency   Syria's emptied out of
All but potential controllers and   Russia has arrived on foot

In the beautiful   collage dead minds make   different sets of constel-
Lations are projected in turn in   mind's eye   I don't remember
Them   They are newly   formed on   the instant   they are notes
You read or this   as you hear   immediate a per-   formed com-

Position   The dead woman and her dead sons   the Syrians   sat
Near my chair   all day yesterday   Last night I communed with
Jimmy   He said he didn't   mind it was me that   he handed his
Blunt packages to   I am a piece of fate   a prodigious

Hole my heart   Everyone   must listen to me   even if
I say nothing   The human surface of earth   in self-
Inflicted danger   from companies and councils   impels all towards
The doom foretold   You knowing this   will soon get up   off your

Fesses and   walk towards your deaths   incapable
Stop con-   suming anything   Listen to my lines   Join my mind
Harmless and lucid   it is vaster   than our planet   overreaching
The ugly power   of men

You Are an Agent

Duly, friends   from the truth of the opaque   I stop   turning a-
Way and face Night   dead in my mind   but a clinger   If
You wage extensive war . . .   Snapped a cable . . .   Can you hear me
She walks towards a hut   on a seacoast flat   and enters

There's writing on these   close walls   which expand
Really to envelop   you in-   visibly   so you can be
Cured   characterized now by the   foolishness of quo-
Tidian chores wherever you are   There is no   mercy there are only

Laws   of compliance to   people exactly like you
Except for within me   There you need do nothing   as I whis-
Per lines that affect you bodily   We will do this ignor-
Ing else   You can find a sand dollar   You don't even have

To listen   Just stay in here   coming back   You have returned to the
Primal site without approval   of external agency   you are the agent
Do you feel that   Or it is our electrical   connection
There are al-   ways moments in   between moments   where you

Don't have to suffer   I show you pul-   ses to   slide between or
I show you   how to be a   sound wave   the flexile   your soul

Thick and unknowing more   unknowing as much   as I can though
Nonetheless en-   closing all in my field   Listen   I'm listening (real)
You are my aching   heart of your crime-tinged   disposals   I
Have always   wanted to reach you be-   cause the universe com-   pletes it-

Self cognitively   and elsewise   as we who are   it recognize that
We are here just here   So tell me a thing: There is   only to care for
These new Syr-   ian dead ones   But they will want to   know what
You are   what they are   Nothing being only   a linguistic idea

What are you . . .   If I saw it (voice says)   I would be separate   from
Myself . . .   You can't project   soul of the light   but if
You get it   you'll know how there's   not nothing   We can sep-
Arate from each   other   maybe but one can't   observe oneself

And not being able to   then that is   what there is   It has no extent
But is everything   Don't separate your-   self from the so-
Called . . . light that needs no   source   I'm   only trying to
Help   the voice concludes   We feel better a some-   one says

Listening to quiet sounds   voices   working through
Thoughts   Perhaps we won't do   much else   for a while

I saw Sandra   on the cross   Or was it I on the cross   I saw one of
Us   as what is called past   inquires   how can you   be ready
Readied by suffering   She died and I   didn't and Kayla   died
How can I cure them   but I already have   tortured hearts for

The time—   the-all-of-time-that-could-ever-elapse—   has gone by
When   In between any two of the   phrases as   we are together in
The pre-dawn   And between those betweens   one is on the cross
Get it?   I am for I'm alive   and can suffer any time the wheel

Stops at me   *Maybe it isn't*   *gonna stop at you*   *any more*   I've
Been on a run of bad   the entire   and am upon of   a sudden
The cross to do it for   everyone again   Because you don't understand
It's just something else you don't get   that this is   the only way to know

Flashes of noise   around   the wounds I mean   lights I mean
You did this to me   Because you want certain things   You don't want to
Know   You just want things

Is the name of power   powerlessness   I mean   physical power or
Electric power   since in the dead world   unphysical   is the most
Power   What are you using   for power   Again   it's only mind
Just mind   How did you or we   ever get mind   There's no getting

For of what there is there *is* it   And you know there is   what you are
Am I a performance   one might ask   The stars might ask   Or a quasar
You are strangely grouped   like a wind   You know how to laugh do you
I was circling you   Tell the truth   It saved my soul   What saved it

You can't lose it after all   Can lose contact with it   for a while
And pretend you're yourself they say   Who pretends then   isn't that you
I lost my spark   in the inquiry   into its origin   Nothing gets lost
Not even a spark of self   Not even a dead man's soul   It left me yes

And I was only fearful   Not in death   I was dead alive   Now that I'm
Actually dead   I can't remember anything true   Remember being dead
I remember   I did   whatever I wanted   or you wanted   I was evil for
You wanted an evil   performance   a powerful leader   I was for you what

Was wanted   I   tortured killed raped   and never begged   You joined me
Am I dead   but I'm alive here   What   can I do   am I doing anything
There is no power   I have no limbs   no hands or locomotion I   understand
What is the power here   For we continue   without time and design

What are we effecting   Who are we with-   out god what's going on
What performance is this   I want power   I still want power   more than
Anyone else has   You can't have that here   We're too connected
I don't want to be connected   We're the same material   the same power

Flash but no light's   here I soul of cress   moss and   flash fritillary
Crawling shade   How gross a soul how noisy   I'm but more and   more ob-
Scure obtuse a-   lone in this one   only this moment   I'm inkblots gi-
Gantic   so one can have no ac-   cess to this form   finding what and

Couldn't hex this   Was I once hexed   a supposed execution   with vul-
Tures I   see who you are   I sped away from   your murder of me
Leave   I am be-   coming an even larger dark-   ness cover-
Ing your piti-   ful ground   You stupid   little figurines

From this chair   And I used   what they   thought happened
But I knew you   couldn't make anything   happen but
Trash   Fixated on each other-   er though   pieces of   similitude
Having pulled a-   way towards death I   have the power it's

Never where it's   thought to be   What do I   want with it   to
Redesign the universe of   course but to de-   scale eyes   is it I
Don't know I just like   to hulk over you   when not cru-
Cified   I am the crucifix the storm   but most   I am the mind

You are so *little*   Monarchs of companies   countries institutions
But like dolls   I am trying to   save you be-   fore you die anyway
Ever-diminished stars   your value ex-   cept being of this sub-
Stance   I've got to find your re-   ality or are   you blank lost

In the nothing room   where you've always seen   objects as trained to
See them they're without ed-   ges   I move towards and swal-   low their forms
Not seeing anymore   I assume my power   Shadow of hand on pa-
Ge writing   as edgeless as   you will be   in the righteousness of my un-rule

I will teach the only known   the blasphemy of loss   And with lost vision
The new collage   of who one is ex-   pands   For it was a robe
That is now casu-   ally draped   folded over and in   without dimensionary
Status   A universe shifts to be   any rose and on   every petal

Glue the qua-   sar's re-   peated melody   stress surrounded by pulling-
Apart   fab-   ric or cue to   another   oscilat-   ing vocal piece
I don't mean vo-   cal I mean   simultaneity   of
Torn-off and glued-on   by my mind   your   needs I don't

Mean   Come within this mind   and perceive   that your shape is
Grossly shadows   flashing with phrases   navy-black-grey-matte
Textured communicant   sudden wings   for letters' con-
Figuration   Each thing you say picture non-   pollutant wisdom grain

MEMORY

What happened   never had edges   though there are events   not quite edged
If you suddenly   witness a death it   happens   exactly at its mo-
Ment when   the hole of it opens   dislodging air   So   you can re-
Member how you felt   if you dare   or his   final expression

I remember the   plastic noose form-   ing in my   hands   Sandra says
Memory is con-   tinuity a low voice says   a dead voice says
I don't remember   what I was an-   other says   What I am I
Still take for granted   as if I can't   forget   to be

Are you yourself   Surely   I remember R says   seeing people's
Hurt faces when   I did   whatever I pleased   experimentally
Why haven't I for-   gotten   It's not guilt   Why   was the experiment
Necessary or   was it   I wanted to   feel it   still must want to

Do you really   say these things   to me I ask them   And someone says
You must be-   lieve you are   hearing us   We continue to
Remember you   who you are   remember we need you   If you were to go
Away . . .   I'm re-   making another says   as you said to   the uni-

Verse   Unedged memory   collage logic   We must remember
What   How to   exist   Do I have to remem-   ber I killed some-
One with my fist?   For how long?   Whenever I know
He's near?   I remember I say   I belong to all you   forever   That's who I am

VISION

I see how you the dead ac-   company me where I go   within my surround
I can't see you but I see you   Sometimes a group   sometimes billions featureless
We don't see you either   one says   even when we're with you   we go to
You we go to your mind   I once literally felt I say   a hand   someone's

Hand   though you have none   on my shoulder   when I doubted you
Really spoke to me   spoke or com-   municated   Saw or sensed
A voice says your language   doesn't apply   In vision I
Always see you I say   without exactness   each a generalized

Self   yourself   I find you as individuals   in a rush to cling
Many I   only remember from   media photos   But I see that you
Have a form   composed of person-   ality   and   swirling volume
Sometimes you talk to   me in *my* voice   But I know   I see   it's you

Now I see chairs in my room   denominated only   'the one that
Looks like that'   If I stop and think what it   looks   like   slowly
Then that's not what   it looks like   Appearance is fast   Making my mental way
About the outer   I love all you in particular   therefore Love's the delineation

It looks for a charac-   teristic to know by   And it finds it in air
It sees in air   Vision has long been a system   Now it is free   to see

Because I lost my life and still live   in an onrush of tragedy and in-
Consequential detail   the goings-on   So I could   find the un-
Syntaxed bearings   or were they logical   is this logical   If
I was hexed —   I think they want me to be un-   happy or dead

But if the wind's steady   can I move   Only with the effort of
Saying   I need a new house   or I'll hurt you if   you attack a-
Gain   I said that to someone   when I awoke   sick of the conceit of popular
Music   What is this   a dead voice says what are you   writing   thinking

Look for the language   of forgetting   in order to think I say   so I can for-
Get to be hexed   Forget duty   even if still im-   mersed in it
Or love   It's Sandra who now moans low   I'm looking for   how you
Talk but   I'm hexed I   say   bone-pointed lots-   cast-against

Out of the unconscious   language of art and   poetry
That is always *against*   at this moment   *against* or only *for* and
I was nowhere   You don't have to   make sense to me   Sandra says
I still don't under-   stand my own   suicide   Because I

Lost my life   And still live I say   and will not be part of living
Cannot live except here   But whose is the ill spell   that reaches me
No one should take   part in this world   as it stands
You live must withdraw from   it   Leave your country   for my force-field

COLLAGE

Torn into as many pieces   as sleep makes   of a suicide
We   and says Kayla I'm ripped up   begin to be re-combined   You will be
Your own col-   lage   And I I say can give   you   pieces   of me if you
Wish   so you can have surprise   Some of my heart-space pieces — when

I made room for distress packages   can be yours   Are asks Sandra   these pieces
Visible   Are we aiming for   what we looked like   before   Take this
Piece of my heart I say   and put it next to what   in your mind
Is most broken   My disposition was so un-   even she says

It looks like a purple torn ocean   And the piece of my   heart's   sere
Some skin ripped and dead   but next to purple a   dried wild-   flower
And so on   Make yourselves any-   thing   Your soul reminds that
It is all you are   but making the beautiful   heals you

And says Kayla   my lost childhood's   stuck to my forehead
Like a jewel   artificial   so what   Behind my transparent temples
Memories of the ripping-out of my fingernails   glued to the light in Oak Creek Canyon
Bump it   they bump   Let me be remade ran-   domly

And my soul me ab-   sorbs the images only   images
I am a soul   and what happened   is a collage   is a collage   the
Universe is a soul   upon which such jumble   as I say
People mistook for order   the collage   of a previous universe's   old parts

Kayla

Remember before you were born   I remember an   old brown house   sag-
Ging   in the woods   Are you going to take my misery   remake it into what
I was before I was born   It goes inside this   cavern of me to be changed
Into the combo of before and after   I re-   member she says   I had no

Need to find myself   That was purely you I say   Now you are al-
Most that stranger   and have given me   your worst memories
Having placed them in a packet   because thinking them is useless   Now
I take the guilt or lump of misery of yours   into the cavern my heart

Or you thrust it in   There was so much last night   There were so many
Who came to my   room to give me theirs   their terrible bundles   How
Does it come to be remade she asks   into the gold soul the universe's   melt
Of transcendence   we are all of   Because you came to me   begging for change

And I have lost my features   I have no face   She is the best friend
You'll ever have   a voice says   Because out of me   pours new soul
Out of my dead   heart and blank face   and from my finger-
Tips it comes forth   and through my skin   I become   the production of

New soul   It flows   towards you and you just   take it in   You can't resist
This enhancement   This knowledge made of   everyone' self-   disgust and sin
Transformed in my alchemical   chamber   or body of origin
That I have never lost   connection with   the communicants'

Pure gold   pure relevance   the speaking star   which is now you

I make my way through the   There's nowhere to go   I wasn't try-
ing to explain how I felt   I was trying to   move things with my mind
The dead have   no matter to move   even at first   Matter must have been
Mind   Opaque and unknown am I   I don't need to move matter   but I walk

And I do it   from within the matter   Lifted I   lifted a molecule
From across the room   called love   I lifted a   red book called Oration
I lifted . . .   You lifted mine eyes   dead man says   What
Are we playing at   The emotion that   the mental motion that   promotes

Physical change   And we told our minds   that a crooked line   was straight
And thus I saw it   I *remember* that   I remem-   ber that a fiery particle
Shot out of a grey void   when I called to it   None of this is
True   Are you true?   You can't lie   Hallucinated motion   on acid

What the dead know one says   is that hallucinated   matter isn't necessary
Though *we did that*   We never saw why we   were there   It was
Because the words became too true   A body   must be left
It isn't true enough   I mean it's too true   a prison a word-like

Prison   Push out its sides   I never asked   for this
What did you ask for   I asked to heal you   first in other
Words I don't want to remember   I lifted   the lamp with my
Mind over-head   So you could see the glass of   water   Does it matter

There is no mat-   ter I repeat   There is some-   thing else
I surpass it now   I surpass what-   ever's   said to be   to be happening or to be

THE BATTLE

I laid down and   the fictive bone was there   next to me   Memory of
A battle   Consciousness   against Unconsciousness   Consciousness won
Consciousness won then   But maybe it won't   this time coming
What language do you speak   I ask the air   Or is it space   or outer space

What lang-   uage do you speak   I ask the outmost edge   of the uni-
Verse   What language   were you are   you I   ask it again
Whatever you speak it says   What a rock speaks   Or piece of fire
Can we go beyond   where we are I ask   this edge or rim   of knowledge

I don't think it's there it   says   I think it's all   inside one
Infinity it's   some rest of   extent inside us . . . .
I haven't found out all   of the unconscious   have I   I ask the dead
How well   do I know   what is called un-   consciousness

For when you're   with me   we seem conscious   a conscious
Unconsciousness   Unconsciousness   says a voice
Is always there   subjected   If you release it more   some-
Thing happens   a battle for   more sovereignty   it wants

To be consciousness   in both the dead and live   Is this
True   Yes   the universe voice says   this is   exact
And the bone   next to me?   So you won't win   unconsciousness back
They are afraid of it   so afraid of   territorial loss   quotidian power

> "Out the window with the window."
> — Gregory Corso

The bone's covered with   writing or marks   You need salt or a cruci-
Fix a voice says   I am a crucifix I say   Leaving the Atrophied Station
The bone's shadowed with   lacy marks lattice-   work   Your work
Isn't simple-   minded enough some-   one says   for earth its

Small mentality   But for the dead   for us it works   If I quote leave
The station do I   have to stop at another one   At the old battle-
Field remember   this time Inter-   galactic intercosmic   Inter Uncon and
Con   Right now you're lying next to a bone   a manuscript or artifact

Last night I lay   next to   a Sonoran boy dead I say   in jeans and short-
Sleeved shirt   still scared   He stayed with me   till his deceased aunt came
There's a changing group   of ill-wishers   like that chain five
Hundred miles long   On every link   someone who   wishes you harm

How can there not   be a battle   Can you nego-   tiate with
People   who won't ac-   knowledge their   malicious desires
She or he   deliberately   stays unclear   Where is this battle-
Field   Somewhere inside   folded-up space   in an opaque zone

What about the   textual rhyming bone   It's not a joke the
Voice says   You should think about   destroying   someone
First   try to read it?   All you do is read   the voice says
I was born read-   ing I say   I surely read be-   fore I was born

I read that ex-   istence   is a hoax   that I'd rewrite   for everyone

"... l'inanité de toute tentative pour se débarrasser de son
sorcier par un affrontement direct ou violent avec lui."
— Jeanne Favret-Saada

I see   how the earth has be-   come dark with fate   It has a fate
But that of the universe   is so diffuse   as not to exist
And   the dimension of the dead   has somewhat of fate
But the earth   a small beloved   is both dark and   distracted

I saw yester-   day ob-   serving within me   that the earth now
Is fully dark with   human ignorance and   destructive force
No one sees beyond   the small frame in front of one   hand-held screen
My screen   is in my mind   But as for the   bone poin-

Ted at me   written on it obscurely's   some script   'You will pay
From the far past   unto the future   This curse affects
You and yours   that you not succeed'   There is a draw-
Ing or fetish   woman with tri-   angular sex   I sup-

Pose that's me   even if I'm un-   gendered now un-   hormonal
Nothing   in the earth's view   Though I'm changing it   lead and heal
In so-far occult or   hidden ways I've devised ...   This bone's not
Material   but I see it   She wants me   dead or un-

Happy   I encroach   on her territory   who would vendi-
Cate herself   But there's no future here   except in death
It is a long curse   a voice says   aimed at you   Will you
Kill her?   Who?   It is a long curse cast by who

I can't   locate its source   And what good is it   if the earth's so dark
She has no future   She can still kill you before you act   the voice says

571

This language comes to me and I'm opaque

We're both   the language and I   dark   and   hard
I don't understand my motions   what I say   where I'm going now
I'm certain   no one on earth   knows a thing   How dark it is   How
Dark I am   I am a purpose   as if that were   an object

I am yours   your purpose   dark to you as   ghosts
The language says   And now   we fight for   What do we fight
For   I don't want to   Everything that we   don't know yet
What you are cursed for   what we the dead   have been sad for

We the alive   say in our dreams   that we are sick   All of us
You will   the language says to me   enter the folds of
The fabric per-   haps becoming disturbed   and will discover
At first then . . .   It's probably a   collage too   space-

Time   Is math a collage   Pieces   pieces   stand-
Ins   uneruptibles   they   don't have math   in outer space or death
Though it's calm   You're going to the un-   hexer   Your aim
Is to make   the enemy   fall into pieces   she is composed of

But that's a side e-   vent   Your aim is to "unearth"
Consciousness   and unconsciousness

And in Death Before the Battle:
You Are Talking About Him Behind His Back

Michael Brown cries out   all the live who name me   hurt me
I have just tran-   scribed your cry and   thus named you   I say
But I want you he says   to tell them   I am not for   them to name a-
Gain   The dead aren't dead and the live are ig-   norant asses!

Michael's image-   face grey with men-   tal pain   I tell you
Truly   And you name him and   name him nam-   ing his namers a-
Gain but   he has never been a name   I thought   it didn't mat-
Ter he says   Because dead I'm free   and I am   But I hear

Them each time   as if they're call-   ing me though they're   ignoring me
I don't care which race you are   Alice why do   I keep hearing them
Because the ear of the dead   opens to us   though we're blocked to them
Why? he asks   I don't know if questions   serve you   serve

Your thought   How you're learning to be   Yes he says   At a cer-
Tain point there are no   questions though there   may be . . .
A door that opens   I'm waiting for that I say   A door to battle
In the mean-   time in our epic   I exhort people   not to name

Michael   unless you love him   For I do   And now
At the end of Fated   I draw a sword

. . . And then you kill—   was it it? her or him   Is that   in the battle
Is the cast-   ing of lots or throwing of spells   The unconscious
World is shutting me out   and I haven't dreamt   for two nights is
That part   'They don't know   which world you're   from' a voice says

I tried for Alabaster Heart   It's a bus stop   Can't come in   Alice
Can't come in   Who can   A warrior for our side   Oh sides I
Don't do them   Who are your lives   Poet leader healer savior
No one   Banished battered hexed   Hearer of Voices   The Complete Songs

Come in   I'm afraid (truly) to   go in this time   Is this what we want
We don't know say the voices
                                        A door that opens   Do I
Know this door   the light inside   Enter   only the bat-
Tered war-   rior enters   Pieced together of   olden words

The loving child   the Childe enters   I am   not for you to
Name   Michael's voice rings   in my ear   Not for you to name
Alive in absolution   all were without   blame when
At the first   we begin to figurate   as selves   or   souls

Come in this door   of what you forgot

574

I see flat trans-   parent hands first why   they're nowhere   other side of
Door   kind of dangling   They might be mine?   to do with
Like gloves   like soul gloves   But I can't put   on anything
I don't know how   Just glide   Why is the floor   fuchsia red

Why is there a window   This room of   where fame stops   nothing's known
Put on the gloves   Why   Won't catch anything   won't leave fingerprints
I don't know   about hands   This isn't an outfit   there's no company
Keep being in   this room   without my body   or any body

Folding chair sit down   Nothing sits down   Or do I   invisible
See the wooden floor   This is an attic   Battle of the Attic?
No one to fight   Have the thoughts   what or whose
I am having your   thoughts whose   being   someone here

Gloves now on the wooden floor   *This species had hands*   I don't
The walls expand out-   wards   I'm coming   towards . . .
Her image   Towards it or being it   Going towards it   No
I reject her and she dis-   solves   Gloves on   the floor still

She was me   *I know*   *I rejected her*   she was too caught
It's so   red in here   And I am the one   left behind I say
It's all in power now   The room's cracking   into pieces   I see be-
Hind the wall   a REHEARSAL word REHEARSAL   spheres in orbit I

See   The planets rehearsing their move-   ments to be   When is this
I blast their order   I blast their paths   away   How how did you do it
I just blasted   The planets?   Figments of human senses   I blast away
So I can be here   Blast with thoughts   Blast them away

Ted says I don't remember her (someone still alive now famous)
Joe and I   we sit inside each other's minds   like sites
Like archeological sites

THE BATTLE OF CHANGES

The act-   ual disorder   contains no sites or   parasites
That I know of   I'm in charge of the battle one   casualty so far un-
Identified   I grew up   in some wheel-shaped   outpost   Is this true
In or on the wheel you   I left my identity to   take over this   area

Don't make meanings   like black holes   and see where   that gets you
It is very scrunched some-   times and changes   rapidly

Hatching   What's really here?   Remember   you're a target
Meat exchange   hair roots bloody   fecal espresso glitter mind
I got a thought   Hold it   I will take over   with some equipment
There's a word for it   righteousness   the buried   deck near the slough

This bludgeoned her   Did you do it? he asks   In the sleep so
Without physicality   You're all   under attack   The battle goes on
Throughout the site   of memory   So many harms to shoot
Comfort is one shoot it up   the house   the laws   translated in-

To scientific ones   easy pigeons   where were we   the bank cos-
Mic covered with   fuchsia ichor   In the fact the   body's there
Again under the bus   I'm trying not to   think   except for the truth
It just screams   Who set in motion   all your lies   Replace them with

Gashes and excisions   And unmolecular eyes   This isn't the unconscious I
Knew a voice says   too gruesome   But   this is where it   happens

Colors for what eyes, sounds for what ears

In among the lights and colors   fighting each other   deep pink and yellow
Dark blue and yellow   Green green no blue   Purple   no red no orange
Yellow it's yellow   pulled fabric cirrus   it's yellow   pink-edged
In among them   What's the matter   What's a position   Hear the

Sounds fighting   mixolydien mode against   simple tritones
No it's tremb-   ling one-notes   middle C   against the house
What's the house   what falls a-   part and reconstitutes   the cards
Where did they come from   Faced with planets   At this stage

On this stage that   collapses of course   ratatat or some shit
Red blue green   F sharp B   What about   seals and signets no
Way that eas-   y   What about microtones   Everywhere   Sta-
Tic   Loss of color   Whiteness then   saturation crimson . . .

The version of the   *universe in un-*   *consciousness*   *is not legal*
Lawful   But the le-   gal one col-   lapses as I   always knew it would
Do you feel how   nothing is certain   You   have no era but
You have no aura   No mouth no hands no   matter   no case

Back in what   room I   love you   Michael says
That doesn't belong I   say then say   Okay   That be-
Longs here too   There was love some-   where in   the battle
Saint Michael slew the   dragon   at the fountain overrun with blood

A guarantee   a guarantee   that there's a universe   and reality
I know a man who'll   give you a guarantee   of your reality

The color is navy-blue tonight   marine-   blue with rhinestones
That's the sky be-   hind the utility company   where the California
Hotel used to be   where the old store was   The vans take off
Full of packed stuff   Too personal   Nothing's personal

Time for the battle again   What kind of stuff   do we need to be
What were we once   what have we been   Colors arias touches   Texture's
Fetid greeting   crows   pulling at dead mouse's tendons   Dream level
The lousy drama   threatens to   rise up like   the old river

The river's been mostly dry for years   But it's in me   It's risen in me
You left me on the street   in curls and a short dress   You didn't know
I was the one   Do I care now   Did I care then
The battle encroaches   Drives away   my personal assumption of

That costume   I'm rich   with impersonality   and could kill
You   Who   So here I am   in all my force   some first element
Who are you   I'm the soul   sweating crystal   vibrations   the truth
I'll walk all over you   Like an angel's   mouth whisper   Spirit's

Running everywhere   Feel it   thick as air   Palpate   it

Let Me Finish Healing the Future

Prescience   to the battle bring   First there was this   silken thought ev-
Erywhere   It knew   Did the hex start there   Let me finish healing the future
They are thrusting their packets   into my chest   as I stand here dis-
Covering   aggression   twoness   I'm condemned   to oneness I say

The fabric or silk or thought   becomes my   sculpted face out-thrust
I haven't dreamed yet   ever   Counting backwards to . . .
There's no direction   home   Comes into the   space   a monad
Says I am here   to make up   your mind for you   I push it

Down awakening stairs   My face now a doily   of nebulae
Blank   I have a sword again   like that archangel   Slash the
Colors and sounds some more   And they are bleeding   aghast that
Being   can be rent   by the force that I am   alone

No mind none   to make up   Stay away from   me so
I can heal   you or me   Cutting up every-   thing I see
You can't see   says someone   And the worm's   in three parts   Our
Ouroboros   Forget what it was   There's an X   on my heart where *it* is

Where Is the War Now Everywhere

The X chest of me   so full of black sub-   stance   turning to gold
Presses   The X chest   shudders   at the uni-   verse's remaking
Out of bad mind   combus-   tion fumes and dead suns
Keep fighting keep fight-   ing the hexer the   vain one

As I took in the dead from   the bombed Afghan hospital   the Syr-
Ian rebel forces   and the sunken ship   As they mob   my actual bed
For love and forgiveness   as the myriad dead   among the or-
Ganic and non-organic   being of all us   pushes its shitty sin   into my heart

I am also lying near   the lots the bone the   spell cast
Did self-obsession shatter oneness   Is it the mirror's regard   or a love of control
That caused some as-   pect of the fab-   ric to tear a-   way   and come out
The other side of death the real   Someone was lying there   pretending

To know me well   Now stand and kill the hexer   and let it place its —
Or her or his —   bundle into my chest sub-   sequently   I know you I say

She wants to con-   trol my strength   so we would remain small in mind
Small enough that   there can be fame   and she can have it
She poses no diffi-   cult confrontation   another photo
In the small world   I'll stand and tower now   too tall   to be killed

Or bother with   the subtle   complainants   I call for
Their language   to leave them   Isn't that death   the invalidation
Of their power   allowed at origin   that any would be-
Lieve   another   that matter would believe humans   that you

Would believe I was weak-   ened   I'm killing   your words
I have not been clear   You had en-   tered my house   in order
To know it small   But it was larger than   a palisade   or abyss
You had befriended me   to share my   breath   take

Of it then   declare it wanting   You stole   from my books
Disclaiming all source but   yourselves   But here at
Origin I am the victor   denying   you a tongue
No one dependent on con-   sciousness   will flourish   and there

Is no reign or rule   You will have to   learn how to   talk again   Can you
You wanted   to be famous   when we needed   a new universe

You wanted to be famous on earth   when we needed a new universe

Dream

I prepare two veal's hearts stuck everywhere with pins and give them to George.
He has prepared one for me. I'm not sure who the sorcerers are.

Everything's rising up within   This is how it works   This is the universe work-
Ing   the river of force rising   you stick the pins   in the calf's heart   as
Mine was once stuck   before I became   everyone's heart-   space
You turn the   curse back on them   who   And I know who   and

Don't name   All of historical time   earth time   can be seen like a labyrinth
From this mental height   and I see fate   handed on   and around by
Un-   caring ones   who want themselves   Do I   want myself
But the fate stops here   like the buck   I'm sending it back to   its last handler

You want me   to be wrong   If right and wrong is   your commodity   you
Will be wrong   If outrage is   your commodity I   am going to
Outrage you   I stuck the pins in   the calf's heart   methodically   by rule
This is at the first   I've taken my force back   from you   You disappear in-

To the fabric squealing   I've taken your false   language   away from you
I've taken your false heart   your cunning   rage from you   your power of
Intimidation   that once worked   apparently   Creature of   appearance
The ground of   poetic   thieves and thugs

They are killing you   They are killing you   You   are killing them
When it comes up la-   ter the river   who are   you the river
In the de-   sert someone's kidnapping   the fat lady's children   I get it
Then you   give them back   But it's too late   She's singing

The fat lady sings I've   got something bad to   tell you
What a hot desert where   the river of the un-   conscious floods its
Banks   Are you a whim   Is your planet a whim   Is a hex-
Er a fact   You walked into one of my   internal rooms

With your most humorless expression   But now   I was the
Crucifix the salt little else   Likewise the planet was   Are you glad
To be fam-   ous in its last   hours are you   glad
You get the veal's heart   You also get the   sputtering sparkler

The Unconscious   rises up   Once more drowning   you take offense
When it's a bullying po-   et is it a poet   Each bit of
Universal form-   ation is it a poet   humming The End
I per-   ceived my thoughts   had not to   do with my brain

My meat   I separated out   from your dominion fame   that was dying
I am anywhere the soul   Some body's fighting   on automatic pilot
I watch your false molecules riot   Then the   river then the river
Of real memory over-   takes you   You were   never in this

Story   Who are you   Are you dying in   the wrong story   who are you
I've got some-   thing bad to say   the fat   lady sings
My children are kidnapped   I've got them you   say but   it's
Too late   the fat lady's singing   I've got something   bad to say

583

You can on-   ly change the   world with mind re-   make matter with mind
Open your mind   Don't touch the hexers though   even internally
Meanwhile matter   flies across the   heavens   hurls itself a-   cross space
I am the cross space   space and time intersecting   in me my chest wound

How shall I conduct   this war further   The war is al-   ways within
Concept of matter with-   in and the rain's com-   posed of soul   new round rain
I'm pelted with inside this felt fold   of the discovered   dimension in grand
I'm so over-   come with the ele-   ment I am I   give into it the rain

Of infinitesimal drops of soul   Is it grace   whose   penetrating mine
The hour we don't have hours   has arrived   casually then   the new
Particles will emerge   from the mix in me   the touch of   any evil is
Degraded   broken down into   this new essence   we can emerge as   after

After the ex-   terior planet   has changed so   much we can't live on it
Is that what you   mean who are you   talking to   You can start
Now   Let yourself be   bombarded with soul   in this battle for the
Universe   not even the world and   what dies   who kills   have I killed my

Hexers   Would you please   negate your sorcerers   Out of my heart flow
The new heterodox particles   the new golden mesh   the new   of death and life
Is this the uncon   the unconscious doorless   the one where you park
Thinking with these   new particles   pervasive   What are we now

(At building door yesterday   sensation of rising   my mind rising   above my brain)

Before the world you knew the   ones you've been with
You knew mountains

I press to go   the chance but-   ton   Does it exist   *Not for you*
Can never le-   ave where you've known all   I'm not fighting enough?
New essence pours   out of my chest   and I whirl be-   sworded but

Not a person ex-   cept in your eyes I   can drop it   True is it
Truth is pour-   ing out of   my nightmare   chest where
Every-   one's craftiness has been de-   graded into   common grace
Like at the first?   I don't know   I still need to   kill someone

Became bodies dis-   crete bags of common fluids   meat   No
See that   no parts   My soul slipped out and   looked at me
She's chang-   ing into   You have to see me   Again I lie?   No
You can't see   It doesn't *do* these words   word-things   Just speak

Make you hap-   pen but I   To save us   your body's chang-
Ing   And flooded into a   Your chest   really is
Full of our most re-   pulsive characterist-   ics   mixed with
The sub-   stance or   underconsciousness   which is every-

Where   It she my-   self says   So please be true   The battle
Goes on   Be true to ev-   eryone   You are their only real leader
And the heavens follow you   into their new   presentation

Corp-   ses everywhere   What we have is   a memory   of bodies
Are we aery   images now   Or were we   never really   flesh a word
I am   a dead word are you   a word   Walk a-   long I walk
A further fold of   the universe arena   into and down   Image glide

Among these down   where go   On every level be-   hind every cur-
Tain corpses   not only peo-   ple and their attenu-   ated guts   but ev-
Ery idea you con-   tained   Hey are you the   dead-dead or dead-live or
Who was it any-   one spoke of   did you speak   I glide   on

If conscious-   ness is dead   I am uncon-   scious   not in a
Dream   I don't know   what to call it   Slip inside here   black a
Soothing fold   Corridor opens   Words latticed   ir-
Regular arise as I go   Walk   Alone   Keep lov-   ing along I

Am loving along   Souls following   of who's gone   or even sleeping
Or even awake not a-   ware part of it's   with me   There are no
Images   Imago tar-   get on a wing   There are   no wings no
Theater   in which to act for others   Red stretched thin   sound faroff bullet

It was . . .   And now   in the dist . . . .   no method   so I
Dropped it   And I turn and say   Start being here   You haven't brought a thing

I'm the universe source   all of it   coming from my chest   Giants'
Souls rocklike   souls of planets geo-   logical form-   ations their
Suns   and dying eyes of constellations   stars red and yellow   have
Thrust their sad pasts   their form-   al after-   math of sigh-

Ing empty plain   and mountain range   the guilt   of creation   into
My chest   I'm the universe source I   feel an X   being inscribed
Against my breast-   bone I am willing it   telekinesis with
Carver
          At the end of Fated   who can   anything be

The hexers' corpses   lie too among their   toylike ambitions
Just three peo-   ple who had once   had dental work done
All the pathologists   are dead   all the   keepers of identities
So get up now   you're dead you're blank   you're renewed at the

End of Fated   You're un-   conscious   Who are   you face-
Less shining dum-   mies is it   And are you   already some-
One else?   Don't let that happen   It's beautiful   to be null
The stories   lie on the ground   black limp   cords like bullsnakes

But snakes have souls   And a bird's soul   calls   Hadn't there
There had been too   many patches   on the folds of ex-
Istence hadn't there   I don't doonn't   haaave   *there*
You are no long-   er located located located   who

587

Walk there   not like a camera   There is no 'like'   Or meta-   phor for
No for   What's traversed   not a descript-   ive set-up
Characterization   Cosmic plug-in   sense of reward or   award
Did you really   knock the planets   out of their   orbits

I think it's up   to what you . . .   Have you ever   lost track
In such a trough   where systems break down   and no one
Looks at it   that way just   it stopped hap-   pening   I wasn't
Ever doing that   as planet   *I regretted*   *the mot-*

Ion of sol-   ipsistic bod-   ies in the eyes of   *other solipsists*
I don't remem-   ber anyone now   just a couple   Enter another
Passageway   dragging my sword   Lack of recollection   Lack
Of prompters   I'll start it   up with amber   light   No wait

And no psychology   Just a tired butterfly   Don't start it up
The shades sit down   There are these words   clanking around
In my   head   I still don't get   what you're proposing
I remember   we were suddenly   here   Why I couldn't

Say   Or was it only me   drifting form-   lessly   Did I
Have an apt-   itude or was it   Do it with-   out trying
Aptitude   for living

"They clank a-   round in my lo-   cation"

I remember the   broadsides of   convenience   'I need that car   or that machismo'
But when the president   the present   was pas-   sive it was worse   That's why
I take over   And then blank   Or these ner-   vous clanks   superscript

The weight left   There was this ap-   pearance of   void   Ap-
Peared to you   I can't feel   and there's nothing   to reason about
Whatever there is   is still being   made in my   chest I
Mean the new   primal substance   And act-   ual dead people

Are still laying their   guilt on me   But the un-   conscious that's it and
It's what I'm   producing   must have   taken over   That's it
There has been a stick-   y jealousy   Or a sick   viscosity
Or near-lethal gas   Lurking near the . . .   I remember . . .   the corpses

Of the self-   satisfied   My gaping heart no one can see   Can't it be
Marked X or Tau   My cross   Then there is some   singing un-
Gentle to com-   memorate   'I was the bat-   tle it was me / I
Did not destroy tenderly /   And what rushes in to replace   the olden

Will not necessarily   be . . . lovely'   'I am calling to the unfamiliar'
'I am the unfamiliar . . .'   Stop prolonging   our arrival

Shimmer be-   becomes more e-   lectrified   If you open that
Shocking gate   On the wet grass   barefoot   There's broken glass
To glide above   Cross-   roads I was the god there   What choices now
The personal shell   broke added   to the litter   I have no

So I go on   have no   you dig   until it's this   huge no I have
Everything   It could be-   come hallucinatory   but that
Falls too   images and tones   You could pick one or   just no   But these syl-
Lables   visual audi-   tory labels oh no   No   Errant

Not haz-   y   What's haze for   The old partitas   flouncing van-
Ish   Notes van-   ish   Are you finally   more than
It   Was al-   ways hidden   How much more   And the rays
Of ne-   on gas   redden   This   inconsist-   ency a song not

A song an   in-   consistent op-   era   on-going   Notes fall
Over edge   Size-   less   Beats swelling   Have no   Have no

Sandra calls   you on-   ly have to   kill the bad nights . . .

The beginning fate-   ful first scratches   Letters on parti-   cles would form
And as   new substance   issues from   STOP   before you de-
Sign   Stop says   Sandra the   first little move-   ments
Locked in the   unconscious es-   caping towards me   and joining with

The from-my-gaping-heart   new   element   the new
Medium   This was sup-   pressed   how   the initial   gesture
Was done   The going towards   The sense we un-   consciously de-
Vised ourselves   It was first done   by some part   of us unknown

And now   But I'm con-   sciously unconscious   HOLD IT A MOMENT someone
Else says   We need to man-   age it I say   I know how   But it *is* us

And the element or medium ac-   quires a grain   a sense of partition
But we are one con-   sistent kind of   particle I say   Every-   thing we
Are or have been   has been used   This this us   is one thing but
Newly   Are we dream-   ing it   Sandra asks   No the

World you died from   is the dream the   what you thought you
Thought   The medium's particles —   see —   begin to permeate us

Clementa

What you are now   becoming   a consistency of   That it was al-
Ways there   That it is others'   sins as well broken   down   Others' re-
Morse   and yours   crimes   aggressions   enmeshed   until a partic-
Ulate is a-   chieved   I feel in my soul   I on-   ly feel it there   the

Enormity   of your   crimes and how close   to what I was   they were
But a sophisti-   cation is now en-   gendered a   sympathy that can't
Fail   Dead or alive   one will be wanted   in simili-   tude and simple ex-
Tension of self   Yes says Clementa   but who am I   who am

Still my-   self dead . . .   Oh I see   What do you see?   We have re-
Named   flesh and all mat-   erial also soul   And now   that we have we
See it   You are a form whose   skin is all images   how can I ex-
Plain   and everything is   you me how ex-   plain   We took part

In all   of it   And now we   arise gold-   en without spe-
Cific memory   Because that never was   But on your sur-
Face your skin are   literally the   stars and planets and our e-   vents as
Contiguity totality   I can on-   ly see it   The unconscious the

Undertow   If I love you who   do I love?   Me I say

The wind asway   that I put in the bank   Daddy   comes towards me
The right thing   is happening he says   What   kind of world
A lot of streets re-   membered   from dreams I say   I al-
Ways had a dream version   of Chicago   and the Lower East Side   I

Know where I am   when I'm back in them   Dream version of a
Desert town that   doesn't exist   somewhere a-   round Searchlight
Repeated and real   Where are you going   in this argument he says
Places too I say down the   river where there   are pink flowers I'm

Not going any-   where   Memory is for   remembering anything
So you can ex-   ist   in your mind   I keep remembering
Dreams   How many places am I in   I have fought   this battle to
Win back   all of memory   and presence   I   you   will remember

Not *versions*   but gross expanses   of uni-   versal and indi-
Vidual e-   vents   not in time but   here   Sing it   of the
Middle of it   And now   we are where   remembering what
In the tules float-   ing silence   I remem-   ber giving you

A flower   That never happened   Nothing happened
Butterfly wings   Memories aren't of things   I remember you
I hear you   I am re-   creating the universe   out of my
Own love   and other's foul dis-   cards   Keep remembering I'm doing this

Dreams now   Woman dying   a woman's dying   she dies with
Her hands on her breasts   Others are with her and   they call her
Woman with   hands on her breasts   That turns out to   have been her name
All along: woman-with-hands-on-her-breasts   How meaning gets

Made   Did the words or gest-   ure come first   or did the words or gen-
Der come first or   when were words first dreamed   in the night or
In the night of death   I awoke with my   hands on my breasts
Holding open my heart   for wrapped-up discards of   the dead—

And I have fought too   and killed for you   No dream no metaphor
I have been killing words   which are more like   flesh than flesh
As they cover you in pub-   lic   as they're   bent by you
To make your way   as they fill in for   love and action

So in the second   dream I discover   my hair   is now light red
Hair and eyebrows   red for blood shed   In the dream I was pleased

From all the sta-   tic from all the cries and   messages   the thinking
Select   How am I to be now   And there's more   static then
What shape are we   Slanted script   our minds are writ-
Ing   all over the sky   Who is there   the battle where   did it

Take place   where was it played   I sent it out to all and now speech   dis-
Rupted   stag-   gers   Anyone   is in your space   or body who
Am I   the fabric shift-   ed I'm not   doing   what I used to
Or do you   know   When you   dream you   lose your memory

And you don't know   you're not remembering   I don't   I
May have once   been other   says a voice   and I   do I know
What I could · remember   What planet is   this ugliness
Someone wants   me to do things   Why?   Says I should eat

But I say   I don't mind dying   I Alice open   my chest now
To allow the   egress of   the new primal ele-   ment   It is
Everyone's   as there always was   a basic One   nothing's
Divided up in   not even Con and   Uncon   Let it in-   to yourself

And the static   shaping itself cries   No   windup universe
It I   as usual   here forever   form memory   the waves of color   and tone

Who are all these dead friends all scattered like dry leaves

Who is it   what is it who   I don't have to be   any I know
What I remem-   ber Allen says   is that my feast day   was called Jewels
What I   remember Rudy   says is that I'm   dying of colors
They pull out   my force but   then it comes back   like you say

From your heart Alice   I remember some-   thing like that
I remember   Sandra says that   I am let out   of myself
I wanted to be   When I talk now it comes from   steel lips
But steel has its own   soul and we're   together talking I

Can always ex-   alt and have   steel   everlastingness
I remember Ted   says that I   stopped   being guil-
Ty   I had hung around a-   while   though I couldn't
Think of what this   weight was I   finally gave   to your

Heart   I remember I killed   says someone   someone I don't
Know   the wind   I shot it   till there was blood   whirling in the air
It was people   as if you were supposed to   kill them in school or
Church   Let me forget   Small parts of   what you did

Are everywhere   everyone   I say   I remember the asteroid says
That I was a com-   position   and had velocity con-   demned
I remember   says onyx   I remember   I remember I say
That an equation   can be made   for the circumference of

The rip   in my chest   as it has grown   and for the spin of   soul's
New particles   as they pour out of me   But their spin shakes
All of me trem-   bles in   an ultimate strength   of sufferance
Trembles as the e-   quations shift   constantly   to be free

Don't want to be the same   each time

This Syrian woman   looked like a face   in a cave   Wore a dark red shawl
I was a doctor   she said I'll help you   For I was al-   most hysterical
She touched places   on my body   and a man rubbed my feet   Others watched
There were animals here   cats   I had the impression   of a cluster of

Points   on my shoulder   Visible dots   What was wrong   I'm sorry I said
I was given   a tablet to swallow   You let yourself she said   become
Big for us   You can be weak sometimes   Can you I asked   see the
Future now   She shrugged   The panic I've seen   can become widespread

All there is   War for nothing   Anyone   fighting anyone
Saying   it's for the usual   God   territory   water maybe   but
For nothing   I just fought for us some-   where I say   You fought in
Heaven   no one's dead of it   What of your cul-   ture I say what

Of cultures   People don't die   but maybe cultures do
Question of memory   and of form held close   To the chest? she
Joked   about my gaping   frontal hole   We take things with us
Even dead   Though I'll forget won't I   But I'm inscribed

Like a stele   Or a divinatory   liver   Don't even   have to read my-
Self   Uncompelled now   and the new soul   permeates me

Have you noticed the change   What do you need   Nothing
Is it too late   For what   What do you do a-   bout all the lies
You learned at   school do you un-   learn them   I
Just forget them   My memory's now   for being here

All these tattoos   on my surface   remember   my experience for me
Destroy the cars no   walk away from them   the dead cars every-
Where   in life not in death   We killed a planet with cars   it was
Obvious   I'm not afraid   to die now   I'm not afraid of you

Who do you think   knows anything   you want to know
No one at all   But I'll talk to you   Don't use anything don't
Make anything   Get rid of your   devices   and listen
Listen to the voices   in your head   They are the dead

Don't con-   ceive of another social   structure   another pol-
Itics   leave it   No one wants to be   organized   by you
No one wants to vote   No one needs to choose   Essentially
There is nothing   but   communication   which is ev-

Erywhere   there is no structure but memory   Remember re-
Member this poem   We begin again   with just a few words
We begin with   memory   There is memory   Even without lin-
Earity   without a line to re-   member in   Held   I am perfectly held

So we looked at the new   stuff the particles   out of my heart   so
I'm *looking*   Who can see them really   I saw someone's   face change
Before me   Because I saw it   I saw new   words on my hands per-
Meated by   the graceful   frightening thus truthful   substance we've

Become   On my hand did it say Radar   On the other hand No Need
Because the murderous   projects of others   are shared by us as one
Grace would be offset   And I saw me   She looked like   a drawing of her
She changed again   Her hair seemed longer   And she didn't

Care about   anything but   standing there   The particles are like
That   Where did they   come from   Although who thought of them
I did   I'm the only one who knows   what we're doing   making
I think *things*   objects   res   stations   out on the edge or   in a

Note's heart   I can touch and change   it or you though
The dead   can't be touched   But with words I touch   and change any-
One   You were listening   to the static wind   in which I sang
Callibrate   callibrate   your-   self as   you love along

I hover above words I am reading   They change in-   to the new sub-
Stance don't need   to be read   exactly   Blending with the world
I know   what they say   They were al-   ready   written   what
Isn't   This   Bear down   my zoophilic semblant

And my heart space full of   glassine tremb-   ling vibra-
Tory syllables   from everyone's agony   and repulsive crime
Sounds out ex-   tends its sound-   ing   What's a crime
Asks a mount-   ain's soul   When you were hit   When you took

That asteroid's   hit   at a pri-   mal moment   when the ele-
Ments were set   against each other   so they say   When the
Cards were dealt   by imagination's   hands   imagination be-
Ing imagined by all us   but   I have killed   this percept-

Ion of our form   And we are no longer formed   Do what you wish
Souls don't wish   a voice says   They remember to be   another says

I care not for your stories or   words that were   They are al-
Ready gone   Like what you thought   to be   Hovering over it some
Marks on skin or pa-   per burnt   An interpretation   An est-
Ablishment of advantage   Walked out on those people's words   though

I seem to be drag-   ging your souls a-   long   the only thing you couldn't
Mass-produce   your souls   also known as the one all-mass   the love
I am its spokes-   person   A voice says now   I beg your mer-
Cy at this junct-   ure between ever-known   and unknown

You aren't frightened I say   No and I under-   stand I am changed
But what am I   in the same sense as   what   was I before
What is this set-up   I know that it's what is   And that's one
Answer   And nothing's *for*   anything   And no one's in charge

But—aren't you in charge?   I don't know I say   I was the on-
Ly one willing   to be   what I am   from forever   This is the un-
Conscious in full lib-   eration   We aren't in the old   Noth-
Ing looks the same be-   cause anything has lost its   importance

Is blurred now   Something to ignore   until it perhaps disappears
Who you are is what ig-   nores   humankind and other kind
That you are called derived from   The set-up   is that we
Made it   but we change   and I as Change   exhort you to stay with me

I am a soul I   I ac-   quired a sort of writing   upon me then   shrugged it off
What I should be like   how I should love   and who be loyal to   I renounce now
I cannot be   humane   I cannot be in a known   kinship   I can-
Not be   the shape of a life   as you know it   Or a keeper   of wisdom

I came here   to change you   I suffered for you   not to be like you
I am here   to change everything   Whether you see the change   at once or later
Is not important   Nor will I listen to   your replies to me
Your arguments   based on self-interest   though seeming selfless

You have been hypocrites   a hypocrite race   But your soul   is itself   soul
And what that is   I have become   entirely   Stop lying   You need nothing
Stop lying   You have no enemies   There is   no other party
I've changed your skin   Do you see that   The same sur-   face is what

You all are   Admixed with   all you fear   and hate   is what you are
The phenomenal world   has become   with my victory over
It   over your view of it   a gentle chaos   gently work with that
Who are the dead   Who are the live   are we becoming one   it's a necessity

THE OTHER SIDE OF THE ANGEL

Betrayed Again: Nov 13 Attentats

And time went forwards and backwards   there were bullets   either way
I walked there   see you tomorrow   For I am   in life again
My ears ring   And you are a   hoax not   part of me
The jet-black af-   fect plastic over-   lay after   an attack

Then I'm god   again please crowd me   come back into
My room strangers   *You can't zigzag so*   *and be a savior*   The sav-
Ior   traditionally   trembles and doubts but   Change the nature of
Flesh   I'm changing the nature of flesh   And deny guns' efficacy

Stupid fuckers bullets   all over my parish   my Paris   So shapes
Enter my room in   full cloudy No-   vember daylight
And are you   crying Alice   or are you receiving   packets of
Violent sins   once again   in your chest   wound to

Remix the one soul   And tell the world   says a dead man
Not to emphasize   any fierceness   whenas I've just found out
There's only love   I died and found out love   I was naive alive
To read e-   vil action as   more than a thing   Glucksmann says

But how can   one alive not be fright-   ened or out-   raged

So in a mat-   itudinal   light of sirens   jogging   I con-
Sider the shoot-   out at St. Denis   the cop cars coming from
St. Denis   Two dead in-   cluding a female   jihadist like. . .
Not like me   Later   at night   the new-   ly dead woman

Enters my room   Shaking all o-   ver an   up and down tremb-
Ling   Where am I   Dead I say   Who are you   You may owe
Me an ex-   planation I say   For my violence?   Your stupidity
Not knowing   that you would not die   into   the paradise

Promised by words   male words I   mean that are   pasted on dis-
Gruntled mouths   devious lips   powerful   as you
Give him power   I gave him pow-   er she   says shak-
Ing where am I   My apartmental un-   conscious consciousness

With all the others   the all of you I say   What can I do she says
About your con-   dition?   Accept my heart   which open bleeds and
Acquires your crime   Use me   or do nothing   There's nothing
To do here   but talk   You have   less of   nothing

Than when alive   You don't have a life   Don't have to have one

So much hap-   and yet is   it happening   Here is our fab-
Ric   I am ex-   uding   in a call or rain   From the huis ouvert
See it with   hidden   eyes once ob-   scured see our new parti-
Cles   sparkling   new color   I have conceived   a new hue

Or are the   particles our eyes   our new eyes   The color's blue and rose a-
Cross chang-   ing with these sparkles   How more   do you say
What this is   I spoke a new lang-   uage last night   It was your mat-
Ter   There were more sounds   I cut off ends of words   to go on

There's more just voiced or   sung   Chalk it up   to magisterially
You place your in-   credulity of a shootout   beside   your in-
Credulity   of   a new substance to be   Choose one as more substantial
I choose myself you say   transformed by you   your internal

Effort   And I I say   can be told by you   what further to say
As I stand be-   fore us di-   vided   to convince   the violence I   uni-
Versally was   to convince   the thug I might be   now to stand down
And remember more   what were you   when we ex-   panded opened up

Last Night's Terrorist

He's a-   symmetric jagged   image blood   on the visage and   all blood
Dried   Last night's terrorist   imploring me for . . .   assuagement
Of self-terror   and a change   I allow him to lie   beside me with
All his image and blood   Says I have no body now   I have   to locate you I

Say   so I see you   I will convert you in-   to new substance   I want he says
To warn oth-   ers that there's no para-   dise no   god they
Won't be-   lieve it   Tell them I say   tell them   and pass on to them
If they can hear you   this change of   substance   Change them

Change them in their dreams and thoughts   Break down the door
Between life and death   Look at me I'm alive and dead   Let me rest he says
You have no rights mass-mur-   derer   No rights here either   But
No one can hurt you   You have changed al-   ready   as the dead

Are all   renewed cloth   How is this working   Nothing works
We're just un-   stable enough   to ad-   mit gross trans-
Formation   if you tip it in   You're a mind now   Tip this in
My chest opens or   my mind opens and   gold sparks pour out

Take it in   You've no body   You're just a site   Take some in

Take this you changer   stupidly merciless   as you were
If we're all same thing   as the doors be-   tween our minds with-
In our minds open   And then I   become   sick again
Later my brother says it's be-   cause your   brain's changing in

Order to understand us   A vertiginous night   How much of my story can
You take   Yes I'll pro-   bably go to the doctor   The black leaves
Run in the gut-   ter depressed   I think I   once asked to *be*
Must've   No being without re-   membering   how to be

What is the power voice says   My heart   How does it work
Ac-   ceptance of all we've done   newly electrifies us and we . . .   go on
The particle flip-flops in-   to   it comes nearby   then goes else-
Where   but nothing's that far   in one mind   more and more . . .   im-

Pure   You will lay   your burden down   right now
No one cares   how heavy it is   how wicked you are
Stick it in   my heart   Doors are all   goddammed open
And you my   terrorist ripped up the   order   of the day   *but I'm*

Destroying   your molecular   particular   habits

Introducing Reality

It goes into you   But were you already there   I'm taking over
The guy re-   fuses to go   He only has to trans-   Then syllables
You will no long-   er be anyone's   syllables   If dead speak
Now   *I have begun to*   syllables   I'm trying to under-   get it

Something happens last night   I become so overwrought   about the terror-
Ist attacks   that I am hysteri-   start to déja-vu   Pierced in-
To a   syllable   I remember dreaming while a-   wake   at the Gare Montpar-
Nasse   the cafes and stores become cubicles   Like syllable   that each is a

Not-there doubled   No that's not it   Al-   ways two levels   con-
Scious and un-   conscious the syllables sing   A-   lso there when my
Brain   is it my brain   changes   birds spar-   rows fly up
What are these syl-   lables   I mean particles   They are you

Saying it   But if you're a rock
                              Affirms   it is firm-
Ly syllabic   to the air   unanthropo-   morphically   but meta-
Morphically   will resist science   Instability   No it's ability
I am the first sub-   stance   under the stance   the rock's

Syllable bits soul   I am that   so stick it!   Intro-   ducing reality . . .

I have to tell the truth with no ache   no trance   As I state that the old
Game is over   Nothing is holding it up   I've collapsed at least
Twice this last week   But I've made the new mat-   ter   The guy says
Blatant   that your lives are lies   and not just the top per cent

This is hard   Because at the mo-   ment you were   shot to pieces I say
And in shock must list-   en to me   Soft grief and hard   grief the tones sins
As young men   with mere guns   shoot the   world I
Put on two slender crowns   of thorns and of   crystal   but when

I try to proclaim some-   thing come out with   It is as far   from here to
Chihuahua   as it is from   Chihuahua   to here
I am so tired of ex-   plaining   Nothing is holding you up
He told me   weeks ago   that everyone would   come to me

Now   of the live ones   the dead   ever   chez moi   Listen listen
To the facts   That beneath the floor   the new soul con-
Structs its   hive or infinite   suite of   rooms   out
Of and I am so ex-   hausted   my true   heart's sub-

Stance   gold and black   that's being made   continuously

The ruins of worlds col-   lapsed buildings   I per-   haps am malleable
And the grey loft planks of wood   Everything stands in   for itself
Whenever you   seem outside and fixed   though usually in your head
Remember   how to be so many   things or ones at once   There are

Rooms or cells stretching   out from my right ear   differently tonal
I look forward to   gradually   including   more of the floor
Of squares of fake lino   in my sight   I wouldn't have to see it exactly
Tears in my ad-   jacent eyes   And I find in my   mind a dove with

Scalloped wings shuttle   up and down   the effect   up and down the effect
There was an old man   I had forgotten   was dead whose hair long had grown
I was trying to climb   further up   from even lower down   than usual
And who I was now   was anyone's guess   I brought up glancing

And disrupting   straight lines   and tangled ash   from the place of
But it didn't   burn up   aventurine   from what planet
You have to be our   savior still   said everyone   Okay but
Inside the   and you can see it too   there's smoke's eye   under the stairs

(The old man was Herman)

Phrases Possessed of Their Own

Transpla-   the name of the ma-   transl-   I go down   up grou-
Transfo-   E square on the jaw   Remember jaws   I throw off shel-
These mess-   ages seeking you   to be said   A long empt-   time
In the chair   of soul   My eyes aren't seeing   what you sa-

There open   cubicles ap-   proached from   above on
Am I fly-   ing out of them   I being   precise nothing
I was noth-   ing com-   ing out of those   grey cement text-
Ure   For nothing too remembers   that is est-   ablishes it-

Self   Con-   nected via   enclaves of   itself to   itself
Not even air   as in song   I nothing have   gone below the
Drea-   Where phra-   come from   stars be-   neath the feet
I remember   black lines   drew things and   I nothing

Didn't identify   Phra-   ses possessed   of their own   exist-
As the thought comes   comely   watch phrase   glisten
I latterly   The broke   was spent   and nothing   manufact-
Spl-   can you say   Gives you blue agates   a brace-

Above God

I have filled the stars   with juice already   A nervous gesture
Above nerves is better   I am a cur-   rent am I
You can see yourself if   you look down voice   says   Lying there
Try not for detail   putting back or up   So   there's no resemblance

Between different fish or rocks   Each is   nothing a
Different case of it   But first I am gestur-   al nothing a
Current juiced   there's no resemblance   no one re-   sembles me
That's what god is   resemblance   in the juice   I'm above it

I'm above god   would be same as   below   below dreams above god
Below language as little let-   ters and photos   Above the cubicles and
Further   There's one light   on the green hill   it isn't
Person   No go back above   above   And in the current

Above all   see that this is the in-   side of   the particle chanced
I see it   it's a changing thought   Outside of it is better
Are you both at once   I need to be a-   bove god when I
Care about you   if you're all god   And this current

And above   there are no houses   there is no tribe
I brought my   words from home but   they are juiced
From here   And if I for-   get them come   back on their own
Go above them   No   they change into   better ones

Bring up this one of them   There's adjacence but   there's jacinth sparkle
My tongue's bleeding   A certain pressure to accede to   humanity is resisted
I like air resist it   and another brilliant is ex-   truded green   and pressed down
Into what   the cubicle of the   particle   or is it molecule or are they   no more

She sits to show us   an open asymmetrical   struct-   ure that
Changes as I   remember it so   I might never do   it the same way twice
Lay them   framed next to each other   in the room or under trees
I was only watch-   ing   Particles   may be no more   as I bring up

By watching   more of the un-   consciously fashioned gems   Because they're in
My soul   its tongue is bleeding   from building   this house or civil-
Ized structure   casually   Keep remembering memory   that it's all
That there is   So I'll know what   I'm doing   Another brilliant and a-

Nother   a blue zircon they say   You have to re-   member the repeating
That it's that   the facets   repeat holding still   but allow   my vision
To change their hue to other blues   She sits showing   us the crude frame a-
Round each cu-   bicle   Not a grid   though the   cubicles are parts of

An ir-   regular growing ag-   glomerate of one's   full of   not just
Brilliants which   slice at one but   old things like some   newspaper pieces old words

Who's in-   side you as you   cross the street   I sat down in a cave or
Cube as I crossed   I sit down ill-   ish and they   crown me with a slen-
Der coronet   You don't have time   to be sick   No time in these col-
Laged together com-   partments   Long red dress I'm wearing

Too many dead ones need to   thrust their sins into you   I
Need to rend-   er the remaking final   I can't get   the new soul dis-
Tributed enough   You haven't had e-   nough time   There is no
Time except lived   You've got to   No you've got to he says   Temporal

Life must be   for making these changes to death   Are they   You're
The one who knows he says   You're the one chang-   ing the dead   I
Need to   change the   living faster I'm   almost dead   They don't
Understand   can't under-   stand anything   Just keep your

Crown on he says   No one can see it   The trillions   of souls here see it
And see my heart that o-   pens to   the dark   refractory

I am she . . . everyone's guilty

Place this irregularity onto   Pose it brief-   ly and let it go   to itself
So you can see what it   is   Because what we do   telekinetically
Or via the con-   nection be-   tween eye and object   called world
She moves within the   cubic I guess cub-   ical form some-   one says

As you make art and   other's eyes move   inside it   anywhere you go
I refuse to destroy you so   we are elemental   together   Going on
The memorial   put you in place   as murderers   Privation
You needed some-   thing further   to pre-   vent you from

Monstrous   acts it was said   Inside the cube   that I'm maintain-
Ing with parts of me an-   cient anguish as   dark grit or scum
Inter-   mixes with my re-   flectiveness   Some more of
Grid in my chest   For yes Allen says as our maker you're al-

Lowed any-   thing   so she takes my love seen   red and gold
And touches war and terror to it   I mean an-   guish as herself
It is a strange universe   without justice   since   every-
One's guilty   Can you see it   it's visible that   everyone's guilty

Among the living   The dead know they   are and are sad
When I figured I owed   everything I am   to the dead   I was
Released some-   times to hover   as nothing   I'm trying to show
You living how to look   The fabrication will   always have

Patched edges   But we can put a new thing in   It shines and keens
What would be the   point if I   killed you   The smell of death is back
Al-   bert says   I guess they like it   Should we remove
Liking   from the new universe   I don't see it anymore I say   But I'm nothing now

Take it and place it   Wound or rough sound   I've got   a lot of it
From that same source   Shadow half-cocked   but you're here
Even if you don't bleed   Fortunate as dice   So we put   this one on
Because it got made   in the eon   I found   yellow tinge

Or something fast   both swift   and sticking   Press red there
And then ignition   Think the spark   It's still   but it goes
Trees over there   I'm in your   writing hand   Need bare
Ecru lace   need outer space   glued-down   gneiss pieces

Why   So I can see it   I want this   liberty of   Corpse night coun-
Ter to starring   The star you say   the star had qual-   ities of myself
That was what they   bought   half-dumb   hypocrites
These words   play out of   the cube sung out   of it   all

The things I make   come out of your hand   I am just a
Dead sucker   Remake me as   this   new de-   sign   your
Heart   I can be your heart   your chest of gold and woe   or
A part   Signed   All of in-   animate   memory

CUBE

It isn't straight-edged it   wavers and curves some-   times   Okay
Or o-   pens into space   with a dark . . .   chute
It's unanthro-   pomorphic mem-   ory tak-   ing hold again
On the other side of words   I'm being crowned with   gold thorns

Why were we born   why is there a universe   we weren't born   I
Beg to differ says   one's mother   How many dimen-   sions mental   in the
Cube-thing I'm fashioning   set against the fire of your   I-was-born-to-
Love   dimension   So the fire glows without   tinder or ag-

Gression   in one corner   I fall down the chute   Who is as barren
As the mountain   where I go   with one existential   olive tree
Cube I'm fashioning   to attach to   the burgeoning   dimensionality of
Take my hand and write   Conquered a planet once   now tremble to con-

Struct real   reality   beaten by the inner   gods the dimension-
Ally   estranged   first times we were   remember   I re-
Member some ob-   jects being like these   vibrant cubicles
They're just like what you see   aren't they   with your eyes

I remember the beauty   of the souls of my   words   grouped
People in reds greens and blues   attaining the vocal bandwidth ar-
Ticulating how we're to be   as they climb   the desolate mount
Smiling   all intermixed   all experience   fit exchange

(Seizes my hand)

I seize your hand   to write (I'm dead)   The real   becomes big-
Ger now   the black-gold stuff   cubes opening up   space malleable as
Always   I'm taking your construct part-   ly of evil   the sub-
Stance   and I'm smearing it   all over   the sky of   the dead be-

Cause   it's real   the dead are   and you Alice   The live don't seem very
Real though full   of blood   But I'm telling them   trying to break   the
Mind-mind barrier   that   There is no god as they think it   Violence won't
Be a success   I'm be-   lieving you   Alice   cubes or un-   stable small

Rooms   of structure   opening up   Now they're   rounder opening
Cluster of dimen-   sions you are not cata-   strophic   strophe of
I'm opening   Colors streak in the   firmament   and gigantic souls
Of whales   elephants and alps   turn somersaults   together

I am to tell you (Alice)   be brave   they've e-   volved from cube-
Spheres to   this kind of memory   infinitesimally made   memory it-
Self is changing   keeping up   I see the   memory cube-
Spheres with scenes at-   tached   glued   of my   saying

This   So aren't you rich   with this know-   ledge of the spirit   our home

Piece

I take your pen   Lots of in-   vention   but what if   there's no room
You have to be able to be there   so climb or de-   scend stairs
Want you to see us   the souls take up   the room of   can't make this word come out
It means *soul-room*   You can put it in an   ashtray   or   sur-   reality   which is

Above my shoulder — I write   Yes — it writes   But not to be cute
So in the room you en-   ter (or   cube or round)   we sit we all have   to fit
We worship you be-   cause we   fit in your   mind but   not worship
Attend   for you hold   us   it's warmly lit how   you're accustomed to

Light so it's like it   And that same red again   We're assembled I tell
You my hand writes   the word is spacious   I mean *The Word*
And I was nev-   er flesh but I   was word it   writes   I am
Covered by rocks I'm hill-   ish like under   a cairn   Now *you* speak to *us*:

We make these rooms   for our grad-   ual cogni-   zance of our exist-   ence
But   we are all that exists   We must need to   tell it to   ourselves as
Shimmery com-   ponents of the   choir   The voices so   infinite a-   cross
See the tissue that's you —   and I'm leading —   It's very strong gauze   moth's wing

The cub-   icles   of a bombed-out building   in Aleppo   are grey and un-
Evenly edged now   These wounds   these wounds will   make good build-
Ing blocks   Shadowed   back corners   the guys are   hanging out
They could be   souls of   lunar   rock formations   or any-

One who   talks to me   Souls or shadows   I am in knowing   one says
And can tell you thing or two   pasting sequins and   braid in-   to the mind's
Cursive script here a-   round these so-   called edges   They are just part of
The thought   'destruction of   made thing   into memory'   this is

Memory   inhabited by   the conver-   sation of . . .   Voice takes my hand
Writes   Hieroglyphics were once   and then bombed be-   came new language
You write in blocks   you write on air   you write upon the night not
Unfriendly   It wasn't hu-   man destiny it was   soul scripture lingering

Aleppo with two p's   a cube in each that's round   I remember   the night I
Left   my mind was dead and legs   did my   work for me
I remember birds   written everywhere on the sky   Remember death
The deaths of others   factual   then I too was   in the sky'

I Remember

A moment when   a pinpoint minute   when all   your structure vanishes
And now it isn't there   the city   named by you city   whose reality has been pro-
Jected by your mentality   believing it   believing in it and   your body in it empty fool
I'm   not   that   I'm leading you into   that pinpoint   No one else is I am

Let fall away   the phantoms or   ideas of   you and others   the mak-
Ing of caring   now the un-   raveling of   a trillion stories   gone to air
Gone to texture of   new universe   Built from   ragged torn glyphs   call-
Ing to you   that know   Colored know   Dazzling know like other

Self of you   I've seen my life wind up   seen it   disappear in several dreams
Because   I'd perceived it   as a thread or line   We're destroying the order of
Events do   you remember   I remember finding out   there is only   one moment
I remember dis-   covering   that my mind is in-   scribed with hieroglyphs

Coming to focus   I remember know-   ing my stony   mind is engraved
With poems   being uncovered with-   in me as   I learn to know
Each one or   aggregate half-   ragged yet   permanent   I remember
Whatever I make   is permanent   its iotas being where   the dimensions play

Will enable   those sounds in stone   to be heard   by me
Because I could   see them   in my mind engraved   You'll find
Them someone says   Not stone   that belies their quickness
No need to be con-   sistent the sounds braid   then snap off

A mental move like   *I find you* but then   it slides
I have to con-   struct a glyph   a room you
Know   voice says I remember   promises that   depended upon
A story's validity   This magic tone alone will   create you

But I'm here   at the beginning   mid-circumstance   I re-
Member   how to be   the glyphs told me how   But I had writ-
Ten them   All because there is no line   Knowledge is in
No special or-   der   I remember talk to it   Just go out and

Talk   I remember that I might   lose my con-   sciousness   Then
Saith the stone   or glyph in tone   You will at-   tain another consciousness

ORATOR

In as-   sumption of proper power   board ship with   the only orator
Somewhere like Fecamp's harbor   There are two   sizes of power
I'm choosing the larger   I pledge my soul   a new though
Perhaps indifferent — as a style assumed it's   just deployed —

Outwardness   To display your power board   ship in harbor and
Sail away   We went on board on   a purple-grey day   the orator
And I   to travel to   significant ports and   make speeches
The runes in my brain   would tell me what to say   I'd been shy

Before   not eloquent extempor-   aneously I thought   But the ora-
Tor   who at first hadn't   wanted to come   finally assented:
Your brain will tell you   Is this day a cubicle   or canticle
This day of embarkment   The orator said: You will say 'There

Is no death'   then perhaps nothing else   You might add 'On the
Other hand the planet is dying'   You will say   'Find your way
I will help you   accept the vast-   ness of your   soul and let
Go of all you stood for   For you were only   symbolic   to be

Seen as something familiar   but now and I   and I am talking to
Myself as well   know that   no one has ever known   you nor you them
Those who at this mo-   ment assume out-   ward power in the world
Are callous devious potential —   ly brutal un-   masked every day then re-

Accepted   They would describe to you what you'd want   But you don't want any-
Thing   no one ever has   Contrary to the teachings   were not born to
Desire but to be   Leave this perverse   memorization   of the details of
Other people's   imaginations   and come with me   I promise nothing but

To be in touch   forever   You've broken my heart   by being so lost
But now I don't mind   A broken heart stays open   And as the dead do
You can place in it   in my heart   your crimes and   mischievous thoughts
I forgive you   in a promise of   transformation   I am the forgiver'

Then I said to the live / I won't be a spy any / longer /
and must re- / veal myself

A piece of bone in mind: Forgotten your name it   says   Revert to older
This one   Knowledges of no less-   ons   I was your   matter once
When you were . . .   In the future?   No time line   I wasn't ev-
Er a thing   but   waves   petrified radio activity   remember

Words like that   sitting here squat-   ly blip   blip one long
Note of   no mode   mode then no mode separ-   ate sound
If you separ-   ate the sound   eliminate   necessity
I'll e-   liminate   it anyway   I say   One just sings

I I say being a   very grand power   am en-   veloping with
Radiance   every thing and   disclosing the hid-   ing discover
You gracious relic   In my story I was   martyred   in my
Continuing ex-   istence it says   can teach   your throat

Hold me to it thr   throat   What you are   found-
Ing   alread-   y here   It was a black note or   knowledge or
A not-nature   It has to be true   I can't get the sound   of . . .   But it's
Here   the truth   I have it hold it it   says   I am the   truth it says

Place me in your con-   struction   you who are now   power

I don't have to offer an alternative
I don't have to control you

You don't have to learn anything

In this vision   we the folk are   individually recog-   nizable but when
Looked at hard   are wavery have   shifting   boundaries about
Our forms and are hued tinted   as if by a dif-   ferent   artist than
We're used to   A man I know is more   grey-blue in his   skin of brown but

As you know   if you look lovingly you   don't see   you blend
We the folk are   sometimes blended from   within   sometimes more mo-
Tile in boundary   In this vision we are   not in need   not being de-
Sirous and I   for one am taller and   expansive with   golden love on all sides

That becomes much of   what I do   actively loving though   I com-
Pose poems   transcribed from my mind   to a   surface like paper
Or directly to your mind   My lips and throat   move   I am hold-
Ing many people in my arms   though this isn't possible   Both the dead and live

Allen (for I must have been in doubt)

Alice you have to take part   In what   The   ongoing dis-
Memberment of e-   volution   Or it's unwind-   ing like a snake
Around a   tree trunk   the tree of life then dis-   solves   it's dust
We're this other thing Alice   place your hands on   my upturned palms

They're an image   Do it please   you who have healed   of me my wound I
What wound   I couldn't really   think with   what I saw   I couldn't
Combine images of others   and my . . . self   I couldn't   think of
Us as one   As we unite more   going backwards   till we reprocess the

Dark   I still need your love he con-   tinues   Why   It seems to
Be the on-   ly real power   and inside me it   melts anguish   you
Knew we   wanted you for this   You will use   me for ever   That's a
Moment play-   ing back on it-   self   a   note gently rewound

Have I nothing to say   about it   This was   your . . . fate   Or
This is what you always were un-   changing   I almost
Saw it when I   was alive   I thought it   was maternal but
That's just a hu-   man de-   tail   You could   love anything and

Ignore it at the same time   Because you're   with it   in one time
The condition we have re-   turned to   every thing not only equal
But mixed   Your love glues it   Don't be a-   fraid for me to say this
(My hands re-   main on   his palms   which I can't see)

In dolor in grief   they implore me never to   leave   berobed in
Modest image cloth   the ones left   skeletal and   nude from Assad's
Torture rooms   You've seen the photos the   men are tagged
I must never leave my   rooms here but   that is myself   I can-

Not pretend normality   teaching a Subject   as if poetry   Were that
When they the dead   and all the dead   are alive   *In* poetry   for
Isn't our universe   measured articulate rhythmic   anyone's   mind as
It goes   All I know of meta-   physics and   aesthetics

You are hold-   ing the whole thing to-   gether   Allen says   It
Is thus   the white snow dove   the onyx bead   the scream scar-
Ring us of   the epic contralto   the deer's ree   the waves and
Broken prism tossed   into outer space   a memory or alpha-

Bet   structured   massive or massless   You must not
Be like others   pretend-   ing that poetry ever   lives in the academy
It lives on the kill-   ing floor   It lives in the   saturation of
Soul in pain   until soul snaps   really snaps   They want you

Because you will al-   ways   love them   with your voice

The green knob or hill   cube or sphere   *is*   so green but for my
Soul's eyes   And is gently   placed ad-   jacent to our   castle or new uni-
Verse   A color to be lost in   for a moment that spreads   through your time
And all around green I wrote   in script   what my hand sudden knew   seized:

Whi or go or make it   is it that ever to struct   is rightful
And I said are we not 'struct'   And my hand   of who now   wrote
Dead I am partly fashioned of   my form I   was   but
Coming more to   be am loose   And what we're   build-

Ing on-   ly allows what   already is   reperceived in   malleability
We are that fast-   changing says my hand and I   will change *and*
Change   even the cells   the particles   whose ex-   istence at all is
Human definition   I am founding I say   our material   in-

Constancy in beauty   The point of living not   to be defined as
What one was   And the point of death   not   to be defined as such a
Mass-ridden entity   Oh I have the eyes   of   crows or coals
Or have none   but the panorama of a mind   now will see past an-

Y body   past the castle one might make   into no ground

The end-   ing disap-   pears   I only see   the   parts of words

I walk up-   not down-   stairs   without count-
Ing   I walk up to   a chair   up a red   staircase   ziggurat to a
Brown chair   wood chair with slats throne   And sit down
In my long grey hair: "Elements of the uni-   verse

We now understand who   we are   those who slip back and
Forth between   life and death   lit and dark mat-
Ters   because we can   Our concentration   is all we are
Mental and   sometimes material   We speak   sweetly   play-

Fully   fulsomely adroitly and master-   fully   to each oth-
Er in minds   We are in fact   destroying   sorrow though
Destroy may be   too strong a word   But we   are done with
It   and with regret and self-   searing guiltiness   If you are

Maimed of your own   evil acts you must   now stand free
Loathing and self-   loathing   have no place here   for you
Are all my love   The psyche is abolished   Explanations
Cannot thrive in this   exalted and en-   during moment

No one cares what   happened to anyone   or thing   Start-
Ing over   over and over   in the reign of the   particles
Of bliss   though they re-   member hints and   mood of other eras
That is moments   within this moment   they are above and anew

We are above god   somewhere never trav-   elled   yet known in
Part be-   fore   and we make and we talk   for no reason   This could
Be known as love   as could my soul's em-   brace of every soul
But as we have nev-   er had to   know a thing   or learn

To speak   continue now   The castle we build   dis-
Solves and resumes   as it will   or as we build   our will that is
Memory   into it   'colors I can re-   call'   you say   in the
Heart of non-   dominion   any open   heart my dark

Wedge-shaped entrée   the color of dark   woven air
And you may still   place cares there if they   arise   but that
May be rare in oc-   curence   I ac-   cept any-
One anything   and so do you   of our   fabric our lab-

Oratory's invention   our transcendent   product the price
Paid   throughout and melded   our oneness   the only substance
We have fought for   and won   love caritas   charity grace we
Are   and no one   can be ex-   cluded   For the new memory

Is now   and the glints of past   are only   particles glisten-
Ing   if the liquid is tears that's all   you re-   member it is so
Intermixed and gone into   a living texture   Let none think
There was an ease in ar-   riving   But all   is forgotten and the

Forgiveness pat-   tern worn out   Certain olden words dissolve
Like written fire   Already gone   And I am   here for-
Ever   as you wish   the figure *of*   the new memory   the
New particles the new   mind   Am yours   and no other

You could carry it around   I have no arms   In your mind you
Could open the scene   changing as you watched   There might be
A story   if it were never   the same   A language that mutated
Of a mo-   ment   Darkly attached and then be-   come you so

I present-   ly cough   like a crow   near was it   a goal   to be brave
Why   I the cruci-   fix fail   Then the magi too tall
For their cubicle   became stars   became stars   One moves
Too fast   Trying to guide   the mountain   that once traveled with

Me   sliding across the plain af-   ter my   mother died   Do
You remem-   ber the fool's tongue French   I can speak in cross-
Hatches or kr-krs   I spik with ac-   centual   aggravation
Sometimes I don't re-   member what I'm saying   I remember

Calling out mountain mountain   and a crown   appears on its
Peak   I hear it say a very quiet kr-kr   I hear   some
Gravel slide   The white elk has come back   Look its eyes
I don't know how man-   y cubicles or rounds   or cookie-

Cut crescents   The red shiny sphere had a tinny   sliding square
On its round   surface and there was a bell   I want the lang-
Uage to have a bell sound sometimes   They were a people who
Never called it Death   Fury or a gust   A lament sound only the

Sound   I told the story singing it   closeup   to your mind

I parleyed in sound   of plain angel   and one said   I don't care how
Sad at the table   which later became   in the retable
Your garment's part of you   not imposed with   its soft folds
Of sleeves   a pinkish dawn color   Feet slap the floor in time

To what ancient pilgrimage   My words were on it   Speak-
Ing in signs it was   said   But what was   there to stand
For   Pleasant and   like a bird of crystal tones   a wren a-
Gain click click   or cling cling!   I real-   ize the syn-

Tax of dead angel   So far politesse   Now and sudden   fate comes
As a kind of   love   Kind?   The singular   curve forced
High tones   But are they in time   We the dead   polite say no
No to un-   bearable   time and its hyster-   ical jig

A white   patch on un-   polished dark   Who told you   life was ab-
Stracted from the pass-   ing matter   I didn't   let it pass
I held it   in arms   mental   it held me   in arms mental
All this hap-   pens on the other   side of   the angel

You can't run away from   me can't leave   my heart or arms
Can't run   You can't leave my mind   you can al-   ways see in-
To mine   You will nev-   er leave me   You can't disgust me   You and
We   extending each other   from the greenest   most un-

Stable   first   the first color   it was al-   ways green
Or the color nothing like   almost silver air   I am mak-
Ing ours   Making us ac-   cording to   various conflicting
Descriptions that are true   It's all true   Your soul of our

Particles   Face of a cubicle   or thought   a thought like a or
The   photo of that   unstably   This is our   first universe all
It is unstable   in the sense of   mutational   at its edges
And what we're mak-   ing as if tangible   a dream of struct-

Ure   not abiding   germinal   You can't run   I see your
Mind with its   unstable   scripted thought intoned   I see
Your syntax   like dark green ex-   tended cubic or round
Nests of it   And my arms   enfolding   all of it

All the mind im-   material   Connected   without mechani-
Cal   conventions   There's no time   there are pauses
What is language soul and memory   what   eternal we
Speaking   soul and memory   what there is   our gravity

Our lightness   our release from   dolorousness   Our release from
Wishes   From the notion of   events   From story   as a hard trap
A drab trap   From doing bad from do-   ing evil
From being weighted   not to say measured   From having to

Stay alive   from having to survive   From   above all
Having to   survive   Nothing has to be   No compulsion
No teachings   No size   Above all there is no size   No
Comparison   The mind flows and   cannot be found

I have never been forced   You have now   never been forced
What do you remember   Read my mind   Read my mind

June–December 2015

Entirety of Series Jan 2013–2015, then revised until 2020

APPENDIX

The following is a more detailed table of contents for Books I and IV, containing a list of the inset poems in Book I, *The House Gone* and all the poems in Book IV, *To Paste On*. These are poems that have acquired a life of their own outside the narrative of the whole series. *To Paste On* is, in fact, a collection as well as a narrative.

I. *The House Gone*

IV. *To Paste On*

ACKNOWLEDGMENTS

Some of this work first appeared in the chapbook *Undo*, published by above/ ground press. "Malorum Sanatio" was chosen for *Best American Experimental Writing 2020*. "The Woman Who Counted Crossties" was first published in *50 Favorite US Poets: A Little American Anthology of New Writing*, from Green Integer. "Victorious" was first published in the *Iowa Review*, and "Postscript: Happened" was published in *Volt*. A number of poems first appeared in *THE EQUALIZER*. "And the beautiful recollection" became a broadside from Woodland Pattern in Milwaukee. "You're Sick at the Filling Station" was published in the *Seneca Review*. Finally the poem "The Story" first appeared in my book *Certain Magical Acts*, and is published here with the permission of Penguin Poets, Penguin Random House.

Other Fonograf Editions titles

Fonograf Editions is a registered 501(c)(3) nonprofit organization.
Find more information about the press at: fonografeditions.com.